HEAVENLY SECRETS

(ARCANA CÆLESTIA)

WHICH ARE CONTAINED IN
THE HOLY SCRIPTURE OR
WORD OF THE LORD

DISCLOSED

FROM THE LATIN OF
EMANUEL SWEDENBORG

VOL. I

GENESIS, CHAPTERS I–VII

NOS. 1–823

1972

SWEDENBORG FOUNDATION (INCORPORATED)
139 EAST 23 STREET
NEW YORK, NEW YORK

First published in Latin, London 1749
First English Translation published in London 1813
First English Translation Published in USA in 1837
40th Printing in USA 1967
Standard Book Number 0–87785–053–4

PREFACE

For centuries Judaic and Christian scholars have endeavored to distil moral and spiritual values from Genesis and Exodus, but only a single work out of numberless volumes can rightfully be considered scientific in its approach and undiluted in its essence.

Arcana Cælestia by Emanuel Swedenborg stands apart, unique and unparalleled, as a systematized explanation of the spiritual import contained within the imagery, fable and history of the Old Testament.

The familiar narratives of the Scripture take on new and profound meanings. This book offers to the persevering reader the key to the understanding of divine revelation. But the work is by no means esoteric or cultish. It presents an organized, rational approach to Scriptural interpretation; one which recognized the boundless depths of divine wisdom and also the perfection of the Word of God.

With greater clarity than any of his predecessors, or successors, Swedenborg emphasizes that the Holy Scripture was never intended to be merely an account of worldly creation, Hebrew history, or an anthology of ancient lore, but rather an unfoldment of the nature of God and His providence in the lives of men.

This is a book which belongs in the library of all

students of the Old and New Testaments. All spiritual wayfarers in quest of Scripture insights will find in it an invaluable source of inspiration.

The references to the chapters and verses of Scripture are printed in accordance with the enumeration of the Authorized Version of the English Bible, even where Swedenborg, quoting from another Version, or translating from the Hebrew, employs a different enumeration.

The translation of the passages from Scripture is made from the Latin of Swedenborg, and is not copied from the English Bible.

The figures in the margin are intended to facilitate references from the *Swedenborg Concordance*.

INTRODUCTION

SWEDENBORG'S works, especially the "Arcana Cælestia" (*Heavenly Secrets*), confirm much of what Inger-
soll and other critics of the Bible say about the un-
trustworthiness of its literal statements; but at the
same time it is demonstrated that they are quite wrong
in their conclusions about its value from a different
point of view. I have had abundant opportunity to
learn how defective the sense of the letter is in the
light of modern science, how strange some of the stories
are, and how often they lack outward harmony.
Nevertheless, I have also observed that there is a
meaning beneath the letter that cannot be read in
word but only in symbol, and this meaning holds good
throughout the parts where it occurs. There is a compelling example of it in Psalm 78:

"I will open my mouth in a parable; I will utter
dark sayings of old, which we have heard and known,
and our fathers have told us."

Then follows in the Psalm a summary of the experiences of the Israelites in Egypt and their pilgrim-
age to Canaan. This record is true history; but here
it is pronounced to be a parable which only the initiated can fully grasp. And what a deep parable it is!

It describes perfectly our exodus from materialism and ignorance, and our slow, difficult progress toward the happier life, which the beautiful, fertile land of Canaan represents. I am giving this simply as an illustration of how Swedenborg always regards the Bible as a vehicle of Divine Truth.

It is of interest to recall that in the year 1753 Astruc made his famous discovery of two or more documents in the Pentateuch and at that very time Swedenborg was publishing, anonymously, in London, the "Arcana" explaining Genesis and Exodus. The latter did not believe that Scripture had anything to do with the physical creation or a literal deluge, or that the first eleven chapters of Genesis were about individuals named Adam and Noah. It was a very different phase of the subject which came to his attention. He was enabled by the study of Hebrew and by his mental illumination to see that the early chapters gave an account in an ancient parabolical style of the spiritual life of the race from the beginning down to the Jewish era. He pointed out that the first chapter contains the stages of evolution by which the mind of man, at first dark and chaotic, was developed until it reached the Eden of simple truth and happiness. This age continued until self-interest asserted its power, and the innocence of childhood was gradually lost. At last wrong ideas flooded the world. Then a keen race of men, denoted by Noah in the ark, began a new age. Intelligence grew rapidly, and the rod of conscience replaced the voice of the pure soul. The symbol was no longer a garden but a vineyard. Mankind grew up like an ambitious youth, building the great empires of the East whose records we are recovering year by year. The civilization of that period was extensive; but in time it declined. Polytheism and idolatry came into being. War and violence threatened to cover the face of the earth with ruins, and another dispensation had to be established. That was the beginning of the Jewish Church which kept monotheism alive until, in the fullness of time, Christianity dawned upon the world.

The first Christian Church, or civilization, was essentially a continuation of the Mosaic one—full of the rough makeshifts and tallow candles and flickering torches of a faith fitted to a turbulent society. The sense-pictures and fair engravings of ritual and the sceptre of authority beheld, as it were, in the margin of the Word were superstitiously revered; but the Divine Meaning remained unread. So passed the perverse manhood of the world, and we continue to feel its passionate outbreaks and downfalls and unhappy moods. But now the arc light of a more enlightened faith shines upon humanity, and the creation of a new man goes on step by step; yea, the Sabbath of peace in all hearts and in the outer world shall yet come, and the reign of selfish, blind instincts shall vanish forever. Thus the Bible is portrayed as one vast glorious parable. All the way one may read in it lessons of life and its phases—its first innocence, its youthful waywardness, its saving conversion, and its incalculable possibilities of service and joy. It is a complete circle from paradise to paradise—"the circle of the earth upon which sitteth the Lord forever." The limited language and imperfect modes of thought of days long gone by are only the body of a heavenly message that declares God to be always with us, imparting new and higher gifts and capabilities.

Helen Keller

from *My Religion*, pages 79–82

CONTENTS

CONTENTS.

THE

BOOK OF GENESIS

1. From the mere letter of the Word of the Old Testament no one would ever see that this part of the Word contains heavenly arcana, and that everything within it both in general and in particular has reference to the Lord, to His heaven, to the church, to faith, and to all things connected therewith : for from the letter or sense of the letter all that any one can see is that—to speak generally —everything therein has reference to the external rites of the Jewish Church. Yet the truth is that everywhere in that Word there are internal things which never appear in the external things, except a very few which the Lord revealed and explained to the Apostles ; such as that the sacrifices signify the Lord ; that the land of Canaan and Jerusalem signify heaven—on which account they are called the Heavenly Canaan and Jerusalem—and that Paradise has a similar signification.

2. The Christian world, however, is as yet profoundly ignorant of the fact that all things in the Word both in general and in particular, indeed, the very smallest particulars down to the least iota, signify and enfold within them spiritual and heavenly things ; and for this reason the Old Testament is but little cared for. Yet that the Word is really of this character might be known

from the single consideration that, being the Lord's
and from the Lord, it could not possibly be given
unless it contained within it such things as belong
to heaven, to the church, and to faith, and that
unless it did so it could not be called the Lord's
Word, nor could it be said to have any life in it.
For whence comes its life except from those things
that belong to life, that is to say, except from the
fact that everything in it both in general and in
particular has reference to the Lord, who is the
very Life itself ; so that anything which does not
inwardly look towards Him is not alive ? And it
may be truly said that any expression in the Word
that does not embrace Him within it, that is, which
does not in its own way refer to Him, is not Divine.

3. Without such a Life, the Word as to the
letter is dead. The case is the same as it is with
man, who, as is known in the Christian world, is
both internal and external. When separated from
the internal man, the external man is the body, and
is therefore dead ; for it is the internal man that
lives and causes the external man to live, the
internal man being its soul. So the Word, as to
the letter alone, is like the body without the soul.

4. While the mind is taken up with the sense
of the letter alone, no one can see that it contains
such things.   Thus in these first chapters of
Genesis, nothing is discoverable from the sense of
the letter other than that the creation of the world
is treated of, and the garden of Eden which is called
Paradise, and Adam as the first created man.
Who imagines anything else ?   But it will be
sufficiently established in the following pages that
these matters contain arcana which have never
yet been revealed ; and in fact that the first

10

chapter of Genesis in the internal sense treats in general of the new creation of man, or of his regeneration, and specifically of the Most Ancient Church ; and this in such a manner that there is not the least expression which does not represent, signify, and enfold within it these things.

5. That this is really the case no one can ever know except from the Lord. It may, therefore, be stated in advance that of the Lord's Divine mercy it has been granted me now for some years to be constantly and uninterruptedly in company with spirits and angels, hearing them speak and in turn speaking with them. In this way it has been granted me to hear and see wonderful things in the other life, which have never before come to the knowledge of any man, nor entered into his idea. I have been instructed in regard to the different kinds of spirits ; the state of souls after death ; hell, or the lamentable state of the unfaithful ; heaven, or the blessed state of the faithful ; and especially in regard to the doctrine of faith which is acknowledged in the universal heaven ; on which subjects, of the Lord's Divine mercy, more will be said in the following pages.

CHAPTER I.

1. In the beginning God created the heavens and the earth.

2. And the earth was a void and emptiness, and thick darkness was upon the faces of the deep. And the Spirit of God moved upon the faces of the waters.

3. And God said, Let there be light, and there was light.

4. And God saw the light, that it was good ; and God distinguished between the light and the darkness.

5. And God called the light day, and the darkness He called night. And the evening and the morning were the first day.

6. And God said, Let there be an expanse in the midst of the waters, and let it divide between the waters in the waters.

7. And God made the expanse, and divided between the waters which were under the expanse, and the waters which were above the expanse ; and it was so.

8. And God called the expanse heaven. And the evening and the morning were the second day.

9. And God said, Let the waters under the heaven be gathered together to one place, and let the dry [land] appear ; and it was so.

10. And God called the dry [land] earth, and the gathering together of the waters called He seas ; and God saw that it was good.

11. And God said, Let the earth bring forth the tender herb, the herb yielding seed, and the fruit-tree bearing fruit after its kind, whose seed is in itself, upon the earth ; and it was so.

12. And the earth brought forth the tender herb, the herb yielding seed after its kind, and the tree bearing fruit, whose seed was in itself, after its kind ; and God saw that it was good.

13. And the evening and the morning were the third day.

14. And God said, Let there be lights in the expanse of the heavens, to distinguish between the day and the night ; and let them be for signs, and for seasons, and for days, and for years.

15. And let them be for lights in the expanse

of the heavens to give light upon the earth ; and it was so.

16. And God made two great lights, the great light to rule by day, and the lesser light to rule by night ; and the stars.

17. And God set them in the expanse of the heavens, to give light upon the earth ;

18. And to rule in the day, and in the night, and to distinguish between the light and the darkness : and God saw that it was good.

19. And the evening and the morning were the fourth day.

20. And God said, Let the waters cause to creep forth the creeping thing, the living soul ; and let fowl fly above the earth upon the faces of the expanse of the heavens.

21. And God created great whales, and every living soul that creepeth, which the waters caused to creep forth after their kinds, and every winged fowl after its kind ; and God saw that it was good.

22. And God blessed them, saying, Be fruitful and multiply, and fill the waters in the seas, and the fowl shall be multiplied in the earth.

23. And the evening and the morning were the fifth day.

24. And God said, Let the earth bring forth the living soul after its kind ; the beast, and the thing moving itself, and the wild animal of the earth, after its kind ; and it was so.

25. And God made the wild animal of the earth after its kind, and the beast after its kind, and everything that creepeth on the ground after its kind ; and God saw that it was good.

26. And God said, Let us make man in our image, after our likeness ; and let them have dominion over the fish of the sea, and over the

fowl of the heavens, and over the beast, and over all the earth, and over every creeping thing that creepeth upon the earth.

27. And God created man in His own image, in the image of God created He him ; male and female created He them.

28. And God blessed them, and God said unto them, Be fruitful, and multiply, and replenish the earth, and subdue it ; and have dominion over the fish of the sea, and over the fowl of the heavens, and over every living thing that creepeth upon the earth.

29. And God said, Behold, I give you every herb bearing seed which is upon the faces of all the earth, and every tree in which is fruit ; the tree yielding seed, to you it shall be for food.

30. And to every wild animal of the earth, and to every fowl of the heavens, and to everything that creepeth upon the earth wherein is a living soul, every green herb for food ; and it was so.

31. And God saw everything that He had made, and behold it was very good. And the evening and the morning were the sixth day.

THE CONTENTS.

6. The six days, or periods, which are so many successive states of the regeneration of man, are in general as follows.

7. The *first* state is that which precedes, including both the state from infancy, and that immediately before regeneration. This is called " a void," " emptiness," and " thick darkness." And the first motion, which is the Lord's mercy, is " the Spirit of God moving upon the faces of the waters."

8. The *second* state is when a distinction is made between those things that are of the Lord, and those that are proper to man. The things that are the Lord's are called in the Word " remains," and here are especially cognitions of faith, which have been learned from infancy, and which are stored up, and are not manifested until the man comes into this state. At the present day this state seldom exists without temptation, misfortune, or sorrow, by which the things of the body and the world, that is, such as are proper to man, are brought into quiescence, and as it were die. Thus the things that belong to the external man are separated from those that belong to the internal man. In the internal man are the remains, stored up by the Lord unto this time, and for this use.

9. The *third* state is that of repentance, in which the man, from his internal man, speaks piously and devoutly, and brings forth goods, like works of charity, but which, nevertheless, are inanimate, because he thinks they are from himself. These goods are called the " tender grass," and also the " herb yielding seed," and afterwards the " tree bearing fruit."

10. The *fourth* state is when the man is affected with love, and illuminated by faith. He indeed previously discoursed piously, and brought forth goods, but he did so in consequence of the temptation and straitness under which he laboured, and not from faith and charity ; wherefore faith and charity are now enkindled in his internal man, and are called two " lights."

11. The *fifth* state is when the man speaks from faith, and thereby confirms himself in truth and good : the things then produced by him are

animate, and are called the " fish of the sea," and the " birds of the heavens."

12. The *sixth* state is when, from faith, and thence from love, he speaks what is true, and does what is good : the things which he then brings forth are called the " living soul " and the " beast." And as he then begins to act at once and together from both faith and love, he becomes a spiritual man, who is called an " image." His spiritual life is delighted and sustained by such things as belong to the cognitions of faith, and to works of charity, which are called his " food " ; and his natural life is delighted and sustained by those which belong to the body and the senses ; whence a combat arises, until love reigns, and he becomes a celestial man.

13. Those who are being regenerated do not all arrive at this state. The greatest part, at this day, attain only the first state ; some only the second ; others the third, fourth, or fifth ; few the sixth ; and scarcely any one the seventh.

THE INTERNAL SENSE.

14. In the following work, by the name LORD is meant the Saviour of the world, Jesus Christ, and Him only ; and He is called " the Lord " without the addition of other names. Throughout the universal heaven He it is who is acknowledged and adored as Lord, because He has all power in the heavens and on earth. He also commanded His disciples so to call Him, saying, " Ye call Me Lord, and ye say well, for I am " (*John* xiii. 13). And after His resurrection His disciples called Him " the Lord."

16

15. In the universal heaven they know no other Father than the Lord, because He and the Father are one, as He Himself has said :

I am the way, the truth, and the life. Philip saith, Show us the Father ; Jesus saith to him, Am I so long time with you, and hast thou not known Me, Philip ? he that hath seen Me hath seen the Father ; how sayest thou then, Show us the Father ? believest thou not that I am in the Father, and the Father in Me ? believe Me that I am in the Father and the Father in Me (*John* xiv. 6, 8–11).

16. Verse 1. **In the beginning God created the heavens** (cœlum) **and the earth.** The most ancient time is called " the beginning." By the prophets it is in various places called the " days of old " and also the " days of eternity." The " beginning " also involves the first period when man is being regenerated, for he is then born anew, and receives life. Regeneration itself is therefore called a " new creation " of man. The expressions to " create," to " form," to " make," in almost all parts of the prophetic writings signify to regenerate, yet with a difference in the signification. As in *Isaiah* :

Every one that is called by My name, I have created him for My glory, I have formed him, yea, I have made him (xliii. 7).

And therefore the Lord is called the " Redeemer," the " Former from the womb," the " Maker," and also the " Creator " ; as in the same Prophet :

I am Jehovah your Holy One, the Creator of Israel, your King (xliii. 15).

In *David* :

The people that is created shall praise Jah (*Ps.* cii. 18).

17

Again :

Thou sendest forth Thy spirit, they are created,
and Thou renewest the faces of the ground
(*Ps.* civ. 30).

That " heaven " signifies the internal man ; and
" earth " the external man before regeneration,
may be seen from what follows.

17. Verse 2. **And the earth was a void and
emptiness, and darkness was upon the faces of the
deep ; and the Spirit of God moved upon the faces
of the waters.** Before his regeneration, man is
called the " earth void and empty," and also the
" ground " wherein nothing of good and truth
has been sown ; " void " denotes where there is
nothing of good, and " empty " where there is
nothing of truth. Hence comes " thick darkness,"
that is, stupidity, and ignorance of all things
belonging to faith in the Lord, and, consequently,
of all things belonging to spiritual and heavenly
life. Such a man is thus described by the Lord
through *Jeremiah* :

My people is stupid, they have not known Me ;
they are foolish sons, and are not intelligent ;
they are wise to do evil, but to do good they have
no knowledge. I beheld the earth, and lo a void
and emptiness, and the heavens, and they had
no light (iv. 22, 23).

18. The " faces of the deep " are the lusts of
the unregenerate man, and the falsities thence
originating, of which he wholly consists and in
which he is totally immersed. In this state, having
no light, he is like a " deep," or something obscure,
and confused. Such persons are also called
" deeps," and " depths of the sea," in many parts

18

of the Word, which are " dried up," or " wasted,"
before man is regenerated. As in *Isaiah* :

> Awake as in the ancient days, in the genera-
> tions of old. Art not thou it that drieth up the
> sea, the waters of the great deep, that maketh the
> depths of the sea a way for the ransomed to pass
> over ? Therefore the redeemed of Jehovah shall
> return (li. 9–11).

Such a man also, when seen from heaven, appears
like a black mass, destitute of life. The same
expressions, likewise, in general involve the vastation of man, frequently spoken of by the Prophets,
which precedes regeneration ; for before man can
know what is true, and be affected with what is
good, there must be a removal of such things as
hinder and resist their admission ; thus the old
man must needs die, before the new man can be
conceived.

19. By the " Spirit of God " is meant the Lord's
mercy, which is said to " move," or " brood," as
a hen broods over her eggs. The things over which
it moves are such as the Lord has hidden and
treasured up in man, which in the Word throughout
are called remains or a remnant, consisting of the
cognitions of what is true and good, which never
come into light or day, until external things are
vastated. These cognitions are here called " the
faces of the waters."

20. Verse 3. **And God said, Let there be light,
and there was light.** The first state is when the
man begins to know that the good and the true
are something higher. Men who are altogether
external do not even know what good and truth
are ; for they fancy all things to be good that belong

to the love of self and the love of the world ; and all things to be true that favour these loves ; not being aware that such goods are evils, and such truths falsities. But when man is conceived anew, he then begins for the first time to know that his goods are not goods, and also, as he comes more into the light, that the Lord is, and that He is good and truth itself. That men ought to know that the Lord is, He Himself teaches in *John* :

Except ye believe that I am, ye shall die in your sins (viii. 24).

Also, that the Lord is good itself, or life, and truth itself, or light, and consequently that there is neither good nor truth except from the Lord, is thus declared :

In the beginning was the Word, and the Word was with God, and God was the Word. All things were made by Him, and without Him was not anything made that was made. In Him was life, and the life was the light of men. And the light shineth in darkness. He was the true light, which lighteth every man that cometh into the world (*John* i. 1, 3, 4, 9).

21. Verses 4, 5. **And God saw the light, that it was good, and God distinguished between the light and the darkness. And God called the light day, and the darkness He called night.** Light is called " good," because it is from the Lord, who is good itself. The " darkness " means all those things which, before man is conceived and born anew, have appeared like light, because evil has appeared like good, and falsity like the truth ; yet they are darkness, consisting merely of the things proper to man himself, which still remain.

Whatsoever is of the Lord is compared to " day," because it pertains to light ; and whatsoever is man's own is compared to " night," because it pertains to darkness. These comparisons frequently occur in the Word.

22. Verse 5. **And the evening and the morning were the first day.** What is meant by " evening," and what by " morning," can now be discerned. " Evening " means every preceding state, because it is a state of shade, or of falsity and of no faith ; " morning " is every subsequent state, being one of light, or of truth, and of the cognitions of faith. " Evening," in a general sense, signifies all things that are of man's own ; but " morning," whatever is of the Lord, as is said through *David* :

The spirit of Jehovah spake in me, and His word was on my tongue ; the God of Israel said, the Rock of Israel spake to me ; He is as the light of the morning, when the sun ariseth, even a morning without clouds, when from brightness, from rain, the tender herb springeth out of the earth (2 *Sam.* xxiii. 2–4).

As it is " evening " when there is no faith, and " morning " when there is faith, therefore the coming of the Lord into the world is called " morning " ; and the time when He comes, because then there is no faith, is called " evening," as in *Daniel* :

The Holy One said unto me, Even unto evening when it becomes morning, two thousand and three hundred (viii. 14, 26).

In like manner " morning " is used in the Word to denote every coming of the Lord, consequently, it is an expression of new creation.

21

23. Nothing is more common in the Word than for " day " to be used to denote time itself. As in *Isaiah* :

The day of Jehovah is at hand. Behold, the day of Jehovah cometh. I will shake the heavens, and the earth shall be shaken out of her place, in the day of the wrath of Mine anger. Her time is near to come, and her days shall not be prolonged (xiii. 6, 9, 13, 22).

And in the same Prophet :

Her antiquity is of ancient days. And it shall come to pass in that day that Tyre shall be forgotten seventy years, according to the days of one king (xxiii. 7, 15).

As " day " is used to denote time, it is also used to denote the state of that time, as in *Jeremiah* :

Woe unto us, for the day is gone down, for the shadows of the evening are stretched out (vi. 4).

And again :

If ye shall make vain My covenant of the day, and My covenant of the night, so that there be not day and night in their season (xxxiii. 20, also 25).

And again :

Renew our days, as of old (*Lam.* v. 21).

24. Verse 6. **And God said, Let there be an expanse in the midst of the waters, and let it distinguish between the waters in the waters.** After the spirit of God, or the Lord's mercy, has brought forth into day the cognitions of what is true and good, and has given the first light, that the Lord is, that He is good itself, and truth itself, and that there is no good and truth but from Him, He then makes a distinction between the internal man and

22

the external, consequently, between the cognitions that are in the internal man, and the scientifics that belong to the external man. The internal man is called an " expanse " ; the cognitions which are in the internal man are called " the waters above the expanse " ; and the scientifics of the external man are called " the waters beneath the expanse." Man, before he is being regenerated, does 2 not even know that any internal man exists, much less does he know what its nature is. He supposes the internal and the external man to be not distinct. For, being immersed in bodily and worldly things, he has also immersed in them the things that belong to his internal man, and has made of things that are distinct a confused and obscure unit. Therefore it is first said, " Let there be an expanse in the midst of the waters," and then, " Let it distinguish between the waters in the waters " ; but not, Let it distinguish between the waters which are " under " the expanse and the waters which are " above " the expanse, as is afterwards said in the next verses :

And God made the expanse, and made a distinction between the waters which were under the expanse, and the waters which were above the expanse ; and it was so. And God called the expanse heaven (verses 7, 8).

The next thing, therefore, that man observes in 3 the course of regeneration is that he begins to know that there is an internal man, or that the things which are in the internal man are goods and truths, which are of the Lord alone. Now as the external man, when being regenerated, is of such a nature that he still supposes the goods that he does to be done of himself, and the truths that he speaks to be spoken of himself, and whereas, being such, he

23

is led by them of the Lord, as by things of his own,
to do what is good and to speak what is true,
therefore mention is first made of a distinction
of the waters under the expanse, and afterwards of
those above the expanse. It is also an arcanum of
heaven, that man, by things of his own, as well by
the fallacies of the senses as by lusts, is led and
bent by the Lord to things that are true and good,
and thus that every movement and moment of
regeneration, both in general and in particular,
proceeds from evening to morning, thus from the
external man to the internal, or from " earth " to
" heaven." Therefore the expanse, or internal
man, is now called " heaven."

25. To " spread out the earth and stretch out
the heavens," is a common form of speaking with
the Prophets, when treating of the regeneration
of man. As in *Isaiah* :

Thus said Jehovah thy Redeemer, and He
that formed thee from the womb ; I am Jehovah
that maketh all things, that stretcheth forth the
heavens alone, that spreadeth abroad the earth
by Myself (xliv. 24).

And again, where the advent of the Lord is openly
spoken of :

A bruised reed shall He not break, and the
smoking flax shall He not quench ; He shall
bring forth judgment unto truth.

This means that He does not break fallacies, nor
quench lusts, but bends them to what is true and
good ; and therefore it follows :

Jehovah God createth the heavens, and
stretcheth them out ; He spreadeth out the
earth, and the productions thereof ; He giveth

breath unto the people upon it, and spirit to them that walk therein (xliii. 3–5).

Not to mention other passages of the same purport.

26. Verse 8. **And the evening and the morning were the second day.** The meaning of " evening," of " morning," and of " day," was shown above at verse 5.

27. Verse 9. **And God said, Let the waters under the heaven be gathered together to one place, and let the dry [land] appear ; and it was so.** When it is known that there is both an internal and an external man, and that truths and goods flow in from, or through, the internal man to the external, from the Lord, although it does not so appear, then those truths and goods, or the cognitions of the true and the good in the regenerating man, are stored up in his memory, and are classed among its scientifics ; for whatsoever is insinuated into the memory of the external man, whether it be natural, or spiritual, or celestial, abides there as scientifics, and is brought forth thence by the Lord. These cognitions are the " waters gathered together into one place," and are called " seas," but the external man himself is called the " dry [land]," and presently " earth," as in what follows.

28. Verse 10. **And God called the dry [land] earth, and the gathering together of the waters called He seas ; and God saw that it was good.** It is a very common thing in the Word for " waters " to signify cognitions and scientifics, and, consequently, for " seas " to signify a collection of these. As in *Isaiah* :

The earth shall be full of the knowledge (*scientia*) of Jehovah, as the waters cover the sea (xi. 9).

And in the same Prophet, where a lack of cognitions and scientifics is treated of:

The waters shall fail from the sea, and the river shall be dried up and become utterly dry, and the streams shall recede (xix. 5, 6).

Here, in *Haggai*, a new church is spoken of:

I will shake the heavens and the earth, and the sea and the dry [land]; and I will shake all nations; and the desire of all nations shall come, and I will fill this house with glory (ii. 6, 7).

And concerning man in the process of regeneration, in *Zechariah*:

There shall be one day, it is known to Jehovah; not day, nor night; but it shall come to pass that at evening time it shall be light; and it shall be in that day that living waters shall go out from Jerusalem, part of them toward the eastern sea, and part of them toward the hinder sea (xiv. 7, 8).

In *David* also, describing a vastated man who is to be regenerated and who will worship the Lord:

Jehovah despiseth not His prisoners; let the heavens and the earth praise Him, the seas and everything that creepeth therein (*Ps.* lxix. 33, 34).

That the " earth " signifies a recipient, appears from *Zechariah*:

Jehovah stretcheth forth the heavens, and layeth the foundation of the earth, and formeth the spirit of man in the midst of him (xii. 1).

29.   Verses 11, 12. **And God said, Let the earth bring forth the tender herb, the herb yielding seed, and the fruit-tree bearing fruit after its kind, whose seed is in itself, upon the earth ; and it was so.**

And the earth brought forth the tender herb, the herb yielding seed after its kind, and the tree bearing fruit, whose seed was in itself, after its kind ; and God saw that it was good. When the " earth," or man, has been thus prepared to receive celestial seeds from the Lord, and to produce something of what is good and true, then the Lord first causes some tender thing to spring forth, which is called the " tender herb " ; then something more useful, which again bears seed in itself, and is called the " herb yielding seed " ; and at length something good which becomes fruitful, and is called the " tree bearing fruit, whose seed is in itself," each according to its own kind. The man who is being regenerated is at first of such a quality that he thinks that the good which he does, and the truth which he speaks, are from himself, when in reality all good and all truth are from the Lord, so that whoever supposes them to be from himself has not as yet the life of true faith, which, nevertheless, he may afterwards receive ; for he cannot as yet believe that they are from the Lord, because he is only in a state of preparation for the reception of the life of faith. This state is here represented by things inanimate, and the succeeding one of the life of faith, by animate things. The Lord is He 2 who sows, the " seed " is His Word, and the " earth " is man, as He Himself has deigned to declare (*Matt.* xiii. 19–24, 37–39 ; *Mark* iv. 14–21 ; *Luke* viii. 11–16). To the same purport He gives this description :

So is the kingdom of God, as a man when he casteth seed into the earth, and sleepeth and riseth night and day, and the seed groweth and riseth up, he knoweth not how ; for the earth bringeth forth fruit of herself, first the blade,

27

then the ear, after that the full corn in the ear
(*Mark* iv. 26–28).

By the " kingdom of God," in the universal sense,
is meant the universal heaven ; in a sense less
universal, the true church of the Lord ; and in a
particular sense, every one who is of true faith,
or who is regenerate by a life of faith.   Wherefore,
such a person is also called " heaven," because
heaven is in him ; and also the " kingdom of God,"
because the kingdom of God is in him ; as the
Lord Himself teaches in *Luke* :

Being demanded of the Pharisees when the
kingdom of God should come, He answered
them, and said, The kingdom of God cometh
not with observation ; neither shall they say, Lo
here ! or, Lo there ! for behold, the kingdom
of God is within you (xvii. 20, 21).

This is the third successive stage of the regeneration
of man, being his state of repentance, and in like
manner proceeding from shade to light, or from
evening to morning ; wherefore it is said (v. 13),
*and the evening and the morning were the third
day.*

30.   Verses 14–17.   **And God said, Let there
be lights in the expanse of the heavens, to distinguish
between the day and the night ; and let them be
for signs, and for seasons, and for days, and for
years ; and let them be for lights in the expanse
of the heavens, to give light upon the earth ; and
it was so.   And God made two great lights, the
great light to rule by day, and the lesser light to
rule by night ; and the stars.   And God set them
in the expanse of the heavens, to give light upon
the earth.**   What is meant by " great lights "
cannot be clearly understood unless it is first

known what is the essence of faith, and also what
is its progress with those who are being created
anew. The very essence and life of faith is the
Lord alone, for he who does not believe in the Lord
cannot have life, as He Himself has declared in
John :

> He that believeth on the Son hath eternal
> life ; but he that believeth not on the Son shall
> not see life, but the wrath of God shall abide upon
> him (iii. 36).

The progression of faith with those who are being 2
created anew is as follows. At first they have no
life, for there is none in what is evil and false,
but only in what is good and true is there life ;
afterwards they receive life from the Lord by faith,
first by faith of the memory, which is a faith of
mere scientifics ; next by faith in the understanding, which is an intellectual faith ; lastly by faith
in the heart, which is the faith of love, or saving
faith. The first two kinds of faith are represented
from verse 3 to verse 13, by things inanimate, but
faith vivified by love is represented from verse 20
to verse 25, by animate things. For this reason
love, and faith thence derived, are now here first
treated of, and are called " lights " ; love being
" the great light which rules by day " ; faith
derived from love " the lesser light which rules by
night " ; and as these two lights ought to make a
one, it is said of them, in the singular number, " Let
there be lights (*sit luminaria*)," and not in the
plural (*sint luminaria*). Love and faith in the 3
internal man are like heat and light in the external
corporeal man, for which reason the former are
represented by the latter. It is on this account
that lights are said to be " set in the expanse of
heaven," or in the internal man ; a great light in

its will, and a lesser one in its understanding ; but they appear in the will and the understanding only as does the light of the sun in its recipient objects. It is the Lord's mercy alone that affects the will with love, and the understanding with truth or faith.

31. That the " great lights " signify love and faith, and are also called " sun, moon, and stars," is evident from the Prophets, as in *Ezekiel* :

When I shall extinguish thee, I will cover the heavens and make the stars thereof black ; I will cover the sun with a cloud, and the moon shall not give her light ; all the luminaries of the light of heaven will I make black over thee, and I will set darkness upon thy land (xxxii. 7, 8).

In this passage Pharaoh and the Egyptians are treated of, by whom are meant, in the Word, the sensual and scientific ; and here, that by sensuous things and scientifics, love and faith had been extinguished. So in *Isaiah* :

The day of Jehovah cometh to set the land in desolation, for the stars of heaven and the constellations thereof shall not give their light ; the sun is darkened in his going forth, and the moon shall not cause her light to shine (xiii. 9, 10).

Again, in *Joel* :

The day of Jehovah cometh, a day of darkness and of thick darkness ; the earth trembleth before Him, the heavens are in commotion ; the sun and the moon are blackened, and the stars withdraw their brightness (ii. 1, 2, 10).

2 Again, in *Isaiah*, speaking of the advent of the Lord and the enlightening of the Gentiles, consequently, of a new church, and in particular of all

30

who are in darkness, and receive light, and are being regenerated :

Arise, shine, for thy light is come ; behold darkness covers the earth, and thick darkness the peoples, and Jehovah shall arise upon thee, and the Gentiles shall come to thy light, and kings to the brightness of thy rising, Jehovah shall be to thee a light of eternity, thy sun shall no more go down, neither shall thy moon withdraw itself, for Jehovah shall be to thee a light of eternity (lx. 1–3, 20).

So in *David* :

Jehovah in intelligence maketh the heavens, He stretcheth out the earth above the waters ; He maketh great lights ; the sun to rule by day, the moon and stars to rule by night (*Ps.* cxxxvi. 5–9).

And again :

Glorify ye Jehovah, sun and moon ; glorify Him, all ye stars of light ; glorify Him, ye heavens of heavens, and ye waters that are above the heavens (*Ps.* cxlviii. 3, 4).

In all these passages, " lights " signify love and 3 faith. It was because " lights " represented and signified love and faith towards the Lord that it was ordained in the Jewish Church that a perpetual light should be kept burning from evening till morning, for every ordinance in that church was representative of the Lord. Of this light it is written :

Command the sons of Israel that they take oil for the light, to cause the lamp to ascend continually : in the tabernacle of the congregation without the veil, which is before the testi-

mony, shall Aaron and his sons order it from
evening even until morning, before Jehovah
(*Exod.* xxvii. 20, 21).

That these things signify love and faith, which the
Lord kindles and causes to give light in the internal
man, and through the internal man in the external,
will, of the Lord's Divine mercy, be shown in its
proper place.

32. Love and faith are first called " great
lights," and afterwards love is called a " great
light," and faith a " lesser light " ; and it is said
of love that it shall " rule by day," and of faith
that it shall " rule by night." As these are arcana
which are hidden, especially in this end of days,
it is permitted, of the Lord's Divine mercy, to
explain them. The reason why these arcana are
more especially concealed in this end of days is
that now is the consummation of the age, when
there is scarcely any love, and, consequently,
scarcely any faith, as the Lord Himself foretold
in the Evangelists in these words :

The sun shall be darkened, and the moon
shall not give her light, and the stars shall
fall from heaven, and the powers of the heavens
shall be shaken (*Matt.* xxiv. 29).

By the " sun " is here meant love, which is darkened ; by the " moon " faith, which does not give
light ; and by the " stars," the cognitions of faith,
which fall from heaven, and which are the " virtues
2 and powers of the heavens." The Most Ancient
Church acknowledged no other faith than love
itself. The celestial angels also do not know what
faith is except that which is of love. The universal
heaven is a heaven of love, for there is no other
life in the heavens than the life of love. From this

32

is derived all heavenly happiness, which is so great that it does not admit of description, nor can it ever be conceived by any human idea. Those who are under the influence of love, love the Lord from the heart, but yet know, declare, and perceive, that all love, and, consequently, all life—which is of love alone—and thus all happiness, come solely from the Lord, and that they have not the least love, life, or happiness, from themselves. That it is the Lord from whom all love comes, was also represented by the great light or " sun," at His transfiguration, for it is written :

His face did shine as the sun, and His raiment was white as the light (*Matt.* xvii. 2).

Inmost things are signified by the face, and the things that proceed from them by the raiment. Thus the Lord's Divine was signified by the " sun," or love ; and His Human by the " light," or wisdom proceeding from love.

33. It is in every one's power to know quite well that no life is possible without some love, and that no joy is possible except that which flows from love. Such, however, as is the love, such is the life, and such the joy ; if you were to remove loves, or what is the same thing, desires—for these are of love—thought would instantly cease, and you would become like a dead person, as has been shown me to the life. The loves of self and of the world have in them some resemblance to life and to joy, but as they are altogether contrary to true love, which consists in a man's loving the Lord above all things, and his neighbour as himself, it must be evident that they are not loves, but hatreds, for in proportion as any one loves himself and the world, in the same proportion he hates his

B   **33**

neighbour, and thereby the Lord. Wherefore true
love is love to the Lord, and true life is the life of
love from Him, and true joy is the joy of that life.
There can be but one true love, and therefore
but one true life, whence flow true joys and true
felicities, such as are those of the angels in the
heavens.

34. Love and faith admit of no separation,
because they constitute one and the same thing;
and therefore when mention is first made of
" lights " they are regarded as one, and it is said,
" let there be (*sit*) lights in the expanse of the
heavens." Concerning this circumstance it is
permitted me to relate the following wonderful
particulars. The celestial angels, by virtue of the
celestial love in which they are from the Lord,
are from that love in all the cognitions of faith, and
are in such a life and light of intelligence that
scarcely anything of it can be described. But, on
the other hand, spirits who are in the knowledge
of the doctrinals of faith, without love, are in such
a coldness of life and obscurity of light that they
cannot even approach the first threshold of the
court of the heavens, but flee back again. Some
of them say that they have believed in the Lord,
but they had not lived according to His precepts,
and it was of such that the Lord said in *Matthew* :

Not every one that saith unto Me, Lord, Lord,
shall enter into the kingdom of the heavens,
but he that doeth My will : many will say to
Me in that day, Lord, Lord, have we not prophesied through Thy name ? (vii. 21, 22, to the
end).

2 Hence it is evident that those who are in love are
also in faith, and thereby in heavenly life, but not

34

those who say they are in faith, and are not in the life of love. The life of faith without love is like the light of the sun without heat, as in the time of winter, when nothing grows, but all things are torpid and dead ; whereas faith proceeding from love is like the light of the sun in the time of spring, when all things grow and flourish in consequence of the sun's fructifying heat. It is precisely similar in regard to spiritual and heavenly things, which are usually represented in the Word by such as exist in the world and on the face of the earth. No faith, and faith without love, are also compared by the Lord to "winter," where He foretells the consummation of the age, in *Mark* :

> Pray ye that your flight be not in the winter, for those shall be days of affliction (xiii. 18, 19).

" Flight " means the last time, and also that of every man when he dies. " Winter " is a life destitute of love ; the " day of affliction " is its miserable state in the other life.

35. Man has two faculties : the will and the understanding. When the understanding is governed by the will they together constitute one mind, and thus one life, for then what the man wills and does he also thinks and intends. But when the understanding is at variance with the will, as with those who say they have faith, and yet live in contradiction to faith, then the one mind is divided into two, one of which desires to exalt itself into heaven, while the other tends towards hell ; and since the will is the doer in every act, the whole man would plunge headlong into hell if it were not that the Lord has mercy on him.

35

36. Those who have separated faith from love do not even know what faith is. When thinking of faith, some imagine it to be mere thought, some that it is thought directed towards the Lord, few that it is the doctrine of faith. But faith is not only a knowledge and acknowledgment of all things that the doctrine of faith comprises, but especially is it an obedience to all things that the doctrine of faith teaches. The primary point that it teaches, and that which men should obey, is love to the Lord, and love towards the neighbour, for if a man is not in this, he is not in faith. This the Lord teaches so plainly as to leave no doubt concerning it, in *Mark* :

> The first of all the commandments is, Hear, O Israel, the Lord our God is one Lord ; therefore thou shalt love the Lord thy God with all thy heart, and with all thy soul, and with all thy mind, and with all thy strength : this is the first commandment ; and the second is like, namely this, Thou shalt love thy neighbour as thyself ; there is none other commandment greater than these (xii. 29–31).

In *Matthew*, the Lord calls the former of these the " first and great commandment," and says that " on these commandments hang all the Law and the Prophets " (xxii. 37–41). The " Law and the Prophets " are the universal doctrine of faith, and the whole Word.

37. It is said that the lights shall be " for signs, and for seasons, and for days, and for years." In these words are contained more arcana than can at present be unfolded, although in the sense of the letter nothing of the kind appears. Suffice it here to observe that there are alternations of

things spiritual and celestial, both in general and
in particular, which are compared to the changes
of days and of years. The changes of days are
from morning to mid-day, thence to evening, and
through night to morning ; and the changes of
years are similar, being from spring to summer,
thence to autumn, and through winter to spring.
Hence come the alternations of heat and light,
and also of the productions of the earth. To these
changes are compared the alternations of things
spiritual and celestial. Life without such alternations and varieties would be uniform, consequently,
no life at all ; nor would good and truth be discerned or distinguished, much less perceived. These
alternations are in the Prophets called "ordi-
nances," as in *Jeremiah* :

> Said Jehovah, who giveth the sun for a light
> by day, and the ordinances of the moon and
> of the stars for a light by night (xxxi. 35, 36).

And in the same Prophet :

> Said Jehovah, If My covenant of day and
> night stand not, and if I have not appointed
> the ordinances of heaven and earth (xxxiii. 25).

But concerning these things, of the Lord's Divine
mercy, we will treat at *Genesis* viii. 22.

38. Verse 18. **And to rule in the day, and in the
night, and to distinguish between the light and the
darkness; and God saw that it was good.** By the
"day" is meant good, by the "night," evil ;
and therefore goods are called works of the day,
but evils works of the night ; by the "light" is
meant truth, and by the "darkness" falsity, as
the Lord says :

> Men loved darkness rather than light. He

that doeth truth cometh to the light (*John* iii. 19, 21).

Verse 19. **And the evening and the morning were the fourth day.**

39. Verse 20. **And God said, Let the waters cause to creep forth the creeping thing, the living soul ; and let fowl fly above the earth upon the faces of the expanse of the heavens.** After the great lights have been kindled and placed in the internal man, and the external receives light from them, then the man first begins to live. Heretofore he can scarcely be said to have lived, inasmuch as the good which he did he supposed that he did of himself, and the truth which he spoke that he spoke of himself ; and since man of himself is dead, and there is in him nothing but what is evil and false, therefore whatsoever he produces from himself is not alive, insomuch that he cannot, from himself, do good that in itself is good. That man cannot even think what is good, nor will what is good, consequently, cannot do what is good, except from the Lord, must be plain to every one from the doctrine of faith, for the Lord says in *Matthew* :

He that soweth the good seed is the Son of man (xiii. 37).

Nor can any good come except from the real Fountain of good, which is One only, as He says in another place :

None is good save One, God (*Luke* xviii. 19).

2 Nevertheless, when the Lord is resuscitating man to life, that is, regenerating him, He permits him at first to suppose that he does what is good and speaks what is true from himself, for at that time he is incapable of conceiving otherwise, nor can he

in any other way be led to believe, and afterwards
to perceive, that all good and truth are from the
Lord alone.- While man is thinking in such a way
his truths and goods are compared to the " tender
grass," and also to the " herb yielding seed,"
and lastly to the " tree bearing fruit," all of which
are inanimate ; but now that he is vivified by
love and faith, and believes that the Lord works
all the good that he does and all the truth that he
speaks, he is compared first to the " creeping
things of the water," and to the " fowls which fly
above the earth," and also to " beasts," which are
all animate things, and are called " living souls."

40. By the " creeping things which the waters
bring forth," are signified the scientifics which
belong to the external man ; by " birds " in
general, rational and intellectual things, of which
the latter belong to the internal man. That the
" creeping things of the waters," or " fishes,"
signify scientifics, is plain from *Isaiah* :

I came and there was no man ; at My rebuke
I dry up the sea, I make the rivers a wilderness ;
their fish shall stink because there is no water
and shall die for thirst ; I clothe the heavens
with blackness (l. 2, 3).

But it is still plainer from *Ezekiel*, where the Lord 2
describes the new temple, or a new church in
general, and the man of the church, or a regenerate person ; for every one who is regenerate
is a temple of the Lord :

The Lord Jehovih said unto me, These waters
that shall issue to the boundary toward the
east, and shall come toward the sea, being led
into the sea, and the waters shall be healed ; and
it shall come to pass that every living soul that

shall creep forth, whithersoever the water of the rivers shall come, shall live, and there shall be exceeding much fish, because those waters shall come thither, and they shall heal, and everything shall live whither the river cometh ; and it shall come to pass that fishers shall stand upon it from En-gedi to En-eglaim, with the spreading of nets shall they be ; their fish shall be according to its kind, as the fish of the great sea, exceeding many (xlvii. 8–10).

3 " Fishers from En-gedi unto En-eglaim," with the " spreading of nets," signify those who shall instruct the natural man in the truths of faith. That " birds " signify rational and intellectual things, is evident from the Prophets ; as in *Isaiah* :

Calling a bird from the east, the man of My counsel from a distant land (xlvi. 11).

And in *Jeremiah* :

I beheld and lo there was no man, and all the birds of the heavens were fled (iv. 25).

In *Ezekiel* :

I will plant a shoot of a lofty cedar, and it shall lift up a branch, and shall bear fruit, and be a magnificent cedar : and under it shall dwell every fowl of every wing, in the shadow of the branches thereof shall they dwell (xvii. 22, 23).

And in *Hosea*, a new church is spoken of or a regenerate man.

And in that day will I make a covenant for them with the wild beast of the field, and with the fowls of heaven, and with the moving thing of the ground (ii. 18).

That " wild beast " does not signify wild beast, nor " bird " bird, must be evident to every one, for the Lord is said to " make a new covenant " with them.

41. Whatever is of man's proprium has no life in itself, and whenever it is made manifest to the sight it appears hard, like a bony and black substance ; but whatever is from the Lord has life, containing within it that which is spiritual and celestial, which, when presented to view, appears human and living. It may seem incredible but is nevertheless most true, that every single expression, every single idea, and every least thought in an angelic spirit, is alive, containing in its minutest particulars an affection that proceeds from the Lord, who is Life itself. And therefore whatsoever things are from the Lord, have life in them, because they contain faith towards Him, and are here signified by the " living soul " : they have also a species of body, here signified by " what moves itself," or " creeps." These truths, however, are as yet profound arcana to man, and are now mentioned only because the " living soul," and the " thing moving itself," are treated of.

42. Verse 21. **And God created great whales, and every living soul that creepeth, which the waters made to creep forth, after their kinds, and every winged fowl after its kind ; and God saw that it was good.** " Fishes," as before said, signify scientifics, now animated by faith from the Lord, and thus alive. " Whales " signify their general principles, in subordination to which, and from which, are the particulars ; for there is nothing in the universe that is not under some general principle, as a means that it may exist and subsist. " Whales," or " great fishes," are sometimes mentioned by the Prophets, and they there signify

the generals of scientifics. Pharaoh the king of Egypt (by whom is represented human wisdom or intelligence, that is, knowledge in general), is called a " great whale." As in *Ezekiel* :

Behold, I am against thee, Pharaoh king of Egypt, the great whale that lieth in the midst of his rivers, that hath said, My river is mine own, and I have made myself (xxix. 3).

2 And in another place :

Take up a lamentation for Pharaoh king of Egypt, and say unto him, Thou art as a whale in the seas, and hast gone forth in thy rivers, and hast troubled the waters with thy feet (xxxii. 2).

By these words are signified those who desire to enter into the mysteries of faith by means of scientifics, and thus from themselves. In *Isaiah* :

In that day Jehovah, with His hard and great and strong sword, shall visit upon leviathan the long serpent, even leviathan the crooked serpent, and He shall slay the whales that are in the sea (xxvii. 1).

By " slaying the whales that are in the sea," is signified that such persons are ignorant of even the general principles of truth. So in *Jeremiah* :

Nebuchadnezzar the king of Babylon hath devoured me, he hath troubled me, he hath made me an empty vessel, he hath swallowed me as a whale, he hath filled his belly with my delicacies, he hath cast me out (li. 34).

This denotes that he had swallowed the cognitions of faith, here called " delicacies," as the whale did Jonah ; a " whale " denoting those who possess the general principles of the cognitions of faith as scientifics, and act in this manner.

43. Verse 22. **And God blessed them, saying, Be fruitful, and multiply, and fill the waters in the seas, and the fowl shall be multiplied in the earth.** Everything that has in itself life from the Lord fructifies and multiplies itself immensely ; not so much while the man lives in the body, but to an amazing degree in the other life. To " be fruitful," in the Word, is predicated of the things that pertain to love, and to " multiply," of the things that pertain to faith ; the " fruit " which is of love contains "seed," by which it so greatly multiplies itself. The Lord's " blessing " also in the Word signifies fructification and multiplication, because they proceed from it.

Verse 23. **And the evening and the morning were the fifth day.**

44. Verses 24, 25. **And God said, Let the earth bring forth the living soul after its kind, the beast, and the moving thing, and the wild animal of the earth after its kind ; and it was so. And God made the wild animal of the earth after its kind, and the beast after its kind, and everything that creepeth on the ground after its kind ; and God saw that it was good.** Man, like the earth, can produce nothing good unless the cognitions of faith are first sown in him, whereby he may know what is to be believed and done. It is the office of the understanding to hear the Word, and of the will to do it. To hear the Word and not to do it, is like saying that we believe when we do not live according to our belief ; in this case we separate hearing and doing, and have a divided mind, and are those whom the Lord calls " foolish " in the following passage :

Whosoever heareth My words, and doeth them, I will liken unto a wise man who built his house upon a rock : but every one that heareth My words, and doeth them not, I will liken to a foolish man, who built his house upon the sand (*Matt.* vii. 24, 26).

The things that belong to the understanding are signified, as before shown, by the " creeping things which the waters bring forth," and also by the " fowl upon the earth," and " upon the faces of the expanse " ; but those which belong to the will are signified here by the " living soul which the earth produces," and by the " beast " and "creeping thing," and also by the " wild animals of that earth."

45. Those who lived in the most ancient times thus signified the things relating to the understanding and to the will ; and therefore in the Prophets, and constantly in the Word of the Old Testament, similar things are represented by different kinds of animals. Beasts are of two kinds ; the evil, so called because they are hurtful ; and the good, which are harmless. Evils in man are signified by evil beasts, as by bears, wolves, dogs ; and the things which are good and gentle, by beasts of a similar nature, as by heifers, sheep, and lambs. The " beasts " here referred to are good and gentle ones, and thus signify affections, because it here treats of those who are being regenerated. The lower things in man, which have more connection with the body, are called " wild animals of that earth," and are lusts and pleasures.

46. That " beasts " signify man's affections—. evil affections with the evil, and good affections with the good—is evident from numerous passages in the Word, as in *Ezekiel* :

Behold, I am for you, and I will look back

to you, that ye may be tilled and sown, and I will multiply upon you man and beast, and they shall be multiplied and bring forth fruit ; and I will cause you to dwell as in your ancient times (xxxvi. 9, 11, treating of regeneration).

In *Joel* :

Be not afraid ye beasts of My field, for the dwelling-places of the wilderness are become grassy (ii. 22).

In *David* also :

So foolish was I, I was as a beast before Thee (*Ps.* lxxiii. 22).

In *Jeremiah,* treating of regeneration :

Behold the days come, saith Jehovah, that I will sow the house of Israel and the house of Judah with the seed of man, and with the seed of beast, and I will watch over them to build and to plant (xxxi. 27, 28).

" Wild animals " have a similar signification, as 2 in *Hosea* :

In that day will I make a covenant for them with the wild animal of the field, and with the fowl of the heavens, and with the creeping thing of the earth (ii. 18).

In *Job* :

Thou shalt not be afraid of the wild animals of the earth, for thy covenant is with the stones of the field, and the wild animals of the field shall be at peace with thee (v. 22, 23).

In *Ezekiel* :

I will make with you a covenant of peace, and will cause the evil wild animal to cease out of the land, that they may dwell confidently in the wilderness (xxxiv. 25).

45

In *Isaiah* :

> The wild animals of the field shall honour me,
> because I have given waters in the wilderness
> (xliii. 20).

In *Ezekiel* :

> All the fowls of the heavens made their nests
> in his boughs, and under his branches did all
> the wild animals of the field bring forth their
> young, and under his shadow dwelt all great
> nations (xxxi. 6).

This is said of the Assyrian, by whom is signified
the spiritual man, and who is compared to the
garden of Eden.

In *David* :

> Glorify ye Him, all His angels, glorify Jehovah
> from the earth, ye whales, fruit-trees, wild
> animal, and every beast, creeping thing, and
> flying fowl (*Ps.* cxlviii. 2, 7, 9, 10).

Here mention is made of the same things—as
" whales," the " fruit-tree," " wild animal," the
" beast," " creeping thing," and " fowl," which,
unless they had signified living principles in man,
could never have been called upon to glorify
3 Jehovah. The Prophets carefully distinguish
between " beasts " and " wild animals " " of the
earth," and " beasts " and " wild animals " " of
the field." Nevertheless, goods in man are called
" beasts," just as those who are nearest the Lord in
heaven are called " animals," both in *Ezekiel* and
in *John* :

> All the angels stood round about the throne,
> and the elders, and the four animals, and fell
> before the throne on their faces, and worshipped
> the Lamb (*Rev.* vii. 11 ; xix. 4).

Those also who have the gospel preached to them are called " creatures," because they are to be created anew :

Go ye into all the world, and preach the gospel to every creature (*Mark* xvi. 15).

47. That these words contain arcana relating to regeneration, is evident also from its being said in the foregoing verse that the earth should bring forth " the living soul, the beast, and the wild animal of the earth," whereas in the following verse the order is changed, and it said that God made " the wild animal of the earth," and likewise " the beast " ; for at first, and afterwards until he becomes celestial, man brings forth as of himself ; and thus regeneration begins from the external man, and proceeds to the internal ; therefore here there is another order, and external things are mentioned first.

48. Hence it appears that man is in the fifth state of regeneration when he speaks from a principle of faith, which belongs to the understanding, and thereby confirms himself in what is true and good. The things then brought forth by him are animate, and are called the " fishes of the sea," and the " fowl of the heavens." He is in the sixth state, when from faith, which is of the understanding, and from love thence derived, which is of the will, he speaks truths, and does goods ; what he then brings forth being called the " living soul," and the " beast." And as he then begins to act from love, as well as from faith, he becomes a spiritual man, who is called an " image of God," which is the subject now treated of.

47

49. Verse 26. **And God said, Let us make man in our image, after our likeness ; and let them have dominion over the fish of the sea, and over the fowl of the heavens, and over the beast, and over all the earth, and over every creeping thing that creepeth upon the earth.** In the Most Ancient Church, with the members of which the Lord conversed face to face, the Lord appeared as a Man ; concerning which much might be related, but the time has not yet arrived. On this account they called no one " man " but the Lord Himself, and the things which pertained to Him ; neither did they call themselves " men," but only those things in themselves—as all the good of love and all the truth of faith—which they perceived they had from the Lord. These they said were " of man," because they were of the Lord. Hence in the Prophets, by " man " and the " Son of man," in the highest sense, is meant the Lord ; and, in the internal sense, wisdom and intelligence ; thus every one who is regenerate. As in *Jeremiah* :

2

I beheld the earth, and lo, it was void and emptiness, and the heavens, and they had no light. I beheld, and lo, there was no man, and all the birds of the heavens were fled (iv. 23, 25).

In *Isaiah*, where, in the internal sense, by " man " is meant a regenerate person, and in the highest sense, the Lord Himself, as the One Man :

Thus saith Jehovah the Holy One of Israel, and his Former, I have made the earth, and created man upon it ; I, even My hands, have stretched out the heavens, and all their host have I commanded (xlv. 11, 12).

3 The Lord therefore appeared to the prophets as a man, as in *Ezekiel* :

Above the expanse, as the appearance of a
sapphire stone, the likeness of a throne, and
upon the likeness of the throne was the likeness as
the appearance of a man above upon it (i. 26).

And when seen by Daniel He was called the " Son
of man," that is, the Man, which is the same
thing :

I saw, and behold, one like the Son of man
came with the clouds of heaven, and came to the
Ancient of days, and they brought Him near
before Him ; and there was given Him dominion,
and glory, and a kingdom, that all people, and
nations, and languages should serve Him ; His
dominion is an everlasting dominion, which
shall not pass away, and His kingdom that which
shall not be destroyed (vii. 13, 14).

The Lord also frequently calls Himself the " Son of 4
man," that is, the Man, and, as in *Daniel*, foretells
His coming in glory :

Then shall they see the Son of man coming in
the clouds of heaven with power and great
glory (*Matt*. xxiv. 30).

The " clouds of heaven " are the literal sense of the
Word ; " power and great glory " are the internal
sense of the Word, which in all things, both in
general and in particular, has reference solely to
the Lord and His kingdom ; and it is from this
that the internal sense derives its power and glory.

50. The Most Ancient Church understood by
the " image of the Lord " more than can be
expressed.   Man is altogether ignorant that he
is governed by the Lord through angels and
spirits, and that with every one there are at least
two spirits, and two angels.   By spirits he has

communication with the world of spirits, and by angels with heaven. Without communication by means of spirits with the world of spirits, and by means of angels with heaven, and thus through heaven with the Lord, man could not live at all ; his life entirely depends on this conjunction, so that if the spirits and angels were to withdraw, he 2 would instantly perish. While man is unregenerate he is governed quite otherwise than when regenerated. While unregenerate there are evil spirits with him, who so domineer over him that the angels, though present, are scarcely able to do anything more than merely guide him so that he may not plunge into the lowest evil, and bend him to some good—in fact, bend him to good by means of his own lusts, and to truth by means of the fallacies of the senses. He then has communication with the world of spirits through the spirits who are with him, but not so much with heaven, because evil spirits rule, and the angels only avert 3 their rule. But when the man is regenerate, the angels rule, and inspire him with all goods and truths, and with fear and horror of evils and falsities. The angels indeed lead, but only as ministers, for it is the Lord alone who governs man through angels and spirits. And as this is done through the ministry of angels, it is here first said, in the plural number, " Let us make man in our image " ; and yet because the Lord alone governs and disposes, it is said in the following verse, in the singular number, " God created him in His own image." This the Lord also plainly declares in *Isaiah* :

Thus saith Jehovah thy Redeemer, and He that formed thee from the womb, I Jehovah make all things, stretching forth the heavens

alone, spreading abroad the earth by Myself
(xliv. 24).

The angels themselves, moreover, confess that
there is no power in them, but that they act from
the Lord alone.

51. As regards the " image " ; an image is not
a likeness, but is according to the likeness ; it is
therefore said, " Let us make man in our image,
after our likeness." The spiritual man is an
" image," and the celestial man a " likeness," or
similitude. In this chapter the spiritual man is
treated of ; in the following, the celestial. The
spiritual man, who is an " image," is called by the
Lord a " son of light," as in *John* :

> He that walketh in the darkness knoweth not
> whither he goeth. While ye have the light,
> believe in the light, that ye may be sons of
> light (xii. 35, 36).

He is called also a " friend " :

> Ye are My friends if ye do whatsoever I
> command you (*John* xv. 14, 15).

But the celestial man, who is a " likeness," is
called a " son of God," in *John* :

> As many as received Him, to them gave He
> power to become sons of God, even to them that
> believe on His name ; who were born not of
> bloods, nor of the will of the flesh, nor of the
> will of man, but of God (i. 12, 13).

52. So long as man is spiritual, his dominion
proceeds from the external man to the internal, as
is here said : " Let them have dominion over the
fish of the sea, and over the fowl of the heavens,
and over the beast, and over all the earth, and over

every creeping thing that creepeth upon the earth."
But when he becomes celestial, and does good from
love, then his dominion proceeds from the internal
man to the external, as the Lord, in *David*, describes
Himself, and thereby also the celestial man, who
is His likeness :

> Thou madest him to have dominion over the
> works of Thy hands ; Thou hast put all things
> under his feet, the flock and all cattle, and also
> the beasts of the fields, the fowl of the heavens,
> and the fish of the sea, and whatsoever passeth
> through the paths of the seas (*Ps.* viii. 6–8).

Here therefore " beasts " are first mentioned, and
then " fowl," and afterwards the " fish of the sea,"
because the celestial man proceeds from love,
which belongs to the will, differing herein from
the spiritual man, in describing whom " fishes "
and " fowl " are first named, which belong to the
understanding, and this to faith ; and afterwards
mention is made of " beasts."

53. Verse 27. **And God created man in His own
image, in the image of God created He him.** The
reason why " image ' is here twice mentioned,
is that faith, which belongs to the understanding,
is called " His image " ; whereas love, which
belongs to the will, and which in the spiritual man
comes after, but in the celestial man precedes, is
called the " image of God."

54. **Male and female created He them.** What
is meant by " male and female," in the internal
sense, was well known to the Most Ancient Church,
but when the interior sense of the Word was lost
among their posterity, this arcanum also perished.
Their marriages were their chief sources of happi-

ness and delight, and whatever admitted of the
comparison they likened to marriage, in order
that in this way they might perceive its felicity.
Being also internal men, they were delighted only
with internal things. External things they merely
saw with the eyes, but they thought of what was
represented. So that outward things were nothing
to them, save as these could in some measure be
the means of causing them to turn their thoughts
to internal things, and from these to celestial
things, and so to the Lord who was their All, and
consequently to the heavenly marriage, from which
they perceived the happiness of their marriages
came. The understanding in the spiritual man
they therefore called male, and the will female,
and when these acted as one they called it a
marriage. From that church came the form of
speech which became customary, whereby the
church itself, from its affection of good, was called
" daughter " and " virgin," as the " virgin of
Zion," the " virgin of Jerusalem," and also " wife."
But on these subjects see the following chapter,
at verse 23, and chapter iii., verse 15.

55. Verse 28. **And God blessed them, and God
said unto them, Be fruitful, and multiply, and
replenish the earth, and subdue it ; and have
dominion over the fish of the sea, and over the
fowl of the heavens, and over every living thing
that creepeth upon the earth.** As the most ancient
people called the conjunction of the understanding
and the will, or of faith and love, a marriage,
everything of good produced from that marriage
they called " fructifications," and everything of
truth, " multiplications." Hence they are so
called in the Prophets, as for instance in *Ezekiel* :

I will multiply upon you man and beast, and they shall multiply and be fruitful, and I will cause you to dwell as in your ancient times, and will do better unto you than at your beginnings, and ye shall know that I am Jehovah, yea, I will cause man to walk upon you, even My people Israel (xxxvi. 11, 12).

By " man " is here meant the spiritual man who is called Israel ; by " ancient times," the Most Ancient Church ; by " beginnings," the Ancient Church after the flood. The reason why " multiplication," which refers to truth, is first mentioned, and " fructification," which refers to good, afterwards, is that the passage treats of one who is to become regenerated, and not of one who is already
2 regenerated. When the understanding is united with the will, or faith with love, the man is called by the Lord " a married land," as in *Isaiah* :

Thy land shall be no more termed waste, but thou shalt be called [Hephzibah] My delight is in her, and thy land [Beulah] married, for Jehovah delighteth in thee, and thy land shall be married (lxii. 4).

The fruits thence issuing, which pertain to truth, are called " sons," and those which pertain to good are called " daughters," and this very frequently
3 in the Word. The earth is " replenished," or filled, when there are many truths and goods ; for when the Lord blesses and speaks to man, that is, works upon him, there is an immense increase of good and truth, as the Lord says in *Matthew* :

The kingdom of the heavens is like to a grain of mustard-seed, which a man took and sowed in his field, which indeed is the least of all seeds, but when it is grown, it is the greatest among

herbs, and becometh a tree, so that the birds
of the heavens come and build their nests in
the branches thereof (xiii. 31, 32).

A "grain of mustard-seed" is man's good before
he becomes spiritual, which is "the least of all
seeds," because he thinks that he does good of
himself, and what is of himself is nothing but
evil. But as he is in a state of regeneration, there
is something of good in him, but it is the least of
all. At length, as faith is joined with love, it 4
grows larger, and becomes an "herb"; and
lastly, when the conjunction is completed, it
becomes a "tree," and then the "birds of the
heavens" (in this passage also denoting truths,
or things intellectual) "build their nests in its
branches," which are scientifics. When man is
spiritual, as well as during the time of his becoming
spiritual, he is in a state of combat, and therefore
it is said, "subdue the earth and have dominion."

56. Verse 29. **And God said, Behold, I give you
every herb bearing seed which is upon the faces of
all the earth; and every tree in which is fruit;
the tree yielding seed, to you it shall be for food.**
The celestial man is delighted with celestial things
alone, which, being in agreement with his life,
are called celestial food. The spiritual man is
delighted with spiritual things, and as these are
in agreement with his life they are called spiritual
food. The natural man in like manner is delighted
with natural things, which, being of his life, are
called food, and consist chiefly of scientifics. As
the spiritual man is here treated of, his spiritual
food is described by representatives, as by the
"herb bearing seed," and by the "tree in which is
fruit," which are called, in general, the "tree

yielding seed." His natural food is described in the following verse.

57. The " herb bearing seed " is every truth which regards use ; the " tree in which is fruit " is the good of faith ; " fruit " is what the Lord gives to the celestial man, but " seed producing fruit " is what He gives to the spiritual man ; and therefore it is said, the " tree yielding seed, to you it shall be for food." That celestial food is called fruit from a tree, is evident from the following chapter, where the celestial man is treated of. In confirmation of this we will here cite only these words of the Lord from *Ezekiel* :

> By the river, upon the bank thereof, on this side and on that side, there cometh up every tree of food, whose leaf shall not fade, neither shall the fruit thereof be consumed ; it is born again in its month ; because these its waters issue out of the sanctuary ; and the fruit thereof shall be for food, and the leaf thereof for medicine (xlvii. 12).

" Waters issuing out of the sanctuary," signify the life and mercy of the Lord, who is the " sanctuary." " Fruit " is wisdom, which shall be food for them ; the " leaf " is intelligence which shall be for their use, and this use is called " medicine." But that spiritual food is called " herb," appears from *David* :

> My shepherd, I shall not want ; Thou makest me to lie down in pastures of herb (*Ps.* xxiii. 1, 2).

58. Verse 30. **And to every wild animal of the earth, and to every fowl of the heavens, and to everything that creepeth upon the earth, wherein**

there is a living soul, I give every green herb for food ; and it was so. The natural meat of the same man is here described. His Natural is signified by the " wild animal of the earth " and by the " fowl of the heavens," to which there are given for food the vegetable and the green of the herb. Both his natural and his spiritual food are thus described in *David* :

> Jehovah causeth the grass to grow for the beast, and herb for the service of man, that he may bring forth bread out of the earth (*Ps.* civ. 14).

Here the term " beast " is used to express both the wild animal of the earth and the fowl of the heavens, which are mentioned in verses 11 and 12 of the same Psalm.

59. The reason why the " vegetable and the green of the herb " only are here described as food for the natural man, is this. In the course of regeneration, when man is being made spiritual, he is continually engaged in combat, on which account the church of the Lord is called militant ; for before regeneration lusts have the dominion, because the whole man is composed of mere lusts and the falsities thence derived. During regeneration, these lusts and falsities cannot be instantaneously abolished, for this would be to destroy the whole man, such being the only life which he has acquired ; and therefore evil spirits are suffered to continue with him for a long time, that they may excite his lusts, and that these may thus be loosened, in innumerable ways, even to such a degree that they can be inclined by the Lord to good, and the man be thus reformed. In the

57

time of combat, the evil spirits, who bear the
utmost hatred against everything good and true,
that is, against whatever pertains to love and
faith towards the Lord—which things alone are
good and true, because they have eternal life in
them—leave the man nothing else for food but
what is compared to the vegetable and the green
of the herb ; nevertheless, the Lord gives him
also a food which is compared to the herb bearing
seed, and to the tree in which is fruit, which are
states of tranquillity and peace, with their joys and
delights ; and this food the Lord gives the man
2 at intervals. Unless the Lord defended man every
moment, yea, even the smallest part of every
moment, he would instantly perish, in consequence
of the indescribably intense and mortal hatred
which prevails in the world of spirits against the
things relating to love and faith towards the Lord.
The certainty of this fact I can affirm, having been
now for some years, although still in the body,
associated with spirits in the other life, even with
the worst of them, and I have sometimes been
surrounded by thousands, who were allowed to
spit forth their venom, and infest me by all possible
methods, yet without their being able to hurt a
single hair of my head, so secure was I under the
Lord's protection. From so many years' experience I have been thoroughly instructed concerning
the world of spirits and its nature, as well as
concerning the combat which those being
regenerated must needs endure, in order to attain
the happiness of eternal life. But as no one can be
so well instructed in such subjects by a general
description as to believe them with an undoubting
faith, the particulars will, of the Lord's Divine
mercy, be related in the following pages.

60. Verse 31. **And God saw everything that He had made, and behold it was very good. And the evening and the morning were the sixth day.** This state is called " very good," the former ones being merely called " good " ; because now the things which are of faith make one with those which are of love, and thus a marriage is effected between spiritual things and celestial things.

61. All things relating to the cognitions of faith are called spiritual, and all that are of love to the Lord and our neighbour are called celestial ; the former belong to man's understanding, and the latter to his will.

62. The times and states of man's regeneration in general and in particular are divided into six, and are called the days of his creation ; for, by degrees, from being not a man at all, he becomes at first something of one, and so by little and little attains to the sixth day, in which he becomes an image of God.

63. Meanwhile the Lord continually fights for him against evils and falsities, and by combats confirms him in truth and good. The time of combat is the time of the Lord's working ; and therefore in the Prophets the regenerate man is called the work of the fingers of God. Nor does He rest until love acts as principal ; then the combat ceases. When the work has so far advanced that faith is conjoined with love, it is called " very good " ; because the Lord then actuates him, as His likeness. At the end of the sixth day the evil spirits depart, and good spirits take their place, and the man is introduced into heaven, or into the celestial paradise ; concerning this we will treat in the following chapter.

64. This then is the internal sense of the Word, its veriest life, which does not at all appear from the sense of the letter. But so many are its arcana that volumes would not suffice for the unfolding of them. A very few only are here set forth, and these such as may confirm the fact that regeneration is here treated of, and that this proceeds from the external man to the internal. It is thus that the angels perceive the Word. They know nothing at all of what is in the letter, not even the proximate meaning of a single word; still less do they know the names of the countries, cities, rivers, and persons, that occur so frequently in the historical and prophetical parts of the Word. They have an idea only of the things signified by the words and the names. Thus by Adam in paradise they perceive the Most Ancient Church, yet not that church, but the faith in the Lord of that church. By Noah they perceive the church that remained with the descendants of the Most Ancient Church, and that continued to the time of Abram. By Abraham they by no means perceive that individual, but a saving faith, which he represented; and so on. Thus they perceive spiritual and celestial things entirely apart from the words and names.

65. Certain ones were taken up to the first entrance-court of heaven, when I was reading the Word, and from there conversed with me. They said they could not there understand one whit of any word or letter therein, but only what was signified in the nearest interior sense, which they declared to be so beautiful, in such order of sequence, and so affecting them, that they called it Glory.

66. There are in the Word, in general, four different styles. The *first* is that of the Most Ancient Church. Their mode of expression was such that when they mentioned terrestrial and worldly things they thought of the spiritual and celestial things which these represented. They therefore not only expressed themselves by representatives, but also formed these into a kind of historical series, in order to give them more life ; and this was to them delightful in the very highest degree. This is the style of which Hannah prophesied, saying :

Speak what is high ! high ! Let what is ancient come out of your mouth (1 *Sam.* ii. 3). Such representatives are called in *David*, " Dark sayings of old " (*Ps.* lxxviii. 2–4). These particulars concerning the creation, the garden of Eden, etc., down to the time of Abram, Moses had from the descendants of the Most Ancient Church. The *second* style is historical, which is found in the books of Moses from the time of Abram onward, and in the books of *Joshua*, *Judges*, *Samuel*, and the *Kings*. In these books the historical facts are just as they appear in the sense of the letter ; and yet they all contain, both in general and particular, quite other things in the internal sense, of which, by the Lord's Divine mercy, we will treat in their order in the following pages. The *third* style is the prophetical one, which was born of that which was so highly venerated in the Most Ancient Church. This style, however, is not in connected and historical form like the most ancient style, but is broken, and is scarcely ever intelligible except in the internal sense, wherein are the deepest arcana, which follow in beautiful connected order, and relate to the external and the internal man ; to the many states of the church ; to heaven itself ; and, in the inmost sense, to the Lord. The *fourth* style is that of the *Psalms of David*, which is intermediate between the prophetical style and that of common speech. The Lord is there treated of in the internal sense, under the person of David as a king.

CHAPTER THE SECOND.

67. As of the Lord's Divine mercy it has been granted me to know the internal meaning of the Word, in which are contained the deepest arcana that have not before come to any one's knowledge, nor can come unless the nature of the other life is known (for very many things of the Word's internal sense have regard to, describe, and involve those of that life), I am permitted to disclose what I have heard and seen during some years in which it has been granted me to be in the company of spirits and angels.

68. I am well aware that many will say that no one can possibly speak with spirits and angels so long as he lives in the body; and many will say that it is all a phantasy, others that I relate such things in order to gain credence, and others will make other objections. But by all this I am not deterred, for I have seen, I have heard, I have felt.

69. Man was so created by the Lord as to be able while living in the body to speak with spirits and angels, as in fact was done in the most ancient times; for, being a spirit clothed with a body, he is one with them. But because in process of time men so immersed themselves in corporeal and worldly things as to care almost nothing for aught besides, the way was closed. Yet as soon as the corporeal things recede, in which man is immersed, the way is again opened, and he is among spirits, and in a common life with them.

70. As it is permitted me to disclose what for several years I have heard and seen, it shall here be told, first, how the case is with man when he is being resuscitated ; or how he enters from the life of the body into the life of eternity. In order that I might know that men live after death, it has been given me to speak and be in company with many who were known to me during their life in the body ; and this not merely for a day or a week, but for months, and almost a year, speaking and associating with them just as in this world. They wondered exceedingly that while they lived in the body they were, and that very many others are, in such incredulity as to believe that they will not live after death ; when in fact only a few days intervene after the death of the body before they are in the other life ; for death is a continuation of life.

71. But as these matters would be scattered and disconnected if inserted among those contained in the text of the Word, it is permitted, of the Lord's Divine mercy, to append them in some order, at the beginning and end of each chapter ; besides those which are introduced incidentally.

72. At the end of this chapter, accordingly, I am allowed to tell how man is raised from the dead and enters into the life of eternity.

CHAPTER II.

1. And the heavens and the earth were finished, and all the host of them.

2. And on the seventh day God finished His work which He had made ; and He rested on the seventh day from all His work which He had made.

3. And God blessed the seventh day, and hallowed it, because that in it He rested from all His work which God in making created.

4. These are the nativities of the heavens and of the earth when He created them, in the day in which Jehovah God made the earth and the heavens.

5. And there was no shrub of the field as yet in the earth, and there was no herb of the field as yet growing, because Jehovah God had not caused it to rain upon the earth. And there was no man to till the ground.

6. And He made a mist to ascend from the earth, and watered all the faces of the ground.

7. And Jehovah God formed man, dust from the ground, and breathed into his nostrils the breath of lives, and man became a living soul.

8. And Jehovah God planted a garden from the east in Eden, and there He put the man whom He had formed.

9. And out of the ground made Jehovah God to grow every tree desirable to behold, and good for food ; the tree of lives also, in the midst of the garden ; and the tree of the knowledge of good and evil.

10. And a river went out of Eden to water the garden, and from thence it was parted, and became four heads.

11. The name of the first is Pishon ; that is it which compasseth the whole land of Havilah, where there is gold.

12. And the gold of that land is good ; there is bdellium and the onyx stone.

13. And the name of the second river is Gihon ; the same is it that compasseth the whole land of Cush.

14. And the name of the third river is Hiddekel ; that is it which goeth eastward toward Assyria ; and the fourth river is Euphrates.

15. And Jehovah God took the man, and put him in the garden of Eden, to till it and take care of it.

16. And Jehovah God commanded the man, saying, Of every tree of the garden eating thou mayest eat.

17. But of the tree of the knowledge of good and evil, thou shalt not eat of it ; for in the day that thou eatest thereof, dying thou shalt die.

THE CONTENTS.

73. When from being dead a man has become spiritual, then from spiritual he becomes celestial, as is now treated of (verse 1).

74. The celestial man is the seventh day, on which the Lord rests (verses 2, 3).

75. His Scientific and his Rational are described by the shrub and the herb out of the ground watered by the mist (verses 5, 6).

76. His life is described by the breathing into him of the breath of lives (verse 7).

77. Afterwards his intelligence is described by the garden in Eden, from the east ; in which trees pleasant to the sight are perceptions of truth, and the trees good for food are perceptions of good. Love is meant by the tree of lives, faith by the tree of knowledge (verses 8, 9).

78. Wisdom is meant by the river in the garden. From thence were four rivers, the first of which is

good and truth ; the second is the cognition of all things of good and truth, or of love and faith. These are of the internal man. The third is reason, and the fourth is knowledge, which pertain to the external man. All are from wisdom, and this is from love and faith in the Lord (verses 10–14).

79. The celestial man is such a garden. But as the garden is the Lord's, it is permitted this man to enjoy all these things, and yet not to possess them as his own (verse 15).

80. He is also permitted to know what is good and true by means of every perception from the Lord, but he must not do so from himself and the world, nor search into the mysteries of faith by means of the things of sense and of scientifics ; which would cause the death of his celestial nature (verses 16, 17).

———

THE INTERNAL SENSE.

81. This chapter treats of the celestial man, as the preceding one did of the spiritual, who was formed out of a dead man. But as it is unknown at this day what the celestial man is, and scarcely what the spiritual man is, or a dead man, it is permitted me briefly to state the nature of each, that the difference may be known. *First*, then, a dead man acknowledges nothing to be true and good but what belongs to the body and the world, and this he adores. A spiritual man acknowledges spiritual and celestial truth and good ; but he does so from a principle of faith, which is likewise the ground of his actions, and not so much from love. A celestial man believes and perceives spiritual

67

and celestial truth and good, acknowledging no other faith than that which is from love, from which also he acts. *Secondly* : The ends which influence 2 a dead man regard only bodily and worldly life, nor does he know what eternal life is, or what the Lord is ; or should he know, he does not believe. The ends which influence a spiritual man regard eternal life, and thereby the Lord. The ends which influence a celestial man regard the Lord, and 3 thereby His kingdom and eternal life. *Thirdly* : A dead man, when in combat almost always yields, and when not in combat, evils and falsities have dominion over him, and he is a slave. His bonds are external, such as the fear of the law, of the loss of life, of wealth, and gain, and of the reputation which he values for their sake. The spiritual man is in combat, but is always victorious ; the bonds by which he is restrained are internal, and are called the bonds of conscience. The celestial man is not in combat, and when assaulted by evils and falsities, he despises them, and is therefore called a conqueror. He is apparently restrained by no bonds, but is free. His bonds, which are not apparent, are perceptions of good and truth.

82. Verse 1. **And the heavens and the earth were finished, and all the host of them.** By these words is meant that man is now rendered so far spiritual as to have become the " sixth day " ; " heaven " is his internal man, and " earth " his external ; " the host of them " are love, faith, and the cognitions thereof, which were previously signified by the great lights and the stars. That the internal man is called " heaven," and the external " earth," is evident from the passages of the Word already cited in the preceding chapter,

68

to which may be added the following from *Isaiah* :

I will make a man more rare than solid gold, even a man than the precious gold of Ophir ; therefore I will smite the heavens with terror, and the earth shall be shaken out of its place (xiii. 12, 13).

Thou forgettest Jehovah thy Maker, that stretcheth forth the heavens, and layeth the foundations of the earth ; but I will put My words in thy mouth, and I will hide thee in the shadow of My hand, that I may stretch out the heaven, and lay the foundation of the earth (li. 13, 16).

From these words it is evident that both " heaven " and " earth " are predicated of man ; for although they refer primarily to the Most Ancient Church, yet the interiors of the Word are of such a nature that whatever is said of the church may also be said of every individual member of it, who, unless he were a church, could not possibly be a part of the church, just as he who is not a temple of the Lord cannot be what is signified by the temple, namely, the church and heaven. It is for this reason that the Most Ancient Church is called " man," in the singular number.

83. The " heavens and the earth and all the host of them " are said to be " finished," when man has become the " sixth day," for then faith and love make one. When they do this, love, and not faith, or in other words the Celestial, and not the Spiritual, begins to be the principal, and this is to be a celestial man.

84. Verses 2, 3. **And on the seventh day God finished His work which He had made ; and He**

69

rested on the seventh day from all His work which He had made. And God blessed the seventh day, and hallowed it ; because that in it He rested from all His work which God in making created. The celestial man is the " seventh day," which, as the Lord has worked during the six days, is called " His work " ; and as all combat then ceases, the Lord is said to " rest from all His work." On this account the seventh day was sanctified, and called the Sabbath, from a Hebrew word meaning " rest." And thus was man created, formed, and made. These things are very evident from the words.

85. That the celestial man is the " seventh day," and that the seventh day was therefore hallowed, and called the Sabbath, are arcana which have not hitherto been discovered. For none have been acquainted with the nature of the celestial man, and few with that of the spiritual man, whom in consequence of this ignorance they have considered to be the same as the celestial man, notwithstanding the great difference that exists between them, as may be seen in n. 81. As regards the seventh day, and as regards the celestial man being the " seventh day " or " Sabbath," this is evident from the fact that the Lord Himself is the Sabbath ; and therefore He says :

The Son of man is Lord also of the Sabbath (*Mark* ii. 27).

These words imply that the Lord is Man himself, and the Sabbath itself. His kingdom in the heavens and on the earth is called, from Him, a 2 Sabbath, or eternal peace and rest. The Most Ancient Church, which is here treated of, was the Sabbath of the Lord above all that succeeded it.

70

Every subsequent inmost church of the Lord is also a Sabbath ; and so is every regenerate person when he becomes celestial, because he is a likeness of the Lord. The six days of combat or labour precede. These things were represented in the Jewish Church by the days of labour, and by the seventh day, which was the Sabbath ; for in that church there was nothing instituted which was not representative of the Lord and of His kingdom. The same was also represented by the ark when it went forward, and when it rested, for by its journeyings in the wilderness were represented combats and temptations, and by its rest a state of peace ; and therefore, when it set forward, Moses said :

> Rise up, Jehovah, and let Thine enemies be scattered, and let them that hate Thee flee before Thy faces. And when it rested, he said, Return, Jehovah, unto the ten thousands of the thousands of Israel (*Num.* x. 35, 36).

It is there said of the ark that it went from the Mount of Jehovah " to search out a rest for them " (verse 33). The rest of the celestial man is described 3 by the Sabbath in *Isaiah* :

> If thou bring back thy foot from the Sabbath, so that thou doest not thy desire in the day of My holiness, and callest the things of the Sabbath delights to the holy of Jehovah, honourable ; and shalt honour it, not doing thine own ways, nor finding thine own desire, nor speaking a word ; then shalt thou be delightful to Jehovah, and I will cause thee to be borne above the lofty things of the earth, and will feed thee with the heritage of Jacob (lviii. 13, 14).

Such is the quality of the celestial man that he

71

acts not according to his own desire, but according to the good pleasure of the Lord, which is his "desire." Thus he enjoys internal peace and happiness—here expressed by " being uplifted over the lofty things of the earth "—and at the same time external tranquillity and delight, which is signified by " being fed with the heritage of Jacob."

86. When the spiritual man, who has become the " sixth day," is beginning to be celestial, which state is here first treated of, it is the " eve of the Sabbath," represented in the Jewish Church by the keeping holy of the Sabbath from the evening. The celestial man is the " morning " to be spoken of presently.

87. Another reason why the celestial man is the " Sabbath," or " rest," is that combat ceases when he becomes celestial. The evil spirits retire, and good ones approach, as well as celestial angels ; and when these are present, evil spirits cannot possibly remain, but flee far away. And since it was not the man himself who carried on the combat, but the Lord alone for the man, it is said that the Lord " rested."

88. When the spiritual man becomes celestial, he is called the " work of God," because the Lord alone has fought for him, and has created, formed, and made him ; and therefore it is here said, " God finished His work on the seventh day " ; and twice, that " He rested from all His work." By the Prophets man is repeatedly called the " work of the hands and of the fingers of Jehovah " ; as in *Isaiah*, speaking of the regenerate man :

Thus hath said Jehovah the Holy One of Israel, and his Former, Seek ye signs of Me,

signs concerning My sons, and concerning the
work of My hands command ye Me. I have made
the earth, and created man upon it ; I, even
My hands, have stretched out the heavens, and
all their host have I commanded. For thus
hath said Jehovah that createth the heavens, God
Himself that formeth the earth and maketh it ;
He establisheth it, He created it not a void,
He formed it to be inhabited ; I am Jehovah and
there is no God else besides Me (xlv. 11, 12,
18, 21).

Hence it is evident that the new creation, or
regeneration, is the work of the Lord alone. The
expressions to " create," to " form," and to
" make," are employed quite distinctively, both
in the above passage—" creating the heavens,
forming the earth, and making it "—and in other
places in the same Prophet, as :

Every one that is called by My name, I have
created him for My glory, I have formed him,
yea, I have made him (xliii. 7).

Also in both the preceding chapter and this one of
Genesis ; as in the passage before us : " He rested
from all His work which God in making created."
In the internal sense this usage always conveys a
distinct idea ; and the case is the same where the
Lord is called " Creator," " Former," or " Maker."

89. Verse 4. **These are the nativities of the
heavens and of the earth, when He created them,
in the day in which Jehovah God made the earth
and the heavens.** The " nativities of the heavens
and of the earth," are the formations of the
celestial man. That his formation is here treated
of is very evident from all the particulars which

c*   73

follow, as that no herb was as yet growing ; that
there was no man to till the ground, as well as
that Jehovah God formed man, and afterwards,
that He made every beast and bird of the heavens,
notwithstanding that the formation of these had
been treated of in the foregoing chapter ; from
all which it is manifest that another man is here
treated of.　This, however, is still more evident
from the fact, that now for the first time the Lord
is called " Jehovah God," whereas, in the preceding passages, which treat of the spiritual man,
He is called simply " God " ; and, further, that
now " ground " and " field " are mentioned, while
in the preceding passages only " earth " is mentioned.　In this verse also " heaven " is first
mentioned before " earth," and afterwards " earth "
before " heaven " ; the reason of which is that
" earth " signifies the external man, and " heaven "
the internal, and in the spiritual man reformation
begins from " earth," that is, from the external
man, while in the celestial man, who is here treated
of, it begins from the internal man, or from
" heaven."

90. Verses 5, 6.　**And there was no shrub of the
field as yet in the earth, and there was no herb of
the field as yet growing, because Jehovah God had
not caused it to rain upon the earth ; and there
was no man to till the ground.　And He made a
mist to ascend from the earth, and watered all the
faces of the ground.**　By the " shrub of the field,"
and the " herb of the field," are meant in general
all that his external man produces.　The external
man is called " earth " while he remains spiritual,
but " ground " and also " field " when he becomes
celestial.　" Rain," which is soon after called

" mist," is the tranquillity of peace when combat ceases.

91. But what these things involve cannot possibly be perceived unless it is known what man's state is while, from being spiritual, he is becoming celestial, for they are deeply hidden. While he is spiritual, the external man is not yet willing to yield obedience to and serve the internal, and therefore there is a combat ; but when he becomes celestial, then the external man begins to obey and serve the internal, and therefore the combat ceases, and tranquillity ensues (see n. 87). This tranquillity is signified by "rain" and "mist," for it is like a vapour with which the external man is watered and bedewed from the internal ; and it is this tranquillity, the offspring of peace, which produces what are called the " shrub of the field," and the " herb of the field," which, specifically, are rational things and scientifics from a celestial spiritual origin.

92. The nature of the tranquillity of peace of the external man, on the cessation of combat, or of the unrest caused by lusts and falsities, can be known only to those who are acquainted with a state of peace. This state is so delightful that it surpasses every idea of delight : it is not only a cessation of combat but is life proceeding from interior peace, and affecting the external man in such a manner as cannot be described ; the truths of faith, and the goods of love, which derive their life from the delight of peace, are then born.

93. The state of the celestial man, thus gifted with the tranquillity of peace—refreshed by the rain—and delivered from the slavery of what is

75

evil and false, is thus described by the Lord in *Ezekiel* :

I will make with them a covenant of peace, and will cause the evil wild beast to cease out of the land, and they shall dwell confidently in the wilderness, and sleep in the woods ; and I will make them and the places round about My hill a blessing ; and I will cause the rain to come down in his season ; rains of blessing shall they be. And the tree of the field shall yield its fruit, and the earth shall yield its increase, and they shall be upon the ground in confidence, and shall know that I am Jehovah, when I have broken the reins of their yoke, and delivered them out of the hand of those that make them to serve them ; and ye My flock, the flock of My pasture, ye are a man, and I am your God (xxxiv. 25–27, 31).

And that this is effected on the " third day," which in the Word signifies the same as the " seventh," is thus declared in *Hosea* :

After two days will He vivify us ; in the third day He will raise us up, and we shall live before Him ; and we shall know, and shall follow on to know Jehovah : His going forth is prepared as the dawn, and He shall come unto us as the rain, as the late rain watering the earth (vi. 2, 3).

And that this state is compared to the " growth of the field " is declared by *Ezekiel*, when speaking of the Ancient Church :

I have caused thee to multiply as the growth of the field, and thou hast increased and hast grown up, and hast come to excellent ornaments (xvi. 7).

76

And it is also compared to

A shoot of the Lord's planting, and a work of the hands of Jehovah God (*Isa.* lx. 21).

94. Verse 7. **And Jehovah God formed man, dust from the ground, and breathed into his nostrils the breath of lives, and man became a living soul.** To " form man, dust from the ground," is to form his external man, which before was not man ; for it is said (verse 5) that there was " no man to till the ground." To " breathe into his nostrils the breath of lives," is to give him the life of faith and love ; and by " man became a living soul," is signified that his external man also was made alive.

95. The life of the external man is here treated of—the life of his faith or understanding in the two former verses, and the life of his love or will in this verse. Hitherto the external man has been unwilling to yield to and serve the internal, being engaged in a continual combat with him, and therefore the external man was not then " man." Now, however, being made celestial, the external man begins to obey and serve the internal, and it also becomes " man," being so rendered by the life of faith and the life of love. The life of faith prepares him, but it is the life of love which causes him to be " man."

96. As to its being said that " Jehovah God breathed into his nostrils," the case is this : In ancient times, and in the Word, by " nostrils " was understood whatever was grateful in consequence of its odour, which signifies perception. On this account it is repeatedly written of Jehovah, that He " smelled an odour of rest " from the

77

burnt-offerings, and from those things which represented Him and His kingdom ; and as the things
relating to love and faith are most grateful to
Him, it is said that " He breathed through his
nostrils the breath of lives." Hence the anointed
of Jehovah, that is, of the Lord, is called the
" breath of the nostrils " (*Lam.* iv. 20). And the
Lord Himself signified the same by " breathing
on His disciples," as written in *John* :

> He breathed on them and said, Receive ye
> the Holy Spirit (xx. 22).

97. The reason why life is described by " breathing " and by " breath," is also that the men of the
Most Ancient Church perceived states of love and
of faith by states of respiration, which were successively changed in their posterity. Of this respiration nothing can as yet be said, because at this
day such things are altogether unknown. The
most ancient people were well acquainted with
it, and so are those who are in the other life, but
no longer any one on this earth, and this was the
reason why they likened spirit or life to " wind."
The Lord also does this when speaking of the
regeneration of man, in *John* :

> The wind bloweth where it listeth, and thou
> hearest the voice thereof, and knowest not
> whence it cometh, or whither it goeth ; so is
> every one that is born of the spirit (iii. 8).

So in *David* :

> By the word of Jehovah were the heavens
> made, and all the host of them by the breath
> of His mouth (*Ps.* xxxiii. 6).

And again :

> Thou gatherest their breath, they expire, and

78

return to their dust ; Thou sendest forth Thy spirit, they are created, and Thou renewest the faces of the ground (*Ps.* civ. 29, 30).

That the " breath " is used for the life of faith and of love, appears from *Job* :

He is the spirit in man, and the breath of Shaddai giveth them understanding (xxxii. 8).

Again in the same :

The Spirit of God hath made me, and the breath of Shaddai hath given me life (xxxiii. 4).

98. Verse 8. **And Jehovah God planted a garden eastward in Eden, and there He put the man whom He had formed.** By a " garden " is signified intelligence ; by " Eden," love ; by the " east," the Lord ; consequently, by the " garden of Eden eastward," is signified the intelligence of the celestial man, which flows in from the Lord through love.

99. Life, or the order of life, with the spiritual man, is such that although the Lord flows in, through faith, into the things of his understanding, his reason, and his scientifics, yet as his external man fights against his internal man, it appears as if intelligence did not flow in from the Lord, but from the man himself, through scientifics and reasonings. But the life, or order of life, of the celestial man, is such that the Lord flows in through love and the faith of love into the things of his understanding, his reason, and his scientifics, and as there is no combat between the internal and the external man, he perceives that this is really so. Thus the order which up to this point had been inverted with the spiritual man, is now described as restored with the celestial man, and

79

this order, or man, is called a " garden in Eden in
the east." In the highest sense, the " garden
planted by Jehovah God in Eden in the east " is
the Lord Himself. In the inmost sense, which is
also the universal sense, it is the Lord's kingdom,
and the heaven in which man is placed when
he has become celestial. His state then is such
that he is with the angels in heaven, and is, as it
were, one among them ; for man has been so
created that while living in this world he may,
at the same time, be in heaven. In this state all
his cognitions and the ideas of his cognitions, and
even his words and actions, are open, even from
the Lord, and contain within them what is celestial
and spiritual ; for there is in every man the life
of the Lord, which causes him to have perception.

100. That a " garden " signifies intelligence, and
" Eden " love, appears also from *Isaiah* :

> Jehovah will comfort Zion, He will comfort all
> her waste places, and He will make her wilder-
> ness like Eden, and her desert like the garden of
> Jehovah ; joy and gladness shall be found
> therein, confession and the voice of singing
> (li. 3).

In this passage, " wilderness," " joy," and " confession," are terms expressive of the celestial
things of faith, or such as relate to love ; but
" desert," " gladness," and " the voice of singing,"
of the spiritual things of faith, or such as belong
to the understanding. The former have relation
to " Eden," the latter to " garden " ; for with
this Prophet two expressions constantly occur
concerning the same thing, one of which signifies
celestial, and the other spiritual things. What is

80

further signified by the " garden in Eden," may be seen in what follows at verse 10.

101. That the Lord is the " east " also appears from the Word, as in *Ezekiel* :

He brought me to the gate, even the gate that looketh the way of the east, and behold the glory of the God of Israel came from the way of the east ; and His voice was as the voice of many waters, and the earth shone with His glory (xliii. 1, 2, 4).

It was in consequence of the Lord's being the " east " that a holy custom prevailed in the representative Jewish Church, before the building of the temple, of turning their faces towards the east when they prayed.

102. Verse 9. **And out of the ground made Jehovah God to grow every tree desirable to behold, and good for food ; the tree of lives also, in the midst of the garden, and the tree of the knowledge of good and evil.** A " tree " signifies perception ; a " tree desirable to behold," the perception of truth , a " tree good for food," the perception of good ; the " tree of lives," love and the faith thence derived ; the " tree of the knowledge of good and evil," faith derived from what is sensuous, or from knowledge.

103. The reason why " trees " here signify perceptions is that the celestial man is treated of, but it is otherwise when the subject is the spiritual man, for on the nature of the subject depends that of the predicate.

104. At this day it is unknown what perception is. It is a certain internal sensation, from the Lord

81

alone, as to whether a thing is true and good ; and
it was very well known to the Most Ancient Church.
This perception is so perfect with the angels, that
by it they are aware and have knowledge of what
is true and good ; of what is from the Lord, and
what from themselves ; and also of the quality of
any one who comes to them, merely from his
approach, and from a single one of his ideas. The
spiritual man has no perception, but has conscience.
A dead man has not even conscience ; and very
many do not know what conscience is, and still
less what perception is.

105. The " tree of lives " is love and the faith
thence derived ; " in the midst of the garden,"
is in the will of the internal man. The will, which
in the Word is called the " heart," is the primary
possession of the Lord with man and angel. But
as no one can do good of himself, the will or heart
is not man's, although it is predicated of man ;
cupidity, which he calls will, is man's. Since then
the will is the " midst of the garden," where the
tree of lives is placed, and man has no will, but
mere cupidity, the " tree of lives " is the mercy
of the Lord, from whom come all love and faith,
consequently all life.

106. But the nature of the " tree of the garden,"
or perception ; of the " tree of lives," or love and
the faith thence derived ; and of the " tree of
knowledge," or faith originating in what is sensuous
and in knowledge, will be shown in the following
pages.

107. Verse 10. **And a river went out of Eden,
to water the garden, and from thence it was parted
and became four heads.** A " river out of Eden,"

signifies wisdom from love, for " Eden," is love ;
" to water the garden," is to bestow intelligence ;
to be " thence parted into four heads," is a
description of intelligence by means of the four
rivers, as follows.

108. The most ancient people, when comparing
man to a " garden," also compared wisdom, and
the things relating to wisdom, to " rivers " ; nor
did they merely compare them, but actually so
called them, for such was their way of speaking.
It was the same afterwards in the Prophets, who
sometimes compared them, and sometimes called
them so. As in *Isaiah* :

> Thy light shall arise in darkness, and thy
> thick darkness shall be as the light of day ; and
> thou shalt be like a watered garden, and like an
> outlet of waters, whose waters deceive not
> (lviii. 10, 11).

This treats of those who receive faith and love.
Again, speaking of the regenerate :

> As the valleys are they planted, as gardens by
> the river's side ; as lignaloes* which Jehovah
> hath planted, as cedar-trees beside the waters
> (*Num.* xxiv. 6).

In *Jeremiah* :

> Blessed is the man who trusteth in Jehovah ;
> he shall be as a tree planted by the waters, and
> that sendeth forth her roots by the river (xvii.
> 7, 8).

In *Ezekiel* the regenerate are not compared to a
garden and a tree, but are so called :

> The waters made her to grow, the deep of

* The Latin is *tentoria,* " tents," seemingly a misprint
for *santalos.* See Schmidius. [REVISER.]

83

waters uplifted her, the river ran round about
her plant, and sent out its channels to all the
trees of the field ; she was made beautiful in
her greatness, in the length of her branches, for
her root was by many waters. The cedars in the
garden of God did not hide her   the fir-trees
were not like her boughs, and the plane-trees
were not like her branches, nor was any tree in
the garden of God equal to her in her beauty ;
I have made her beautiful by the multitude of
her branches, and all the trees of Eden that were
in the garden of God envied her (xxxi. 4, 7–9).

From these passages it is evident that when the
most ancient people compared man, or the things
in man, to a " garden," they added the " waters "
and " rivers " by which he might be watered, and
by these waters and rivers meant such things as
would cause his growth.

109. That although wisdom and intelligence
appear in man, they are, as has been said, from
the Lord alone, is plainly declared in *Ezekiel* by
means of similar representatives :

Behold, waters issued out from under the
threshold of the house eastward ; for the face
of the house is the east ; and he said, These
waters issue out to the border toward the east,
and go down into the plain, and come to the
sea, which being led into the sea, the waters shall
be healed ; and it shall come to pass that every
living soul which creepeth, whithersoever the
water of the rivers shall come, shall live. And
by the river upon the bank thereof, on this side
and on that side, there come up all trees for
food, whose leaf shall not fade, neither shall the
fruit thereof be consumed ; it is born again in its

months, because these its waters issue out of the
sanctuary, and the fruit thereof shall be for food,
and the leaf thereof for medicine (xlvii. 1, 8, 9, 12).

Here the Lord is signified by the " east," and by the
" sanctuary," whence the waters and rivers issued.
Similarly in *John* :

> He showed me a pure river of water of life,
> bright as crystal, going forth out of the throne
> of God and of the Lamb.   In the midst of the
> street thereof, and of the river on this side and
> that, was the tree of life, which bare twelve
> [manner of] fruits, and yielded her fruit every
> month ;   and the leaf of the tree was for the
> healing of the nations (*Rev.* xxii. 1, 2).

110. Verses 11, 12. **The name of the first is
Pishon ;   that is it which compasseth the whole
land of Havilah, where there is gold ;   and the gold
of that land is good ;   there is bdellium and the
onyx stone.**   The " first " river, or " Pishon,"
signifies the intelligence of the faith that is from
love ;   " the land of Havilah " signifies the mind ;
" gold " signifies good ;   " bdellium and the onyx
stone," truth.   " Gold " is mentioned twice because
it signifies the good of love and the good of faith
from love ;   and " bdellium and the onyx stone "
are mentioned because the one signifies the truth
of love, and the other the truth of faith from love.
Such is the celestial man.

111. It is, however, a very difficult matter to
describe these things as they are in the internal
sense, for at the present day no one knows what is
meant by faith from love, and what by the wisdom
and intelligence thence derived.   For external men
scarcely recognize anything but knowledge, which

85

they call intelligence and wisdom, and faith. They do not even know what love is, and many do not know what the will and understanding are, and that they constitute one mind. And yet each of these things is distinct, indeed, most distinct, and the universal heaven is arranged by the Lord in the most distinct manner according to the differences of love and faith, which are innumerable.

112. Be it known, moreover, that there is no wisdom which is not from love, thus from the Lord ; nor any intelligence except from faith, thus also from the Lord ; and that there is no good except from love, thus from the Lord ; and no truth except from faith, thus from the Lord. What are not from love and faith, and thus from the Lord, are indeed called by these names, but they are spurious.

113. Nothing is more common in the Word than for the good of wisdom or of love to be signified and represented by " gold." All the gold in the ark, in the temple, in the golden table, in the candlestick, in the vessels, and upon the garments of Aaron, signified and represented the good of wisdom or of love. So also in the Prophets, as in *Ezekiel* :

> In thy wisdom and in thine intelligence thou hast gotten thee riches, and hast gotten gold and silver in thy treasures (xxviii. 4).

Here it is plainly said that from wisdom and intelligence are " gold and silver," or the good and the true, for " silver " here signifies truth, as it does also in the ark and in the temple. In *Isaiah* :

> The multitude of camels shall cover thee, the dromedaries of Midian and Ephah ; all they from Sheba shall come, they shall bring gold

and incense, and they shall show forth the praises of Jehovah (lx. 6).

Thus also :

The wise men from the east, who came to Jesus when He was born, fell down and worshipped Him ; and when they had opened their treasures, they presented unto Him gifts ; gold, and frankincense, and myrrh (*Matt.* ii. 1, 11).

Here also " gold " signifies good ; " frankincense and myrrh," things that are grateful because from love and faith, which are therefore called " the praises of Jehovah." Wherefore it is said in *David* :

He shall live, and to him shall be given of the gold of Sheba ; prayer also shall be made for him continually, and every day shall He bless him (*Ps.* lxxii. 15).

114. The truth of faith is signified and represented in the Word by precious " stones," as by those in the breast-plate of judgment, and on the shoulders of Aaron's ephod. In the breast-plate, " gold, blue, bright crimson, scarlet double-dyed, and fine-twined linen," represented such things as are of love, and the precious " stones " such as are of faith from love ; as did likewise the two " stones of memorial " on the shoulders of the ephod, which were onyx stones, set in ouches of gold (*Exod.* xxviii. 9–22). This signification of precious stones is also plain from *Ezekiel*, where, speaking of a man possessed of heavenly riches, which are wisdom and intelligence, it is said :

Full of wisdom, and perfect in beauty, thou hast been in Eden the garden of God ; every precious stone was thy covering, the ruby, the

87

topaz, the diamond, the beryl, the onyx, and the
jasper ; the sapphire, the chrysoprase, the
emerald, and gold ; the workmanship of thy
tabrets and of thy pipes was in thee ; in the day
that thou wast created they were prepared ;
thou wast perfect in thy ways from the day that
thou wast created (xxviii. 12, 13, 15).

It must be evident to every one that these do not
signify stones, but the celestial and spiritual things
of faith ; yea, each stone represented some essential
of faith.

115. When the most ancient people spoke of
" lands," they understood what they signified ;
just as those at the present day who have an idea
that the land of Canaan and Mount Zion signify
heaven do not so much as think of any land or
mountain when these places are mentioned, but
only of the things which they signify. It is so
here with the " land of Havilah," which is mentioned again in *Genesis* xxv. 18, where it is said of
the sons of Ishmael, that they " dwelt from Havilah
even unto Shur, which is before Egypt, as thou
goest toward Assyria." Those who are in a
heavenly idea perceive from these words nothing
but intelligence, and what flows from intelligence.
So by to " compass "—as where it is said that the
river Pishon " compasseth the whole land of
Havilah "—they perceive a flowing in ; as also in
the onyx stones on the shoulders of Aaron's ephod
being encompassed with ouches of gold (*Exod.*
xxviii. 11), they perceive that the good of love
should inflow into the truth of faith. And so in
many other instances.

116. Verse 13. **And the name of the second river
is Gihon ; the same is it that compasseth the whole**

land of Cush. The " second river," which is called
" Gihon," signifies the cognition of all things that
belong to the good and the true, or to love and
faith, and the " land of Cush " signifies the mind
or faculty. The mind is constituted of the will and
the understanding ; and what is said of the first
river has reference to the will, and what of this
one to the understanding to which belong the
cognitions of good and of truth.

117. The " land of Cush," or Ethiopia, moreover,
abounded in gold, precious stones, and spices,
which, as before said, signify good, truth, and the
things thence derived which are pleasant, such as
are those of the cognitions of love and faith. This is
evident from the passages above cited (n. 113)
from *Isa.* lx. 6 ; *Matt.* ii. 1, 11 ; *David, Ps.* lxxii. 15.
That similar things are meant in the Word by
" Cush " or " Ethiopia," and also by " Sheba," is
evident from the Prophets, as in *Zephaniah*, where
also the " rivers of Cush " are mentioned :

In the morning He will give His judgment for
light ; for then will I turn to the people with
a clear language, that they may all call upon
the name of Jehovah, to serve Him with one
shoulder ; from the passage of the rivers of
Cush My suppliants shall bring Mine offering
(iii. 5, 9, 10).

And in *Daniel*, speaking of the king of the north
and of the south :

He shall have power over the treasures of
gold and of silver, and over all the desirable things
of Egypt ; and the Lybians and the Ethiopians
shall be under his steps (xi. 43).

2 Here " Egypt " denotes scientifics, and the " Ethiopians " cognitions. So in *Ezekiel* :

> The merchants of Sheba and Raamah, these were thy merchants, in the chief of all spices, and in every precious stone, and in gold (xxvii. 22),

by whom in like manner are signified cognitions of faith. So in *David*, speaking of the Lord, consequently, of the celestial man :

> In his days shall the righteous flourish, and abundance of peace until there shall be no moon ; the kings of Tarshish and of the isles shall bring presents ; the kings of Sheba and Seba shall offer a gift (*Ps.* lxxii. 7, 10).

These words, as is plain from their connection with the preceding and subsequent verses, signify celestial things of faith. Similar things were signified by the queen of Sheba, who came to Solomon, and proposed hard questions, and brought him spices, gold, and precious stones (1 *Kings* x. 1, 2). For all things contained in the historical parts of the Word, as well as in the Prophets, signify, represent, and involve arcana.

118. Verse 14. **And the name of the third river is Hiddekel ; that is it which goeth eastward toward Asshur ; and the fourth river is Euphrates.** The " river Hiddekel " is reason, or the clearsightedness of reason. " Asshur " is the rational mind ; the " river which goeth eastward toward Asshur," signifies that the clearsightedness of reason comes from the Lord through the internal man into the rational mind, which is of the external man ; " Phrath," or Euphrates, is knowledge, which is the ultimate or boundary.

119. That " Asshur " signifies the rational mind, or the Rational of man, is very evident in the Prophets, as in *Ezekiel* :

Behold, Asshur was a cedar in Lebanon, with fair branches and a shady grove, and lofty in height ; and her offshoot was among the thick boughs. The waters made her grow, the deep of waters uplifted her, the river ran round about her plant (xxxi. 3, 4).

The Rational is called a " cedar in Lebanon " ; the " offshoot among the thick boughs," signifies the scientifics of the memory, which are in this state. This is still clearer in *Isaiah* :

In that day shall there be a way from Egypt to Asshur, and Asshur shall come into Egypt, and Egypt into Asshur, and the Egyptians shall serve Asshur. In that day shall Israel be the third with Egypt and with Asshur, a blessing in the midst of the land, that Jehovah Zebaoth shall bless, saying, Blessed be Egypt My people, and Asshur the work of My hands, and Israel Mine inheritance (xix. 23–25).

By " Egypt " in this and various other passages is signified knowledge, by " Asshur " reason, and by " Israel " intelligence.

120. As by " Egypt," so also by " Euphrates," are signified knowledges or scientifics, and also the sensuous things from which these scientifics come. This is evident from the Word in the Prophets, as in *Micah* :

My she-enemy hath said, Where is Jehovah thy God ? The day in which He shall build thy walls, that day shall the decree be far removed ;

that day also He shall come even to thee from
Asshur, and to the cities of Egypt, and to the
river (Euphrates) (vii. 10–12).

So did the prophets speak concerning the coming
of the Lord, who should regenerate man so that
he might become like the celestial man.   In
Jeremiah :

What hast thou to do in the way of Egypt, to
drink the waters of Sihor ? or what hast thou to
do in the way of Asshur, to drink the waters of
the river (Euphrates)? (ii. 18).

Here " Egypt " and " Euphrates " likewise signify
scientifics, and " Asshur " reasonings thence derived.
In *David* :

Thou hast made a vine to go forth out of
Egypt ; Thou hast cast out the nations ; Thou
hast planted her ; Thou hast sent out her shoots
even to the sea, and her branches to the river
(Euphrates) (*Ps.* lxxx. 8, 11).

Here also the " river Euphrates " signifies what is
sensuous and of mere knowledge.   For the Euphrates was the boundary of the dominions of Israel
towards Assyria, as the knowledge of the memory
is the boundary of the intelligence and wisdom of
the spiritual and celestial man.   The same is
signified by what was said to Abraham :

Unto thy seed will I give this land, from the
river of Egypt unto the great river the river
Euphrates (*Gen.* xv. 18).

These two boundaries have a similar signification.

121. The nature of celestial order, or how the
things of life proceed, is evident from these rivers,
namely, from the Lord, who is the " East," and

that from Him proceeds wisdom, through wisdom intelligence, through intelligence reason, and so by means of reason the scientifics of the memory are vivified. This is the order of life, and such are celestial men ; and therefore, since the elders of Israel represented celestial men, they were called "wise, intelligent, and knowing" (*Deut.* i. 13, 15). Hence it is said of Bezaleel, who constructed the ark, that he was

Filled with the spirit of God, in wisdom, in understanding, and in knowledge, and in all work (*Exod.* xxxi. 3 ; xxxv. 31 ; xxxvi. 1, 2).

122. Verse 15. **And Jehovah God took the man, and put him in the garden of Eden, to till it and take care of it.** By the " garden of Eden " are signified all things of the celestial man, as described ; by to " till it and take care of it," is signified that it is permitted him to enjoy all these things, but not to possess them as his own, because they are the Lord's. *ne + mine*

123. The celestial man acknowledges, because he perceives, that all things both in general and in particular are the Lord's. The spiritual man does indeed acknowledge the same, but with the mouth, because he has learned it from the Word. The worldly and corporeal man neither acknowledges nor admits it ; but whatever he has he calls his own, and imagines that were he to lose it, he would altogether perish.

124. That wisdom, intelligence, reason, and knowledge are not of man, but of the Lord, is very evident from all that the Lord taught ; as in *Matthew*, where the Lord compares Himself to a householder, who planted a vineyard, and hedged

it round, and let it out to husbandmen (xxi. 33) ;
and in *John* :

> The Spirit of truth shall guide you into all
> truth ; for He shall not speak of Himself, but
> what things soever He shall hear, He shall
> speak ; He shall glorify Me, for He shall receive
> of Mine, and shall declare it unto you (xvi. 13, 14).

And in another place :

> A man can receive nothing except it be given
> him from heaven (iii. 27).

That this is really so is known to every one who is
acquainted with even a few of the arcana of
heaven.

125. Verse 16. **And Jehovah God commanded
the man, saying, Of every tree of the garden, eating
thou mayest eat.** To " eat of every tree," is to
know from perception what is good and true ;
for, as before observed, a " tree " signifies perception. The men of the Most Ancient Church had
the cognitions of true faith by means of revelations,
for they conversed with the Lord and with angels,
and were also instructed by visions and dreams,
which were most delightful and paradisal to them.
They had from the Lord continual perception, so
that when they reflected on what was treasured up
in the memory they instantly perceived whether it
was true and good, so that when anything false
presented itself, they not only avoided it but even
regarded it with horror : such also is the state of the
angels. In place of this perception of the Most
Ancient Church, however, there afterwards succeeded the cognition of what is true and good from
what had been previously revealed, and afterwards
from what was revealed in the Word.

94

126. Verse 17. **But of the tree of the knowledge of good and evil, thou shalt not eat of it ; for in the day that thou eatest thereof, dying thou shalt die.** These words, taken together with those just explained, signify that it is allowable to become acquainted with what is true and good by means of every perception derived from the Lord, but not from self and the world ; that is, we are not to inquire into the mysteries of faith by means of the things of sense and of scientifics, for in this case the celestial of faith is destroyed.

127. A desire to investigate the mysteries of faith by means of the things of sense and of scientifics, was not only the cause of the fall of the posterity of the Most Ancient Church, as treated of in the following chapter, but it is also the cause of the fall of every church ; for hence come not only falsities, but also evils of life.

128. The worldly and corporeal man says in his heart, If I am not instructed concerning the faith, and everything relating to it, by means of the things of sense, so that I may see, or by means of scientifics, so that I may understand, I will not believe ; and he confirms himself in this by the consideration that natural things cannot be contrary to spiritual. Thus he is desirous of being instructed from things of sense in what is celestial and Divine, which is as impossible as it is for a camel to go through the eye of a needle ; for the more he desires to grow wise by such means, the more he blinds himself, till at length he believes nothing, not even that there is anything spiritual, or that there is eternal life. This comes from the principle which he assumes. And this is to " eat of the tree of the knowledge of good and evil," of which the

95

more any one eats, the more dead he becomes. But he who would be wise from the Lord, and not from the world, says in his heart that the Lord must be believed, that is, the things which the Lord has spoken in the Word, because they are truths ; and according to this principle he regulates his thoughts. He confirms himself by things of reason, by scientifics, by sensuous and natural things, and those which are not confirmatory he casts aside.

129. Every one may know that man is governed by the principles he assumes, be they ever so false, and that all his knowledge and reasoning favour his principles ; for innumerable considerations tending to support them present themselves to his mind, and thus he is confirmed in what is false. He therefore who assumes as a principle that nothing is to be believed until it is seen and understood, can never believe, because spiritual and celestial things cannot be seen with the eyes, or conceived by the imagination. But the true order is for man to be wise from the Lord, that is, from His Word, and then all things follow, and he is also enlightened in matters of reason and of science. For it is by no means forbidden to learn the sciences; since they are useful for his life and delightful ; nor is he who is in faith prohibited from thinking and speaking as do the learned of the world ; but it must be from this principle—to believe the Word of the Lord, and, so far as possible, confirm spiritual and celestial truths by natural truths, in terms familiar to the learned world. Thus his starting-point must be the Lord, and not himself ; for the former is life, but the latter is death.

130. He who desires to be wise from the world, has for his " garden " sensuous things and

scientifics ; the love of self and the love of the world
are his " Eden " ; his " east " is the west, or
himself ; his " river Euphrates " is all his knowledge, which is condemned ; his " second river,"
where is " Assyria," is infatuated reasoning pro-
ductive of falsities ; his " third river," where is
" Ethiopia," is the principles of evil and falsity
thence derived, which are the cognitions of his
faith ; his " fourth river " is the wisdom thence
derived, which in the Word is called " magic."
And therefore " Egypt," which signifies knowledge,
after it became magical, signifies such a man,
because, as may be seen from the Word, he desires
to be wise from self.   Of such it is written in
Ezekiel :

> Thus hath said the Lord Jehovih, Behold, I
> am against thee, Pharaoh king of Egypt, the
> great whale that lieth in the midst of his rivers,
> who hath said, My river is mine own, and I have
> made myself.   And the land of Egypt shall be
> for a solitude, and a waste, and they shall know
> that I am Jehovah, because he hath said, The
> river is mine, and I have made it (xxix. 3, 9).

Such men are also called " trees of Eden in hell,"
in the same Prophet, where also Pharaoh, or the
Egyptian, is treated of in these words :

> When I shall have made him descend into
> hell with them that descend into the pit ; to
> whom art thou thus made like in glory and in
> greatness among the trees of Eden ? yet shalt
> thou be made to descend with the trees of Eden
> into the lower earth, in the midst of the uncir-
> cumcised, with them that be slain by the sword.
> This is Pharaoh and all his crew (xxxi. 16, 18).

Here the " trees of Eden " denote scientifics and cognitions from the Word, which they thus profane by reasonings.

———

18. And Jehovah God said, It is not good that the man should be alone, I will make him a help as with him.

19. And Jehovah God formed out of the ground every beast of the field, and every fowl of the heavens, and brought it to the man to see what he would call it ; and whatsoever the man called every living soul, that was the name thereof.

20. And the man gave names to every beast, and to the fowl of the heavens, and to every wild animal of the field ; but for the man there was not found a help as with him.

21. And Jehovah God caused a deep sleep to fall upon the man, and he slept ; and He took one of his ribs, and closed up the flesh in the place thereof.

22. And the rib which Jehovah God had taken from the man, He built into a woman, and brought her to the man.

23. And the man said, This now is bone of my bones, and flesh of my flesh ; therefore she shall be called wife, because she was taken out of man (*vir*).

24. Therefore shall a man (*vir*) leave his father and his mother, and shall cleave unto his wife, and they shall be one flesh.

25. And they were both naked, the man and his wife, and were not ashamed.

———

THE CONTENTS.

131. The posterity of the Most Ancient Church, which inclined to their proprium, is here treated of.

132. Since man is such as not to be content to be led by the Lord, but desires to be led also by himself and the world, or by his proprium, therefore the proprium which was granted him is here treated of (verse 18).

133. And first it is given him to know the affections of good and the knowledges of truth with which he is endowed by the Lord ; but still he inclines to his proprium (verses 19, 20).

134. Wherefore he is let into a state of his proprium, and a proprium is given him, which is described by the rib built into a woman (verses 21 to 23).

135. Celestial and spiritual life are adjoined to the man's proprium, so that they appear as a one (verse 24).

136. And innocence from the Lord is insinuated into this proprium, so that it still might not be unacceptable (verse 25).

THE INTERNAL SENSE.

137. The first three chapters of Genesis treat in general of the Most Ancient Church which is called " Man " (*homo*), from its first period to its last, when it perished : the preceding part of this chapter treats of its most flourishing state, when it was a celestial man ; here it now treats of those who inclined to their proprium, and of their posterity.

138. Verse 18. **And Jehovah God said, It is not good that the man should be alone ; I will make him a help as with him.** By " alone " is signified that he was not content to be led by the Lord, but desired to be led by self and the world ; by a " help as with him," is signified man's proprium, which is subsequently called a " rib built into a woman."

139. In ancient times those were said to " dwell alone " who were under the Lord's guidance as celestial men, because such were no longer infested by evils, or evil spirits. This was represented in the Jewish Church also by their dwelling alone when they had driven out the nations. On this account it is sometimes said of the Lord's church, in the Word, that she is " alone," as in *Jeremiah* :

Arise, get you up to a quiet nation that dwelleth confidently, saith the Lord, which hath neither gates nor bar ; they dwell alone (xlix. 31).

In the prophecy of Moses :

Israel hath dwelt confidently alone (*Deut.* xxxiii. 28).

And still more clearly in the prophecy of Balaam :

Lo, the people dwelleth alone, and shall not be reckoned among the nations (*Num.* xxiii. 9).

Here " nations " signify evils. This posterity of the Most Ancient Church was not disposed to dwell alone, that is, to be a celestial man, or to be led by the Lord as a celestial man, but, like the Jewish Church, desired to be among the nations. And because they desired this, it is said, " it is not good that the man should be alone," for he who desires is already in evil, and it is permitted to him.

100

140. That by " a help as with him " is signified the man's proprium, is evident both from the nature of this proprium, and from what follows. As, however, the man of the church who is here treated of was well disposed, a proprium was granted him, but of such a kind that it appeared his own, as it were, and therefore it is said " a help as with him."

141. Innumerable things might be said about the man's proprium in describing its nature with the corporeal and worldly man, with the spiritual man, and with the celestial man. With the corporeal and worldly man, his proprium is his all, he knows of nothing else than his proprium, and imagines, as before said, that if he were to lose this proprium he would perish. With the spiritual man also his proprium has a similar appearance, for although he knows that the Lord is the life of all, and gives wisdom and understanding, and, consequently, the power to think and to act, yet this knowledge is rather the profession of his lips than the belief of his heart. But the celestial man discerns that the Lord is the life of all and gives the power to think and to act, for he perceives that it is really so. He never desires his proprium, nevertheless a proprium is given him by the Lord, which is conjoined with all perception of what is good and true, and with all happiness. The angels are in such a proprium, and are at the same time in the highest peace and tranquillity, for in their proprium are those things which are the Lord's, who governs their proprium, or them by means of their proprium. This proprium is the veriest celestial itself, whereas that of the corporeal man is infernal. But concerning this proprium more hereafter.

142. Verses 19, 20. **And Jehovah God formed out of the ground every beast of the field, and every fowl of the heavens, and brought it to the man to see what he would call it ; and whatsoever the man called every living soul, that was the name thereof. And the man gave names to every beast, and to the fowl of the heavens, and to every wild animal of the field ; but for the man there was not found a help as with him.** By " beasts " are signified celestial affections, and by " fowls of the heavens," spiritual affections ; that is to say, by " beasts " are signified things of the will, and by " fowls " things of the understanding. To " bring them to the man to see what he would call them," is to enable him to know their quality, and his " giving them names," signifies that he knew it. But notwithstanding that he knew the quality of the affections of good and of the cognitions of truth that were given him by the Lord, still he inclined to the proprium, which is expressed in the same terms as before—that " there was not found a help as with him."

143. That by " beasts " and " animals " anciently signified affections and similar things in man, may appear strange at the present day ; but as the men of those times were in a celestial idea, and as such things are represented in the world of spirits by animals, and in fact by such animals as they are like, therefore when they spoke in that way they meant nothing else. Nor is anything else meant in the Word in those places where beasts are mentioned either generally or specifically. The whole prophetic Word is full of such things, and therefore one who does not know what each beast specifically signifies, cannot possibly under-

stand what the Word contains in the internal
sense. But, as before observed, beasts are of two
kinds—evil or noxious beasts, and good or harmless
ones—and by the good beasts are signified good
affections, as for instance by sheep, lambs, and
doves ; and as it is the celestial, or the celestial
spiritual man, who is treated of, such are here
meant. That " beasts " in general signify affections, may be seen above, confirmed by some
passages in the Word (n. 45, 46), so that there is no
need of further confirmation.

144. That to " call by name " signifies to know
the quality, is because the ancients, by the " name,"
understood the essence of a thing, and by " seeing
and calling by name," they understood to know
the quality. The reason was that they gave names
to their sons and daughters according to the things
which were signified, for every name had something
peculiar in it, from which, and by which, they might
know the origin and the nature of their children,
as will be seen in a future part of this work, when,
of the Lord's Divine mercy, we come to treat of
the twelve sons of Jacob. As therefore the names
implied the source and quality of the things named,
nothing else was understood by " calling by name."
This was the customary mode of speaking among
them, but one who does not understand this may
wonder that such things should be signified.

145. In the Word also by " name " is signified
the essence of a thing, and by " seeing and calling
by name " is signified to know the quality. As in
Isaiah :

I will give thee the treasures of darkness, and
hidden riches of secret places, that thou mayest
know that I, Jehovah, who call thee by thy

name, am the God of Israel. For Jacob My
servant's sake, and Israel My chosen, I have
even called thee by thy name, I have surnamed
thee, and thou hast not known Me (xlv. 3, 4).

In this passage, to " call by name," and to " sur-
name " signifies to foreknow the quality. Again :

Thou shalt be called by a new name, which the
mouth of Jehovah shall declare (lxii. 2).

This signifies to become of another character, as
appears from the preceding and subsequent
verses. Again :

Fear not, O Israel, for I have redeemed thee,
I have called thee by thy name ; thou art Mine
(xliii. 1).

This denotes that He knew their quality. Again
in the same Prophet :

Lift up your eyes on high, and behold who
hath created these things, that bringeth out
their army by number. He will call them all by
name (xl. 26).

This means that He knew them all. In the *Revelation* :

Thou hast a few names even in Sardis who
have not defiled their garments : he that over-
cometh, the same shall be clothed in white
raiment, and I will not blot out his name out
of the book of life, but I will confess his name
before My Father, and before His angels (iii. 4, 5).

And in another place :

Whose names are not written in the Lamb's
book of life (xiii. 8).

By " names " in these passages are by no means
meant names, but qualities ; nor is the name of any
one ever known in heaven, but his quality.

104

146. From what has been stated, the connection of what is signified may be seen. In verse 18 it is said, " It is not good that the man should be alone, I will make him a help as with him," and presently " beasts " and " birds " are spoken of, which nevertheless had been treated of before, and immediately it is repeated that " for the man there was not found a help as with him," which denotes that although he was permitted to know his quality as to the affections of good and knowledges of truth, still he inclined to his proprium ; for those who are such as to desire the proprium, begin to despise the things of the Lord, however plainly they may be represented and shown to them.

147. Verse 21. **And Jehovah God caused a deep sleep to fall upon the man, and he slept ; and He took one of his ribs, and closed up the flesh in the place thereof.** By a " rib," which is a bone of the chest, is meant man's proprium, in which there is but little life, and indeed a proprium which is dear to him ; by " flesh in the place of the rib," is meant a proprium in which there is life ; by a " deep sleep " is meant the state into which he was let so that he might seem to himself to have a proprium, which state resembles sleep, because while in it he knows not but that he lives, thinks, speaks, and acts, from himself. But when he begins to know that this is false, he is then roused as it were out of sleep, and becomes awake.

148. The reason why man's proprium, and indeed a proprium which is dear to him, is called a " rib," which is a bone of the chest, is that among the most ancient people the chest signified charity, because it contains both the heart and the lungs ; and bones signified the viler things, because they

D*   105

possess a minimum of life ; while flesh denoted such as had life. The ground of these significations is one of the deepest arcana known to the men of the Most Ancient Church, concerning which of the Lord's Divine mercy more will be said hereafter.

149. In the Word also, the man's proprium is signified by " bones," and indeed a proprium vivified by the Lord, as in *Isaiah* :

Jehovah shall satisfy thy soul in droughts, and make thy bones alert, and thou shalt be like a watered garden (lviii. 11).

Again :

Then shall ye see, and your heart shall rejoice, and your bones shall sprout as the blade (lxvi. 14).

In *David* :

All my bones shall say, Jehovah, who is like unto Thee ? (*Ps.* xxxv. 10).

This is still more evident from *Ezekiel*, where he speaks of bones receiving flesh and having spirit put into them :

The hand of Jehovah set me in the midst of the valley, and it was full of bones ; and He said to me, Prophesy upon these bones, and say unto them, O ye dry bones, hear the word of Jehovah ; thus saith the Lord Jehovih to these bones ; behold, I bring breath (*spiritus*) into you, and ye shall live, and I will lay sinews upon you, and will make flesh come upon you, and cover you with skin, and I will put breath (*spiritus*) in you, and ye shall live, and ye shall know that I am Jehovah (xxxvii. 1, 4–6).

2 The proprium of man, when viewed from heaven, appears like a something that is wholly bony,

inanimate, and very ugly, consequently, as being in itself dead, but when vivified by the Lord it looks like flesh. For man's proprium is a mere dead thing, although to him it appears as something, indeed as everything. Whatever lives in him is from the Lord's life, and if this were withdrawn he would fall down as dead as a stone ; for man is only an organ of life, and such as is the organ, such is the life's affection. The Lord alone has Proprium ; by this Proprium He redeemed man, and by this Proprium He saves him. The Lord's Proprium is Life, and from His Proprium, man's proprium, which in itself is dead, is made alive. The Lord's Proprium is also signified by the Lord's words in *Luke* :

A spirit hath not flesh and bones as ye see Me have (xxiv. 39).

It was also meant by not a bone of the paschal lamb being broken (*Exod*. xii. 46).

150. The state of man when in his proprium, or when he supposes that he lives from himself, is compared to "deep sleep," and indeed by the ancients was called deep sleep ; and in the Word it is said of such that they have " poured out upon them the spirit of deep sleep " (*Isa.* xxix. 10), and that they sleep a sleep (*Jer.* li. 57). That man's proprium is in itself dead, and that no one has any life from himself, has been shown so clearly in the world of spirits, that evil spirits who love nothing but their proprium, and obstinately insist that they live from themselves, were convinced by sensible experience, and were forced to confess that they do not live from themselves. For a number of years I have been permitted in an especial manner to know how the case is with what is man's

107

proprium, and it has been granted to me to perceive
clearly that I could think nothing from myself,
but that every idea of thought flows in, and sometimes I could perceive how and whence it flowed in.
The man who supposes that he lives from himself
is therefore in what is false, and by believing that
he lives from himself appropriates to himself
everything evil and false, which he would never do
if his belief were in accordance with the real truth
of the case.

151. Verse 22. **And the rib which Jehovah God
had taken from the man He built into a woman,
and brought her to the man.** By to " build " is
signified to raise up what has fallen ; by the " rib,"
man's proprium not vivified ; by a "woman," the
proprium vivified by the Lord ; by " He brought
her to the man," that a proprium was granted him.
The posterity of this church did not wish, like
their parents, to be a celestial man, but to be under
their own self-guidance ; and, thus inclining to their
proprium, it was granted to them, but still a proprium vivified by the Lord, and therefore called
a " woman," and afterwards a " wife."

152. It requires but little attention in any one
to discern that woman was not formed out of the
rib of a man, and that deeper arcana are here
implied than any person has heretofore been aware
of. And that by the " woman " is signified the
proprium, may be known from the fact that it was
the woman who was deceived ; for nothing ever
deceives man but his proprium, or what is the
same, the love of self and of the world.

153. The rib is said to be " built into a woman,"
but it is not said that the woman was " created,"

108

or " formed," or " made," as before when treating
of regeneration. The reason of this is that to
" build " is to raise up that which has fallen ; and
in this sense it is used in the Word, where to
" build " is predicated of evils ; to " raise up," of
falsities ; and to " renew," of both ; as in *Isaiah* :

> They shall build the wastes of eternity, they
> shall set up again the ancient desolations,
> and they shall renew the cities of the waste,
> the desolations of generation and generation
> (lxi. 4).

" Wastes " in this and other passages signify
evils ; " desolations," falsities ; to " build " is
applied to the former, to " set up again " to the
latter, and this distinction is carefully observed
in other places by the prophets, as where it is said
in *Jeremiah* :

> Yet still will I build thee, and thou shalt be
> built, O virgin of Israel (xxxi. 4).

154. Nothing evil and false is ever possible which
is not the proprium, and from the proprium, for
the proprium of man is evil itself, and, consequently, man is nothing but evil and falsity. This
has been evident to me from the fact that when
the things of the proprium are presented to view
in the world of spirits, they appear so deformed that
it is impossible to depict anything more ugly,
yet with a difference according to the nature of the
proprium, so that he to whom the things of the
proprium are visibly exhibited is struck with
horror, and desires to flee from himself as from a
devil. But truly the things of the proprium that
have been vivified by the Lord appear beautiful
and lovely, with variety according to the life to
which the celestial of the Lord can be applied ;

109

and indeed those who have been endowed with
charity, or vivified by it, appear like boys and
girls with most beautiful countenances ; and those
who are in innocence, like naked infants, variously
adorned with garlands of flowers encircling their
bosoms, and diadems upon their heads, living and
sporting in a diamond-like aura, and having a perception of happiness from the very inmost.

155. The words " a rib was built into a woman,"
have more things inmostly concealed in them than
it is possible for any one ever to discover from the
letter ; for the Word of the Lord is such that its
inmost contents regard the Lord Himself and His
kingdom, and from this comes all the life of the
Word. And so in the passage before us, it is the
heavenly marriage that is regarded in its inmost
contents. The heavenly marriage is of such a
nature that it exists in the proprium, which, when
vivified by the Lord, is called the " bride and
wife " of the Lord. The proprium thus vivified has
a perception of all the good of love and truth of
faith, and consequently possesses all wisdom and
intelligence conjoined with inexpressible happiness.
But the nature of this vivified proprium, which is
called the " bride and wife " of the Lord, cannot
be concisely explained. Suffice it therefore to
observe that the angels perceive that they live
from the Lord, although when not reflecting on the
subject they know no otherwise than that they
live from themselves ; but there is a general
affection of such a nature that at the least departure
from the good of love and truth of faith they
perceive a change, and, consequently, they are in
the enjoyment of their peace and happiness, which
is inexpressible, while they are in their general

110

perception that they live from the Lord. It is this proprium also that is meant in *Jeremiah*, where it is said :

> Jehovah hath created a new thing in the earth, a woman shall compass a man (xxxi. 22).

It is the heavenly marriage that is signified in this passage also, where by a " woman " is meant the proprium vivified by the Lord, of which woman the expression " to compass " is predicated, because this proprium is such that it encompasses, as a rib made flesh encompasses the heart.

156. Verse 23. **And the man said, This now is bone of my bones and flesh of my flesh ; therefore she shall be called wife, because she was taken out of man** (*vir*). " Bone of bones and flesh of flesh," signify the proprium of the external man ; " bone," the proprium not so much vivified, and " flesh," the proprium that is vivified. Man (*vir*), moreover, signifies the internal man, and from his being so coupled with the external man as is stated in the subsequent verse, the proprium which was before called " woman," is here denominated " wife." " Now," signifies that it was thus effected at this time because the state was changed.

157. Inasmuch as " bone of bones and flesh of flesh " signified the proprium of the external man in which was the internal, therefore in ancient times all those were called " bone of bones and flesh of flesh " who could be called their own, and were of one house, or of one family, or in any degree of relationship. Thus Laban said of Jacob,

> Surely thou art my bone and my flesh (*Gen.* xxix. 14).

111

And Abimelech said of his mother's brethren, and of the family of the house of his mother's father,

> Remember that I am your bone and your flesh (*Judges* ix. 2).

The tribes of Israel also said of themselves to David,

> Behold, we are thy bone and thy flesh (2 *Sam.* v. 1).

158. That man (*vir*) signifies the internal man, or what is the same, one who is intelligent and wise, is plain from *Isaiah*:

> I behold, and there is no man (*vir*), even among them, and there is no counsellor (xli. 28).

This means there is none wise and intelligent. Also in *Jeremiah*:

> Run ye to and fro through the streets of Jerusalem, and see if ye can find a man, if there be any executing judgment, seeking the truth (v. 1).

"One who executes judgment" means a wise person; and "one who seeks the truth," an intelligent one.

159. But it is not easy to perceive how the case is with these things unless the state of the celestial man is understood. In the celestial man the internal man is distinct from the external, indeed so distinct that the celestial man perceives what belongs to the internal man, and what to the external, and how the external man is governed through the internal by the Lord. But the state of the posterity of this celestial man, in consequence of desiring the proprium, which belongs to the external man, was so changed that they no longer perceived the

internal man to be distinct from the external, but imagined the internal to be one with the external, for such a perception takes place when man inclines to the proprium.

160. Verse 24. **Therefore shall a man leave his father and his mother, and shall cleave unto his wife, and they shall be one flesh.** To " leave father and mother," is to recede from the internal man, for it is the internal which conceives and brings forth the external ; to " cleave unto his wife," is that the internal may be in the external ; to " be one flesh," that they are there together ; and because previously, the internal man, and the external from the internal, was spirit, but now they have become flesh. Thus was celestial and spiritual life adjoined to the proprium, that they might be as one.

161. This posterity of the Most Ancient Church was not evil, but was still good ; and because they desired to live in the external man, or in their proprium, this was permitted them by the Lord, what is spiritual celestial, however, being mercifully insinuated therein. How the internal and external act as one, or how they appear as one, cannot be known unless the influx of the one into the other is known. In order to have some idea of it, take for example an action. Unless in an action there is charity, that is, love and faith, and in these the Lord, that action cannot be called a work of charity, or the fruit of faith.

162. All the laws of truth and right flow from celestial beginnings, or from the order of life of the celestial man. For the whole heaven is a celestial man because the Lord alone is a celestial

113

Man, and as He is the all in all of heaven and the celestial Man, they are thence called celestial. As every law of truth and right descends from celestial beginnings, or from the order of life of the celestial man, so in an especial manner does the law of marriages. It is the celestial (or heavenly) marriage from and according to which all marriages on earth must be derived ; and this marriage is such that there is one Lord and one heaven, or one church whose head is the Lord. The law of marriages thence derived is that there shall be one husband and one wife, and when this is the case they represent the celestial marriage, and are an exemplar of the celestial man. This law was not only revealed to the men of the Most Ancient Church, but was also inscribed on their internal man, wherefore at that time a man had but one wife, and they constituted one house. But when their posterity ceased to be internal men, and became external, they married many wives. Because the men of the Most Ancient Church in their marriages represented the celestial marriage, conjugial love was to them a kind of heaven and heavenly happiness, but when the Church declined they had no longer any perception of happiness in conjugial love, but in pleasure from a number, which is a delight of the external man. This is called by the Lord " hardness of heart," on account of which they were permitted by Moses to marry many wives, as the Lord Himself teaches :

For the hardness of your heart Moses wrote you this precept, but from the beginning of the creation God made them male and female. For this cause shall a man leave his father and mother, and shall cleave unto his wife, and they twain shall be one flesh ; wherefore they are
114

no more twain but one flesh ; what therefore God hath joined together let not man put asunder (*Mark* x. 5–9).

163. Verse 25. **And they were both naked, the man and his wife, and were not ashamed.** Their being " naked, and not ashamed," signifies that they were innocent, for the Lord had insinuated innocence into their proprium, to prevent its being unacceptable.

164. The proprium of man, as before stated, is mere evil, and when exhibited to view is most deformed, but when charity and innocence from the Lord are insinuated into the proprium, it then appears good and beautiful (as before observed, n. 154). Charity and innocence not only excuse the proprium (that is, what is evil and false in man), but as it were abolish it, as may be observed in little children, in whom what is evil and false is not merely concealed, but is even pleasing, so long as they love their parents and one another, and their infantile innocence shows itself. Hence it may be known why no one can be admitted into heaven unless he possesses some degree of inno-cence ; as the Lord has said :

Suffer the little children to come unto Me, and forbid them not, for of such is the kingdom of God. Verily I say unto you, whosoever shall not receive the kingdom of God as a little child, he shall not enter therein. And He took them up in His arms, put His hands upon them, and blessed them (*Mark* x. 14–16).

165. That the " nakedness of which they were not ashamed " signifies innocence, is proved by what follows, for when integrity and innocence

115

departed they were ashamed of their nakedness, and it appeared to them disgraceful, and they therefore hid themselves. The same is evident also from the representations in the world of spirits, for when spirits wish to exculpate themselves and prove their guiltlessness, they present themselves naked in order to testify their innocence. Especially is it evident from the innocent in heaven, who appear as naked infants decorated with garlands according to the nature of their innocence ; while those who have not so much innocence are clad in becoming and shining garments (of diamond silk, as you might say), as the angels were occasionally seen by the prophets.

----

166. Such are some of the things contained in this chapter of the Word, but those here set forth are but few. And as the celestial man is treated of, who at the present day is known to scarcely any one, even these few things cannot but appear obscure to some.

167. If any one could know how many arcana each particular verse contains, he would be amazed, for the number of arcana contained is past telling, and this is very little shown in the letter. To state the matter shortly : the words of the letter, exactly as they are, are vividly represented in the world of spirits, in a beautiful order. For the world of spirits is a world of representatives, and whatever is vividly represented there is perceived, in respect to the minute things contained in the representatives, by the angelic spirits who are in the second heaven ; and the things thus perceived by the angelic spirits are perceived abundantly and fully in expressible angelic ideas by the angels who are in the third heaven, and thus in boundless variety in accordance with the Lord's good pleasure. Such is the Word of the Lord.

CONCERNING THE RESUSCITATION OF MAN FROM THE DEAD, AND HIS ENTRANCE INTO ETERNAL LIFE.

168. Being permitted to describe in connected order how man passes from the life of the body into the life of eternity, in order that the way in which he is resuscitated might be known, this has been shown me, not by hearing, but by actual experience.

169. I was reduced into a state of insensibility as to the bodily senses, thus almost into the state of dying persons, retaining however my interior life unimpaired, attended with the power of thinking, and with sufficient breathing for life and finally with a tacit breathing, that I might perceive and remember what happens to those who have died and are being resuscitated.

170. Celestial angels were present who occupied the region of the heart, so that as to the heart I seemed united with them, and so that at length scarcely anything was left to me except thought, and the consequent perception, and this for some hours.

171. I was thus removed from communication with spirits in the world of spirits, who supposed that I had departed from the life of the body.

172. Beside the celestial angels, who occupied the region of the heart, there were also two angels sitting at my head, and it was granted me to perceive that it is so with every one.

173. The angels who sat at my head were perfectly silent, merely communicating their thoughts by the face, so that I could perceive that another face was as it were induced upon me ; indeed two, because there were two angels. When the angels perceive that their faces are received, they know that the man is dead.

174. After recognizing their faces, they induced certain changes about the region of the mouth, and thus communicated their thoughts, for it is customary with the celestial angels to speak by the province of the mouth, and it was permitted me to perceive their cogitative speech.

175. An aromatic odour was perceived, like that of an embalmed corpse, for when the celestial angels are present, the cadaverous odour is perceived as if it were aromatic, this when perceived by evil spirits prevents their approach.

176. Meanwhile I perceived that the region of the heart was kept very closely united with the celestial angels, as was also evident from the pulsation.

177. It was insinuated to me that man is kept engaged by the angels in the pious and holy thoughts which he entertained at the point of death ; and it was also insinuated that those who are dying usually think about eternal life, and seldom of salvation and happiness, and therefore the angels keep them in the thought of eternal life.

178. In this thought they are kept for a considerable time by the celestial angels before these angels depart, and those who are being resuscitated are then left to the spiritual angels, with whom they are next associated. Meanwhile they have a dim idea that they are living in the body.

118

179. As soon as the internal parts of the body grow cold, the vital substances are separated from the man, wherever they may be, even if inclosed in a thousand labyrinthine interlacings, for such is the efficiency of the Lord's mercy (which I had previously perceived as a living and mighty attraction), that nothing vital can remain behind.

180. The celestial angels who sat at the head remained with me for some time after I was, as it were, resuscitated, but they conversed only tacitly. It was perceived from their cogitative speech that they made light of all fallacies and falsities, smiling at them not indeed as matters for derision, but as if they cared nothing about them. Their speech is cogitative, devoid of sound, and in this kind of language they begin to speak with the souls with whom they are at first present.

181. As yet the man, thus resuscitated by the celestial angels, possesses only an obscure life ; but when the time comes for him to be delivered to the spiritual angels, then after a little delay, when the spiritual angels have approached, the celestial depart ; and it has been shown me how the spiritual angels operate in order that the man may receive the benefit of light, as described in the continuation of this subject prefixed to the following chapter.

CHAPTER THE THIRD.

CONTINUATION CONCERNING THE ENTRANCE
INTO ETERNAL LIFE OF THOSE WHO ARE RAISED
FROM THE DEAD.

182. When the celestial angels are with a resuscitated person, they do not leave him, for they love every one ; but when the soul is of such a character that he can no longer be in the company of the celestial angels, he is eager to depart from them ; and when this takes place the spiritual angels arrive, and give him the use of light, for previously he had seen nothing, but had only thought.

183. I was shown how these angels work. They seemed as it were to roll off the coat of the left eye towards the septum of the nose, in order that the eye might be opened and the use of light be granted. To the man it appears as if this were really done, but it is only an appearance.

184. After this little membrane has been thus in appearance rolled off, some light is visible, but dim, such as a man sees through his eyelids when he first awakes out of sleep ; and he who is being resuscitated is in a tranquil state, being still guarded by the celestial angels. There then appears a kind of shadow of an azure colour, with a little star, but I perceived that this takes place with variety.

185. Afterwards there seems to be something gently unrolled from the face, and perception is

120

communicated to him, the angels being especially cautious to prevent any idea coming from him but such as is of a soft and tender nature, as of love ; and it is now granted him to know that he is a spirit.

186. He then commences his life. This at first is happy and glad, for he seems to himself to have come into eternal life, which is represented by a bright white light that becomes of a beautiful golden tinge, by which is signified his first life, to wit, that it is celestial as well as spiritual.

187. His being next taken into the society of good spirits is represented by a young man sitting on a horse and directing it towards hell, but the horse cannot move a step. He is represented as a youth because when he first enters upon eternal life he is among angels, and therefore appears to himself to be in the flower of youth.

188. His subsequent life is represented by his dismounting from the horse and walking on foot, because he cannot make the horse move from the place ; and it is insinuated to him that he must be instructed in the cognitions of what is true and good.

189. Afterwards pathways were seen sloping gently upwards, which signify that by the cognitions of what is true and good, and by self-acknowledgment, he should be led by degrees towards heaven ; for no one can be conducted thither without such self-acknowledgment, and the cognitions of what is true and good. A continuation of this subject may be seen at the end of this chapter.

CHAPTER III.

1. And the serpent was more subtle than any wild animal of the field which Jehovah God had made ; and he said unto the woman, Yea, hath God said, Ye shall not eat of every tree of the garden ?

2. And the woman said unto the serpent, We may eat of the fruit of the tree of the garden ;

3. But of the fruit of the tree which is in the midst of the garden, God hath said, Ye shall not eat of it, neither shall ye touch it, lest ye die.

4. And the serpent said unto the woman, Ye shall not surely die.

5. For God doth know that in the day ye eat thereof, then your eyes shall be opened, and ye shall be as God, knowing good and evil.

6. And the woman saw that the tree was good for food, and that it was pleasant to the eyes, and a tree to be desired to give intelligence, and she took of the fruit thereof and did eat, and she gave also to her man (*vir*) with her, and he did eat.

7. And the eyes of them both were opened, and they knew that they were naked ; and they sewed fig-leaves together and made themselves girdles.

8. And they heard the voice of Jehovah God going to itself in the garden in the air of the day ; and the man and his wife hid themselves from the face of Jehovah God in the midst of the tree in the garden.

9. And Jehovah God cried unto the man (*homo*), and said unto him, Where art thou ?

10. And he said, I heard Thy voice in the garden, and I was afraid, because I was naked ; and I hid myself.

122

11. And He said, Who told thee that thou wast naked ? hast thou eaten of the tree whereof I commanded thee that thou shouldest not eat ?

12. And the man (*homo*) said, The woman whom Thou gavest to be with me, she gave me of the tree, and I did eat.

13. And Jehovah God said unto the woman, Why hast thou done this ? And the woman said, The serpent beguiled me, and I did eat.

THE CONTENTS.

190. The third state of the Most Ancient Church is treated of, which so desired the proprium as to love it.

191. Because from the love of self, that is, their own love, they began to believe nothing that they did not apprehend by the senses, the Sensual is represented by the " serpent " ; the love of self, or their proprium, by the " woman " ; and the Rational by the " man."

192. Hence the " serpent," or Sensual, persuaded the woman to inquire into matters pertaining to faith in the Lord in order to see whether they are really so, which is signified by " eating of the tree of knowledge " ; and that the Rational of man consented, is signified by " the man that he did eat " (verses 1–6).

193. But they perceived that they were in evil ; from which remnant of perception, signified by their " eyes being opened," and by their " hearing the voice of Jehovah " (verses 7, 8), and from the fig-leaves of which they made themselves girdles (verse 7), and from their shame, or hiding in the

123

midst of the tree of the garden (verses 8, 9), as well as from their acknowledgment and confession (verses 10–13), it is evident that natural goodness still remained in them.

THE INTERNAL SENSE.

194. Verse 1. **And the serpent was more subtle than any wild animal of the field which Jehovah God had made ; and he said unto the woman, Yea, hath God said, Ye shall not eat of every tree of the garden ?** By the " serpent " is here meant the Sensual of man in which he trusts ; by the " wild animal of the field," here, as before, every affection of the external man ; by the " woman," man's proprium ; by the serpent's saying, " Yea, hath God said, Ye shall not eat of every tree ? " that they began to doubt. The subject here treated of is the third posterity of the Most Ancient Church, which began not to believe things revealed unless they saw and felt them. Their first state, that it was one of doubt, is described in this and in the next verse.

195. The most ancient people did not compare all things in man to beasts and birds, but they so named them ; and this their manner of speaking remained even in the Ancient Church after the flood, and was preserved among the prophets. The sensual things in man they called " serpents," because as serpents live close to the earth, so sensuous things are those next the body. Hence also reasonings concerning the mysteries of faith, founded on the evidence of the senses, were called by them the " poison of a serpent," and the reasoners themselves " serpents "; and because

124

such persons reason much from sensual, that is, from visible things, such as are things terrestrial, corporeal, mundane, and natural, it is said that " the serpent was more subtle than any wild animal of the field." And so in *David*, speaking of those 2 who seduce man by reasonings :

They sharpen their tongue like a serpent ; the poison of the asp is under their lips (*Ps.* cxl. 3).

And again :

They go astray from the womb, speaking a lie. Their poison is like the poison of a serpent, like the deaf poisonous asp that stoppeth her ear, that she may not hear the voice of the mutterers, of a wise one that charmeth charms (*Ps.* lviii. 3–6).

Reasonings that are of such a character that the men will not even hear what a wise one says, or the voice of the wise, are here called the " poison of a serpent." Hence it became a proverb among the ancients, that " The serpent stoppeth the ear." In *Amos* :

As if a man came into a house, and leaned his hand on the wall, and a serpent bit him. Shall not the day of Jehovah be darkness and not light ? even thick darkness, and no brightness in it ? (v. 19, 20).

The " hand on the wall " means self-derived power, and trust in sensual things, whence comes the blindness which is here described. In *Jeremiah* :   3

The voice of Egypt shall go like a serpent, for they shall go in strength, and shall come to her with axes as hewers of wood. They shall cut down her forest, saith Jehovah, because it will not be searched ; for they are multiplied more than the locust, and are innumerable. The daughter of Egypt is put to shame ; she shall be delivered into the hand of the people of the north (xlvi. 22–24).

" Egypt " denotes reasoning about Divine things from sensuous things and scientifics. Such reasonings are called the " voice of a serpent " ; and the blindness thereby occasioned, the " people of the north." In *Job* :

He shall suck the poison of asps ; the viper's tongue shall slay him. He shall not see the brooks, the flowing rivers of honey and butter (xx. 16, 17).

" Rivers of honey and butter " are things spiritual and celestial, which cannot be seen by mere reasoners ; reasonings are called the " poison of the asp " and the " viper's tongue." See more respecting the serpent below, at verses 14 and 15.

196. In ancient times those were called " serpents " who had more confidence in sensuous things than in revealed ones. But it is still worse at the present day, for now there are persons who not only disbelieve everything they cannot see and feel, but who also confirm themselves by scientifics unknown to the ancients, and thus occasion in themselves a far greater degree of blindness. In order that it may be known how those blind themselves, so as afterwards to see and hear nothing, who form their conclusions concerning heavenly matters from the things of sense, scientifics, and philosophy, and who are not only " deaf serpents," but also the " flying serpents " frequently spoken of in the Word, which are much more pernicious, we will take as an example what they believe about
2 the spirit. The sensuous man, or he who only believes on the evidence of his senses, denies the

126

existence of the spirit because he cannot see it, saying, " It is nothing because I do not feel it : that which I see and touch I know exists." The man of knowledge (*scientificus*), or he who forms his conclusions from knowledges, says, " What is the spirit, except perhaps vapour or heat, or some other entity of his science, that presently vanishes into thin air ? have not the animals also a body, senses, and something analogous to reason ? and yet it is asserted that these will die, while the spirit of man will live." Thus they deny the existence of the spirit. Philosophers also, who would be more acute than the rest of mankind, speak of the spirit in terms which they themselves do not understand, for they dispute about them, contending that not a single expression is applicable to the spirit which derives anything from what is material, organic, or extended ; thus they so abstract it from their ideas that it vanishes from them, and becomes nothing. The more sane, however, assert that the spirit is thought ; but in their reasonings about thought, in consequence of separating from it all substantiality, they at last conclude that it must vanish away when the body expires. Thus all who reason from the things of sense, scientifics, and philosophy, deny the existence of the spirit, and therefore believe nothing of what is said about the spirit and spiritual things. Not so the simple in heart : if these are questioned about the existence of spirit, they say they know it exists, because the Lord has said that they will live after death ; thus instead of extinguishing their Rational, they vivify it by the Word of the Lord.

197. Among the most ancient people, who were celestial men, by the " serpent " was signified

circumspection, and also the Sensual through which they exercised circumspection so as to be secure from injury. This signification of a " serpent " is evident from the Lord's words to His disciples :

> Behold, I send you forth as sheep into the midst of wolves ; be ye therefore prudent as serpents, and simple as doves (*Matt.* x. 16).

And also from the " brazen serpent " that was set up in the wilderness, by which was signified the Sensual in the Lord, who alone is the celestial Man, and alone takes care of and provides for all ; wherefore all who looked upon it were preserved.

198. Verses 2, 3. **And the woman said unto the serpent, We may eat of the fruit of the tree of the garden ; but of the fruit of the tree which is in the midst of the garden, God hath said, Ye shall not eat of it, neither shall ye touch it, lest ye die.** The " fruit of the tree of the garden," is the good and truth revealed to them from the Most Ancient Church ; the " fruit of the tree which is in the midst of the garden, of which they were not to eat," is the good and truth of faith, which they were not to learn from themselves ; " not to touch it," is a prohibition against thinking of the good and truth of faith from themselves, or from what is of sense and scientifics ; " lest ye die," is because thus faith, or all wisdom and intelligence, would perish.

199. That the " fruit of the tree of which they might eat," signifies the good and truth of faith revealed to them from the Most Ancient Church, or the cognitions of faith, is evident from the fact that it is said to be the " fruit of the tree of the garden of which they might eat," and not the " tree of the garden," as before when treating of the celestial man, or the Most Ancient Church

128

(ii. 16). The " tree of the garden," as it is there called, is the perception of what is good and true ; which good and truth, because they are from that source, are here called " fruit," and are also frequently signified by " fruit " in the Word.

200. The reason why the " tree of knowledge " is here spoken of as being " in the midst of the garden," although previously (ii. 9), the tree of lives was said to be in the midst of the garden, and not the tree of knowledge, is that the " midst " of the garden signifies the inmost ; and the inmost of the celestial man, or of the Most Ancient Church, was the " tree of lives," which is love and the faith thence derived ; whereas with this man, who may be called a celestial spiritual man, or with this posterity, faith was the " midst " of the garden, or the inmost. It is impossible more fully to describe the quality of the men who lived in that most ancient time, because at the present day it is utterly unknown, their genius being altogether different from what is ever found with any one now. For the purpose, however, of conveying some idea of their genius, it may be mentioned that from good they knew truth, or from love they knew what is of faith. But when that generation expired, another succeeded of a totally different genius, for instead of discerning the true from the good, or what is of faith from love, they acquired the knowledge of what is good by means of truth, or what is of love from the cognitions of faith, and with very many among them there was scarcely anything but knowledge. Such was the change made after the flood to prevent the destruction of the world.

201. Seeing, therefore, that such a genius as that of the most ancient people anterior to the

E   129

flood is not found and does not exist at the present day, it is no easy matter to explain intelligibly what the words of this passage in their genuine sense imply. They are, however, perfectly under-stood in heaven, for the angels and angelic spirits who are called celestial are of the same genius as the most ancient people who were regenerate before the flood ; while the angels and angelic spirits who are termed spiritual are of a similar genius to the regenerate after the flood, although in both cases with boundless variety.

202. The Most Ancient Church, which was a celestial man, was of such a character as not only to abstain from " eating of the tree of knowledge," that is, from learning what belongs to faith from sensuous things and scientifics, but was not even allowed to touch that tree, that is, to think of anything that is a matter of faith from sensuous things and scientifics, lest they should sink down from celestial life into spiritual life, and so on down-ward. Such also is the life of the celestial angels, the more interiorly celestial of whom do not even suffer faith to be named, nor anything whatever that partakes of what is spiritual ; and if it is spoken of by others, instead of faith they have a perception of love, with a difference known only to themselves ; thus whatever is of faith they derive from love and charity. Still less can they endure listening to any reasoning about faith, and least of all to anything of knowledge respecting it ; for, through love, they have a perception from the Lord of what is good and true ; and from this perception they know instantly whether a thing is so, or is not so. Therefore when anything is said about faith, they answer simply that it is so, or that

it is not so, because they perceive it from the Lord. This is what is signified by the Lord's words in *Matthew* :

> Let your communication be Yea, yea ; Nay, nay ; for whatsoever is more than these cometh of evil (v. 37).

This then is what was meant by their not being allowed to touch the fruit of the tree of knowledge ; for if they touched it, they would be in evil, that is, they would in consequence " die." Nevertheless, the celestial angels converse together on various subjects like the other angels, but in a celestial language, which is formed and derived from love, and is more ineffable than that of the spiritual angels.

203. The spiritual angels, however, converse about faith, and even confirm the things of faith by those of the intellect, of the reason, and of scientifics, but they never form their conclusions concerning matters of faith on such grounds : those who do this are in evil. They are also endowed by the Lord with a perception of all the truths of faith, although not with such a perception as that of the celestial angels. The perception of the spiritual angels is a kind of conscience which is vivified by the Lord, and which indeed appears like celestial perception, yet is not so, but is only spiritual perception.

204. Verses 4, 5. **And the serpent said unto the woman, Ye shall not surely die. For God doth know that in the day ye eat thereof, then your eyes shall be opened, and ye shall be as God, knowing good and evil.** Their " eyes being opened by eating of the fruit of the tree," signifies that if they were to examine the things of faith from what is of sense

131

and knowledge, that is, from themselves, they would plainly see those things as if erroneous. And that they would be " as God, knowing good and evil," denotes that if they did so from themselves, they would be as God, and could guide themselves.

205. Every verse contains a particular state, or change of state, in the church : the preceding verses, that although thus inclined they nevertheless perceived it to be unlawful ; these verses, an incipient doubt whether it might not be lawful for them, since they would thus see whether the things they had heard from their forefathers were true, and so their eyes would be opened. At length, in consequence of the ascendancy of self-love, they began to think that they could lead themselves, and thus be like the Lord ; for such is the nature of the love of self that it is unwilling to submit to the Lord's leading, and prefers to be self-guided, and being self-guided to consult the things of sense and scientifics as to what is to be believed.

206. Who have a stronger belief that their eyes are open, and that as God they know what is good and evil, than those who love themselves, and at the same time excel in worldly learning ? And yet who are more blind ? Only question them, and it will be seen that they do not even know, much less believe in, the existence of spirit ; with the nature of spiritual and celestial life they are utterly unacquainted ; they do not acknowledge an eternal life ; for they believe themselves to be like the brutes which perish ; neither do they acknowledge the Lord, but worship only themselves and nature. Those among them who wish to be guarded in their expressions, say that a certain Supreme Existence (*Ens*), of the nature of which

they are ignorant, rules all things. These are the principles in which they confirm themselves in many ways by things of sense and of knowledge, and if they dared, they would do the same before all the universe. Although such persons desire to be regarded as gods, or as the wisest of men, if they were asked whether they know what it is to have no proprium, they would answer that it is to have no existence, and that if they were deprived of the proprium, they would be nothing. If they are asked what it is to live from the Lord, they think it a phantasy. If asked whether they know what conscience is, they would say it is a mere creature of the imagination, which may be of service in keeping the vulgar under restraint. If asked whether they know what perception is, they would merely laugh at it and call it enthusiastic rubbish. Such is their wisdom, such " open eyes " have they, and such " gods " are they. Principles like these, which they think clearer than the day, they make their starting-point, and so continue on, and in this way reason about the mysteries of faith ; and what can be the result but an abyss of darkness ? These above all others are the " serpents " who seduce the world. But this posterity of the Most Ancient Church was not as yet of such a character. That which became such is treated of from verse 14 to verse 19 of this chapter.

207. Verse 6. **And the woman saw that the tree was good for food, and that it was pleasant to the eyes, and a tree to be desired to give intelligence, and she took of the fruit thereof and did eat, and she gave also to her husband (vir) with her, and he did eat.** " Good for food " signifies lust ; " pleasant to the eyes," phantasy ; and " desirable to give

133

intelligence," pleasure : these are of the proprium, or " woman ": by the " husband eating," is signified the consent of the Rational (n. 265).

208. This was the fourth posterity of the Most Ancient Church, who suffered themselves to be seduced by self-love, and were unwilling to believe what was revealed. unless they saw it confirmed by the things of sense and of knowledge.

209. The expressions here employed, as that " the tree was good for food, pleasant to the eyes, and desirable for giving intelligence," are such as were adapted to the genius of those who lived in that most ancient time, having especial reference to the will, because their evils streamed out from the will. Where the Word treats of the people who lived after the flood, such expressions are used as relate not so much to the will as to the understanding ; for the most ancient people had truth from good, but those who lived after the flood had good from truth.

210. What the proprium is may be stated in this way. Man's proprium is all the evil and falsity that springs from the love of self and of the world, and from not believing in the Lord or the Word but in self, and from supposing that what cannot be apprehended sensuously and by means of scientifics is nothing. In this way men become mere evil and falsity, and therefore regard all things pervertedly ; things that are evil they see as good, and things that are good as evil ; things that are false they see as true, and things that are true as false ; things that really exist they suppose to be nothing, and things that are nothing they suppose to be everything. They call hatred love, darkness light, death life, and the converse. In

the Word, such men are called the " lame " and
the " blind." Such then is the proprium of man,
which in itself is infernal and accursed.

211. Verse 7. **And the eyes of them both were
opened, and they knew that they were naked.**
Their " eyes being opened," signifies their knowing
and acknowledging, from an interior dictate, that
they were " naked," that is, no longer in innocence, as before, but in evil.

212. That by having the " eyes opened " is
signified an interior dictate, is evident from similar
expressions in the Word, as from what Balaam says
of himself, who in consequence of having visions
calls himself the " man whose eyes are opened "
(*Num.* xxiv. 3). And from Jonathan, who when
he tasted of the honeycomb and had a dictate
from within that it was evil, said that his " eyes
saw," that is, were enlightened, so that he saw
what he knew not (1 *Sam.* xiv. 29). Moreover in
the Word, the " eyes " are often used to denote
the understanding, and thus an anterior dictate
therefrom, as in *David* :

Lighten mine eyes, lest I sleep the sleep of
death (*Ps.* xiii. 3).

Here " eyes " denote the understanding. So in
Ezekiel, speaking of those who are not willing to
understand, who " have eyes to see, and see not "
(xii. 2). In *Isaiah* :

Shut their eyes, lest they see with their eyes
(vi. 10).

This denotes that they should be made blind,
lest they should understand. So *Moses* said to the
people,

Jehovah hath not given you a heart to know,
and eyes to see, and ears to hear (*Deut.* xxix. 4).

Here " heart " denotes the will, and " eyes " denote the understanding. In *Isaiah* it is said of the Lord, that " He should open the blind eyes " (xlii. 7). And in the same Prophet : " The eyes of the blind shall see out of thick darkness and out of darkness " (xxix. 18).

213. By " knowing that they were naked " is signified their knowing and acknowledging themselves to be no longer in innocence as before, but in evil, as is evident from the last verse of the preceding chapter, where it is said " and they were both naked, the man and his wife, and were not ashamed," and where it may be seen that " not to be ashamed because they were naked " signifies to be innocent. The contrary is signified by their " being ashamed," as in this verse, where it is said that they " sewed fig-leaves together, and hid themselves " ; for where there is no innocence, nakedness is a scandal and disgrace, because it is attended with a consciousness of thinking evil. For this reason " nakedness " is used in the Word as a type of disgrace and evil, and is predicated of a perverted church, as in *Ezekiel* :

Thou wast naked and bare, and trampled on in thy blood (xvi. 22).

Again :

They shall leave her naked and bare, and the nakedness shall be uncovered (xxiii. 29).

In *John* :

I counsel thee to buy of Me white raiment that thou mayest be clothed, and that the shame of thy nakedness do not appear (*Rev.* iii. 18).

And concerning the last day :

Blessed is he who watcheth, and keepeth his

garments, lest he walk naked and they see his shame (*Rev.* xvi. 15).

In *Deuteronomy* :

If a man hath found some nakedness in his wife, let him write her a bill of divorcement (xxiv. 1).

For the same reason Aaron and his sons were commanded to have linen breeches when they came to the altar, and to minister, to " cover the flesh of their nakedness, lest they should bear iniquity, and die " (*Exod.* xxviii. 42, 43).

214. They are called " naked " because left to the proprium ; for those who are left to the proprium, that is, to themselves, have no longer anything of intelligence and wisdom, or of faith, and consequently are " naked " as to truth and good, and are therefore in evil.

215. That the proprium is nothing but evil and falsity has been made evident to me from the fact that whatever spirits have at any time said from themselves has been so evil and false, that whenever it was made known to me that they spoke from themselves I at once knew that it was false, even though while speaking they were themselves so thoroughly persuaded of the truth of what they said as to have no doubt about it. The case is the same with men who speak from themselves. And in the same way, whenever any persons have begun to reason concerning the things of spiritual and celestial life, or those of faith, I could perceive that they doubted, and even denied, for to reason concerning faith is to doubt and deny. And as it is all from self or the proprium, they sink into mere falsities, consequently, into an abyss of thick

darkness, that is, of falsities, and when they are in this abyss the smallest objection prevails over a thousand truths, just as a minute particle of dust in contact with the pupil of the eye shuts out the universe and everything it contains. Of such persons the Lord says in *Isaiah*:

Woe unto those who are wise in their own eyes, and intelligent before their own faces (v. 21).

And again :

Thy wisdom and thy knowledge, it hath turned thee away, and thou hast said in thine heart, I, and none else besides me ; and evil shall come upon thee, thou shalt not know from whence it riseth, and mischief shall fall upon thee, which thou shalt not be able to expiate, and vastation shall come upon thee suddenly, of which thou art not aware (xlvii. 10, 11).

In *Jeremiah*:

Every man is made stupid by knowledge (*scientia*), every founder is confounded by the graven image, for his molten image is falsehood, neither is there breath in them (li. 17).

A " graven image " is the falsity, and a " molten image " the evil, of the proprium.

216. And they sewed fig-leaves together, and made themselves girdles. To " sew leaves together " is to excuse themselves ; the " fig-tree " is natural good ; and to " make themselves girdles " is to be affected with shame. Thus spake the most ancient people, and thus they described this posterity of the church, signifying that instead of the innocence they had formerly enjoyed, they possessed only natural good, by which their evil was concealed ; and being in natural good, they were affected with shame.

138

217. That the " vine " is used in the Word to signify spiritual good, and the " fig-tree " natural good, is at this day utterly unknown, because the internal sense of the Word has been lost ; nevertheless, wherever these expressions occur, they signify or involve this meaning ; as also in what the Lord spake in parables concerning a " vineyard " and a " fig-tree " ; as in *Matthew* :

Jesus seeing a fig-tree in the way, came to it, but found nothing thereon save leaves only, and He said unto it, Let no fruit grow on thee henceforward forever ; and presently the fig-tree withered away (xxi. 19).

By this is meant, that no good, not even natural good, was to be found upon the earth. Similar is the meaning of the " vine " and " fig-tree " in *Jeremiah* :

Were they ashamed when they had committed abomination ? Nay, they were not at all ashamed, and they knew not how to blush ; therefore I will surely gather them, saith Jehovah ; there shall be no grapes on the vine, nor figs on the fig-tree, and the leaf hath fallen (viii. 12, 13).

By this is signified that all good, both spiritual and natural, had perished, since they were so depraved as to have lost even the sense of shame, like those at the present day who are in evil, and who, so far from blushing for their wickedness, make it their boast. In *Hosea* :

I found Israel like grapes in the wilderness ; I saw your fathers as the first ripe in the fig-tree in the beginning (ix. 10).

And in *Joel* :

Be not afraid, ye beasts of My fields, for the tree shall bear its fruit, the fig-tree and the vine shall yield their strength (ii. 22).

The " vine " here denotes spiritual good, and the
" fig-tree " natural good.

218. Verse 8. **And they heard the voice of
Jehovah God going to itself in the garden in the air
of the day ; and the man and his wife hid themselves from the face of Jehovah God in the midst
of the tree of the garden.** By the " voice of Jehovah
God going to itself in the garden," is signified an
internal dictate which caused them to feel afraid,
this dictate being the residue of the perception
which they had possessed ; by the " air " or
" breath " of the " day," is denoted a period
when the church still possessed some residue of
perception ; to " hide themselves from the face of
Jehovah God " is to fear the dictate, as is wont
to be the case with those who are conscious of
evil ; by the " midst of the tree of the garden," in
which they hid themselves, is signified natural good ;
that which is inmost is called the " midst " ; the
" tree " denotes perception as before ; but because
there was little perception remaining, the tree is
spoken of in the singular number, as if there were
only one remaining.

219. That by the " voice of Jehovah God going
to itself in the garden," is meant an internal dictate
of which they were afraid, is evident from the
signification of " voice " in the Word, where the
" voice of Jehovah " is used to designate the
Word itself, the doctrine of faith, conscience or a
taking notice inwardly, and also every reproof
thence resulting ; whence it is that thunders are
called the " voices of Jehovah," as in *John* :

The angel cried with a loud voice, as a lion
roareth, and when he had cried seven thunders
uttered their voices (*Rev.* x. 3).

140

This denotes that there was then a voice both external and internal. Again :

> In the days of the voice of the seventh angel the mystery of God shall be consummated (*Rev.* x. 7).

In *David* :

> Sing unto God, sing praises unto the Lord, who rideth upon the heavens of heavens which were of old ; lo, He shall send out His voice, a voice of strength (*Ps.* lxviii. 32, 33).

The " heavens of heavens which were of old," denote the wisdom of the Most Ancient Church ; " voice," revelation, and also an internal dictate. Again :

> The voice of Jehovah is upon the waters ; the voice of Jehovah is in power ; the voice of Jehovah is in glory ; the voice of Jehovah breaketh the cedars ; the voice of Jehovah divideth the flames of fire ; the voice of Jehovah maketh the wilderness to shake ; the voice of Jehovah maketh the hinds to calve, and un-covereth the forests (*Ps.* xxix. 3–5 and 7–9).

And in *Isaiah* :

> Jehovah shall cause the excellency of His voice to be heard, for through the voice of Jehovah shall Asshur be beaten down (xxx. 30, 31).

220. By the " voice going to itself," is meant that there was but little perception remaining, and that alone, as it were, by itself and unheard, as is manifest also from the following verse where it is said, " Jehovah called to the man." So in *Isaiah* :

> The voice of one crying in the wilderness ; the voice said, Cry (xl. 3, 6).

The " wilderness " is a church where there is no faith ; the " voice of one crying " is the

141

annunciation of the Lord's advent, and in general
every announcement of His coming, as with
the regenerate, with whom there is an internal
dictate.

221. That by the " air " or " breath " " of the
day," is signified a period when the church had
still somewhat of perception remaining, is evident
from the signification of " day " and of " night."
The most ancient people compared the states of the
church to the times of the day and of the night,
to the times of the day when the church was still
in light, wherefore this state is compared to the
breath or air " of the day," because there was still
some remnant of perception by which they knew
that they were fallen. The Lord also calls the state
of faith " day," and that of no faith " night " ;
as in *John* :

> I must work the works of Him that sent Me,
> while it is day ; the night cometh when no man
> can work (ix. 4).

The states of the regeneration of man were for the
same reason called " days " in Chapter I.

222. That to " hide themselves from the face of
Jehovah," means to be afraid of the dictate, as is
wont to be the case with those who are conscious of
evil, is evident from their reply (verse 10) : " I
heard Thy voice in the garden, and I was afraid
because I was naked." The " face of Jehovah,"
or of the Lord, is mercy, peace, and every good,
as is clearly evident from the benediction :

> Jehovah make His faces to shine upon thee,
> and be merciful unto thee ; Jehovah lift up His
> faces upon thee, and give thee peace (*Num.*
> vi. 25, 26).

142

And in *David* :

God be merciful unto us, and bless us, and cause His faces to shine upon us (*Ps.* lxvii. 1).

And in another place :

There be many that say, Who will show us any good ? Jehovah, lift Thou up the light of Thy faces upon us (*Ps.* iv. 6).

The mercy of the Lord is therefore called the " angel of faces," in *Isaiah* :

I will make mention of the mercies of Jehovah ; He hath requited them according to His mercies, and according to the multitude of His mercies ; and He became their Saviour. In all their affliction He was afflicted, and the angel of His faces saved them ; in His love and in His pity He redeemed them (lxiii. 7-9).

223. As the " face of the Lord " is mercy, peace, and every good, it is evident that He regards all from mercy, and never averts His countenance from any ; but that it is man, when in evil, who turns away his face, as is said by the Lord in *Isaiah* :

Your iniquities have separated between you and your God, and your sins have hid His face from you (lix. 2).

And here, " they hid themselves from the face of Jehovah, because they were naked."

224. Mercy, peace, and every good, or the " faces of Jehovah," are the cause of the dictate with those who have perception, and also, although in a different manner, with those who have conscience, and they always operate mercifully, but are received according to the state in which the man is. The state of this man, that is, of this posterity of the

Most Ancient Church, was one of natural good ; and those who are in natural good are of such a character that they hide themselves through fear and shame because they are naked : while such as are destitute of natural good do not hide themselves, because they are not susceptible of shame ; concerning whom, in *Jeremiah* viii. 12, 13. (See above, n. 217.)

225. That the " midst of the tree of the garden," signifies natural good, in which there is some perception which is called a " tree," is also evident from the " garden " in which the celestial man dwelt ; for everything good and true is called a " garden," with a difference according to the man who cultivates it. Good is not good unless its inmost is celestial, from which, or through which, from the Lord, comes perception. This inmost is here called the " midst," as also elsewhere in the Word.

226. Verses 9, 10. **And Jehovah God cried unto the man, and said unto him, Where art thou ? And he said, I heard Thy voice in the garden, and I was afraid, because I was naked ; and I hid myself.** The meaning of " crying," of the " voice in the garden," of their " being afraid because they were naked," and of " hiding themselves," has been previously explained. It is common in the Word for man to be first asked where he is and what he is doing, although the Lord previously knew all things ; but the reason for asking is that man may acknowledge and confess.

227. As it is desirable that the origin of perception, internal dictate, and conscience, should be known, and as at the present day it is altogether unknown, I may relate something on the subject.

It is a great truth that man is governed by the Lord by means of spirits and angels. When evil spirits begin to rule, the angels labour to avert evils and falsities, and hence arises a combat. It is this combat of which the man is rendered sensible by perception, dictate, and conscience. By these, and also by temptations, a man might clearly see that spirits and angels are with him, were he not so deeply immersed in corporeal things as to believe nothing that is said about spirits and angels. Such persons, even if they were to feel these combats hundreds of times, would still say that they are imaginary, and the effect of a disordered mind. I have been permitted to feel such combats, and to have a vivid sense of them, thousands and thousands of times, and this almost constantly for several years, as well as to know who, what, and where they were that caused them, when they came, and when they departed ; and I have conversed with them.

228. It is impossible to describe the exquisite perception whereby the angels discover whether anything gains admission that is contrary to the truth of faith and the good of love. They perceive the quality of what enters, and when it enters, a thousand times more perfectly than the man himself, who scarcely knows anything about it. The least of thought in a man is more fully perceived by the angels than the greatest is by himself. This is indeed incredible, yet is most true.

229. Verses 11–13. **And He said, Who told thee that thou wast naked ? hast thou eaten of the tree whereof I commanded that thou shouldest not eat ? And the man said, The woman whom Thou gavest to be with me, she gave me of the tree, and I**

did eat. And Jehovah God said unto the woman, Why hast thou done this ? And the woman said, The serpent beguiled me, and I did eat. The signification of these words is evident from what has been explained before, namely, that the Rational of man suffered itself to be deceived by the proprium, because this was dear to him (that is, by the love of self), so that be believed nothing but what he could see and feel. Every one can see that Jehovah God did not speak to a serpent, and indeed that there was no serpent, neither did He address the Sensual that is signified by the " serpent " ; but that these words involve a different meaning, namely, that they perceived themselves to be deluded by the senses, and yet, in consequence of self-love, were desirous of ascertaining the truth of what they had heard concerning the Lord, and concerning faith in Him, before they believed it.

230. The ruling evil of this posterity was the love of self, without their having at the same time so much of the love of the world as exists at the present day ; for they dwelt within their own households and families, and had no desire to accumulate wealth.

231. The evil of the Most Ancient Church which existed before the flood, as well as that of the Ancient Church after the flood, and also that of the Jewish Church, and subsequently the evil of the new church, or church of the Gentiles, after the coming of the Lord, and also that of the church of the present day, was and is that they do not believe the Lord or the Word, but themselves and their own senses. Hence there is no faith, and where there is no faith there is no love of the neighbour, consequently all is false and evil.

146

232. At this day however it is much worse than in former times, because men can now confirm the incredulity of the senses by scientifics unknown to the ancients, and this has given birth to an indescribable degree of darkness. If men knew how great is the darkness from this cause they would be astounded.

233. To explore the mysteries of faith by means of scientifics is as impossible as it is for a camel to go through the eye of a needle, or for a rib to govern the finest fibrils of the chest and of the heart. So gross, indeed, much more so, is that which pertains to our senses and mere knowledge relatively to what is spiritual and celestial. He would investigate the hidden things of nature, which are innumerable, discovers scarcely one, and while investigating them falls into errors, as is well known. How much more likely is this to be the case while investigating the hidden truths of spiritual and celestial life, where myriads of mysteries exist for one that is invisible in nature ! As an illustration, take this single example : Of 2 himself man cannot but do what is evil, and turn away from the Lord. Yet man does not do these things, but the evil spirits who are with him. Nor do these evil spirits do them, but the evil itself which they have made their own. Nevertheless, man does evil and turns himself away from the Lord, and is in fault ; and yet he lives only from the Lord. So, on the other hand, of himself man cannot possibly do what is good, and turn to the Lord, but this is done by the angels. Nor can the angels do it, but the Lord alone. And yet a man is able as of himself to do what is good, and to turn himself to the Lord. These facts can never

147

be apprehended by our senses, science, and philosophy ; if these are consulted, they will be denied in spite of their truth. And it is the same all 3 through. From what has been said it is evident that those who consult sensuous things and scientifics in matters of belief, plunge themselves not only into doubt, but also into denial, that is, into thick darkness, and consequently into all lusts. For as they believe what is false, they also do what is false. And as they believe that what is spiritual and celestial has no existence, so they believe that there is nothing but what pertains to the body and the world. And so they love everything that belongs to self and the world, and in this way cupidities and evils spring from what is false.

---

14. And Jehovah God said unto the serpent, Because thou hast done this, thou art cursed above every beast, and above every wild animal of the field ; upon thy belly shalt thou go, and dust shalt thou eat all the days of thy life.

15. And I will put enmity between thee and the woman, and between thy seed and her seed ; He shall trample upon thy head, and thou shalt bruise His heel.

16. And unto the woman He said, I will greatly multiply thy sorrow and thy conception ; in sorrow thou shalt bring forth sons, and thine obedience shall be to thy man (*vir*), and he shall rule over thee.

17. And unto the man He said, Because thou hast hearkened unto the voice of thy wife, and hast eaten of the tree of which I commanded thee, saying, Thou shalt not eat of it ; cursed is the ground for thy sake ; in great sorrow shalt thou eat of it all the days of thy life.

18. And the thorn and the thistle shall it bring forth unto thee, and thou shalt eat the herb of the field.

19. In the sweat of thy face shalt thou eat bread, till thou return unto the ground ; for out of it wast thou taken ; for dust thou art, and unto dust shalt thou return.

THE CONTENTS.

234. The subsequent state of the church down to the flood is here described ; and as at that time the church utterly destroyed itself, it is foretold that the Lord would come into the world and save the human race.

235. Being unwilling to believe anything that could not be apprehended by the senses, the Sensual which is the " serpent," cursed itself, and became infernal (verse 14).

236. Therefore, to prevent all mankind from rushing into hell, the Lord promised that He would come into the world (verse 15).

237. The church is further described by the " woman," which so loved self or the proprium as to be no longer capable of apprehending truth, although a Rational was given them that should " rule " (verse 16).

238. The quality of the Rational is then described, in that it consented, and thus cursed itself, and became infernal, so that reason no longer remained, but ratiocination (verse 17).

149

239. The curse and vastation are described, and also their ferine nature (verse 18).

240. Next, their aversion to everything of faith and love ; and that thus from being man they became not men (verse 19).

THE INTERNAL SENSE.

241. The most ancient people, being celestial men, were so constituted that every object they beheld in the world or upon the face of the earth, they indeed saw, but they thought about the heavenly and Divine things the objects signified or represented. Their sight was merely an instrumental agency, and so, consequently, was their speech. Any one may know how this was from his own experience, for if he attends closely to the meaning of a speaker's words, he does indeed hear the words, but it is as if he did not hear them, taking in only the sense ; and one who thinks more deeply does not attend even to the sense of the words, but to a more universal sense. But the posterities that are here treated of were not like their fathers, for when they beheld the objects in the world and on the face of the earth, since they loved them, their minds cleaved to them, and they thought about them, and from them about things heavenly and Divine. Thus with them what is sensuous began to be the chief thing, and not as with their fathers the instrumental. And when that which is of the world and of the earth becomes the chief thing, then men reason from this about the things of heaven, and so blind themselves. How this is may also be known by any one from his own experience ; for he who attends to the

150

words of a speaker, and not to the sense of the words, takes in but little of the sense, and still less of the universal import of the sense, and sometimes judges of all that a man says from a single word, or even from a grammatical peculiarity.

242. Verse 14. **And Jehovah God said unto the serpent, Because thou hast done this, cursed art thou above every beast, and above every wild animal of the field ; upon thy belly shalt thou go, and dust shalt thou eat all the days of thy life.** By " Jehovah God said unto the serpent," is signified that they perceived their Sensual to be the cause. " The serpent cursed above every beast and above every wild animal of the field," signifies that their Sensual averted itself from that which is heavenly, and turned itself to that which is of the body, and thus cursed itself ; the " beast," and the " wild animal of the field," here signify affections, as before. The " serpent going upon its belly," signifies that their Sensual could no longer look upwards to the things of heaven, but only downwards to those of the body and the earth. Its " eating dust all the days of its life," signifies that their Sensual became such that it could not live from anything but that which is of the body and the earth, that is to say, it became infernal.

243. In the most ancient celestial men the sensuous things of the body were of such a character as to be compliant and subservient to their internal man, and beyond this they did not care for them. But after they had begun to love themselves, they set the things of sense before the internal man, and therefore those things were separated, became corporeal, and so were condemned.

244. Having before shown that by " Jehovah God speaking to the serpent " is signified their perceiving the Sensual to be the cause of their fall, no more need be said in regard to these words.

245. That " He said to the serpent, Thou art cursed above every beast, and above every wild animal of the field " signifies that the Sensual averted itself from that which is heavenly, turned itself to that which is of the body, and thus cursed itself, may be clearly shown from the internal sense of the Word. Jehovah God or the Lord never curses any one. He is never angry with any one, never leads any one into temptation, never punishes any one, and still less does He curse any one. All this is done by the infernal crew, for such things can never proceed from the Fountain of mercy, peace, and goodness. The reason of its being said, both here and in other parts of the Word, that Jehovah God not only turns away His face, is angry, punishes, and tempts, but also kills and even curses, is that men may believe that the Lord governs and disposes all and everything in the universe, even evil itself, punishments, and temptations ; and when they have received this most general idea, may afterwards learn how He governs and disposes all things by turning the evil of punishment and of temptation into good. In teaching and learning the Word, the most general truths must come first ; and therefore the literal sense is full of such things.

246. That the " beast and the wild animal of the field " signify affections, is evident from what was previously said concerning them (n. 45 and 46), to which it is permitted to add the following passage from *David* :

152

Thou, O God, dost send the rain of Thy kindnesses; Thou confirmest Thy labouring inheritance; Thy wild animal shall dwell therein (*Ps.* lxviii. 9, 10).

Here also " wild animal " denotes the affection of good, because it is said that it shall " dwell in the inheritance of God." The reason why here, and also in Chapter II, 19, 20, the " beast and the wild animal of the field " are mentioned, while in Chapter I, 24, 25, the " beast and the wild animal of the earth " are named, is that the present passage treats of the church or regenerated man, whereas the first chapter related to what was as yet not a church, or to man about to become regenerate; for the word " field " is applied to the church, or to the regenerate.

247. That the " serpent going on his belly " denotes that their Sensual could no longer look upwards to the things of heaven, but only downwards to those of the body and the earth, is evident from the fact that in ancient times by the " belly " such things are signified as are nearest to the earth; by the " chest " such as are above the earth; and by the " head," what is highest. It is here said that the Sensual, which in itself is the lowest part of man's nature, "went upon its belly," because it turned to what is earthly. The depression of the belly even to the earth, and the sprinkling of dust on the head, had a similar signification in the Jewish Church. Thus we read in *David* :

Wherefore hidest Thou Thy faces, and forgettest our misery and our oppression ? For our soul is bowed down to the dust, and our belly cleaveth to the earth. Arise, a help for

153

us, and redeem us for Thy mercy's sake (*Ps.* xliv. 24–26).

Here also it is evident that when man averts himself from the face of Jehovah, he " cleaves by his belly to the dust and to the earth." In *Jonah* likewise, by the " belly " of the great fish, into which he was cast, are signified the lower parts of the earth, as is evident from his prophecy :

Out of the belly of hell cried I, and Thou heardest my voice (ii. 2).

Here " hell " denotes the lower earth.

248. When, therefore, man had regard to heavenly things, he was said to " walk erect," and to " look upward," or " forward," which means the same ; but when he had regard to corporeal and earthly things, he was said to be " bowed to the earth," and to " look downward " or " backward." As in *Leviticus* :

I am Jehovah your God, who brought you forth out of the land of Egypt, that ye should not be their bondmen ; and I have broken the bonds of your yoke, and made you to go erect (xxvi. 13).

In *Micah* :

Ye shall not thence remove your necks, neither shall ye go erect (ii. 3).

In *Jeremiah* :

Jerusalem hath sinned a sin, therefore they despise her, because they have seen her nakedness ; yea, she groaned and hath turned backward. From on high hath He sent fire into my bones, and hath made me to return backward ; He hath made me desolate (*Lam.* i. 8, 13).

154

And in *Isaiah* :

> Jehovah thy Redeemer, that turneth wise men backward, and maketh foolish their knowledge (xliv. 24, 25).

249. That to " eat dust all the days of its life " signifies that their Sensual became such that it could not live from anything except that which is of the body and the earth, that is to say, that it became infernal, is evident also from the signification of " dust " in the Word ; as in *Micah* :

> Feed thy people as in the days of eternity. The nations shall see and shall blush at all their might ; they shall lick the dust like a serpent, they shall be shaken out of their holds like creeping things (*serpentes*) of the earth (vii. 14, 16, 17).

The " days of eternity," mean the Most Ancient Church ; the " nations," those who trust in their proprium, of whom it is predicated that " they shall lick the dust like a serpent." In *David* :

> Barbarians shall bow themselves before God, and His enemies shall lick the dust (*Ps.* lxxii. 9).

" Barbarians " and " enemies " are those who regard only earthly and worldly things. In *Isaiah* :

> Dust shall be the serpent's bread (lxv. 25).

As " dust " signifies those who do not regard spiritual and celestial things, but only what is corporeal and earthly, therefore the Lord enjoined His disciples that if the city or house into which they entered was not worthy, they should " shake off the dust of their feet " (*Matt.* x. 14). That " dust " signifies what is condemned and infernal, will be further shown at verse 19.

250. Verse 15. **And I will put enmity between thee and the woman, and between thy seed and her seed ; He shall trample upon thy head, and thou shalt bruise His heel.** Every one is aware that this is the first prophecy of the Lord's advent into the world ; it appears indeed clearly from the words themselves, and therefore from them and from the prophets even the Jews knew that a Messiah was to come. Hitherto, however, no one has understood what is specifically meant by the " serpent," the " woman," the " serpent's seed," the " woman's seed," the " head of the serpent which was to be trodden upon," and the " heel which the serpent should bruise." They must therefore be explained. By the " serpent " is here meant all evil in general, and specifically the love of self ; by the " woman " is meant the church ; by the " seed of the serpent," all infidelity ; by the " seed of the woman," faith in the Lord ; by " He," the Lord Himself ; by the " head of the serpent," the dominion of evil in general, and specifically that of the love of self ; by to " trample upon," depression, so that it should " go upon the belly and eat dust " ; and by the " heel," the lowest Natural, as the Corporeal, which the serpent should " bruise."

251. The reason why the " serpent " means all evil in general, and specifically the love of self, is that all evil has had its rise from the Sensual, and also from the Scientific, which at first were signified by the " serpent " ; and therefore it here denotes evil of every kind, and specifically the love of self, or hatred against the neighbour and the Lord, which is the same thing. As this evil or hatred was various, consisting of numerous genera and still more numerous species, it is described in the Word

156

by various kinds of serpents, as " snakes," " cocka-trices," " asps," " adders," " fiery serpents," " serpents that fly " and " that creep," and " vipers," according to the differences of the poison, which is hatred. Thus we read in *Isaiah* :

> Rejoice not thou, whole Philistia, because the rod which smiteth thee is broken, for out of the serpent's root shall go forth a cockatrice, and his fruit shall be a flying fire-serpent (xiv. 29).

The " serpent's root " denotes that part of the mind, or that principle, which is connected with the Sensual and the Scientific ; the " cockatrice " denotes evil originating in the falsity thence derived ; and the " flying fire-serpent," the lust that comes from the love of self. By the same Prophet also similar things are elsewhere thus described :

> They hatch cockatrice's eggs, and weave the spider's web ; he that eateth of their eggs dieth, and when it is crushed there cometh out a viper (lix. 5).

The serpent described here in *Genesis* is called in the *Revelation* the " great and red dragon," and the " old serpent," and also the " devil and satan," that " deceives the whole world " (xii. 3, 9 ; xx. 2), where, and also in other places, by the " devil " is not meant any particular devil who is prince over the others, but the whole crew of evil spirits, and evil itself.

252. That by the " woman " is meant the church, is evident from what was said above (n. 155) concerning the heavenly marriage. Such is the nature of the heavenly marriage, that heaven, and, consequently, the church, is united

157

to the Lord by the proprium, insomuch that these are in their proprium, for without the proprium there can be no union. When the Lord in mercy insinuates innocence, peace, and good into this proprium, it still retains its identity, but becomes heavenly and most happy (as may be seen at n. 164). The quality of a heavenly and angelic proprium from the Lord, and the quality of a proprium, which, because from self, is infernal and diabolical, cannot be told. The difference is like that between heaven and hell.

253. It is by virtue of a heavenly and angelic proprium that the church is called a " woman," and also a " wife," a " bride," a " virgin," and a " daughter." She is called a " woman " in the *Revelation* :

> A woman clothed with the sun, and the moon under her feet, and upon her head a crown of twelve stars. And the dragon persecuted the woman who brought forth the man child (xii. 1, also 4 to 13).

In this passage by a " woman " is meant the church ; by the " sun," love ; by the " moon," faith ; by " stars," as before, the truths of faith, all of which evil spirits hate, and persecute to the utmost. The church is called a " woman," and also a " wife," in *Isaiah* :

> Thy Maker is thy Husband, Jehovah of hosts is His name, and thy Redeemer the Holy One of Israel, the God of the whole earth is He called ; for as a woman forsaken and afflicted in spirit hath Jehovah called thee, and as a wife of youth (liv. 5, 6).

Here the " Maker " is called also the " husband,"

because united to the proprium ; and a " woman afflicted," and a " wife of youth," signify specifically the Ancient and Most Ancient Churches. Likewise in *Malachi* :

Jehovah hath borne witness between thee and the wife of thy youth (ii. 14).

She is called a " wife " and a " bride " in the *Revelation* :

I saw the holy city New Jerusalem coming down from God out of heaven, prepared as a bride adorned for her husband : come hither, I will show thee the bride, the Lamb's wife (xxi. 2, 9).

The church is called a " virgin " and a " daughter " throughout the Prophets.

254. That by the " seed of the serpent " is meant all infidelity, is evident from the signification of a " serpent," as being all evil ; " seed " is that which produces and is produced, or that which begets and is begotten ; and as the church is here spoken of, this is infidelity. In *Isaiah*, in reference to the Jewish Church in its perverted state, it is called a " seed of evil doers," a " seed of adultery," a " seed of falsehood " :

Woe to the sinful nation, a people laden with iniquity, a seed of evildoers, sons that are destroyers ; they have forsaken Jehovah, they have provoked the Holy One of Israel, they have estranged themselves backward (i. 4).

Again :

Draw near hither, ye sons of the sorceress, the seed of the adulterer. Are ye not children of transgression, a seed of falsehood ? (lvii. 3, 4).

159

And again, speaking of the " serpent " or " dragon,"
who is there called Lucifer :

> Thou art cast out of thy sepulchre like an
> abominable shoot, because thou hast corrupted
> thy land, thou hast slain thy people ; the seed of
> evildoers shall not be called to eternity (xiv.
> 19, 20).

255. That the " seed of the woman " signifies
faith in the Lord, is evident from the signification
of " woman " as being the church, whose " seed "
is nothing but faith, for it is from faith in the Lord
that the church is called the church. In *Malachi*,
faith is called the " seed of God " :

> Jehovah hath witnessed between thee and the
> wife of thy youth ; and not one hath done so
> who had a residue of the spirit ; and wherefore
> one, seeking the seed of God ? but observe ye in
> your spirit, lest he deal treacherously against the
> wife of thy youth (ii. 14, 15).

In this passage the " wife of youth " is the Ancient
and Most Ancient Churches, of whose " seed," or
faith, the prophet speaks. In *Isaiah* also, in
reference to the church :

> I will pour waters upon the thirsty, and floods
> upon the dry ; I will pour My spirit upon thy
> seed, and My blessing upon thine offspring
> (xliv. 3).

In the *Revelation* :

> The dragon was wroth with the woman, and
> went to make war with the remnant of her seed,
> who were keeping the commandments of God,
> and have the testimony of Jesus Christ (xii. 17).

And in *David* :

> I have made a covenant with Mine elect, I

have sworn unto David My servant, even to eternity will I establish thy seed, and his seed will I make to endure forever, and his throne as the days of the heavens ; his seed shall endure to eternity, and his throne as the sun before me (*Ps.* lxxxix. 3, 4, 29, 36).

Here by " David " is meant the Lord ; by " throne," His kingdom ; by the " sun," love ; and by " seed," faith.

256. Not only is faith, but also the Lord Himself is called the " seed of the woman," both because He alone gives faith, and thus is faith, and because He was pleased to be born, and that into such a church as had altogether fallen into an infernal and diabolical proprium through the love of self and of the world, in order that by His Divine power He might unite the Divine celestial proprium with the human proprium in His human essence, so that in Him they might be one ; and unless this union had been effected, the whole world must have utterly perished. Because the Lord is thus the seed of the woman, it is not said, " it," but " He."

257. That by the " head of the serpent " is meant the dominion of evil in general, and specifically of the love of self, is evident from its nature, which is so direful as not only to seek dominion, but even dominion over all things upon earth ; nor does it rest satisfied with this, but aspires even to rule over everything in heaven, and then, not content with this, over the Lord Himself, and even then it is not satisfied. This is latent in every spark of the love of self. If it were indulged, and freed from restraint, we should perceive that it would at

once burst forth, and would grow even to that aspiring height. Hence it is evident how the "serpent," or the evil of the love of self, desires to exercise dominion, and how much it hates all those who refuse its sway. This is that "head of the serpent" which exalts itself, and which the Lord "tramples down," even to the earth, that it may "go upon its belly and eat dust," as stated in the verse immediately preceding. Thus also is described the "serpent" or "dragon" called "Lucifer" in *Isaiah* :

O Lucifer, thou hast said in thy heart, I will ascend the heavens, I will exalt my throne above the stars of God, and I will sit upon the mount of the congregation, in the sides of the north, I will ascend above the heights of the cloud, I will be made equal to the Most High ; yet thou shalt be brought down to hell, to the sides of the pit (xiv. 12–15).

The "serpent" or "dragon" is also described in the *Revelation* in regard to the way in which he exalts his head :

A great red dragon, having seven heads, and ten horns, and many diadems upon his heads ; but he was cast into the earth (xii. 3, 9).

In *David* :

The saying of Jehovah to my Lord, Sit Thou at My right hand, until I make Thine enemies Thy footstool : Jehovah shall send the rod of thy strength out of Zion, He shall judge the nations, He hath filled with dead bodies, He hath bruised the head over much land ; He shall drink of the brook in the way, therefore shall He lift up the head (*Ps.* cx. 1, 2, 6, 7).

258. That by " trampling on " or " bruising," is meant depression, so as to compel it to " go on the belly and eat the dust," is now evident from this and the preceding verses. So likewise in *Isaiah* :

Jehovah hath cast down them that dwell on high ; the exalted city He will humble it ; He will humble it even to the earth ; He will prostrate it even to the dust ; the foot shall tread it down (xxvi. 4–6).

Again :

He shall cast down to the earth with the hand ; they shall be trampled on by feet—a crown of pride (xxviii. 2, 3).

259. That by the " heel " is meant the lowest Natural or Corporeal cannot be known unless the way in which the most ancient people considered the various things in man is known. They referred his celestial and spiritual things to the head and face ; what comes forth from these, as charity and mercy, to the chest ; natural things, to the feet ; lower natural things, to the soles of the feet ; and the lowest natural and corporeal things, to the heel ; nor did they merely refer them, but also so called them. The lowest things of reason, that is, scientifics, were also meant by what Jacob prophesied concerning Dan :

Dan shall be a serpent upon the way, an adder upon the path, biting the horse's heels, and his rider falls backward (*Gen*. xlix. 17).

Also in *David* :

The iniquity of my heels hath compassed me about (*Ps*. xlix. 5).

In like manner by what is related of Jacob, when he came forth from the womb,

163

That his hand laid hold of Esau's heel, whence
he was called Jacob (*Gen.* xxv. 26).

For the name " Jacob " comes from the " heel,"
because the Jewish Church, signified by " Jacob,"
injured the heel.   A serpent can injure only the
lowest natural things, but, unless it is a species of
viper, not the interior natural things in man, still
less his spiritual things, and least of all his celestial
things, which the Lord preserves and stores up in
man without his knowledge.   What are thus stored
up by the Lord are called in the Word " remains."
The mode in which the serpent destroyed those
lowest natural things in the people before the
flood, by the Sensual and the love of self ;   and
among the Jews, by sensuous things, traditions, and
trifles, and by the love of self and of the world ;
and how at this day he has destroyed and continues
to destroy them by the things of sense, of scientifics,
and of philosophy, and at the same time by the
same loves, shall, of the Lord's Divine mercy, be
told hereafter.

260.   From what has been said it is evident that
it was revealed to the church of that time that the
Lord would come into the world to save them.

261.   Verse 16.   **And unto the woman He said, I
will greatly multiply thy sorrow and thy conception ;
in sorrow thou shalt bring forth sons, and thine
obedience shall be to thy man (*vir*), and he shall
rule over thee.**   By the " woman " is now signified
the church as to proprium, which it loved ;   by
" greatly multiplying her sorrow," is signified
combat, and the anxiety it occasions ;   by " conception," every thought ;   by the " sons whom she
would bring forth in sorrow," the truths which she

164

would thus produce ; by " man," here as before, the Rational which it will obey, and which will rule.

262. That the church is signified by the " woman," has been previously shown, but here the church perverted by the proprium, which was itself formerly signified by the " woman," because the posterity of the Most Ancient Church, which had become perverted, is now treated of.

263. When therefore the Sensual averts itself or curses itself, the consequence is that evil spirits begin to fight powerfully, and the attendant angels to labour, and therefore this combat is described by the words, " I will greatly multiply thy sorrow, in relation to the conception and birth of sons," that is, as to the thoughts and productions of truth.

264. That the " conception and birth of sons," in the Word, are taken in a spiritual sense—" conception " for the thought and device of the heart, and " sons " for truths, is evident from *Hosea* :

As for Ephraim, their glory shall fly away like a bird, from the birth, and from the womb, and from the conception ; though they shall have brought up their sons, yet will I bereave them, that they be not man ; yea, woe also to them when I depart from them (ix. 11, 12).

Where " Ephraim " signifies the intelligent, or the understanding of truth ; and " sons," truths themselves. It is likewise said elsewhere concerning Ephraim, or one who is intelligent, who has become foolish :

The sorrows of one in travail have come upon him, he is an unwise son, for at the time he will not stand in the breach of the womb of sons (xiii. 13).

165

And in *Isaiah* :

> Blush, O Zidon, for the sea hath spoken, the fortress of the sea, saying, I have not travailed, nor brought forth, nor have I brought up young men, nor caused girls to grow up ; as at the report concerning Egypt, they shall bring forth according to the report of Tyre (xxiii. 4, 5).

2 Here " Zidon " means those who have been in the cognitions of faith, but have destroyed them by scientifics, and so have become barren. Again in the same prophet, treating of regeneration, and where likewise the truths of faith are signified by " sons " :

> Before she travailed she bringeth forth ; and before her pain came, she was delivered of a man child ; who hath heard such a thing ? who hath seen such things ? shall the earth bring forth in one day ? and shall I not cause to bring forth ? saith Jehovah ; shall I cause to bring forth, and close up ? saith thy God (lxvi. 7–9).

Goods and truths, being conceived and born of the heavenly marriage, are therefore called " sons " by the Lord in *Matthew* :

> He that soweth the good seed is the Son of man ; the field is the world ; and the seed are the sons of the kingdom (xiii. 37, 38).

And the goods and truths of a saving faith He calls " sons of Abraham " (*John* viii. 39) ; for " seed " (as stated n. 255) denotes faith, wherefore " sons," which are of the " seed," are the goods and truths of faith. Hence also the Lord, as being Himself the " seed," called Himself the " Son of man," that is, the faith of the church.

166

265. That by "man (*vir*)" is signified the Rational, appears from verse 6 of this chapter, in that the woman gave to her man with her, and he did eat, by which is meant his consent ; and the same is also evident from what was said of the man in n. 158, where by him is meant one who is wise and intelligent. Here, however, "man" denotes the Rational, because in consequence of the destruction of wisdom and intelligence by eating of the tree of knowledge, nothing else was left ; for the Rational is imitative of intelligence, being as it were its semblance.

266. As every law and precept comes forth from what is celestial and spiritual, as from its true beginning, it follows that this law of marriage does so, which requires that the wife, who acts from desire, which is of the proprium, rather than from reason, like the man, should be subject to his prudence.

267. Verse 17. **And unto the man He said, Because thou hast hearkened unto the voice of thy wife, and hast eaten of the tree of which I commanded thee, saying, Thou shalt not eat of it ; cursed is the ground for thy sake, in great sorrow shalt thou eat of it all the days of thy life.** By the " man hearkening to the voice of his wife," is signified the consent of the man (*vir*), or Rational, by which it also averted or cursed itself, and, consequently, the whole external man, denoted by " cursed is the ground for thy sake." To " eat thereof in sorrow," means that the future state of his life would be miserable, and this even to the end of that church, or " all the days of his life."

268. That the " ground " signifies the external man, is evident from what was previously stated

concerning "earth," "ground," and "field."
When man is regenerate, he is no longer called
"earth," but "ground," because celestial seed
has been implanted in him; he is also compared to
"ground" and is called "ground" in various
parts of the Word. The seeds of good and truth
are implanted in the external man, that is, in his
affection and memory, and not in the internal
man, because there is nothing of one's proprium in
the internal man, but only in the external. In the
internal man are goods and truths, and when these
no longer appear to be present, the man is external
or corporeal; they are however stored up in the
internal man by the Lord, without the man's
knowledge, as they do not come forth except when
the external man, as it were, dies, as is usually the
case during temptations, misfortunes, sicknesses,
and at the hour of death. The Rational belongs
also to the external man (n. 118), and is in itself a
kind of medium between the internal man and the
external; for the internal man, through the
Rational, operates on the Corporeal external. But
when the Rational consents, it separates the external
man from the internal, so that the existence of the
internal man is no longer known, nor, consequently,
the intelligence and wisdom which are of the internal.

269. That Jehovah God (that is, the Lord) did
not "curse the ground," or the external man, but
that the external man averted or separated itself
from the internal, and thus cursed itself, is evident
from what was previously shown (n. 245).

270. That to "eat of the ground in great sorrow"
signifies a miserable state of life, is evident from
what precedes and follows, not to mention that to
"eat," in the internal sense, is to live. The same is

evident also from the fact that such a state of life ensues when evil spirits begin to fight, and the attendant angels to labour. This state of life becomes more miserable when evil spirits begin to obtain the dominion ; for they then govern the external man, and the angels only the internal man, of which so little remains that they can scarcely take anything thence with which to defend the man ; hence arise misery and anxiety. Dead men are seldom sensible of such misery and anxiety, because they are no longer men, although they think themselves more truly so than others ; for they know no more than the brutes what is spiritual and celestial, and what is eternal life, and like them they look downwards to earthly things, or outwards to worldly ones ; they favour only their proprium, and indulge their inclinations and senses with the entire concurrence of the Rational. Being dead, they sustain no spiritual combat or temptation, and were they exposed to it their life would sink under its weight, and they would thereby curse themselves still more, and precipitate themselves still more deeply into infernal damnation : hence they are spared this until their entrance into the other life, where, being no longer in danger of dying in consequence of any temptation or misery, they endure most grievous sufferings, which likewise are here signified by the ground being cursed, and eating of it in great sorrow.

271. That " all the days of thy life " signifies the end of the days of the church, is evident from the fact that the subject here treated of is not an individual man, but the church and its state. The end of the days of that church was the time of the flood.

272. Verse 18. **And the thorn and the thistle shall it bring forth unto thee, and thou shalt eat the herb of the field.** By the " thorn and the thistle," are meant curse and vastation; and by "thou shalt eat the herb of the field," is signified that he should live as a wild animal. Man lives like a wild animal when his internal man is so separated from his external as to operate upon it only in a most general manner, for man is man from what he receives through his internal man from the Lord, and is a wild animal from what he derives from the external man, which, separated from the internal, is in itself no other than a wild animal, having a similar nature, desires, appetites, phantasies, and sensations, and also similar organic forms. That, nevertheless, he is able to reason, and, as it seems to himself, acutely; and this from the spiritual substance by which he receives the influx of life from the Lord, which is, however, perverted in such a man, becoming the life of evil, which is death. Hence he is called a dead man.

273. That the " thorn and the thistle " signify curse and vastation, is evident from harvest and fruit-tree denoting the opposites, which are blessings and multiplications. That the " thorn," the " thistle," the " brier," the " bramble," and the " nettle," have such a signification, is evident from the Word, as in *Hosea* :

Lo, they are gone away because of the vastation; Egypt shall gather them; Memphis shall bury them; their desirable things of silver, the nettle shall inherit them; the bramble shall be in their tents (ix. 6).

Here " Egypt " and " Memphis " denote such as
170

seek to understand Divine things from themselves
and their own scientifics. In the same Prophet :

The lofty places of Aven, the sin of Israel, shall
be destroyed ; the thorn and the thistle shall
come up upon their altars (x. 8).

Here the " lofty places of Aven," signify the love
of self ; and the " thorn and thistle on the altars,"
profanation. In *Isaiah* :

Mourning upon the paps for the fields of
desire, for the fruitful vine ; upon the ground of
My people shall come up the briery thorn
(xxxii. 12, 13).

And in *Ezekiel* :

There shall be no more a pricking brier unto
the house of Israel, nor a painful thorn from all
that are round about them (xxviii. 24).

274. That to " eat the herb of the field," that is,
wild food, denotes to live like a wild animal, is
evident from what is said of Nebuchadnezzar in
Daniel :

They shall drive thee from man, and thy
dwelling shall be with the beast of the field ;
they shall make thee to eat grass as oxen, and
seven times shall pass over thee (iv. 25).

And in *Isaiah* :

Hast thou not heard how I have done it long
ago, and from the days of old have I formed it ;
now have I brought it to pass, and it shall be to
lay waste bulwarks, fenced cities, in heaps ; and
their inhabitants, short of hand, were dismayed
and put to shame ; they were made the grass of
the field, and the green of the herb, the grass of
the house-tops, and a field parched before the
standing corn (xxxvii. 26, 27).

Here it is explained what is signified by the " grass of the field," the " green of the herb," the " grass on the house-tops," and a " field parched " ; for the subject here treated of is the time before the flood, which is meant by " long ago," and the " days of old."

275. Verse 19. **In the sweat of thy face shalt thou eat bread, till thou return unto the ground ; for out of it wast thou taken ; for dust thou art, and unto dust shalt thou return.** By " eating bread in the sweat of the face " is signified to be averse to what is celestial ; to " return to the ground from whence he was taken," is to relapse into the external man, such as he was before regeneration ; and " dust thou art, and unto dust shalt thou return," signifies that he is condemned and infernal.

276. That to " eat bread in the sweat of the face " signifies to be averse to what is celestial, is evident from the signification of " bread." By " bread " is meant everything spiritual and celestial, which is the food of the angels, on the deprivation of which they would cease to live as certainly as men deprived of bread or food. That which is celestial and spiritual in heaven also corresponds to bread on earth, by which, moreover, they are represented, as is shown by many passages in the Word. That the Lord is " bread," because from Him proceeds whatever is celestial and spiritual, He Himself teaches in *John* :

This is the bread that cometh down from heaven ; he that eateth of this bread shall live to eternity (vi. 58).

Wherefore also bread and wine are the symbols

employed in the Holy Supper. This celestial is also represented by the manna. That what is celestial and spiritual constitutes the food of angels, is manifest from the Lord's words :

Man shall not live by bread alone, but by every word that proceedeth out of the mouth of God (*Matt.* iv. 4).

That is, from the life of the Lord, from which comes everything celestial and spiritual. The last posterity of the Most Ancient Church, which existed immediately before the flood, and is here treated of, had become so thoroughly lost and immersed in sensuous and bodily things, that they were no longer willing to hear what was the truth of faith, what the Lord was, or that He would come and save them ; and when such subjects were mentioned they turned away. This aversion is described by " eating bread in the sweat of the face." So also the Jews, in consequence of their being of such a character that they did not acknowledge the existence of heavenly things, and desired only a worldly Messiah, could not help feeling an aversion for the manna, because it was a representation of the Lord, calling it vile " bread," on which account fiery serpents were sent among them (*Num.* xxi. 5, 6). Moreover, the heavenly things imparted to them in states of adversity and misery, when they were in tears, were called by them the " bread of adversity," the " bread of misery," and the " bread of tears." In the passage before us, that which was received with aversion is called the " bread of the sweat of the face."

277. This is the internal sense. He who keeps close to the letter, understands only that man must procure bread for himself out of the ground by

labour, or by the sweat of his face. " Man," however, does not here mean any one man, but the
Most Ancient Church ; nor does " ground " mean
ground, nor " bread " bread, nor " garden "
garden, but celestial and spiritual things, as has
been sufficiently shown.

278. That by " returning to the ground whence
he was taken " is signified that the church would
return to the external man such as it was before
regeneration, is evident from the fact that
" ground " signifies the external man, as previously
stated. And that " dust " signifies what is condemned and infernal, is also evident from what
was said of the serpent, which in consequence of
being cursed is said to " eat dust." In addition
to what was there shown as to the signification of
" dust," we may add the following passage from
David :

All those who go down to the dust shall bow
before Jehovah, and those whose soul He hath
not made alive (*Ps.* xxii. 29).

And in another place :

Thou hidest Thy faces, they are troubled ;
Thou takest away their breath, they expire,
and return to their dust (*Ps.* civ. 29).

This means that when men turn away from the face
of the Lord, they expire or die, and thus " return
to the dust," that is, are condemned and become
infernal.

279. All these verses then, taken in a series,
involve that the Sensual averted itself from the
Celestial (verse 14) ; that the Lord would come
into the world for the purpose of reuniting them
(verse 15) ; that combat arose in consequence of

174

the external man averting itself (verse 16) ; whence resulted misery (verse 17) ; condemnation (verse 18) ; and at length hell (verse 19). These things followed in succession in that church, from the fourth posterity down to the flood.

---

20. And the man (*homo*) called his wife's name Eve, because she was the mother of all living.

21. And Jehovah God made for the man and for his wife coats of skin, and clothed them.

22. And Jehovah God said, Behold, the man is become as one of us, knowing good and evil ; and now lest he put forth his hand, and take also of the tree of lives, and eat, and live to eternity.

23. Therefore Jehovah God sent him forth from the garden of Eden, to till the ground from which he was taken.

24. And He cast out the man ; and He made to dwell from the east toward the garden of Eden cherubim, and the flame of a sword turning itself, to keep the way of the tree of lives.

THE CONTENTS.

280. The Most Ancient Church, and those who fell away, are here summarily treated of ; thus also its posterity down to the flood, when it expired.

281. Of the Most Ancient Church which was celestial, and from the life of faith in the Lord, called " Eve," and the " mother of all living " (verse 20).

282. Of its first posterity, in which there was celestial spiritual good ; and of its second and third, in which there was natural good, signified

175

by the " coat of skin which Jehovah God made for the man and his wife " (verse 21).

283. Of the fourth posterity, in which natural good began to be dissipated, and which, had they been created anew or instructed in the celestial things of faith, would have perished, which is meant by, " Lest he put forth his hand, and take also of the tree of lives, and eat, and live to eternity " (verse 22).

284. Of the fifth posterity, which was deprived of all good and truth, and was reduced to the state in which they had been previous to regeneration, which is meant by his being " sent forth out of the garden of Eden to till the ground from which he was taken " (verse 23).

285. Of the sixth and seventh posterities, in that they were deprived of all knowledge of what is good and true, and were left to their own filthy loves and persuasions ; this being provided lest they should profane the holy things of faith,— which is signified by his being " driven out, and cherubim being made to dwell at the garden, with the flame of a sword, to keep the way of the tree of lives " (verse 24).

THE INTERNAL SENSE.

286. This and the preceding chapters, down to the verses now under consideration, treat of the most ancient people and of their regeneration : first, of those who lived like wild creatures, but at length became spiritual men ; then of those who became celestial men, and constituted the Most Ancient Church ; afterwards of those who fell

away, and their descendants, in regular order through the first, second, and third posterities and their successors, down to the flood. In the verses following, which conclude the chapter, we have a recapitulation of what occurred from the period when the man of the Most Ancient Church was formed, until the flood ; thus it is a conclusion to all that goes before.

287. Verse 20. **And the man called his wife's name Eve, because she was the mother of all living.** By the " man " (*homo*) is here meant the man of the Most Ancient Church, or the celestial man, and by the " wife " and the " mother of all living " is meant the church. She is called " mother," as being the first church ; and " living," in consequence of possessing faith in the Lord, who is life itself.

288. That by " man " is meant the man of the Most Ancient Church, or the celestial man, was previously shown ; and at the same time it was also shown that the Lord alone is Man, and that from Him every celestial man is man, because in His likeness. Hence every member of the church, without exception or distinction, was called a " man," and at length this name was applied to any one who in body appeared as a man, to distinguish him from beasts.

289. It has also been shown above that by " wife " is meant the church, and in the universal sense the kingdom of the Lord in the heavens and on earth ; and from this it follows that the same is meant by " mother." In the Word the church is very frequently called " mother," as in *Isaiah* :

Where is the bill of your mother's divorcement ? (l. 1).

177

In *Jeremiah* :

> Your mother is greatly ashamed : she that bare you was suffused with shame (l. 12).

In *Ezekiel* :

> Thou art thy mother's daughter that loathed her man and her sons ; your mother was a Hittite, and your father an Amorite (xvi. 45).

Here " man " (*vir*) denotes the Lord and all that is celestial ; " sons," the truths of faith ; a " Hittite," what is false ; and an " Amorite," what is evil. In the same :

> Thy mother is like a vine in thy likeness, planted near the waters ; she was fruitful and full of leaves because of many waters (xix. 10).

Here " mother " denotes the Ancient Church. The term " mother " is more especially applicable to the Most Ancient Church, because it was the first church, and the only one that was celestial, and therefore beloved by the Lord more than any other.

290. That she was called the " mother of all living " in consequence of possessing faith in the Lord, who is Life itself, is also evident from what has been already shown. There cannot be more than one Life, from which is the life of all, and there can be no life, which is life, except through faith in the Lord, who is the Life ; nor can there be faith in which is life, except from Him, consequently, unless He is in it. On this account, in the Word, the Lord alone is called " Living," and is named the " Living Jehovah " (*Jer.* v. 2 ; xii. 16 ; xvi. 14, 15 ; xxiii. 7 ; *Ezek.* v. 11) ; " He that liveth to eternity " (*Dan.* iv. 34 ; *Rev.* iv. 10 ; v. 14 ; x. 6) ; the " Fountain of life " (*Ps.* xxxvi. 9) ; the " Fountain of living waters " (*Jer.* xvii.

13). Heaven, which lives by or from Him, is called the " Land of the living " (*Isa.* xxxviii. 11 ; liii. 8 ; *Ezek.* xxvi. 20 ; xxxii. 23–27, 32 ; *Ps.* xxvii. 13 ; lii. 5 ; cxlii. 5). And those are called " Living," who are in faith in the Lord ; as in *David* :

Who putteth our soul among the living (*Ps.* lxvi. 9).

And those who possess faith are said to be " in the Book of lives " (*Ps.* lxix. 28), and " in the Book of Life " (*Rev.* xiii. 8 ; xvii. 8 ; xx. 15). Wherefore also those who receive faith in Him are said to be " made alive " (*Hos.* vi. 2 ; *Ps.* lxxxv. 6). On the other hand it follows that those who are not in faith are called " dead " ; as in *Isaiah* :

The dead shall not live ; the Rephaim shall not rise again, because Thou hast visited and destroyed them (xxvi. 14).

This means those who are puffed up with the love of self ; to " rise again " signifies to enter into life. They are also said to be " pierced " (*Ezek.* xxxii. 23–26, 28–31). They are also called " dead " by the Lord (*Matt.* iv. 16 ; *John* v. 25 ; viii. 21, 24, 51, 52). Hell also is called " death " (*Isa.* xxv. 8 ; xxviii. 15).

291. In this verse is described the first time, when the church was in the flower of her youth, representing the heavenly marriage, on which account she is described by a marriage, and is called " Eve," from a word meaning " life."

292. Verse 21. **And Jehovah God made for the man** (*homo*) **and for his wife coats of skin, and clothed them.** These words signify that the Lord instructed them in spiritual and natural good ; His instructing them is expressed by " making "

179

and " clothing," and spiritual and natural good, by the " coat of skin."

293. It could never appear from the letter that these things are signified ; and yet there is evidently here enfolded some deeper meaning, for every one must be aware that Jehovah God did not make a coat of skin for them.

294. Neither would it be evident to any one that a " coat of skin " signifies spiritual and natural good, except by a revelation of the internal sense, and a subsequent comparison of passages in the Word where similar expressions occur. The general term " skin," is here used, but that of a kid, sheep, or ram, is understood, which animals in the Word signify affections of good, charity, and that which belongs to charity, as was likewise signified by the sheep used in the sacrifices. Those are called " sheep " who are endowed with the good of charity, that is, with spiritual and natural good, and hence the Lord is called the " Shepherd of the sheep," and those who are endowed with charity are called His " sheep," as everybody knows.

295. The reason why they are said to be " clothed with a coat of skin," is that the most ancient people were said to be " naked," on account of their innocence ; but when they lost their innocence they became conscious that they were in evil, which also is called " nakedness." That all things might appear to cohere historically (in accordance with the way of speaking of the most ancient people), they are here said to be " clothed lest they should be naked," or in evil. Their being in spiritual and natural good is evident from what was remarked above concerning them, from verses 1 to 13 of this

chapter, as well as from its being here related that
" Jehovah God made them a coat of skin, and
clothed them " ; for it here treats of the first—and
more especially of the second and third—posterities
of the church, who were endowed with such good.

296. That the skins of kids, sheep, goats, badgers,
and rams signify spiritual and natural goods, is
evident from the internal sense of the Word, where
Jacob is treated of; and also where the ark is
treated of. Of Jacob it is said that he was " clothed
with the raiment of Esau," and on his hands and
on his neck, where he was naked, " with skins of
kids of the goats," and when Isaac smelled them,
he said, " the smell of my son is as the smell of a
field " (*Gen.* xxvii. 15, 16, 27). That these skins
signify spiritual and natural goods, will, of the
Lord's Divine mercy, be seen in that place. Of
the ark it is said that the covering of the tent was
" of rams' skins and badgers' skins " (*Exod.* xxvi.
14 ; xxxvi. 19), and that when they set forward
Aaron and his sons covered the ark with a covering
" of badgers' skins," and likewise the table and its
vessels, the candlestick and its vessels, the altar of
gold, and the vessels of ministry and of the altar
(*Num.* iv. 6–14). Of the Lord's Divine mercy it
will also be seen in that place that these skins
signify spiritual and natural good, for whatever
was in the ark, the tabernacle, or the tent, yea,
whatever was upon Aaron when clothed with the
garments of holiness, signified what is celestial-
spiritual, so that there was not the least thing that
had not its own representation.

297. Celestial good is not clothed, because it is
inmost, and is innocent ; but celestial-spiritual
good is that which is first clothed, and then natural

181

good, for these are more external, and on that
account are compared to and are called
"garments"; as in *Ezekiel*, speaking of the
Ancient Church :

> I clothed thee with broidered work, and shod
> thee with badger, I girded thee about with fine
> linen, and I covered thee with silk (xvi. 10).

In *Isaiah* :

> Put on thy beautiful garments, O Jerusalem,
> the city of holiness (lii. 1).

In the *Revelation* :

> Who have not defiled their garments, and
> they shall walk with me in white, for they are
> worthy (iii. 4, 5).

It is likewise said of the four and twenty elders
that they were "clothed in white raiment" (iv. 4).
Thus the more external goods, which are celestial-
spiritual, and natural, are "garments"; wherefore also those who are endowed with the goods of
charity appear in heaven clothed in shining garments ; but here, because still in the body, with
a "coat of skin."

298. Verse 22. **And Jehovah God said, Behold
the man is become as one of us, knowing good and
evil ; and now lest he put forth his hand, and take
also of the tree of lives, and eat, and live to eternity.**
The reason "Jehovah God" is first mentioned in
the singular, and afterwards in the plural number,
is that by "Jehovah God" is meant the Lord, and
at the same time the angelic heaven. The man's
"knowing good and evil," signifies that he had
become celestial, and thus wise and intelligent ;
"lest he put forth his hand, and take also of the
tree of lives," means that he must not be instructed

in the mysteries of faith, for then never to all eternity could he be saved, which is to "live to eternity."

299. Here are two arcana : first, that " Jehovah God " signifies the Lord, and at the same time heaven ; secondly, that had they been instructed in the mysteries of faith they would have perished eternally.

300. As regards the first arcanum—that by " Jehovah God " is meant the Lord and at the same time heaven—it is to be observed that in the Word, always for a secret reason, the Lord is sometimes called merely " Jehovah," sometimes " Jehovah God," sometimes " Jehovah " and then " God," sometimes the " Lord Jehovih," sometimes the " God of Israel," and sometimes " God " only. Thus in the first chapter of *Genesis*, where it is also said in the plural, " Let *us* make man in our image," He is called " God " only, and He is not called " Jehovah God " until the following chapter, where the celestial man is treated of. He is called " Jehovah " because He alone *is* or lives, thus from Essence ; and " God," because He can do all things, thus from Power ; as is evident from the Word, where this distinction is made (*Isa.* xlix. 4, 5 ; lv. 7 ; *Ps.* xviii. 2, 28, 29, 31 ; xxxi. 14). On this account every angel or spirit who spoke with man, and who was supposed to possess any power, was called " God," as appears from *David* :

God hath stood in the congregation of God, He will judge in the midst of the gods (*Ps.* lxxxii. 1).

And in another place :

Who in the sky shall be compared unto

183

Jehovah ? who among the sons of the gods shall be likened to Jehovah ? (*Ps.* lxxxix. 6).

Again :

Confess ye to the God of gods, confess ye to the Lord of lords (*Ps.* cxxxvi. 2, 3).

Men also, as being possessed of power, are called " gods," as in *Ps.* lxxxii. 6 ; *John* x. 34, 35 ; Moses also is said to be " a god to Pharaoh " (*Exod.* vii. 1). For this reason the word " God " in the Hebrew is in the plural number—" Elohim." But as the angels do not possess the least power of themselves, as indeed they acknowledge, but solely from the Lord, and as there is but one God, therefore by " Jehovah God " in the Word is meant the Lord alone. But where anything is effected by the ministry of angels, as in the first chapter of *Genesis*, He is spoken of in the plural number. Here also because the celestial man, as man, could not be put in comparison with the Lord, but with the angels only, it is said, the man " is become as one of us, knowing good and evil," that is, is wise and intelligent.

301. The other arcanum is that had they been instructed in the mysteries of faith they would have perished eternally, which is signified by the words, " now lest he put forth his hand, and take also of the tree of lives, and eat, and live to eternity." The case is this. When men have become inverted orders of life, and are unwilling to live, or to become wise, except from themselves and from their proprium, they reason about everything they hear respecting faith, as to whether it is so, or not ; and as they do this from themselves and from their

own things of sense and scientifics, it must needs lead to denial, and, consequently, to blasphemy and profanation, so that at length they do not scruple to mix up profane things with holy. When a man becomes like this, he is so condemned in the other life that there remains for him no hope of salvation. For things mixed up by profanation remain so mixed up, that whenever any idea of something holy presents itself, an idea of something profane that is conjoined with it is also there, the consequence of which is that the person cannot be in any society except one of the damned. Whatever is present in any idea of thought in consequence of being conjoined with it, is most exquisitely perceived in the other life, even by spirits in the world of spirits, and much more so by angelic spirits, so exquisitely indeed that from a single idea they know a person's character. The separation of profane and holy ideas when thus conjoined cannot be effected except by means of such infernal torment that, if a man were aware of it, he would as carefully avoid profanation as he would avoid hell itself.

302. This is the reason why the mysteries of faith were never revealed to the Jews. They were not even plainly told that they were to live after death, nor that the Lord would come into the world to save them. So great were the ignorance and stupidity in which they were kept, and still are kept, that they did not and do not know of the existence of the internal man, or of anything internal, for if they had known of it, or if they now knew of it, so as to acknowledge it, such is their character that they would profane it, and there would be no hope of any salvation for them in the

other life. This is what is meant by the Lord in *John* :

> He hath blinded their eyes, and closed their heart, that they should not see with their eyes, nor understand with their heart, and convert themselves, and I should heal them (xii. 40).

And by the Lord speaking to them in parables without explaining to them their meaning, lest, as He Himself says,

> Seeing they should see, and hearing they should hear, and should understand (*Matt*. xiii. 13).

For the same reason all the mysteries of faith were hidden from them, and were concealed under the representatives of their church, and for the same reason the prophetic style is of the same character. It is, however, one thing to know, and another to acknowledge. He who knows and does not acknowledge, is as if he knew not ; but it is he who acknowledges and afterwards blasphemes and profanes, that is meant by these words of the Lord.

303. A man acquires a life by all the things he is persuaded of, that is, which he acknowledges and believes. That of which he is not persuaded, or does not acknowledge and believe, does not affect his mind. And therefore no one can profane holy things unless he has been so persuaded of them as to acknowledge them, and yet denies them. Those who do not acknowledge may know, but are as if they did not know, and are like those who know things that have no existence. Such were the Jews about the time of the Lord's advent, and therefore they are said in the Word to be " vastated " or " laid waste," that is, to have no longer any faith. Under these circumstances it does men no injury to have the interior contents of the Word

opened to them, for they are as persons seeing, and yet not seeing ; hearing, and yet not hearing ; and whose hearts are closed ; of whom the Lord says in *Isaiah* :

Go and tell this people, Hearing ye hear, but ye understand not, and seeing ye see, but know not. Make the heart of this people fat, and make their ears heavy, and smear their eyes, lest they see with their eyes, and hear with their ears, and understand with their heart, and be converted, so that they be healed (vi. 9, 10).

That the mysteries of faith are not revealed until men are in such a state, that is, are so vastated that they no longer believe, in order, as before said, that they may not be able to profane them, the Lord also plainly declares in the subsequent verses of the same Prophet :

Then said I, Lord, how long ? And He said, Even until the cities are desolated, so that there be no inhabitant ; and the houses, so that there be no man, and the ground be utterly desolated, and Jehovah have removed man (vi. 12).

He is called a " man " who is wise, or who acknowledges and believes. The Jews were thus vastated, as already said, at the time of the Lord's advent ; and for the same reason they are still kept in such vastation by their lusts, and especially by their avarice, that although they hear of the Lord a thousand times, and that the representatives of their church are significative of Him in every particular, yet they acknowledge and believe nothing. This then was the reason why the antediluvians were cast out of the garden of Eden, and vastated even until they were no longer capable of acknowledging any truth.

187

304. From all this it is evident what is meant by the words, " lest he put forth his hand, and take also of the tree of lives, and eat, and live to eternity." To " take of the tree of lives and eat," is to know even so as to acknowledge whatever is of love and faith ; for " lives " in the plural denote love and faith, and to " eat " signifies here as before, to know. To " live to eternity," is not to live in the body to eternity, but to live after death in eternal damnation. A man who is " dead " is not so called because he is to die after the life of the body, but because he will live a life of death, for " death " is damnation and hell. The expression to " live," is used with a similar signification by *Ezekiel* :

> Ye hunt souls for My people, and save souls alive for yourselves, and ye have profaned Me among My people, to slay souls that will not die, and to make souls live that will not live (xiii. 18, 19).

305. Verse 23. **Therefore Jehovah God sent him forth from the garden of Eden, to till the ground from which he was taken.** To be " cast out of the garden of Eden," is to be deprived of all intelligence and wisdom ; and to " till the ground from which he was taken," is to become corporeal, as he was previous to regeneration.

That to be " cast out of the garden of Eden " is to be deprived of all intelligence and wisdom, is evident from the signification of a " garden," and of " Eden," as above ; for a " garden " signifies intelligence, or the understanding of truth ; and " Eden," being significative of love, signifies wisdom, or the will of good.

That to " till the ground from which he was

188

taken " signifies to become corporeal, such as he was before regeneration, has been shown above (v. 19), where similar words occur.

306. Verse 24. **And He cast out the man ; and He made to dwell from the east toward the garden of Eden cherubim, and the flame of a sword turning itself, to keep the way of the tree of lives.** To " cast out the man," is to entirely deprive him of all the will of good and understanding of truth, insomuch that he is separated from them, and is no longer man. To " make to dwell cherubim from the east," is to provide against his entering into any secret thing of faith ; for the " east toward the garden of Eden " is the celestial, from which is intelligence ; and by " cherubim " is signified the providence of the Lord in preventing such a man from entering into the things of faith. By the " flame of a sword turning itself," is signified self-love with its insane desires and consequent persuasions, which are such that he indeed wishes to enter, but is carried away to corporeal and earthly things, and this for the purpose of " keeping the way of the tree of lives," that is, of preventing the profanation of holy things.

307. It here treats of the sixth and seventh posterities, which perished by the flood, and were altogether " cast out of the garden of Eden," that is, from all understanding of truth, and became, as it were, not men, being left to their insane lusts and persuasions.

308. As the signification of the " east " and of the " garden of Eden " were given above, it is needless to dwell longer on them ; but that " cherubim " denote the providence of the Lord

189

lest man should insanely enter into the mysteries
of faith from his proprium, and from what is of the
senses and from scientifics, and should thus profane
them, and destroy himself, is evident from all the
passages in the Word where mention is made of
" cherubim." As the Jews were of such a quality
that if they had possessed any clear knowledge
concerning the Lord's coming, concerning the
representatives or types of the church as being
significative of Him, concerning the life after
death, concerning the interior man and the internal
sense of the Word, they would have profaned it,
and would have perished eternally; therefore this
was represented by the " cherubim " on the
mercy-seat over the ark, upon the curtains of the
tabernacle, upon the vail, and also in the temple;
and it was signified that the Lord had them in
keeping (*Exod.* xxv. 18–21; xxvi. 1, 31; 1 *Kings*
vi. 23–29, 32). For the ark, in which was the
testimony, signified the same as the tree of lives
in this passage, namely, the Lord and the celestial
things which belong solely to Him. Hence also
the Lord is so often called the " God of Israel
sitting on the cherubim," and hence He spake with
Moses and Aaron " between the cherubim "
(*Exod.* xxv. 22; *Num.* vii. 89). This is plainly
described in *Ezekiel*, where it is said:

The glory of the God of Israel was uplifted
from upon the cherub whereon He was, to the
threshold of the house. And He called to the
man clothed with linen, and said unto him, Go
through the midst of the city, through the midst
of Jerusalem, and set a mark upon the foreheads
of the men who groan and sigh for all the
abominations done in the midst thereof. And
to the others He said, Go ye after him through

the city, and smite ; let not your eye spare, neither have ye pity ; slay to blotting out the old man, and the young man, and the virgin, the infant, and the women ; defile the house, and fill the courts with the slain (ix. 3–7).

And again :

He said to the man clothed in linen, Go in between the wheel to beneath the cherub, and fill thy palms with coals of fire from between the cherubim, and scatter them over the city ; the cherub put forth his hand from between the cherubim unto the fire which was between the cherubim, and took thereof, and put it into the palms of him that was clothed in linen, who took it and went out (x. 2, 7).

From these passages it is evident that the providence of the Lord in preventing men from entering into the mysteries of faith is signified by the " cherubim " ; and that therefore they were left to their insane lusts, here also signified by the " fire that was to be scattered over the city," and that " none should be spared."

309. That by the " flame of a sword turning itself," is signified self-love with its insane lusts and persuasions, which are such that they desire to enter [into the mysteries of faith], but are carried away to corporeal and earthly things, might be confirmed by so many passages from the Word as would fill pages ; but we will cite only these from *Ezekiel* :

Prophesy and say, Thus saith Jehovah, Say a sword, a sword, it is sharpened, and also burnished to make a sore slaughter ; it is sharpened that it may be as lightning. Let the sword be

doubled the third time, the sword of his slain ;
the sword of a great slaughter, which entereth
into their bed-chambers, that their heart may
melt, and their offences be multiplied, I have set
the terror of the sword in all their gates.   Alas !
it is made as lightning (xxi. 9, 10, 14, 15).

A " sword " here signifies the desolation of man
such that he sees nothing that is good and true, but
mere falsities and things contrary, denoted by
" multiplying offences."   It is also said in Nahum,
of those who desire to enter into the mysteries of
faith, " The horseman mounting, and the flame of
the sword, and the flash of the spear, and a multitude of the slain " (iii. 3).

310. Each particular expression in this verse
involves so many arcana of deepest import,
applicable to the genius of this people who perished
by the flood, a genius totally different from that of
those who lived subsequent to the flood, that it
is impossible to set them forth.   We will briefly
observe that their first parents, who constituted
the Most Ancient Church, were celestial men, and,
consequently, had celestial seeds implanted in
them ; whence their descendants had seed in them
from a celestial origin.   Seed from a celestial origin
is such that love rules the whole mind and makes it
one.   For the human mind consists of two parts,
the will and the understanding.   Love or good
belongs to the will, faith or truth to the understanding ; and from love or good those most
ancient people perceived what belongs to faith or
truth, so that their mind was one.   With the posterity of such a race, seed of the same celestial
origin necessarily remains, so that any falling away
from truth and good on their part is most perilous,

since their whole mind becomes so perverted as to render a restoration in the other life scarcely possible. It is otherwise with those who do not possess celestial but only spiritual seed, as did the people after the flood, and as also do the people of the present day. There is no love in these, consequently, no will of good, but still there is a capability of faith, or understanding of truth, by means of which they can be brought to some degree of charity, although by a different way, namely, by the insinuation of conscience from the Lord grounded in the cognitions of truth and the derivative good. Their state is therefore quite different from that of the antediluvians, concerning which state, of the Lord's Divine mercy, we will treat hereafter. These are arcana with which the present generation are utterly unacquainted, for at the present day none knows what the celestial man is nor even what the spiritual man is, and still less what is the quality of the human mind and life thence resulting, and the consequent state after death.

311. In the other life, the state of those who perished by the flood is such that they cannot be in the world of spirits, or with other spirits, but are in a hell separated from the hells of others, and as it were under a certain mountain. This appears as an intervening mountain in consequence of their direful phantasies and persuasions. Their phantasies and persuasions are such as to produce so profound a stupor in other spirits that they do not know whether they are alive or dead, for they deprive them of all understanding of truth, so that they perceive nothing. Such also was their persuasive power during their abode in the world;

and because it was foreseen that in the other life they would be incapable of associating with other spirits without inducing on them a kind of death, they all became extinct, and the Lord of His Divine mercy induced other states on those who lived after the flood.

312. In this verse, the state of these ante-diluvians is fully described, in that they were " cast out," or separated from celestial good, and in that " cherubim were placed from the east toward the garden of Eden." This expression, " from the east toward the garden of Eden," is applicable only to them, and could not be used in relation to those who lived afterwards, of whom it would have been said, " from the garden of Eden toward the east." In like manner, had the words " the flame of a sword turning itself " been applied to the people of the present day, they would have been " the sword of a flame turning itself." Nor would it have been said the " tree of lives," but the " tree of life " ; not to mention other things in the series that cannot possibly be explained, being understood only by the angels, to whom the Lord reveals them ; for every state contains infinite arcana, not even one of which is known to men.

313. From what is here said of the first man, it is evident that all the hereditary evil existing at the present day did not come from him, as is falsely supposed. For it is the Most Ancient Church that is here treated of under the name of " man " ; and when it is called " Adam," it signifies that man was from the ground, or that from being non-man he became man by regeneration from the Lord. This is the origin and signification of the name. But as to hereditary evil, the case is this. Every one

194

who commits actual sin thereby induces on himself a nature, and the evil from it is implanted in his children, and becomes hereditary. It thus descends from every parent, from the father, grandfather, great-grandfather, and their ancestors in succession, and is thus multiplied and augmented in each descending posterity, remaining with each person, and being increased in each by his actual sins, and never being dissipated so as to become harmless except in those who are being regenerated by the Lord. Every attentive observer may see evidence of this truth in the fact that the evil inclinations of parents remain visibly in their children, so that one family, and even an entire race, may be thereby distinguished from every other.

CONTINUATION CONCERNING MAN'S ENTRANCE INTO ETERNAL LIFE.

314. After the use of light has been given to the resuscitated person, or soul, so that he can look about him, the spiritual angels previously spoken of render him all the kindly services he can desire in that state, and give him information about the things of the other life, but only so far as he is able to receive it. If he has been in faith, and desires it, they show him the wonderful and magnificent things of heaven.

315. But if the resuscitated person or soul is not of such a character as to be willing to be instructed, he then desires to be rid of the company of the angels, which they exquisitely perceive, for in the other life there is a communication of all the ideas of thought. Still, they do not leave him even then, but he dissociates himself from them. The angels love every one, and desire nothing more than to render him kindly services, to instruct him, and to convey him to heaven. In this consists their highest delight.

316. When the soul thus dissociates himself, he is received by good spirits, who likewise render him all kind offices while he is in their company. If, however, his life in the world has been such that he cannot remain in the company of the good, he desires to be rid of these also, and this process is repeated again and again, until he associates himself with those who are in full agreement with his former life in the world, among whom he finds, as it were, his own life. And then, wonderful to say, he leads with them a life like that which he had lived when in the body. But after sinking back into such a life, he makes a new beginning of life ; and some after a longer time, some after a shorter, are from this borne on towards hell ; but such as have been in faith towards the Lord, are from that new beginning of life led step by step towards heaven.

317. Some however advance more slowly towards heaven, and others more quickly. I have seen some who were elevated to heaven immediately after death, of which I am permitted to mention only two instances.

318. A certain spirit came and discoursed with me, who, as was evident from certain signs, had only lately died. At first he knew not where he was, supposing himself still to be in the world ; but when he became conscious that he was in the other life, and that he no longer possessed anything,

196

such as house, wealth, and the like, being in another
kingdom, where he was deprived of all he had
possessed in the world, he was seized with anxiety,
and knew not where to betake himself, or whither
to go for a place of abode. He was then informed
that the Lord alone provides for him and for all,
and was left to himself, that his thoughts might
take their wonted direction, as in the world. He
now considered—for in the other life the thoughts
of all may be plainly perceived—what he must do,
being deprived of all means of subsistence ; and
while in this state of anxiety he was brought into
association with some celestial spirits who belonged
to the province of the heart, and who showed him
every attention that he could desire. This being
done, he was again left to himself, and began to
think, from charity, how he might repay kindness so
great, from which it was evident that while he had
lived in the body he had been in the charity of
faith, and he was therefore at once taken up into
heaven.

319. I saw another also who was immediately
translated into heaven by the angels, and was
accepted by the Lord and shown the glory of
heaven ; not to mention much other experience
respecting others who were conveyed to heaven
after some lapse of time.

CHAPTER THE FOURTH.

ON THE NATURE OF THE LIFE OF THE SOUL OR SPIRIT.

320. With regard to the general subject of the life of souls, that is, of novitiate spirits, after death, I may state that much experience has shown that when a man comes into the other life he is not aware that he is in that life, but supposes that he is still in this world, and even that he is still in the body. So much is this the case that when told he is a spirit, wonder and amazement possess him, both because he finds himself exactly like a man, in his senses, desires, and thoughts, and because during his life in this world he had not believed in the existence of the spirit, or, as is the case with some, that the spirit could be what he now finds it to be.

321. A second general fact is that a spirit enjoys much more excellent sensitive faculties, and far superior powers of thinking and speaking, than when living in the body, so that the two states scarcely admit of comparison, although spirits are not aware of this until gifted with reflection by the Lord.

322. Beware of the false notion that spirits do not possess far more exquisite sensations than during the life of the body. I know the contrary by experience repeated thousands of times. Should any be unwilling to believe this, in consequence of their preconceived ideas concerning the nature of

spirit, let them learn it by their own experience
when they come into the other life, where it will
compel them to believe. In the first place spirits
have sight, for they live in the light, and good
spirits, angelic spirits, and angels, in a light so great
that the noonday light of this world can hardly
be compared to it. The light in which they dwell,
and by which they see, will, of the Lord's Divine
mercy, be described hereafter. Spirits also have
hearing, hearing so exquisite that the hearing of
the body cannot be compared to it. For years they
have spoken to me almost continually, but their
speech also will, of the Lord's Divine mercy, be
described hereafter. They have also the sense of
smell, which also will, of the Lord's Divine mercy,
be treated of hereafter. They have a most exquisite
sense of touch, whence come the pains and torments
endured in hell ; for all sensations have relation to
the touch, of which they are merely diversities and
varieties. They have desires and affections to
which those they had in the body cannot be compared, concerning which, of the Lord's Divine
mercy, more will be said hereafter. Spirits think
with much more clearness and distinctness than
they had thought during their life in the body.
There are more things contained within a single
idea of their thought than in a thousand of the
ideas they had possessed in this world. They
speak together with so much acuteness, subtlety,
sagacity, and distinctness, that if a man could
perceive anything of it, it would excite his aston-
ishment. In short, they possess everything that
men possess, but in a more perfect manner, except
the flesh and bones and the attendant imperfec-
tions. They acknowledge and perceive that even
while they lived in the body it was the spirit that

sensated, and that, although the faculty of sensation manifested itself in the body, still it was not of
the body ; and therefore that when the body is cast
aside, the sensations are far more exquisite and
perfect. Life consists in the exercise of sensation,
for without it there is no life, and such as is the
faculty of sensation, such is the life, a fact that
any one may observe.

323. At the end of the chapter, several examples
will be given of those who, during their abode in
this world, had thought otherwise.

CHAPTER IV.

1. And the man knew Eve his wife, and she
conceived, and bare Cain, and said, I have gotten a
man (*vir*), Jehovah.

2. And she added to bear his brother Abel ; and
Abel was a shepherd of the flock, and Cain was a
tiller of the ground.

3. And at the end of days it came to pass that
Cain brought of the fruit of the ground an offering
to Jehovah.

4. And Abel, he also brought of the firstlings of
his flock, and of the fat thereof. And Jehovah
looked at Abel, and to his offering :

5. And unto Cain and unto his offering He looked
not, and Cain's anger was kindled exceedingly,
and his faces fell.

6. And Jehovah said unto Cain, Why art thou
wroth ? and why are thy faces fallen ?

7. If thou doest well, art thou not exalted ? and
if thou doest not well, sin lieth at the door ; and to
thee is his desire, and thou rulest over him.

8. And Cain talked to Abel his brother ; and it came to pass when they were in the field, that Cain rose up against Abel his brother, and slew him.

9. And Jehovah said to Cain, Where is Abel thy brother ? And he said, I know not, am I my brother's keeper ?

10. And He said, What hast thou done ? the voice of thy brother's bloods crieth to Me from the ground.

11. And now art thou cursed from the ground, which hath opened its mouth to receive thy brother's bloods from thy hand.

12. When thou tillest the ground, it shall not henceforth yield unto thee its strength ; a fugitive and a wanderer shalt thou be in the earth.

13. And Cain said unto Jehovah, Mine iniquity is greater than can be taken away.

14. Behold, Thou hast cast me out this day from the faces of the ground ; and from Thy faces shall I be hid, and I shall be a fugitive and a wanderer in the earth ; and it shall come to pass that every one that findeth me shall slay me.

15. And Jehovah said unto him, Therefore whosoever slayeth Cain, vengeance shall be taken on him sevenfold. And Jehovah set a mark upon Cain, lest any finding him should smite him.

16. And Cain went out from the faces of Jehovah, and dwelt in the land of Nod, toward the east of Eden.

17. And Cain knew his wife, and she conceived and bare Enoch ; and he was building a city, and called the name of the city after the name of his son, Enoch.

18. And unto Enoch was born Irad ; and Irad begat Mehujael ; and Mehujael begat Methusael ; and Methusael begat Lamech.

19. And Lamech took unto him two wives ; the name of the one was Adah, and the name of the other Zillah.

20. And Adah bare Jabal ; he was the father of the dweller in tents, and of cattle.

21. And his brother's name was Jubal ; he was the father of every one that playeth upon the harp and organ.

22. And Zillah, she also bare Tubal-Cain, an instructor of every artificer in brass and iron ; and the sister of Tubal-Cain was Naamah.

23. And Lamech said unto his wives, Adah and Zillah, Hear my voice, ye wives of Lamech, and with your ears perceive my speech, for I have slain a man to my wounding, and a little one to my hurt.

24. If Cain shall be avenged sevenfold, truly Lamech seventy and sevenfold.

25. And the man knew his wife again, and she bare a son, and called his name Seth ; for God hath appointed me another seed instead of Abel ; for Cain slew him.

26. And to Seth, to him also there was born a son ; and he called his name Enosh ; then began they to call upon the name of Jehovah.

THE CONTENTS.

324. Doctrines separated from the church, or heresies, are here treated of ; and a new church that was afterwards raised up, called " Enosh."

325. The Most Ancient Church had faith in the Lord through love ; but there arose some who separated faith from love. The doctrine of faith separated from love was called " Cain " ; and

charity, which is love towards the neighbour, was called "Abel" (verses 1, 2).

326. The worship of each is described, that of faith separated from love, by the "offering of Cain"; and that of charity, by the "offering of Abel" (verses 3, 4). That worship from charity was acceptable, but not worship from separated faith (verses 4, 5).

327. That the state of those who were of separated faith became evil, is described by Cain's "anger being kindled, and his countenance falling" (verses 5, 6).

328. And that the quality of the faith is known from the charity; and that charity wishes to be with faith, if faith is not made the chief thing, and is not exalted above charity (verse 7).

329. That charity was extinguished in those who separated faith, and set it before charity, is described by "Cain slaying his brother Abel" (verses 8, 9).

330. Charity extinguished is called the "voice of bloods" (verse 10); perverted doctrine, the "curse from the ground" (verse 11); the falsity and evil originating thence, the "fugitive and wanderer in the earth" (verse 12). And as they had averted themselves from the Lord, they were in danger of eternal death (verses 13, 14). But as it was through faith that charity would afterwards be implanted, faith was made inviolable, and this is signified by the "mark set upon Cain" (verse 15). And its removal from its former position is denoted by "Cain dwelling toward the east of Eden" (verse 16).

331. The amplification of this heresy is called " Enoch " (verse 17).

332. The heresies that sprang from this one are also called by their names, in the last of which, called " Lamech," there was nothing of faith remaining (verse 18).

333. A new church then arose, which is meant by " Adah and Zillah," and is described by their sons " Jabal," " Jubal," and " Tubal-Cain " ; the celestial things of the church by " Jabal," the spiritual by " Jubal," and the natural by " Tubal-Cain " (verses 19 to 22).

334. That this church arose when everything of faith and charity was extinguished, and had violence done to it, which was in the highest degree sacrilegious, is described (verses 23, 24).

335. A summary of the subject is given : that after faith, signified by " Cain," had extinguished charity, a new faith was given by the Lord, whereby charity was implanted. This faith is called " Seth " (verse 25).

336. The charity implanted by faith is called " Enosh," or another " man " (*homo*), which is the name of that church (verse 26).

THE INTERNAL SENSE.

337. As this chapter treats of the degeneration of the Most Ancient Church, or the falsification of its doctrine, and, consequently, of its heresies and sects, under the names of Cain and his descendants, it is to be observed that there is no possibility of understanding how doctrine was falsified, or what was the nature of the heresies and sects of that church, unless the nature of the true church be rightly understood. Enough has been said above concerning the Most Ancient Church, showing that it was a celestial man, and that it acknowledged no other faith than that of love to the Lord and love towards the neighbour. Through this love they had faith from the Lord, or a perception of all the things that belonged to faith, and for this reason they were unwilling to mention faith, lest it should be separated from love, as was shown above (n. 200, 203). Such is the celestial man, and 2 such he is described by representatives in *David*, where the Lord is spoken of as the king, and the celestial man as the king's son :

> Give the king Thy judgments, and Thy righteousness to the king's son. The mountains shall bring peace to the people, and the hills in righteousness. They shall fear Thee with the sun, and toward the faces of the moon, generation of generations. In his days shall the righteous flourish, and abundance of peace, until there be no moon (lxxii. 1, 3, 5, 7).

By the " sun " is signified love ; by the " moon," faith ; by " mountains " and " hills," the Most Ancient Church ; by " generation of generations," the churches after the flood ; " until there be no moon," is said because faith shall be love. (See also what is said in *Isaiah* xxx. 26.) Such was the 3 Most Ancient Church, and such was its doctrine. But the case is far different at this day, for now faith takes precedence of charity, but still through faith charity is given by the Lord, and then charity becomes the chief thing. It follows from this that in the most ancient time doctrine was falsified when they made confession of faith, and thus separated it from love. Those who falsified doctrine in this way, or separated faith from love, or made confession of faith alone, were then called "Cain"; and such a thing was then regarded as an enormity.

338. Verse 1. **And the man knew Eve his wife, and she conceived, and bare Cain, and said, I have gotten a man** (*vir*), **Jehovah.** By the "man and Eve his wife" is signified the Most Ancient Church, as has been made known; its first offspring, or firstborn, is faith, which is here called "Cain"; her saying, "I have gotten a man, Jehovah," signifies that with those called "Cain," faith was recognized and acknowledged as a thing by itself.

339. In the three foregoing chapters it has been sufficiently shown that by the "man and his wife" is signified the Most Ancient Church, so that it cannot be doubted, and this being admitted, it is evident that the conception and the birth effected by that church were of the nature we have indicated. It was customary with the most ancient people to give names, and by names to signify things, and thus frame a genealogy. For the things of the church are related to each other in this way, one being conceived and born of another, as in generation. Hence it is common in the Word to call things of the church "conceptions," "births," "offspring," "infants," "little ones," "sons," "daughters," "young men," and so on. The prophetical parts of the Word abound in such expressions.

206

340. That the words " I have gotten a man, Jehovah," signify that with such as are called " Cain " faith is recognized and acknowledged as a thing by itself, is evident from what was said at the beginning of this chapter. Previously, they had been, as it were, ignorant of what faith is, because they had a perception of all the things of faith. But when they began to make a distinct doctrine of faith, they took the things they had a perception of and reduced them into doctrine, calling it, " I have gotten a man, Jehovah," as if they had found out something new ; and thus what was before inscribed on the heart became a mere matter of knowledge. In ancient times they gave every new thing a name, and in this way set forth the things involved in the names. Thus the signification of the name Ishmael is explained by the saying, " Jehovah hath heard her affliction " (*Gen.* xvi. 11) ; that of Reuben, by the expression, " Jehovah hath looked upon my affliction " (*Gen.* xxix. 32) ; the name Simeon, by the saying, " Jehovah hath heard that I was less dear " (*Gen.* xxix. 33) ; and that of Judah by, " This time will I praise Jehovah " (verse 35) ; and an altar built by Moses was called, " Jehovah my banner " (*Exod.* xvii. 15). In like manner the doctrine of faith is here denominated " I have gotten a man, Jehovah," or " Cain."

341. Verse 2. **And she added to bear his brother Abel ; and Abel was a shepherd of the flock, and Cain was a tiller of the ground.** The second offspring of the church is charity, signified by " Abel " and " brother " ; a " shepherd of the flock," denotes one who exercises the good of charity ; and a " tiller of the ground " is one who is devoid of

charity, however much he may be in faith separated from love, which is no faith.

342. That the second offspring of the church is charity, is evident from the fact that the church conceives and brings forth nothing but faith and charity. The same is signified by the first children of Leah from Jacob ; " Reuben " denoting faith ; " Simeon," faith in act ; and " Levi," charity (*Gen.* xxix. 32, 33, 34), wherefore also the tribe of Levi received the priesthood, and represented the " shepherd of the flock." As charity is the second offspring of the church, it is called " brother," and is named " Abel."

343. That a " shepherd of the flock " is one who exercises the good of charity, must be obvious to every one, for this is a familiar figure in the Word of both Old and New Testaments. He who leads and teaches is called a " shepherd," and those who are led and taught are called the " flock." He who does not lead to the good of charity and teach it, is not a true shepherd ; and he who is not led to good, and does not learn what is good, is not of the flock. It is scarcely necessary to confirm this signification of " shepherd " and " flock " by quotations from the Word ; but the following passages may be cited. In *Isaiah* :

> The Lord shall give the rain of thy seed, wherewith thou sowest the ground, and bread of the increase of the ground ; in that day shall He feed thy cattle in a broad meadow (xxx. 23).

Here " bread of the increase of the ground," denotes charity. Again :

> The Lord Jehovih shall feed His flock like a shepherd ; He shall gather the lambs into His

208

arms, and carry them in His bosom, and shall gently lead those that are with young (xl. 11).

In *David* :

Give ear, O Shepherd of Israel, Thou that leadest Joseph like a flock ; Thou that sittest on the cherubim, shine forth (*Ps.* lxxx. 1).

In *Jeremiah* :

I have likened the daughter of Zion to a comely and delicate woman ; the shepherds and their flocks shall come unto her, they shall pitch tents near her round about, they shall feed every one in his own space (vi. 2, 3).

In *Ezekiel* :

Thus saith the Lord Jehovih, I will multiply them as a flock of man, as a hallowed flock, as the flock of Jerusalem in her appointed times ; so shall the waste cities be filled with the flock of man (xxxvi. 37, 38).

In *Isaiah* :

All the flocks of Arabia shall be gathered to-gether unto thee, the rams of Nebaioth shall minister unto thee (lx. 7).

Those who lead the flock to the good of charity are those who " gather the flock " ; but those who do not lead them to the good of charity " scatter the flock " ; for all gathering together and union are of charity, and all dispersion and disunion are from lack of charity.

344. What avails faith, that is, the knowledge, cognition, and the doctrine of faith, but that the man may become such as faith teaches ?   And the primary thing that it teaches is charity (*Mark*

209

xii. 28–35 ; *Matt.* xxii. 34–39). This is the end of all it has in view, and if this be not attained, what is all knowledge or doctrine but a mere empty nothing ?

345. That a " tiller of the ground " is one who is devoid of charity, however much he may be in faith separated from love, which is no faith, is evident from what follows : that Jehovah had no respect to his offering, and that he slew his brother, that is, destroyed charity, signified by " Abel." Those were said to " till the ground " who look to bodily and earthly things, as is evident from what is said in *Gen.* iii. 19, 23, where we read that the man was " cast out of the garden of Eden to till the ground."

346. Verse 3. **And at the end of days it came to pass that Cain brought of the fruit of the ground an offering to Jehovah.** By the " end of days " is meant in process of time ; by the " fruit of the ground," the works of faith without charity ; and by " an offering to Jehovah," worship thence derived.

347. That by the " end of days " is signified in process of time, is evident to all. At first, and while there was simplicity in it, the doctrine here called " Cain " does not appear to have been so unacceptable as it became afterwards, as is evident from the fact that they called their offspring a " Man, Jehovah." Thus at first faith was not so far separated from love as at the " end of days," or in process of time ; as is wont to be the case with every doctrine of true faith.

348. That by the " fruit of the ground " are meant the works of faith without charity, appears

also from what follows ; for the works of faith devoid of charity are works of no faith, being in themselves dead, for they are solely of the external man. Of such it is written in *Jeremiah* :

Wherefore doth the way of the wicked prosper ? Thou hast planted them, they also have taken root ; they have gone on, they also bear fruit ; Thou art near in their mouth, and far from their reins ; how long shall the land mourn, and the herb of every field wither ? (xii. 1, 2, 4).

" Near in the mouth, but far from the reins," denotes those who are of faith separated from charity, concerning whom it is said that " the land mourns." In the same Prophet such works are called the " fruit of works " :

The heart is deceitful above all things, and it is desperately wicked, who can know it ? I Jehovah search the heart, I try the reins, even to give to every man according to his ways, and according to the fruit of his works (*Jer.* xvii. 9, 10).

In *Micah* :

The land shall be desolate because of them that dwell therein, for the fruit of their works (vii. 13). That such " fruit " is no fruit, or that the " work " is dead, and that both fruit and root perish, is thus declared in *Amos* :

I destroyed the Amorite before them, whose height was like the height of the cedars, and he was strong as the oaks ; yet I destroyed his fruit from above, and his roots from beneath (ii. 9).

And in *David* :

Their fruit shalt Thou destroy from the earth, and their seed from the sons of man (*Ps.* xxi. 10).

But the works of charity are living, and of them it is declared that they " take root downward, and bear fruit upward " ; as in *Isaiah* :

> The remnant that is escaped of the house of Judah shall again take root downward, and bear fruit upward (xxxvii. 31).

To " bear fruit upward," is to act from charity. Such fruit is called the " fruit of excellence," in the same Prophet :

> In that day shall the shoot of Jehovah be beautiful and glorious, and the fruit of the earth excellent and comely for them that are escaped of Israel (*Isa.* iv. 2).

It is also the " fruit of salvation," and is so called by the same Prophet :

> Drop down, ye heavens, from above, and let the skies pour down righteousness ; let the earth open, and let them bring forth the fruit of salvation, and let righteousness spring up together ; I Jehovah will create it (*Isa.* xlv. 8).

349. That by an " offering " is meant worship, is evident from the representatives of the Jewish Church, in which, sacrifices of every kind, as well as the first fruits of the earth and of all its produce, and the oblation of the firstborn, were called " offerings," in which their worship consisted. And as they all represented heavenly things, and all had reference to the Lord, it must be obvious to every one that true worship was signified by these offerings. For what is a representative without the thing it represents ? or what is an external religion without an internal but a kind of idol and a thing of death ? The external has life from things internal, that is, through these from the Lord.

From these considerations it is evident that all
the offerings of a representative church signify the
worship of the Lord ; and concerning these of the
Lord's Divine mercy we shall treat in particular
in the following pages. That by " offerings " in
general is meant worship, is evident in the Prophets
throughout, as in *Malachi* :

> Who shall abide the day of His coming ? He
> shall sit as a refiner and purifier of silver, and He
> shall purify the sons of Levi, and purge them as
> gold and silver, and they shall offer unto Jehovah
> an offering in righteousness. Then shall the
> offering of Judah and of Jerusalem be pleasant
> unto Jehovah, as in the days of eternity, and as
> in ancient years (iii. 2, 3, 4).

An " offering in righteousness " is an internal
offering, which the " sons of Levi," that is, holy
worshippers, will offer. The " days of eternity,"
signify the Most Ancient Church, and the " ancient
years," the Ancient Church. In *Ezekiel* :

> In the mountain of My holiness, in the moun-
> tain of the height of Israel, there shall all the
> house of Israel, all that land, worship Me ; there
> will I accept them, and there will I require your
> oblations, and the first-fruits of your offerings,
> in all your sanctifyings (xx. 40).

" Oblations," and the " first-fruits of the offerings
in the sanctifyings," are likewise works sanctified
by charity from the Lord. In *Zephaniah* :

> From beyond the rivers of Ethiopia My
> suppliants shall bring Mine offering (iii. 10).

" Ethiopia " denotes those who are in possession
of celestial things, which are love, charity, and the
works of charity.

350. Verse 4. **And Abel, he also brought of the firstlings of his flock, and of the fat thereof ; and Jehovah looked to Abel, and to his offering.** By " Abel " here as before is signified charity ; and by the " firstlings of the flock " is signified that which is holy, which is of the Lord alone ; by " fat " is signified the celestial itself, which also is of the Lord ; and by " Jehovah looking unto Abel, and to his offering," that the things of charity, and all worship grounded in charity, were well-pleasing to the Lord.

351. That " Abel " signifies charity has been shown before. By charity is meant love towards the neighbour, and mercy ; for he who loves his neighbour as himself is also compassionate towards him in his sufferings, as towards himself.

352. That the " firstlings of the flock " signify that which is of the Lord alone, is evident from the firstlings or firstborn in the representative church, which were all holy, because they had relation to the Lord, who alone is the " firstborn." Love and the faith thence derived are the " firstborn." All love is of the Lord, and not one whit of it is of man, therefore the Lord alone is the " firstborn." This was represented in the ancient churches by the firstborn of man and of beast being sacred to Jehovah (*Exod.* xiii. 2, 12, 15) ; and by the tribe of Levi, which in the internal sense signifies love—though Levi was born after Reuben and Simeon, who in the internal sense signify faith—being accepted instead of all the firstborn, and constituting the priesthood (*Num.* iii. 40-45 ; viii. 14-20). Of the Lord as the firstborn of all, with respect to His human essence, it is thus written in *David* :

He shall call Me, My Father, My God, and the rock of My salvation. I will also make Him My firstborn, high above the kings of the earth (*Ps.* lxxxix. 26, 27).

And in *John* :

Jesus Christ the firstborn of the dead, and the prince of the kings of the earth (*Rev.* i. 5). Observe that the firstborn of worship signify the Lord, and the firstborn of the church, faith.

353. By " fat " is signified the celestial itself, which is also of the Lord. The celestial is all that which is of love. Faith also is celestial when it is from love. Charity is the celestial. All the good of charity is the celestial. All these were represented by the various kinds of fat in the sacrifices, and distinctively by that which covered the liver, or the caul ; by the fat upon the kidneys ; by the fat covering the intestines, and upon the intestines ; these were holy, and were offered up as burnt-offerings upon the altar (*Exod.* xxix. 13, 22 ; *Lev.* iii. 3, 4, 14 ; iv. 8, 9, 19, 26, 31, 35 ; viii. 16, 25). They were therefore called the " bread of the offering by fire for a rest unto Jehovah " (*Lev.* iii. 14, 16). For the same reason the Jewish people were forbidden to eat any of the fat of the beasts, by what is called " a perpetual statute throughout your generations " (*Lev.* iii. 17 ; vii. 23, 25). This was because that church was such that it did not even acknowledge internal much less celestial things. That " fat " signifies celestial things, and 2 the goods of charity, is evident in the Prophets ; as in *Isaiah* :

Wherefore do ye weigh silver for that which is not bread ? and your labour for that which

215

satisfieth not ?   Attend ye diligently unto Me,
and eat ye that which is good, and let your soul
delight itself in fatness (lv. 2).

And in *Jeremiah* :

I will fill the soul of the priests with fatness,
and My people shall be satisfied with My goodness (xxxi. 14).

Here it is very evident that fatness is not meant,
but celestial-spiritual good. So in *David* :

They are filled with the fatness of Thy house,
and Thou makest them drink of the river of Thy
delights. For with Thee is the fountain of lives ;
in Thy light we see light (*Ps*. xxxvi. 8, 9).

Here " fatness " and the " fountain of lives "
signify the celestial, which is of love ; and the
" river of delights," and " light," the spiritual,
which is of faith from love. Again in *David* :

My soul shall be satiated with marrow and
fatness, and my mouth shall praise Thee with
lips of songs (*Ps*. lxiii. 5).

Here in like manner " fat " denotes the celestial,
and " lips of songs " the spiritual. That it is what is
celestial is very evident, because it will satisfy the
soul. For the same reason the first fruits, which
were the firstborn of the earth, are called " fat "
3 (*Num*. xviii. 12). As celestial things are of innumerable genera, and still more innumerable
species, they are described in general in the song
which Moses recited before the people :

Butter of kine, and milk of the flock, with fat
of lambs and of rams, the sons of Bashan, and
of goats, with the fat of the kidneys of wheat ;

216

and thou shalt drink the blood of the grape, unmixed (*Deut.* xxxii. 14).

It is impossible for any one to know the signification of these expressions except from the internal sense. Without the internal sense, such expressions as the " butter of kine," the " milk of sheep," the " fat of lambs," the " fat of rams and goats," the " sons of Bashan," the " fat of the kidneys of wheat," and the " blood of the grape," would be words and nothing more, and yet they all and each signify genera and species of celestial things.

354. That " Jehovah looked to Abel, and to his offering," signifies that the things of charity, and all worship derived from them, are pleasing to the Lord, has been explained before, as regards both " Abel," and his " offering."

355. Verse 5. **But to Cain and his offering He looked not ; and Cain's anger was kindled exceedingly, and his faces fell.** By " Cain," as has been stated, is signified faith separated from love, or such a doctrine as admits of the possibility of this separation ; by his " offering not being looked to," is signified as before that his worship was unacceptable. By " Cain's anger being kindled exceedingly, and his faces falling," is signified that the interiors were changed. By " anger " is denoted that charity had departed ; and by the " faces," the interiors, which are said to " fall " when they are changed.

356. That by " Cain " is signified faith separated from love, or a doctrine that admits of this separation ; and that " to his offering He looked not," signifies that his worship was not acceptable, has been shown before.

357. That " Cain's anger was kindled " signifies
that charity had departed, is evident from what is
afterwards related of his killing his brother Abel,
by whom is signified charity. Anger is a general
affection resulting from whatever is opposed to
self-love and its cupidities. This is plainly perceived
in the world of evil spirits, for there exists there a
general anger against the Lord, in consequence of
evil spirits being in no charity, but in hatred, and
whatever does not favour self-love and the love
of the world, excites opposition, which is manifested
by anger. In the Word, " anger," " wrath," and
even " fury," are frequently predicated of Jehovah,
but they are of man, and are attributed to Jehovah
because it so appears, for the reason mentioned
above. Thus it is written in *David* :

> He sent against them the anger of His nostril,
> and wrath, and fury, and trouble, and an inrush
> of evil angels ; He hath weighed a path for His
> anger, He withheld not their soul from death
> (*Ps.* lxxviii. 49, 50).

Not that Jehovah ever sends anger upon any one,
but that men bring it upon themselves ; nor does
He send evil angels among them, but man draws
them to himself. And therefore it is added, that
He " hath weighed a path for His anger, and withheld not their soul from death " ; and therefore
it is said in *Isaiah*, " To Jehovah shall he come,
and all that were incensed against Him shall be
ashamed " (xlv. 24), whence it is evident that
" anger " signifies evils, or what is the same, a
departure from charity.

358. That by the " faces falling " is signified
that the interiors were changed, is evident from the
signification of the " face " and of its " falling."

218

The face, with the ancients, signified internal things, because internal things shine forth through the face ; and in the most ancient times men were such that the face was in perfect accord with the internals, so that from a man's face every one could see of what disposition or mind he was. They considered it a monstrous thing to show one thing by the face and think another. Simulation and deceit were then considered detestable, and therefore the things within were signified by the face. When charity shone forth from the face, the face was said to be " lifted up " ; and when the contrary occurred, the face was said to " fall " ; wherefore it is also predicated of the Lord that He " lifts up His faces upon man," as in the benediction (*Num.* vi. 26 ; and in *Ps.* iv. 6), by which is signified that the Lord gives charity to man. What is meant by the " face falling," appears from *Jeremiah* :

I will not make My face to fall toward you, for I am merciful, saith Jehovah (iii. 12).

The " face of Jehovah " is mercy, and when He " lifts up His face " upon any one, it signifies that out of mercy He gives him charity ; and the reverse when He " makes the face to fall," that is, when man's face falls.

359. Verse 6. **And Jehovah said unto Cain, Why is thine anger kindled ? and why are thy faces fallen ?** " Jehovah said unto Cain," means that conscience dictated ; that his " anger was kindled, and that his countenance fell," signifies, as before, that charity had departed, and that the interiors were changed.

360. That " Jehovah said unto Cain " means that conscience dictated, needs no confirmation, as a similar passage was explained above.

361. Verse 7. **If thou doest well, is there not an uplifting ? and if thou doest not well, sin lieth at the door ; and to thee is his desire, and thou rulest over him.** " If thou doest well, an uplifting," signifies that if thou art well disposed thou hast charity ; " if thou doest not well, sin lieth at the door," signifies that if thou art not well disposed thou hast no charity, but evil. " To thee is his desire, and thou rulest over him," signifies that charity is desirous to be with thee, but cannot because thou desirest to rule over it.

362. The doctrine of faith called " Cain " is here described, which, in consequence of separating faith from love, separated it also from charity, the offspring of love. Wherever there is any church, there heresies arise, because while men are intent on some particular article of faith they make that the main thing ; for such is the nature of man's thought that while intent on some one thing he sets it before any other, especially when his imagination claims it as a discovery of his own, and when the loves of self and of the world puff him up. Everything then seems to agree with and confirm it, until at last he will swear that it is so, even if it is false. Just in this way those called " Cain " made faith more essential than love, and as, consequently, they lived without love, both the love of self and the phantasy thence derived conspired to confirm them in it.

363. The nature of the doctrine of faith that was called " Cain," is seen from the description of it in this verse, from which it appears that charity could be joined. to faith, but so that charity and not faith should have the dominion. On this account it is first said, " If thou doest well art thou not uplifted ? " signifying, If thou art well disposed, charity may be present ; for to " do well " signifies, in the internal sense, to be well disposed, since doing what is good comes from willing what is good. In ancient times action and will made one ; from the action they saw the will, dissimulation being then unknown. That an " uplifting " signifies that charity is present, is evident from what has been already said about the face, that to " lift up the face " is to have charity, and that for the " face to fall " is the contrary.

364. Secondly, it is said, " If thou doest not well, sin lieth at the door," which signifies, If thou art not well disposed, there is no charity present, but evil. Everybody can see that " sin lying at the door " is evil ready and desirous to enter ; for when there is no charity there are unmercifulness and hatred, consequently all evil. Sin in general is called the " devil," who, that is, his crew of infernals, is ever at hand when man is destitute of charity ; and the only means of driving away the devil and his crew from the door of the mind, is love to the Lord and love towards the neighbour.

365. In the third place it is said, " Unto thee is his desire, and thou rulest over him," by which is signified that charity is desirous to abide with faith, but cannot do so because faith wishes to rule over it, which is contrary to order. So long as faith seeks to have dominion, it is not faith, and only becomes faith when charity rules ; for charity is the chief thing of faith, as was shown above. Charity may be compared to flame, which is the essential of heat and light, for heat and light are from it ; and faith in a state of separation may be compared to light that is without the heat of flame, when

indeed there is light, but it is the light of winter
in which everything becomes torpid and dies.

366. Verse 8. **And Cain spake to Abel his
brother ; and it came to pass when they were in
the field, that Cain rose up against Abel his brother,
and slew him.** " Cain spake to Abel " signifies
an interval of time. " Cain," as before stated,
signifies faith separated from love ; and "·Abel "
charity, the brother of faith, on which account he
is here twice called his " brother." A " field "
signifies whatever is of doctrine. " Cain rose up
against Abel his brother, and slew him," signifies
that separated faith extinguished charity.

367. It is unnecessary to confirm these things by
similar passages from the Word, except so far as to
prove that charity is the " brother " of faith, and
that a " field " signifies whatever is of doctrine.
That charity is the " brother " of faith is evident
to every one from the nature or essence of faith.
This brotherhood was represented by Esau and
Jacob, and was the ground of their dispute about
the birthright and the consequent dominion.   It
was also represented by Pharez and Zarah, the
sons of Tamar by Judah (*Gen.* xxxviii. 28, 29, 30) ;
and by Ephraim and Manasseh (*Gen.* xlviii. 13, 14)
and in both of these, as well as in other similar
cases, there is a dispute about the primogeniture
and the consequent dominion.   For both faith and
charity are the offspring of the church.   Faith is
called a " man," as was Cain, in verse 1 of this
chapter, and charity is called a " brother," as in
Isa. xix. 2 ; *Jer.* xiii. 14 ; and other places.   The
union of faith and charity is called " the covenant
of brethren " (*Amos* i. 9).   Similar to the signification of Cain and Abel, was that of Jacob and

Esau, as just said ; in that Jacob also was desirous of supplanting his brother Esau, as is evident also in *Hosea* :

> To visit upon Jacob his ways, according to his doings will He recompense him ; he supplanted his brother in the womb (xii. 2, 3).

But that Esau, or the charity represented by Esau, should nevertheless at length have the dominion, appears from the prophetic prediction of their father Isaac :

> By thy sword shalt thou live, and shalt serve thy brother ; and it shall come to pass, when thou hast the dominion, that thou shalt break his yoke from off thy neck (*Gen.* xxvii. 40).

Or what is the same, the Church of the Gentiles, or new church, is represented by Esau, and the Jewish Church is represented by Jacob ; and this is the reason for its being so often said that the Jews should acknowledge the Gentiles as brethren ; and in the Church of the Gentiles, or primitive church, all were called brethren from charity. Such as hear the Word and do it are likewise called brethren by the Lord (*Luke* viii. 21) ; those who hear are such as have faith ; those who *do* are such as have charity ; but those who hear, or say that they have faith, and do not, or have not charity, are not brethren, for the Lord likens them unto fools (*Matt.* vii. 24, 26).

368. That a " field " signifies doctrine, and, consequently, whatever belongs to the doctrine of faith and charity, is evident from the Word, as in *Jeremiah* :

> O My mountain in the field, I will give thy possessions and all thy treasures for a spoil (xvii. 3).

In this passage "field" signifies doctrine; "possessions" and "treasures" denote the spiritual riches of faith, or the things that belong to the doctrine of faith. In the same :

Shall the snow of Lebanon fall from the rock of My field ? (xviii. 14).

It is declared concerning Zion, when destitute of the doctrine of faith, that she shall be "plowed like a field" (*Jer.* xxvi. 18 ; *Micah* iii. 12). In *Ezekiel* :

He took of the seed of the land, and set it in a field of sowing (xvii. 5).

This treats of the church and of its faith ; for doctrine is called a "field" from the seed in it. In the same :

And let all the trees of the field know that I Jehovah bring down the high tree (xvii. 24).

In *Joel* :

The field is laid waste, the ground mourneth, for the corn is wasted, the new wine is dried up, the oil languisheth, the husbandmen are ashamed, the harvest of the field is perished, all the trees of the field are withered (i. 10, 11, 12).

Here the "field" signifies doctrine, "trees" knowledges, and "husbandmen" worshippers. In *David* :

The field shall exult and all that is therein ; then shall all the trees of the forest sing (*Ps.* xcvi. 12).

Here it is perfectly evident that the field cannot exult, nor the trees of the forest sing ; but things that are in man, which are the cognitions of faith. In *Jeremiah* :

How long shall the land mourn, and the herb of every field wither ? (xii. 4).

224

Where it is also evident that neither the land nor the herbs of the field can mourn ; but that the expressions relate to something in man while in a state of vastation. A similar passage occurs in *Isaiah* :

> The mountains and the hills shall break forth before you into singing, and all the trees of the field shall clap their hands (lv. 12).

The Lord also in His prediction concerning the consummation of the age calls the doctrine of faith a " field " :

> Then shall two be in the field, the one shall be taken and the other left (*Matt.* xxiv. 40 ; *Luke* xvii. 36).

Here by a " field " is meant the doctrine of faith, both true and false. As a " field " signifies doctrine, whoever receives any seed of faith, whether a man, the church, or the world, is also called a " field."

369. From this then it follows that the words, " Cain rose up against his brother Abel, and slew him, when they were in the field together," denote that while both faith and charity were from the doctrine of faith, yet faith separate from love could not but disregard and thereby extinguish charity ; as is the case at the present day with those who maintain that faith alone saves, without any work of charity, for in this very supposition they extinguish charity, although they know and confess with their lips that faith is not saving unless there is love.

370. Verse 9. **And Jehovah said unto Cain, Where is Abel thy brother ? And he said, I know not, am I my brother's keeper ?** " Jehovah said

H   225 unto Cain," signifies a certain perceptive power from within that gave them a dictate concerning charity or the " brother Abel." Cain's reply, " I know not, am I my brother's keeper ? " signifies that faith considered charity as nothing, and was unwilling to be subservient to it, consequently, that faith altogether rejected everything of charity. Such did their doctrine become.

371. By the " speaking of Jehovah " the most ancient people signified perception, for they knew that the Lord gave them the power to perceive. This perception could continue no longer than while love was the chief thing. When love to the Lord ceased, and, consequently, love towards the neighbour, perception perished ; but in so far as love remained, perception remained. This perceptive power was proper to the Most Ancient Church, but when faith became separated from love, as in the people after the flood, and charity was given through faith, then conscience succeeded, which also gives a dictate, but in a different way, of which, by the Lord's Divine mercy, we will treat hereafter. When conscience dictates, it is in like manner said in the Word that " Jehovah speaks " ; because conscience is formed from things revealed, and from cognitions, and from the Word ; when the Word speaks, or dictates, it is the Lord who speaks ; hence nothing is more common, even at the present day, when referring to any matter of conscience, or of faith, than to say " the Lord says."

372. To be a " keeper " signifies to serve, like the " doorkeepers " and " porters " (that is, the keepers of the threshold), in the Jewish Church. Faith is called the " keeper " of charity, from the

fact that it ought to serve it, but it was according to the principles of the doctrine called " Cain," that faith should rule, as was said in verse 7.

373. Verse 10. **And He said, What hast thou done ? The voice of thy brother's bloods crieth to Me from the ground.** The " voice of thy brother's bloods," signifies that violence had been done to charity ; the " crying of bloods " is the accusation of guilt, and " ground " signifies a schism, or heresy.

374. That the " voice of bloods " signifies that violence had been done to charity, is evident from many passages in the Word, in which " voice " denotes anything that accuses, and " blood " any kind of sin, and especially hatred ; for whosoever hates his brother, kills him in his heart ; as the Lord teaches :

Ye have heard that it was said to them of old, Thou shalt not kill, and whosoever shall kill shall be in danger of the judgment ; but I say unto you, that whosoever is angry with his brother rashly shall be in danger of the judgment ; and whosoever shall say to his brother, Raca, shall be in danger of the council ; but whosoever shall say, Thou fool, shall be in danger of the hell of fire (*Matt.* v. 21, 22).

By these words are meant the degrees of hatred. Hatred is contrary to charity, and kills in whatever way it can, if not with the hand, yet in spirit, and is withheld only by external restraints from the deed of the hand. Therefore all hatred is " blood," as in *Jeremiah* :

Why makest thou thy way good to seek love ? Even in thy skirts are found the bloods of the souls of the needy innocent ones (ii. 33, 34).

2 And as hatred is denoted by " blood," so likewise is every kind of iniquity, for hatred is the fountain of all iniquities. As in *Hosea* :

> Swearing falsely, and lying, and killing, and stealing, and committing adultery, they rob, and bloods, in bloods have they touched ; therefore shall the land mourn, and every one that dwelleth therein shall languish (iv. 2, 3).

And in *Ezekiel*, speaking of unmercifulness :

> Wilt thou judge the city of bloods, and make known to her all her abominations ? a city that sheddeth bloods in the midst of it. Thou art become guilty through thy blood that thou hast shed (xxii. 2, 3, 4, 6, 9).

In the same :

> The land is full of the judgment of bloods, and the city is full of violence (vii. 23).

And in *Jeremiah* :

> For the sins of the prophets of Jerusalem, and the iniquities of her priests, that have shed the blood of the righteous in the midst of her, they wander blind in the streets, they have been polluted with blood (*Lam.* iv. 13, 14).

In *Isaiah* :

> When the Lord shall wash away the filth of the daughters of Zion, and shall have purged the bloods of Jerusalem from the midst, with the spirit of judgment, and with the spirit of burning (iv. 4).

And again :

> Your palms are defiled in blood, and your fingers in iniquity (lix. 3).

228

In *Ezekiel*, speaking of the abominations of Jerusalem, which are called " bloods " :

> I passed by thee, and saw thee trampled in thine own bloods, and I said unto thee, Live in thy bloods, yea, I said unto thee, Live in thy bloods (xvi. 6, 22).

The unmercifulness and hatred of the last times 3 are also described by " blood " in the *Revelation* (xvi. 3, 4). " Bloods " are mentioned in the plural, because all unjust and abominable things gush forth from hatred, as all good and holy ones do from love. Therefore, he who feels hatred towards his neighbour would murder him if he could, and indeed does murder him in any way he can ; and this is to do violence to him, which is here properly signified by the " voice of bloods."

375. A " voice crying," and the " voice of a cry," are common forms of expression in the Word, and are applied to every case where there is any noise, tumult, or disturbance, and also on the occasion of any happy event (as in *Exod*. xxxii. 17, 18 ; *Zeph*. i. 9, 10 ; *Isa*. lxv. 19 ; *Jer*. xlviii. 3). In the present passage it denotes accusation.

376. From this it follows that the " crying of bloods " signifies the accusation of guilt ; for those who use violence are held guilty. As in *David* :

> Evil shall slay the wicked, and they that hate the righteous shall be guilty (*Ps*. xxxiv. 21).

In *Ezekiel* :

> Thou city art become guilty by the blood which thou hast shed (xxii. 4).

377. That the " ground " here signifies a schism or heresy, is evident from the fact that a " field "

signifies doctrine, and therefore the "ground," having the field in it, is a schism. Man himself is the "ground," and also the "field," because these things are inseminated in him, for man is man from what is inseminated in him, a good and true man from goods and truths, an evil and false man from evils and falsities. He who is in any particular doctrine or heresy is named from it, and so in the passage before us the term "ground" is used to denote schism or heresy in man.

378. Verse 11. **And now cursed art thou from the ground, which hath opened its mouth to receive thy brother's bloods from thy hand.** "Cursed art thou from the ground," signifies that through the schism he had become averted; "which hath opened its mouth," signifies that the heresy taught them; to "receive thy brother's bloods from thy hand," signifies that it did violence to charity, and extinguished it.

379. That these things are signified, is evident from what has gone before; and that to be "cursed" is to be averse to good, has been already shown (n. 245). For iniquities and abominations, or hatreds, are what avert man, so that he looks downwards only, that is, to bodily and earthly things, thus to those which are from hell. This takes place when charity is banished and extinguished, for then the bond which connects the Lord with man is severed, since only charity, or love and mercy, are what conjoin, and never faith without charity, for this is no faith, that is knowledge only, such as the infernal crew themselves may possess, and by which they can craftily deceive the good, and feign themselves angels of light ; and as very wicked preachers are sometimes wont to

do, with a zeal like that of piety, although nothing is further from their hearts than that which proceeds from their lips. Can any one be of such weak judgment as to believe that faith alone in the memory, or the thought thence derived, can be of any avail, when everybody knows from his own experience that no one esteems the words or assent of another, no matter of what nature, when they do not come from the will or intention ? It is this that makes them pleasing, and that conjoins one man with another. The will is the real man, and not the thought or speech which he does not will. A man acquires his nature and disposition from the will, because this affects him. But if any one thinks what is good, the essence of faith, which is charity, is in the thought, because the will to do what is good is in it. But if he says that he thinks what is good, and yet lives wickedly, he cannot possibly will anything but what is evil, and there is therefore no faith.

380. Verse 12. **When thou tillest the ground, it shall not henceforth yield unto thee its strength ; a fugitive and a wanderer shalt thou be in the earth.** To " till the ground," signifies to cultivate this schism or heresy ; " it shall not yield unto thee its strength," signifies that it is barren. To be a " fugitive and a wanderer in the earth," is not to know what is good and true.

381. That to " till the ground " means to cultivate this schism or heresy, appears from the signification of " ground," of which we have just now spoken ; and that its " not yielding its strength " denotes its barrenness, is evident both from what was said concerning ground, and from the words themselves, as well as from this considera-

tion, that those who profess faith without charity, profess no faith, as was said above.

382. That to be a " fugitive and a wanderer in the earth " signifies not to know what is good and true, is evident from the signification of " wandering " and " fleeing away " in the Word. As in *Jeremiah* :

> The prophets and priests wander blind in the streets, they have been polluted in blood ; the things they cannot do they touch with garments (*Lam.* iv. 13, 14).

Here " prophets " are those who teach, and " priests," those who live accordingly ; to " wander blind in the streets," is not to know what is true 2 and good. In *Amos* :

> A part of the field was rained upon, and the part of the field whereupon it rained not withered ; so two or three cities shall wander unto one city to drink waters, and shall not be satisfied (iv. 7, 8).

Here by the " part of the field on which it rained " is signified the doctrine of faith from charity ; and by the " part " or " piece " " of the field on which it did not rain," the doctrine of faith without charity. To " wander to drink the waters," like-3 wise denotes to seek after truth. In *Hosea* :

> Ephraim is smitten, their root is dried up, they shall bear no fruit ; my God will cast them away, because they did not hearken unto Him ; and they shall be wanderers among the nations (ix. 16, 17).

" Ephraim " here denotes the understanding of truth, or faith, because he was the firstborn of Joseph ; the " root which was dried up," denotes

232

charity that cannot bear fruit ; " wanderers among
the nations," are those who do not know what is
true and good. In *Jeremiah* : 4

> Go ye up against Arabia, and devastate the
> sons of the east. Flee, wander ye exceedingly ;
> the inhabitants of Hazor have let themselves
> down into the deep for a habitation (xlix. 28, 30).

" Arabia " and the " sons of the east," signify
the possession of celestial riches, or of the things
that are of love, which, when vastated, are said to
" flee," and " wander," that is, to be " fugitives
and wanderers," when they do nothing good. Of
the " inhabitants of Hazor," or those who possess
spiritual riches, which are those of faith, it is said
that they " let themselves down into the deep,"
that is, they perish. In *Isaiah* : 5

> All thy foremost ones wander together, they
> are bound before the bow, they have fled from
> far (xxii. 3).

This refers to the " valley of vision," or the
phantasy that faith is possible without charity.
Hence appears the reason why it is said, in a
subsequent verse (14), that he who professes faith
that is apart from charity is a " fugitive and a
wanderer," that is, knows nothing of good and
truth.

383. Verse 13. **And Cain said unto Jehovah,
Mine iniquity is greater than can be taken away.**
" Cain said unto Jehovah," signifies confession
that he was in evil, induced by some internal
pain ; " mine iniquity is greater than can be
taken away," signifies despair on that account.

384. Hence it appears that some good still
remained in Cain ; but that all the good of charity

afterwards perished is evident from what is said of Lamech (verses 19, 23, 24).

385. Verse 14. **Behold Thou hast cast me out this day from the faces of the ground, and from Thy faces shall I be hid ; and I shall be a fugitive and a wanderer in the earth ; and it shall come to pass that every one that findeth me shall slay me.** To be "cast out from the faces of the ground," signifies to be separated from all the truth of the church ; to be "hid from Thy faces," signifies to be separated from all the good of faith of love ; to be a "fugitive and a wanderer in the earth," is not to know what is true and good ; "every one that findeth me shall slay me," signifies that all evil and falsity would destroy him.

386. That to be "cast out from the faces of the ground" is to be separated from all the truth of the church, is evident from the signification of "ground," which, in the genuine sense, is the church, or the man of the church, and therefore whatever the church professes, as shown above. The meaning of a word necessarily varies with the subject treated of, and therefore even those who wrongly profess faith, that is who profess a schism or heresy, are also called "ground." Here, however, to be "driven out from the faces of the ground" signifies to be no longer in the truth of the church.

387. That to be "hid from Thy faces" signifies to be separated from all the good of the faith of love, is evident from the signification of the "faces of Jehovah." The "face of Jehovah," as before said, is mercy, from which proceed all the goods of the faith of love, and therefore the goods of faith are here signified by His "faces."

234

388. To be a " fugitive and a wanderer in the earth," means, as before, not to know what is true and good.

389. That " every one finding him would slay him " signifies that every evil and falsity would destroy him, follows from what has been said. For the case is this. When a man deprives himself of charity, he separates himself from the Lord, since it is solely charity, that is, love towards the neighbour, and mercy, that conjoin man with the Lord. Where there is no charity, there is disjunction, and where there is disjunction, man is left to himself or to his proprium ; and then whatever he thinks is false, and whatever he wills is evil. These are the things that slay man, or cause him to have no life remaining.

390. Those who are in evil and falsity are in continual dread of being slain, as is thus described in *Moses* :

Your land shall be a desolation, and your cities a waste, and upon them that are left of you I will bring softness into their heart in the land of their enemies, and the sound of a driven leaf shall chase them, and they shall flee as fleeing from a sword, and they shall fall when none pursueth, and shall stumble every one upon his brother, as it were before a sword, when none pursueth (*Lev.* xxvi. 33, 36, 37).

In *Isaiah* :

The treacherous deal treacherously, yea, in the treachery of the treacherous they deal treacherously. And it shall come to pass that he who fleeth from the noise of the fear shall fall into the pit, and he that cometh up out of the midst

of the pit shall be taken in the snare ; the transgression thereof shall be heavy upon it, and it
shall fall, and not rise again (xxiv. 16–20).

In *Jeremiah* :

Behold, I bring a dread upon thee, from all
thy circuits shall ye be driven out every man
toward his faces, and none shall gather up him
that wandereth (xlix. 5).

In *Isaiah* :

We will flee upon the horse, therefore shall ye
flee ; and, We will ride upon the swift, therefore
shall they that pursue you be rendered swift ;
one thousand shall flee at the rebuke of one, at
the rebuke of five shall ye flee (xxx. 16, 17).

In these and other passages of the Word, those who
are in falsity and evil are described as " fleeing,"
and as in " fear of being slain." They are afraid
of everybody, because they have no one to protect them. All who are in evil and falsity hate
their neighbour, so that they all desire to kill one
another.

391. The state of evil spirits in the other life
shows most clearly that those who are in evil and
falsity are afraid of everybody. Those who
have deprived themselves of all charity wander
about, and flee from place to place. Wherever
they go, if to any societies, these at once perceive
their character by their mere coming, for such is
the perception that exists in the other life ; and
they not only drive them away, but also punish
them severely, and with such animosity that they
would kill them if they could. Evil spirits take
the greatest delight in punishing and tormenting
one another ; it is their highest gratification. Not

until now has it been known that evil and falsity themselves are the cause of this, for whatever any one desires for another returns upon himself. Falsity has in itself the penalty of falsity, and evil has in itself the penalty of evil, and consequently they have in themselves the fear of these penalties.

392. Verse 15. **And Jehovah said unto him, Therefore whosoever slayeth Cain, vengeance shall be taken on him sevenfold. And Jehovah set a mark upon Cain, lest any finding him should smite him.** By " vengeance being taken sevenfold on any one who slays Cain," is signified that to do violence to faith even when thus separated would be a sacrilege ; " Jehovah set a mark upon Cain, lest any finding him should smite him," signifies that the Lord distinguished faith in a particular manner, in order that it might be preserved.

393. Before we proceed to elucidate the internal sense of the words before us, it is necessary to know how the case is with faith. The Most Ancient Church was of such a character as to acknowledge no faith except that which is of love, insomuch that they were unwilling even to mention faith, for through love from the Lord they perceived all things that belong to faith. Such also are the celestial angels of whom we have spoken above. But as it was foreseen that the human race could not be of this character, but would separate faith from love to the Lord, and would make of faith a doctrine by itself, it was provided that they should indeed be separated, but in such a way that through faith, that is, through the cognitions of faith, men might receive from the Lord charity, so that cognition or hearing should come first, and then through cognition or hearing, charity, that is, love towards

237

the neighbour, and mercy, might be given by the
Lord, which charity should not only be inseparable
from faith, but should also constitute the chief
thing of faith. And then instead of the perception
they had in the Most Ancient Church, there
succeeded conscience, acquired through faith joined
to charity, which dictated not what is true, but
that it is true, and this because the Lord has so
said in the Word. The churches after the flood
were for the most part of this character, as also
was the primitive or first church after the Lord's
advent, and by this the spiritual angels are distinguished from the celestial.

394. Now as this was foreseen, and was provided, lest the human race should perish in eternal
death, it is here declared that none should do
violence to Cain, by whom is signified faith separated
from charity ; and further that a mark was set
upon him, which means that the Lord distinguished
faith in a particular manner, in order to secure its
preservation. These are arcana hitherto undis-
covered, and are referred to by the Lord in what
He said respecting marriage, and eunuchs, in
Matthew :

> There are eunuchs who were so born from their
> mother's womb ; and there are eunuchs who
> were made eunuchs of men ; and there are
> eunuchs who have made themselves eunuchs
> for the kingdom of God's sake ; he that is able
> to receive it let him receive it (xix. 12).

Those in the heavenly marriage are called
" eunuchs " ; those so " born from the womb," are
such as resemble the celestial angels ; those " made
of men," are such as are like the spiritual angels ;
and those " made so by themselves," are like angelic

spirits, who act not so much from charity as from obedience.

395. That the words " whosoever slayeth Cain, vengeance shall be taken on him sevenfold," signify that to do violence to faith even when thus separated would be sacrilege, is evident from the signification of " Cain," which is faith separated from charity, and from the signification of " seven," which is what is sacred. The number " seven " was esteemed holy, as is well known, by reason of the six days of creation, and of the seventh, which is the celestial man, in whom is peace, rest, and the sabbath. Hence this number occurs so frequently in the rites of the Jewish Church, and is everywhere held sacred, and hence also both longer and shorter periods of time were distinguished into sevens, and were called " weeks," such as the great intervals of time to the coming of the Messiah (*Dan.* ix. 24, 25) ; and the time of seven years was called a " week " by Laban and Jacob (*Gen.* xxix. 27, 28). For the same reason, wherever it occurs, the number seven is accounted holy or inviolable. Thus we read in *David* :

Seven times a day do I praise Thee (*Ps.* cxix. 164).

In *Isaiah* :

The light of the moon shall be as the light of the sun, and the light of the sun shall be sevenfold, as the light of seven days (xxx. 26).

Here the " sun " denotes love, and the " moon " faith from love, which should be as love. As the periods of man's regeneration are distinguished into six, before the seventh arrives, that is, the celestial man, so also are the periods of his vastation, up to the time when nothing celestial remains. This was represented by the several captivities of the Jews, and by the last or Babylonish captivity, which lasted seven decades, or seventy years. It is also said several times that the earth should rest on its sabbaths. The same is represented by Nebuchadnezzar, in *Daniel* :

> His heart shall be changed from man, and a beast's heart shall be given unto him, and seven times shall pass over him (iv. 16, 23, 32).

And in *John*, concerning the vastation of the last times :

> I saw another sign in heaven, great and marvellous, seven angels, having the seven last plagues (*Rev.* xv. 1, 6, 7, 8).

And that :

> The Gentiles should tread the holy city under foot forty and two months, or six times seven (*Rev.* xi. 2).

And again :

> I saw a book written within and on the back, sealed with seven seals (*Rev.* v. 1).

For the same reason the severities and augmentations of punishment were expressed by the number seven ; as in *Moses* :

> If ye will not yet for all this obey Me, then I will chastise you sevenfold for your sins (*Lev.* xxvi. 18, 21, 24, 28).

And in *David* :

> Render unto our neighbours sevenfold into their bosom (*Ps.* lxxix. 12).

Now as it was a sacrilege to do violence to faith— since as has been said it was to be of service—it

240

is said that " whosoever should slay Cain, vengeance should be taken on him sevenfold."

396. That " Jehovah set a mark on Cain, lest any should smite him," signifies that the Lord distinguished faith in a particular manner in order that it might be preserved, is evident from the signification of a " mark," and of " setting a mark " on any one, as being a means of distinction. Thus in *Ezekiel*:

Jehovah said, Go through the midst of the city, through the midst of Jerusalem, and set a mark (that is, " mark out ") upon the foreheads of the men groaning and sighing for all the abominations (ix. 4).

Here by " marking out the foreheads," is not meant a mark or line upon the front part of their heads, but to distinguish them from others. So in *John*, it is said that

The locusts should hurt only those men who had not the mark of God on their foreheads (*Rev.* ix. 4).

Here also to have the mark means to be distinguished. And in the same book we read of a 2 " mark on the hand and on the forehead " (*Rev.* xiii. 16). The same thing was represented in the Jewish Church by binding the first and great commandment on the hand and on the forehead, concerning which we read in *Moses*:

Hear, O Israel, Jehovah our God is one Jehovah ; and thou shalt love Jehovah thy God with all thy heart, and with all thy soul, and with all thy strength, and thou shalt bind these words for a sign upon thy hand, and they shall

be as frontlets between thine eyes (*Deut.* vi.
4, 8 ; xi. 13, 18).

By this was represented that they should distinguish the commandment respecting love above
every other, and hence the signification of " marking the hand and the forehead " becomes manifest.
3 So in *Isaiah* :

> I come to gather all nations and tongues ;
> and they shall come· and shall see My glory ;
> and I will set a mark upon them (lxvi. 18, 19).

And in *David* :

> O turn unto me, and have mercy upon me,
> give Thy strength unto Thy servant, and save the
> son of Thy handmaid. Set upon me a mark for
> good, and they that hate me shall see and be
> ashamed (*Ps.* lxxxvi. 16, 17).

From these passages the meaning of a mark is
now evident. Let no one, therefore, imagine that
any mark was set upon a particular person called
Cain, for the internal sense of the Word contains
things quite different from those contained in the
sense of the letter.

397. Verse 16. **And Cain went out from the
faces of Jehovah, and dwelt in the land of Nod,
toward the east of Eden.** By the words " Cain
went out from the faces of Jehovah " is signified
that faith was separated from the good of the
faith of love ; " he dwelt in the land of Nod,"
signifies outside truth and good ; " toward the
east of Eden," is near the intellectual mind, where
love reigned before.

398. That to " go out from the faces of Jehovah "
signifies to be separated from the good of the faith
of love, may be seen in the explanation of verse

242

14 ; that to " dwell in the land of Nod " signifies outside truth and good, is evident from the signification of the word " Nod," which is to be a wanderer and a fugitive ; and that to be " a wanderer and a fugitive " is to be deprived of truth and good, may be seen above. That " toward the east of Eden " signifies near the intellectual mind, where love had previously reigned, and also near the rational mind, where charity had previously reigned, is evident from what has been said of the signification of " the east of Eden," namely, that " the east " is the Lord, and " Eden " love. With the men of the Most Ancient Church, the mind, consisting of the will and the understanding, was one ; for the will was all in all, so that the understanding was of the will. This was because they made no distinction between love, which is of the will, and faith, which is of the understanding, because love was the all in all, and faith was of love. But after faith was separated from love, as was the case with those who were called " Cain," no will reigned any longer, and as in that mind the understanding reigned instead of the will, or faith instead of love, it is said that he " dwelt toward the east of Eden " ; for as was just now observed faith was distinguished, or " had a mark set upon it," that it might be preserved for the use of mankind.

399. Verse 17. **And Cain knew his wife, and she conceived, and bare Enoch; and he was building a city, and called the name of the city after the name of his son, Enoch.** The words " Cain knew his wife, and she conceived and bare Enoch," signify that this schism or heresy produced another from itself that was called " Enoch." By " the city which he

243

built " is signified all that was doctrinal and heretical therefrom, and because the schism or heresy was called " Enoch," it is said that " the name of the city was called after the name of his son, Enoch."

400. That " Cain knew his wife, and she conceived, and bare Enoch," signifies that this schism or heresy produced another from itself, is evident from what has been previously said, as well as from what is stated in the first verse, that the Man and Eve his wife produced Cain ; so that the things which now follow are similar conceptions and births, whether of the church, or of heresies, whereof they formed a genealogy, for these are similarly related to each other. From one heresy that is conceived there is born a host of them.

401. That it was a heresy with all its doctrinal or heretical teaching that was called " Enoch," is in some measure evident from this name, which means the instruction so begun or initiated.

402. That by the " city that was built " is signified all the doctrinal and heretical teaching that came from that heresy, is evident from every passage of the Word in which the name of any city occurs ; for in none of them does it ever mean a city, but always something doctrinal or else heretical. The angels are altogether ignorant of what a city is, and of the name of any city ; since they neither have nor can have any idea of a city, because they are in spiritual and celestial ideas, as was shown above. They perceive only what a city and its name signify. Thus by the " holy city," which is also called the " holy Jerusalem," nothing else is meant but the kingdom of the Lord in general, or in each individual in particular in whom

is that kingdom. The " city " and " mountain "
" of Zion " also are similarly understood ; the
latter denoting the celestial of faith, and the former
its spiritual. The celestial and spiritual itself is 2
also described by " cities," " palaces," " houses,"
" walls," " foundations of walls," " ramparts,"
" gates," " bars," and the " temple " in the midst ;
as in *Ezekiel* xlviii. ; in the *Revelation* xxi. 15 to
the end, where it is also called the Holy Jerusalem,
verses 2, 10 ; and in *Jeremiah* xxxi. 38. In *David*
it is called " the city of God, the holy place of the
tabernacles of the Most High " (*Ps.* xlvi. 4) ; in
Ezekiel, " the city, Jehovah there " (xlviii. 35),
and of which it is written in *Isaiah* :

> The sons of the stranger shall build thy walls,
> all they that despised thee shall bow themselves
> down at the soles of thy feet, and they shall call
> thee the city of Jehovah, the Zion of the Holy
> One of Israel (lx. 10, 14).

In *Zechariah* :

> Jerusalem shall be called the city of truth ;
> and the mountain of Zion, the mountain of
> holiness (viii. 3).

Here the " city of truth," or " Jerusalem," signifies
the spiritual things of faith ; and the " mountain
of holiness," or " of Zion," the celestial things of
faith. As the celestial and spiritual things of faith 3
are represented by a city, so also are all doctrinal
things signified by the cities of Judah and of Israel,
each of which when named has its own specific
signification of something doctrinal, but what that
is no one can know except from the internal sense.
As doctrinal things are signified by " cities," so
also are heresies, and in this case every particular city, according to its name, signifies some

particular heretical opinion. At present we shall
only show from the following passages of the Word,
that in general a " city " signifies something
doctrinal, or else heretical. Thus we read in
4 *Isaiah* :

> In that day there shall be five cities in the land
> of Egypt speaking with the lip of Canaan, and
> swearing to Jehovah Zebaoth ; one shall be
> called the city of Heres (xix. 18).

Here the subject treated of is the knowledge of
spiritual and celestial things at the time of the
Lord's advent. So again, when treating of the
valley of vision, that is, of phantasy :

> Thou art full of tumults, a tumultuous city,
> an exulting city (xxii. 2).

In *Jeremiah*, speaking of those who are " in the
south," that is, in the light of truth, and who
extinguish it :

> The cities of the south have been shut up, and
> none shall open them (xiii. 19).

Again :

> Jehovah hath purposed to destroy the wall
> of the daughter of Zion ; therefore He maketh
> the rampart and the wall to lament ; they
> languished together. Her gates are sunk into
> the ground ; He hath destroyed and broken her
> bars (*Lam.* ii. 8, 9).

Here any one may see that by a " wall," a " ram-
part," " gates," and " bars," doctrinal things only
5 are meant. In like manner in *Isaiah* :

> This song shall be sung in the land of Judah,
> We have a strong city ; salvation will set the
> walls and the bulwark ; open ye the gates, that

the righteous nation which keepeth fidelities may enter in (xxvi. 1, 2).

Again :

I will exalt thee, I will confess to Thy name, for Thou hast made of a city a heap, of a defenced city a ruin ; a palace of strangers shall not be built of the city forever. Therefore shall the strong people honour Thee, the city of the terrible nations shall fear Thee (xxv. 1, 2, 3).

In this passage there is no reference to any particular city. In the prophecy of Balaam :

Edom shall be an inheritance, and out of Jacob shall one have dominion, and shall destroy the residue of the city (*Num.* xxiv. 18, 19).

Here it must be plain to every one that " city " does not mean a city. In *Isaiah* :

The city of emptiness is broken ; every house is shut, that the cry over wine in the streets cannot enter (xxiv. 10, 11).

Here the " city of emptiness " denotes emptinesses of doctrine ; and " streets " signify here as elsewhere the things which belong to the city, whether falsities or truths. In *John* :

When the seventh angel poured out his vial, the great city was divided into three parts, and the cities of the nations fell (*Rev.* xvi. 17, 19).

That the " great city " denotes something heretical, and that the " cities of the nations " do so too, must be evident to every one. It is also explained that the great city was the woman that John saw (xvii. 18) ; and that the woman denotes a church of that character has been shown before.

403. We have now seen what a " city " signifies. But as all this part of *Genesis* is put into an

247

historical form, to those who are in the sense of the letter it must seem that a city was built by Cain, and was called Enoch, although from the sense of the letter they must also suppose that the land was already populous, notwithstanding that Cain was only the firstborn of Adam. But as we observed above, the most ancient people were accustomed to arrange all things in the form of a history, under representative types, and this was to them delightful in the highest degree, for it made all things seem to be alive.

404. Verse 18. **And unto Enoch was born Irad ; and Irad begat Mehujael, and Mehujael begat Methusael, and Methusael begat Lamech.** All these names signify heresies derived from the first, which was called " Cain " ; but as there is nothing extant respecting them, except the names, it is unnecessary to say anything about them. Something might be gathered from the derivations of the names ; for example, " Irad " means that he " descends from a city," thus from the heresy called " Enoch," and so on.

405. Verse 19. **And Lamech took unto him two wives ; the name of the one was Adah, and the name of the other Zillah.** By " Lamech," who was the sixth in order from Cain, is signified vastation, in consequence of there being no longer any faith ; by his " two wives " is signified the rise of a new church ; by " Adah," the mother of its celestial and spiritual things ; and by " Zillah," the mother of its natural things.

406. That by " Lamech " is signified vastation, or that there was no faith, is evident from the following verses (23, 24), in which it is said that

he " slew a man to his wounding, and a little one to his hurt " ; for there by a " man " is meant faith, and by a " little one " or " little child," charity.

407. The state of a church in general is thus circumstanced. In process of time it departs from the true faith and finally ends in no faith. When there is none it is said to be " vastated." This was the case with the Most Ancient Church among those who were called Cainites, and also with the Ancient Church after the flood, as well as with the Jewish Church. At the time of the Lord's advent this last was in such a state of vastation that they knew nothing about the Lord, that He was to come into the world for their salvation, and they knew still less about faith in Him. Such was also the case with the primitive Christian Church, or that which existed after the Lord's advent, and which at this day is so completely vastated that there is no faith remaining in it. Yet there always remains some nucleus of a church, which those who are vastated as to faith do not acknowledge ; and thus it was with the Most Ancient Church, of which a remnant remained until the time of the flood, and continued after that event. This remnant of the Church is called " Noah."

408. When a church has been so vastated that there is no longer any faith, then and not before, it begins anew, that is, new light shines forth, which in the Word is called the " morning." The reason why the new light or " morning " does not shine forth until the church is vastated, is that the things of faith and of charity have been commingled with things profane ; and so long as they remain

in this state it is impossible for anything of light
or charity to be insinuated, since the " tares "
destroy all the " good seed." But when there is
no faith, faith can no longer be profaned, because
men no longer believe what is declared unto them ;
and those who do not acknowledge and believe,
but only know, cannot profane, as was observed
above. This is the case with the Jews at the present
day, who in consequence of living among Christians
must be aware that the Lord is acknowledged by
Christians to be the Messiah whom they themselves
have expected, and still continue to expect, but
yet they cannot profane this because they do not
acknowledge and believe it. And it is the same
with the Mohammedans and Gentiles who have
heard about the Lord. It was for this reason that
the Lord did not come into the world until the
Jewish Church acknowledged and believed nothing.

409. The case was the same with the heresy
called " Cain," which in process of time was
vastated, for although it acknowledged love, yet
it made faith the chief and set it before love, and
the heresies derived from this one gradually
wandered from it, and Lamech, who was the sixth
in order, altogether denied even faith. When this
time arrived, a new light, or morning, shone forth,
and a new church was formed which is here named
" Adah and Zillah," who are called the " wives of
Lamech." They are called the wives of Lamech,
although he possessed no faith, just as the internal
and external church of the Jews, who also had no
faith, are also in the Word called " wives," being
represented by Leah and Rachel, the two wives of
Jacob—Leah representing the external church and
Rachel the internal. These churches, although

they appear like two, are yet only one ; for the external or representative, separate from the internal, is but as something idolatrous, or dead, whereas the internal together with the external constitute a church, and even one and the same church, as Adah and Zillah do here. As, however, Jacob and his posterity, like Lamech, had no faith, the church could not remain with them, but was transferred to the Gentiles, who lived not in infidelity but in ignorance. The church rarely, if ever, remains with those who when vastated have truths among them, but is transferred to those who know nothing at all of truths, for these embrace faith much more easily than the former.

410. Vastation is of two kinds ; first, of those who know and do not wish to know, or who see and do not desire to see, like the Jews of old, and the Christians of the present day ; and secondly, of those who, in consequence of their ignorance, neither know nor see anything, like both the ancient and modern Gentiles. When the last time of vastation comes upon those who know and do not desire to know, that is, who see and do not desire to see, then a church arises anew, not among them, but with those whom they call Gentiles. This occurred with the Most Ancient Church that was before the flood, with the Ancient Church that was after that event, and also with the Jewish Church. The reason why new light shines forth then and not before is, as has been said, that then they can no longer profane the things revealed, because they do not acknowledge and believe that they are true.

411. That the last time of vastation must exist before a new church can arise, is frequently declared

251

by the Lord in the Prophets, and is there called "vastation" or "laying waste," in reference to the celestial things of faith; and "desolation," in relation to the spiritual things of faith. It is also spoken of as "consummation" and "cutting off." (See *Isa*. vi. 9, 11, 12; xxiii. 8 to the end; xxiv.; xlii. 15–18; *Jer*. xxv.; *Dan*. viii.; ix. 24 to the end; *Zeph*. i.; *Deut*. xxxii.; *Rev*. xv., xvi., and following chapters.)

412. Verse 20. **And Adah bare Jabal; he was the father of the dwellers in tents, and of cattle.** By "Adah" is signified, as before, the mother of the celestial and spiritual things of faith; by "Jabal, the father of the dweller in tents, and of cattle," is signified doctrine concerning the holy things of love, and the goods thence derived, which are celestial.

413. That by "Adah" is signified the mother of the celestial things of faith, is evident from her firstborn Jabal being called the "father of the dwellers in tents, and of cattle," which are celestial because they signify the holy things of love and the goods thence derived.

414. That to "dwell in tents" signifies the holiness of love, is evident from the signification of "tents" in the Word. As in *David*:

Jehovah, who shall abide in Thy tent? Who shall dwell in the mountain of Thy holiness? He that walketh upright, and worketh righteousness, and speaketh the truth in his heart (*Ps.* xv. 1, 2).

In this passage, what it is to "dwell in the tent," or "in the mountain of holiness," is described by holy things of love, namely, the walking uprightly, and working righteousness. Again :

> Their line is gone out through all the earth, and their discourse to the end of the world. In them hath He set a tent for the sun (*Ps.* xix. 4).

Here the " sun " denotes love. Again :

> I will abide in Thy tent to eternities, I will trust in the covert of Thy wings (*Ps.* lxi. 4).

Here the " tent " denotes what is celestial, and the " covert of wings " what is spiritual thence derived. In *Isaiah* :

> By mercy the throne has been made firm, and one hath sat upon it in truth, in the tent of David, judging and seeking judgment, and hasting righteousness (xvi. 5).

Here also the " tent " denotes the holiness of love, as may be seen by the mention of " judging judgment," and " hasting righteousness." Again :

> Look upon Zion, the city of our appointed feast ; thine eyes shall see Jerusalem a quiet habitation, a tent that shall not be moved away (xxxiii. 20).

This treats of the heavenly Jerusalem. In *Jere-* 2 *miah* :

> Thus said Jehovah, Behold, I bring again the captivity of Jacob's tents, and will have mercy on his dwelling-places, and the city shall be builded upon her own heap (xxx. 18).

The " captivity of tents " signifies the vastation of what is celestial, or of the holy things of love. In *Amos* :

> In that day will I raise up the tabernacle of David which is fallen, and will fence up the

253

breaches thereof, and I will raise up its ruins, and I will build it as in the days of eternity (ix. 11).

Here the "tabernacle" in like manner denotes what is celestial and the holy things thereof. In *Jeremiah* :

The whole land is laid waste, suddenly are My tents laid waste, and My curtains in a moment (iv. 20).

And in another place :

My tent is laid waste, and all My cords are plucked out, My sons are gone forth from Me, and they are not ; there is none to stretch My tent any more, and to set up My curtains (x. 20).

Here the "tent" signifies celestial things, and "curtains" and "cords" spiritual things thence derived. Again :

Their tents and their flocks shall they take ; they shall carry off for themselves their curtains, and all their vessels, and their camels (xlix. 29).

This treats of Arabia and the sons of the east, by whom are represented those who possess what is celestial or holy. Again :

Into the tent of the daughter of Zion the Lord hath poured out His wrath like fire (*Lam.* ii. 4).

This treats of the vastation of the celestial or 3 holy things of faith. The reason why the term "tent" is employed in the Word to represent the celestial and holy things of love, is that in ancient times they performed the holy rites of worship in their tents. But when they began to profane the

tents by profane kinds of worship, the tabernacle
was built, and afterwards the temple, and therefore
tents represented all that was subsequently denoted
first by the tabernacle, and afterwards by the
temple. For the same reason a holy man is called
a " tent," a " tabernacle," and a " temple " of
the Lord. That a " tent," a " tabernacle," and a
" temple " have the same signification, is evident
in *David* :

> One thing have I asked of Jehovah, that will
> I seek after, that I may remain in the house of
> Jehovah all the days of my life, to behold
> Jehovah in sweetness, and to visit early in His
> temple ; for in the day of evil He shall hide me
> in His tabernacle ; in the secret of His tent shall
> He hide me ; He shall set me up upon a rock.
> And now shall my head be lifted up against
> mine enemies round about me, and I will offer
> in His tent sacrifices of shouting (*Ps.* xxvii.
> 4, 5, 6).

In the highest sense, the Lord as to His Human 4
essence is the " tent," the " tabernacle," and the
" temple " ; hence every celestial man is so called,
and also everything celestial and holy. Now as the
Most Ancient Church was better beloved of the
Lord than the churches that followed it, and as
men at that time lived alone, that is, in their own
families, and celebrated so holy a worship in their
tents, therefore tents were accounted more holy
than the temple, which was profaned. In remem-
brance thereof the feast of tabernacles was instituted, when they gathered in the produce of the
earth, during which, like the most ancient people,
they dwelt in tents (*Lev.* xxiii. 39–44 ; *Deut.* xvi.
13 ; *Hosea* xii. 9).

415. That by the " father of cattle " is signified
the good that is derived from the holy things of
love, is evident from what was shown above
(verse 2 of this chapter), where it was shown that
a " shepherd of the flock " signifies the good of
charity. Here, however, the term " father " is
employed instead of " shepherd," and " cattle "
instead of " flock " ; and the word " cattle," of
which Jabal is said to be the " father," follows
immediately after " tent," whence it is evident
that it signifies the good that comes from the
holiness of love, and that there is meant a habita-
tion or fold for cattle, or the father of them that
dwell in tents and in folds for cattle. And that
these expressions signify goods from the celestial
things of love, is evident from various passages
in the Word. As in *Jeremiah* :

> I will gather the remnants of My flock out of
> all lands whither I have scattered them, and
> I will bring them again to their folds, that they
> may be fruitful and multiply (xxiii. 3).

In *Ezekiel* :

> I will feed them in a good pasture, and upon
> the mountains of the height of Israel shall their
> fold be ; there shall they lie down in a good fold,
> and in a fat pasture shall they feed upon the
> mountains of Israel (xxxiv. 14).

Here " folds " and " pastures " denote the goods of
love, of which " fatness " is predicated. In *Isaiah* :

> He shall give the rain of thy seed wherewith
> thou shalt sow the ground ; and bread of the
> increase of the ground shall be fat and full of
> oil ; in that day shall He feed thy cattle in a
> broad meadow (xxx. 23).

Here by " bread " is signified what is celestial, and by the " fat " whereon the cattle should feed, the goods thence derived. In *Jeremiah* :

Jehovah hath redeemed Jacob, and they shall come and sing in the height of Zion, and shall flow together to the good of Jehovah, for the wheat, and for the new wine, and for the oil, and for the sons of the flock, and of the herd ; and their soul shall be as a watered garden (xxxi. 11, 12).

Here the Holy of Jehovah is described by " wheat " and " oil," and the goods derived from it by " new wine " and the " sons of the flock and of the herd," or of " cattle." Again :

The shepherds and the flocks of their cattle shall come unto the daughter of Zion ; they shall pitch their tents toward her round about ; they shall feed every one his own space (vi. 3).

The " daughter of Zion " denotes the celestial church, of which " tents " and " flocks of cattle " are predicated.

416. That the holy things of love and the derivative goods are signified, is evident from the fact that Jabal was not the first of those who " dwelt in tents and in folds of cattle," for it is said likewise of Abel, the second son of Man and Eve, that he was " a shepherd of the flock," and Jabal was the seventh in the order of descent from Cain.

417. Verse 21. **And his brother's name was Jubal; he was the father of every one that playeth upon the harp and organ.** By " his brother's name was Jubal " is signified the doctrine of the spiritual

I   257

things of the same church ; by the " father of every one that playeth upon the harp and organ " are signified the truths and goods of faith.

418. The former verse treated of celestial things belonging to love, but this verse treats of spiritual things belonging to faith, and these are expressed by the " harp and organ." That by stringed instruments, such as harps and the like, are signified the spiritual things of faith, is evident from many considerations. Similar instruments, and also the singing, in the worship of the representative church, represented nothing else, and it was on this account that there were so many singers and musicians, the cause of this representation being that all heavenly joy produces gladness of heart, which was expressed by singing, and in the next place by stringed instruments that emulated and exalted the singing. Every affection of the heart is attended with this : that it produces singing, and, consequently, what is connected with singing. The affection of the heart is celestial, but the consequent singing is spiritual. That singing and that which resembles it denote what is spiritual, has been evident to me from the angelic choirs, which are of two kinds, celestial and spiritual. The spiritual choirs are easily distinguished from the celestial by their vibrant singing tone, comparable to the sound of stringed instruments, of which, by the Divine mercy of the Lord, we shall treat hereafter. The most ancient people referred what was celestial to the province of the heart, and what was spiritual to that of the lungs, and, consequently, to whatever pertains to the lungs, as do the singing voice and things like it, and therefore the voices or sounds of such instruments. The reason for this was not merely that the heart and lungs represent a kind of marriage, like that of love and faith, but also because the celestial angels belong to the province of the heart, and the spiritual angels to that of the lungs. That such things are meant in the passage before us, may also be known from the fact that this is the Word of the Lord, and that it would be destitute of life if nothing more were implied than that Jubal was the father of such as play upon the harp and the organ ; nor is it of any use to any one to know this.

419. As celestial things are the holy things of love and the derivative goods, so spiritual things are the truths and goods of faith ; for it belongs to faith to understand not only what is true, but also what is good. The cognitions of faith involve both. But to be such as faith teaches is celestial. As faith involves both of these, they are signified by two instruments, the harp and the organ. The harp, as every one knows, is a stringed instrument, and therefore signifies spiritual truth ; but the organ, being intermediate between a stringed instrument and a wind instrument, signifies spiritual good.

420. In the Word mention is made of various instruments, each having its own signification, as will be shown, of the Lord's Divine mercy, in its proper place ; here, however, we shall adduce only what is said in *David* :

I will sacrifice in the tent of Jehovah sacrifices of shouting, I will sing, yea, I will sing praises unto Jehovah (*Ps.* xxvii. 6).

Here by " tent " is expressed what is celestial,

and by " shouting," " singing," and " singing praises," what is spiritual thence derived. Again :

Sing unto Jehovah, O ye righteous, for His praise is comely for the upright ; confess ye to Jehovah on the harp, sing unto Him with the psaltery, an instrument of ten strings. Sing unto Him a new song, play skilfully with a loud noise ; for the Word of Jehovah is right, and all His work is in the truth (*Ps.* xxxiii. 1–4).

2 This denotes the truths of faith, concerning which these things are said. Spiritual things, or the truths and goods of faith, were celebrated with the harp and psaltery, with singing and analogous instruments, but the holy or celestial things of faith were celebrated with wind instruments, such as trumpets and the like ; and this was why so many instruments were used about the temple and so often, in order that this or that subject might be celebrated with certain instruments ; and, in consequence of this, the instruments came to be taken and understood for the subjects that were 3 celebrated with them. Again :

I will confess to Thee with the psaltery, even Thy truth, O my God ; unto Thee will I sing praises with the harp, O Thou Holy One of Israel ; my lips shall sing when I sing praises unto Thee, and my soul which Thou hast redeemed (*Ps.* lxxi. 22, 23).

Here also the truths of faith are signified. Again :

Answer to Jehovah in confession, sing praises upon the harp unto our God (cxlvii. 7).

" Confession " has respect to the celestial things of faith, and therefore mention is made of " Jehovah " ; and to " sing praises upon the
260

harp " has reference to the spiritual things of
faith, wherefore " God " is spoken of. Again :

> Let them praise the name of Jehovah in the
> dance, let them sing praises unto Him with the
> timbrel and harp (cxlix. 3).

Here the " timbrel " signifies good, and the " harp "
truth, which they praise. Again :   4

> Praise God with the sound of the trumpet ;
> praise Him with the psaltery and harp ; praise
> Him with the timbrel and dance ; praise Him
> with stringed instruments and the organ ; praise
> Him upon the loud cymbals ; praise Him upon
> the cymbals of shouting (cl. 3, 4, 5).

These instruments denote the goods and the truths
of faith which were the subjects of praise ; for
let no one suppose that so many different instruments would have been here mentioned unless
each had a distinct signification. Again :

> O send out Thy light and Thy truth, let them
> lead me, let them bring me unto the mountain
> of Thy holiness, and to Thy habitations, and I
> will go in to the altar of God, unto God, the
> gladness of my exultation ; yea, I will confess
> unto Thee upon the harp, O God, my God
> (*Ps.* xliii. 3, 4).

In *Isaiah*, referring to the things that belong to 5
faith, and the cognitions thereof :

> Take a harp, go about the city, play well, sing
> many songs, that thou mayest be called to
> remembrance (xxiii. 16).

The same is expressed still more plainly in *John* :

> The four animals and the four and twenty
> elders fell down before the Lamb, having every

one of them harps, and golden vials full of incense offerings, which are the prayers of the saints (*Rev.* v. 8).

Here it must be evident to every one that the animals and elders had not harps, but that by " harps " are signified the truths of faith, and by " golden vials full of incense offerings," the goods of faith. In *David* the performances on the instruments are called " praises " and " confessions " (*Ps.* xlii. 5 ; lxix. 31). And in another place in *John* :

I heard a voice from heaven as the voice of many waters, and I heard the voice of harpers harping with their harps, and they sang a new song (*Rev.* xiv. 2, 3).

And in another place :

I saw them standing by the sea of glass having the harps of God (*Rev.* xv. 2).

It is worthy of mention that angels and spirits distinguish sounds according to their differences with respect to good and truth, not only those produced in singing and by instruments, but also those of voices ; and they admit none but such as are in accord, so that there may be a concord of the sounds, and consequently of the instruments, with the nature and essence of what is good and true.

421. Verse 22. **And Zillah, she also bare Tubal-Cain, an instructor of every artificer in brass and iron; and the sister of Tubal-Cain was Naamah.** By " Zillah " is signified, as previously stated, the mother of the natural things of the new church ; by " Tubal-Cain," an instructor of every artificer in brass and iron," the doctrine of natural good and truth, " brass " denoting natural good, and " iron "

natural truth. By " Naamah, the sister of Tubal-Cain," is signified a similar church, or the doctrine of natural good and truth outside of that church.

422. How the case was with this new church may be seen from the Jewish Church, which was both internal and external ; the internal church consisting of celestial and spiritual things, and the external church of natural things. The internal church was represented by Rachel, and the external by Leah. But as Jacob, or rather his posterity understood by " Jacob " in the Word, were such as to desire only external things, or worship in externals, therefore Leah was given to Jacob before Rachel ; and by blear-eyed Leah was represented the Jewish Church, and by Rachel a new church of the Gentiles. For this reason " Jacob " is taken in both senses in the Prophets, in one denoting the Jewish Church in its perverted state, and in the other the true external church of the Gentiles. When the internal church is signified, he is called " Israel " ; but of these matters, by the Divine mercy of the Lord, more will be said hereafter.

423. Tubal-Cain is called the " instructor of every artificer," and not the " father," as was the case with Jabal and Jubal ; and the reason is that previously there were no celestial and spiritual or internal things. And the term " father " is applied to Jabal and Jubal, to denote that such internal things then first began to exist ; whereas natural or external things did exist before, but were now applied to internal things, so that Tubal-Cain is not called the " father," but the " instructor, of every artificer."

263

424. By an " artificer " in the Word is signified
a wise, intelligent, and well-informed man, and
here by " every artificer in brass and iron " are
signified those who are acquainted with natural
good and truth. As in *John* :

With violence shall that great city Babylon be
thrown down, and shall be found no more at all.
And the voice of harpers, and musicians, and
of pipers, and trumpeters, shall be heard no more
at all in her ; and no artificer, of whatsoever
craft, shall be found any more in her (*Rev.*
xviii. 21, 22).

" Harpers " here as above signify truths ; " trumpeters," the goods of faith ; an " artificer of any
craft," one who knows, or the knowledge of truth
and good. In *Isaiah* :

The artificer melteth a graven image, and the
smelter spreadeth it over with gold, and casteth
silver chains ; he seeketh unto him a wise
artificer, to prepare a graven image that shall
not be moved (xl. 19, 20).

This treats of those who from phantasy forge for
themselves what is false—a " graven image "—
and teach it so that it appears true. In *Jeremiah* :

At the same time as they are infatuated they
grow foolish, the doctrine of vanities, it is but a
stock. Silver beaten out is brought from Tarshish, and gold from Uphaz, the work of the
artificer, and of the hands of the smelter ; blue
and raiment ; they are all the work of the wise
(x. 1, 8, 9).

This signifies one who teaches falsities, and collects
from the Word things with which to forge his
invention, wherefore it is called a " doctrine of

vanities," and the "work of the wise." Such persons were represented in ancient times by artificers who forge idols, that is, falsities, which they adorn with gold, that is, with a semblance of good ; and with silver, or an appearance of truth ; and with blue and with raiment, or such natural things as are in apparent agreement.

425. It is unknown to the world at the present day that "brass" signifies natural good, and also that every metal mentioned in the Word has a specific signification in the internal sense—as "gold," celestial good ; "silver," spiritual truth ; "brass," natural good ; "iron," natural truth ; and so on with the other metals, and in like manner "wood" and "stone." Such things were signified by the "gold," "silver," "brass," and "wood," used in the ark and in the tabernacle and in the temple, concerning which, of the Lord's Divine mercy, we will treat hereafter. That such is their signification is manifest from the Prophets, as from *Isaiah* :

> Thou shalt also suck the milk of the Gentiles, and shalt suck the breast of kings. For brass I will bring gold, and for iron I will bring silver, and for wood brass, and for stones iron ; I will also make thy tribute peace, and thine exactors righteousness (lx. 16, 17).

This treats of the Lord's advent, of His kingdom, and of the celestial church. "For brass gold," signifies for natural good celestial good ; "for iron silver," signifies for natural truth spiritual truth ; "for wood brass," signifies for corporeal good natural good ; "for stones iron," signifies for sensuous truth natural truth. In *Ezekiel* :

> Javan, Tubal, and Meshech, these were thy

1*   265

merchants, in the soul of man, and vessels of
brass they gave thy trading (xxvii. 13).

This treats of Tyre, by which are signified those
who possess spiritual and celestial riches ; " vessels
of brass " are natural goods.   In *Moses* :

A land whose stones are iron, and out of whose
mountains thou mayest hew brass (*Deut*. viii. 9).

Here also " stones " denote sensuous truth ;
" iron," natural, that is, rational truth ;   and
" brass," natural good.   Ezekiel saw

Four living creatures, or cherubs, whose feet
sparkled like the appearance of burnished brass
(i. 7).

Here again " brass " signifies natural good, for
the " foot " of man represents what is natural.
In like manner there appeared to *Daniel*,

A man clothed in linen, whose loins were
girded with gold of Uphaz, his body also was
like the beryl, and his arms and his feet like
the appearance of burnished brass (x. 5, 6).

That the " brazen serpent " (*Num*. xxi. 9) represented the sensuous and natural good of the Lord,
may be seen above.

426. That " iron " signifies natural truth, is
further evident from what *Ezekiel* says of Tyre :

Tarshish was thy trader by reason of the
multitude of all riches ; in silver, iron, tin, and
lead, they gave thy traffickings.   Dan, and
Javan, and Meusal furnished bright iron in thy
tradings ;   cassia and calamus were in thy
market (xxvii. 12, 19).

From these words, as well as from what is said
both previously and subsequently in the same

chapter, it is very evident that celestial and spiritual riches are signified ; and that every particular expression, and even the names mentioned, have some specific signification, for the Word of the Lord is spiritual, and not verbal. In *Jeremiah* : 2

> Can one break iron, even iron from the north, and brass ? Thy substance and thy treasures will I give for a spoil without price, and this for all thy sins (xv. 12, 13).

Here " iron " and " brass " signify natural truth and good ; that it came from the " north," signifies what is sensuous and natural ; for what is natural, relatively to what is spiritual and celestial, is like thick darkness (that is, the " north ") relatively to light or the " south " ; or like shade, which is also signified here by " Zillah," who is the " mother." That the " substance " and " treasures " are celestial and spiritual riches, is also very evident. Again in *Ezekiel* : 3

> Take thou unto thee a pan of iron, and set it for a wall of iron between thee and the city, and set thy faces toward it, and let it be for a siege, and thou shalt lay siege against it (iv. 3).

Here also it is evident that " iron " signifies truth. Strength is attributed to truth, because it cannot be resisted, and for this reason it is said of iron—by which is signified truth, or the truth of faith—that it " breaks in pieces " and " crushes " ; as in *Daniel* (ii. 34, 40), and in *John* :

> He that overcometh, to him will I give sovereign **power** over the nations, that he may pasture them with a rod of iron ; as the vessels

of a potter shall they be broken to shivers
(*Rev.* ii. 26, 27).

Again :

The woman brought forth a man child, who
should pasture all nations with a rod of iron
(*Rev.* xii. 5).

4 That a " rod of iron " is the truth which is of the
Word of the Lord, is explained in *John* :

I saw heaven open, and behold a white horse,
and He that sat upon him was called Faithful and
True, and in righteousness He doth judge and
fight ; He was clothed with a vesture dipped in
blood, and His name is called the Word of God ;
out of His mouth goeth a sharp sword, that with
it He should smite the nations ; and He shall
pasture them with a rod of iron (*Rev.* xix. 11,
13, 15).

427. Verse 23. **And Lamech said unto his
wives, Adah and Zillah, Hear my voice, ye wives of
Lamech, and with your ears perceive my speech;
for I have slain a man to my wounding, and a little
one to my hurt.** By " Lamech " is signified vastation, as before ; that he " said unto his wives
Adah and Zillah, With your ears perceive my
speech," signifies confession, which can be made
only where there is a church, which, as has been
said, is signified by his " wives." " I have slain
a man to my wounding," signifies that he had
extinguished faith, for by a " man " is signified
faith ; " a little one to my hurt," signifies that
he had extinguished charity. By a " wound " and
a " hurt " is signified that there was no more
soundness ; by a " wound," that faith was desolated ; by a " hurt," that charity was devastated.

428. From the contents of this and the following verse, it is very evident that by " Lamech " is signified vastation ; for he says that he had " slain a man," and a " little child," and that Cain should be avenged sevenfold, and Lamech " seventy and sevenfold."

429. That by a " man (*vir*) " is signified faith, is evident from the first verse of this chapter, in that Eve said, when she bare Cain, " I have gotten a man, Jehovah " ; by whom was meant the doctrine of faith, called a " man, Jehovah." It is evident also from what was shown above concerning a man or male, that he signifies understanding, which is of faith. That he had also extinguished charity, here called a " little one," or a " little child," follows, for he who denies and murders faith, at the same time also denies and murders the charity that is born from faith.

430. A " little one," or " little child," in the Word, signifies innocence, and also charity, for true innocence cannot exist without charity, nor true charity without innocence. There are three degrees of innocence, distinguished in the Word by the terms " sucklings," " infants," and " little children " ; and as there is no true innocence without true love and charity, therefore also by " sucklings," " infants," and " little children," are signified the three degrees of love : namely, tender love, like that of a suckling towards its mother or nurse ; love like that of an infant towards its parents ; and charity, similar to that of a little child towards its instructor. Thus it is said in *Isaiah* :

The wolf shall dwell with the lamb, and the leopard shall lie down with the kid ; and the

269

calf, and the young lion, and the fatling together,
and a little child shall lead them (xi. 6).

Here a " lamb," a " kid," and a " calf," signify
the three degrees of innocence and love ; a " wolf,"
a " leopard," and a " young lion," their opposites ;
and a " little child," charity. In *Jeremiah* :

> Ye commit this great evil against your souls,
> to cut off from you man and wife, infant and
> suckling, out of the midst of Judah, to leave you
> no remains (xliv. 7).

" Man and wife " denote things of the understanding and of the will, or of truth and of good ; and
" infant and suckling," the first degrees of love.
That an " infant " and a " little child " denote
innocence and charity, is very evident from the
Lord's words in *Luke* :

> They brought unto Him little children that He
> should touch them. And Jesus said, Suffer little
> children to come unto Me, and forbid them not,
> for of such is the kingdom of God. Verily I say
> unto you, Whosoever shall not receive the king-
> dom of God as a little child, shall in no wise enter
> therein (xviii. 15, 17).

The Lord Himself is called a " little one," or
" child " (*Isa.* ix. 6), because He is innocence itself
and love itself, and in the same passage He is
spoken of as " Wonderful, Counsellor, God, Hero,
Father of Eternity, Prince of Peace."

431. That by a " wound " and a " hurt " is
signified that there was soundness no longer, by a
" wound " that faith was desolated, and by a
" hurt " that charity was devastated, is evident
from the fact that " wound " is predicated of a
" man," and " hurt " of a " little one." The

desolation of faith and the vastation of charity
are described in the same terms in *Isaiah* :

From the sole of the foot even unto the head
there is no soundness in it ; but wound and
hurt and a fresh sore ; they have not been pressed
out, neither bound up, neither mollified with
oil (i. 6).

In this passage " wound " is predicated of faith
desolated, " hurt " of charity devastated, and
" sore " of both.

432. Verse 24. **If Cain shall be avenged sevenfold, truly Lamech seventy and sevenfold.** These
words signify that they had extinguished the
faith meant by " Cain," to do violence to which
was sacrilege, and at the same time had extinguished the charity which should be born through
faith, a far greater sacrilege, and that for this there
was condemnation, that is, a " seventy and sevenfold vindication."

433. That Cain's being " avenged sevenfold "
signifies that it was sacrilege to do violence to that
separated faith which is meant by " Cain," has
been already shown at verse 15. And that by a
" seventy and sevenfold vindication " is signified
a far greater sacrilege, the consequence of which is
damnation, is evident from the signification of
" seventy and sevenfold." That the number
" seven " is holy, originates in the fact that the
" seventh day " signifies the celestial man, the
celestial church, the celestial kingdom, and, in the
highest sense, the Lord Himself. Hence the
number " seven," wherever it occurs in the Word,
signifies what is holy, or most sacred ; and this
holiness and sanctity is predicated of, or according

to, the things that are being treated of. From this comes the signification of the number " seventy," which comprises seven ages ; for an age, in the Word, is ten years. When anything most holy or sacred was to be expressed, it was said " seventy and sevenfold," as when the Lord said that a man should forgive his brother not until seven times, but until seventy times seven (*Matt.* xviii. 22), by which is meant that they should forgive as many times as he sins, so that the forgiving should be without end, or should be eternal, which is holy. And here, that Lamech should " be avenged seventy and sevenfold " means damnation, because of the violation of that which is most sacred.

434. Verse 25. **And the man (*homo*) knew his wife again, and she bare a son, and called his name Seth; for God hath appointed me another seed instead of Abel, for Cain slew him.** The " man " and his " wife " here mean the new church signified above by " Adah and Zillah " ; and by her " son," whose name was Seth, is signified a new faith, by which charity might be obtained. By " God appointed another seed instead of Abel, whom Cain slew," is signified that charity, which Cain had separated and extinguished, was now given by the Lord to this church.

435. That the " man " and his " wife " here mean the new church signified above by Adah and Zillah no one could know or infer from the literal sense, because the " man and his wife " had previously signified the Most Ancient Church and its posterity ; but it is very evident from the internal sense, as well as from the fact that immediately afterwards, in the following chapter (v. 1–4), the man and his wife, and their begetting Seth, are

again mentioned, but in entirely different words, and in this case there is signified the first posterity of the Most Ancient Church. If nothing else were signified in the passage before us, there would be no need to say the same thing here : in like manner as in the first chapter the creation of man, and of the fruits of the earth, and of the beasts, is treated of, and then in the second chapter they are treated of again, for the reason, as has been said, that in the first chapter it is the creation of the spiritual man that is treated of, whereas in the second chapter the subject is the creation of the celestial man. Whenever there is such a repetition in the mention of one and the same person or thing, it is always with a difference of signification, but what it is that is signified cannot possibly be known except from the internal sense. Here, the connection itself confirms the signification that has been given, and there is the additional consideration that man (*homo*) and wife are general terms which signify the parent church that is in question.

436. That by her " son," whom she named Seth, is signified a new faith, by which charity may be attained, is evident from what has been previously stated, as well as from its being related of Cain that a " mark was set upon him, lest any one should slay him." For the subject as it stands in a series is as follows : Faith separated from love was signified by " Cain " ; charity, by " Abel " ; and that faith in its separated state extinguished charity, was signified by Cain slaying Abel. The preservation of faith in order that charity might be thereby implanted by the Lord, was signified by Jehovah's setting a mark on Cain lest any one should slay him. That afterwards the holiness of

273

love and the good thence derived were given by
the Lord through faith, was signified by Jabal
whom Adah bare ; and that the spiritual of faith
was given, was signified by his brother Jubal ;
and that from these there came natural good and
truth was signified by Tubal-Cain whom Zillah
bare. In these two concluding verses of *Genesis* iv.
we have the conclusion, and thus the summary, of
all these matters, to this effect, that by the " man
and his wife " is signified that new church which
before was called Adah and Zillah, and that by
" Seth " is signified the faith through which charity
is implanted ; and in the verse which now follows,
by " Enosh " is signified the charity that is
implanted through faith.

437. That " Seth " here signifies a new faith,
through which comes charity, is explained by his
name, which it is said was given him because God
" appointed another seed instead of Abel, whom
Cain slew." That God " appointed another seed "
means that the Lord gave another faith ; for
" another seed " is the faith through which comes
charity. That " seed " signifies faith, may be
seen above (n. 255).

438. Verse 26. **And to Seth, to him also there
was born a son ; and he called his name Enosh ;
then began they to call upon the name of Jehovah.**
By " Seth " is signified the faith through which
comes charity, as was said above ; by his " son,"
whose name was " Enosh," is signified a church
which regarded charity as the chief thing of faith ;
by beginning then to " call on the name of Jehovah,"
is signified the worship of that church from charity.

439. That by " Seth " is signified the faith
through which comes charity, was shown in the

preceding verse. That by his " son, whose name was Enosh," is signified a church that regarded charity as the chief thing of faith, is also evident from what has been said before, as well as from the fact that it is called " Enosh," which name also means a " man," not a celestial man, but that human spiritual man which is here called " Enosh." The same is evident also from the words that immediately follow : " then began they to call upon the name of Jehovah."

440. That by the words just quoted is signified the worship of that church from charity, is evident from the fact that to " call upon the name of Jehovah " is a customary and general form of speech for all worship of the Lord ; and that this worship was from charity is evident from the fact that " Jehovah " is here mentioned, whereas in the preceding verse He was called " God," as well as from the fact that the Lord cannot be worshipped except from charity, since true worship cannot proceed from faith that is not of charity, because it is merely of the lips, and not of the heart. That to " call on the name of Jehovah " is a customary form of speech for all worship of the Lord, appears from the Word ; thus it is said of Abraham, that " he built an altar to Jehovah, and called on the name of Jehovah " (*Gen.* xii. 8 ; xiii. 4) ; and again, that he " planted a grove in Beer-sheba, and called there on the name of Jehovah, the God of eternity" (*Gen.* xxi. 33). That this expression includes all worship, is plain from *Isaiah* :

Jehovah the Holy One of Israel hath said, Thou hast not called upon Me, O Jacob, but thou hast been weary of Me, O Israel. Thou hast not brought to Me the small cattle of thy burnt-

offerings, neither hast thou honoured Me with
thy sacrifices. I have not caused thee to serve
with an offering, nor wearied thee with incense
(xliii. 22, 23).

In this passage a summary is given of all representative worship.

441. That the invocation of the name of Jehovah
did not commence at this time, is sufficiently
evident from what has already been said above
in regard to the Most Ancient Church, which
more than any other adored and worshipped the
Lord ; and also from the fact that Abel brought
an offering of the firstlings of the flock ; so that
in this passage by " calling upon the name of
Jehovah," nothing is signified but the worship of
the new church, after the former church had been
extinguished by those who are called " Cain "
and " Lamech."

442. From the contents of this chapter, as
above explained, it is evident that in the most
ancient time there were many doctrines and
heresies separate from the church, each one of
which had its name, and that these separate
doctrines and heresies were the outcome of much
more profound thought than any at the present day,
because such was the genius of the men of that time.

***

SOME EXAMPLES DRAWN FROM EXPERIENCE WITH
SPIRITS CONCERNING WHAT THEY HAD THOUGHT
ABOUT THE SOUL OR SPIRIT DURING THEIR LIFE IN
THE BODY.

443. In the other life it is granted to perceive
clearly what opinions people had entertained while

they lived in the body concerning the soul, the spirit, and the life after death ; for when kept in a state resembling that of the body they think in the same way, and their thought is communicated as plainly as if they spoke aloud. In the case of one person, not long after his decease, I perceived (he himself confessed it) that he had indeed believed in the existence of the spirit, but had imagined that it must live after death an obscure kind of life, because if the life of the body were withdrawn there would remain nothing but what was dim and obscure ; for he had regarded life as being in the body, and therefore he had thought of the spirit as being a phantom ; and he had confirmed himself in this idea from seeing that brutes also have life, almost as men have it. He now marvelled that spirits and angels live in the greatest light, and in the greatest intelligence, wisdom, and happiness, attended with a perception so perfect that it can scarcely be described ; consequently that their life, so far from being obscure, is most perfectly clear and distinct.

444. Conversing with one who while he lived in this world had believed that the spirit has no extension, and on that ground would admit of no word that implied extension, I asked him what he now thought of himself, seeing that now he was a soul or spirit, and possessed sight, hearing, smell, an exquisite sense of touch, desires, thoughts, insomuch that he supposed himself to be exactly as if in the body. He was kept in the idea which he had when he had so thought in the world, and he said that the spirit is thought. I was permitted to ask him in reply, whether, having lived in the world, he was not aware that there can be no

277

bodily sight without an organ of vision or eye ? and how then can there be internal sight, or thought ? Must it not have some organic substance from which to think ? He then acknowledged that while in the bodily life he had laboured under the delusion that the spirit is mere thought, devoid of everything organic or extended. I added that if the soul or spirit were mere thought, man would not need so large a brain, seeing that the whole brain is the organ of the interior senses ; for if it were not so the skull might be hollow, and the thought still act in it as the spirit. From this consideration alone, as well as from the operation of the soul into the muscles, giving rise to so great a variety of movements, I said that he might be assured that the spirit is organic, that is, an organic substance. Whereupon he confessed his error, and wondered that he had been so foolish.

445. It was further remarked, that the learned have no other belief than that the soul which is to live after death, that is, the spirit, is abstract thought. This is very manifest from their unwillingness to admit of any term that implies extension and what belongs to extension, because thought abstractedly from a subject has no extension, whereas the subject of the thought, and the objects of the thought, have extension ; and as for those objects which have no extension, men define them by boundaries and give extension to them, in order that they may comprehend them. This shows very clearly that the learned have no other conception of the soul or spirit than that it is mere thought, and so cannot but believe that it will vanish when they die.

278

446. I have discoursed with spirits concerning the common opinion that prevails among men at the present day, that the existence of the spirit is not to be credited because they do not see it with their eyes, nor comprehend it by their knowledges, and so they not only deny that the spirit has extension, but also that it is a substance, disputing as to what substance is. And as they deny that it has extension, and also dispute about substance, they also deny that the spirit is in any place, and, consequently, that it is in the human body ; and yet the most simple might know that his soul or spirit is within his body. When I said these things, the spirits, who were some of the more simple ones, marvelled that the men of the present day are so foolish. And when they heard the words that are disputed about such as " parts without parts," and other such terms, they called them absurd, ridiculous, and farcical, that should not occupy the mind at all, because they close the way to intelligence.

447. A certain novitiate spirit, on hearing me speak about the spirit, asked, " What is a spirit ? " supposing himself to be a man. And when I told him that there is a spirit in every man, and that in respect to his life a man is a spirit ; that the body is merely to enable a man to live on the earth, and that the flesh and bones, that is, the body, does not live or think at all ; seeing that he was at a loss, I asked him whether he had ever heard of the soul. " What is a soul ? " he replied, " I do not know what a soul is." I was then permitted to tell him that he himself was now a soul, or spirit, as he might know from the fact that he was over my head, and was not standing on the earth. I asked him whether he could not perceive

this, and he then fled away in terror, crying out,
" I am a spirit ! I am a spirit ! "

A certain Jew supposed himself to be living
wholly in the body, insomuch that he could scarcely
be persuaded to the contrary. And when he was
shown that he was a spirit, he still persisted in
saying that he was a man, because he could see
and hear. Such are those who, during their abode
in this world, have been devoted to the body.

To these examples very many more might be
added, but these have been given merely in order
to confirm the fact, that it is the spirit in man, and
not the body, which exercises sensation.

448. I have conversed with many who had been
known to me in this life (and this I have done for
a long time—for months and years), in as clear a
voice, although an inward one, as with friends in
this world. The subject of our conversation has
sometimes been the state of man after death, and
they have wondered exceedingly that during the
bodily life no one knows or believes that he is so to
live when the bodily life is over, when yet there is
then a continuation of life, and such a continuation that the man passes from an obscure life into
a clear one, and those who are in faith in the Lord
into a life that is more and more clear. They have
desired me to tell their friends that they are alive,
and to write and tell them what their condition is,
even as I had related to themselves many things
about that of their friends here. But I replied
that were I to tell their friends such things, or to
write to them about them, they would not believe,
but would call them delusions, would scoff at them,
and would ask for signs or miracles before they
would believe ; and I should merely expose myself

to their derision. And that these things are true, perchance but few will believe. For at heart men deny the existence of spirits, and even those who do not deny it are unwilling to hear that any one can speak with spirits. In ancient times there was no such state of belief in regard to spirits, but so it is now when by wild reasoning men try to find out what spirits are, and by their definitions and suppositions deprive them of all the senses, and do this the more, the more learned they desire to be.

CHAPTER THE FIFTH.

CONCERNING HEAVEN AND HEAVENLY JOY.

449. Hitherto, the nature of heaven and of heavenly joy has been known to none. Those who have thought about them have formed an idea concerning them so general and so gross as scarcely to amount to any idea at all. What notion they have conceived on the subject I have been able to learn most accurately from spirits who had recently passed from the world into the other life ; for when left to themselves, as if they were in this world, they think in the same way. I may give a few examples.

450. Some who during their abode in this world had seemed to be pre-eminently enlightened in regard to the Word, had conceived so false an idea about heaven that they supposed themselves to be in heaven when they were high up, and imagined that from that position they could rule all things below, and thus be in self-glory and pre-eminence over others. On account of their being in such a phantasy, and in order to show them that they were in error, they were taken up on high, and from there were permitted in some measure to rule over things below ; but they discovered with shame that this was a heaven of phantasy, and that heaven does not consist in being on high, but is wherever there is any one who is in love and charity, or in whom is the Lord's kingdom ; and that neither does it consist in desiring to be more eminent than others, for to desire to be greater than others is not heaven, but hell.

451. A certain spirit, who during his life in the body had possessed authority, retained in the other life the desire to exercise command. But he was told that he was now in another kingdom, which is eternal ; that his rule on earth was dead ; and that where he was now no one is held in estimation except in accordance with the good and truth, and the mercy of the Lord, in which he is ; and further, that it is in that kingdom as it is on earth, where every one is rated according to his wealth, and his favour with his sovereign ; and that there good and truth are wealth, and favour with the sovereign is the Lord's mercy ; and that if he desired to exercise command in any other way, he was a rebel, seeing that he was now in the kingdom of Another. On hearing this he was ashamed.

452. I have conversed with spirits who supposed heaven and heavenly joy to consist in being the greatest. But they were told that in heaven he is greatest who is least, because he who would be the least has the greatest happiness, and, consequently, is the greatest, for what is it to be the greatest except to be the most happy ? It is this that the powerful seek by power, and the rich by riches. They were told, further, that heaven does not consist in desiring ˙ ꞁ be the least in order to be the greatest, for in that case the person really aspires and wishes to be the greatest ; but that heaven consists in this, that from the heart we wish better for others than for ourselves, and desire to be of service to others in order to promote their happiness, and this for no selfish end, but from love.

453. Some entertain so gross an idea of heaven that they suppose it to be mere admission, in fact

that it is a room into which they are admitted
through a door, which is opened, and then they
are let in by the doorkeepers.

454. Some think that heaven consists in a life
of ease, in which they are served by others ; but
they are told that there is no possible happiness
in being at rest as a means of happiness, for so
every one would wish to have the happiness of
others made contributory to his own happiness ;
and when every one wished this, no one would have
happiness. Such a life would not be an active life,
but an idle one, in which they would grow torpid,
and yet they might know that there is no happiness
except in an active life. Angelic life consists in
use, and in the goods of charity ; for the angels
know no greater happiness than in teaching and
instructing the spirits that arrive from the world ;
in being of service to men, controlling the evil
spirits about them lest they pass the proper
bounds, and inspiring men with good ; and in
raising up the dead to the life of eternity, and then,
if the souls are such as to render it possible, intro-
ducing them into heaven. From all this they
perceive more happiness than can possibly be
described. Thus are they images of the Lord ;
thus do they love the neighbour more than
themselves ; and for this reason heaven is heaven.
So that angelic happiness is in use, from use, and
according to use, that is, it is according to the goods
of love and of charity. When those who have the
idea that heavenly joy consists in living at ease,
idly breathing in eternal joy, have heard these
things, they are given to perceive, in order to
shame them, what such a life really is, and they
perceive that it is a most sad one, that it is

destructive of all joy, and that after a short time they would loathe and nauseate it.

455. One who in this world had been very learned in regard to the Word, had the idea that heavenly joy consists in being in a glorious light, like that which exists when the solar rays appear of a golden hue, so that he too supposed it to consist in a life of ease. In order that he might know himself to be in error, such a light was granted him, and he, being in the midst of light, was as delighted as if he were in heaven, as indeed he said. But he could not remain long in it, for it gradually wearied him and became no joy at all.

456. The best instructed of them all said that heavenly joy consists solely in praising and glorifying the Lord, being a life destitute of any doing of the goods of charity, and that this is an active life. But they were told that praising and celebrating the Lord is not such an active life as is meant, but is an effect of that life; for the Lord has no need of praises, but wills that they should do the goods of charity, and that it is according to these that they will receive happiness from the Lord. But still these best instructed persons could form no idea of joy, but of servitude, in doing these goods of charity. But the angels testified that such a life is the freest of all, and that it is conjoined with happiness unutterable.

457. Almost all who pass from this world into the other life suppose that hell is the same for every one, and that heaven is the same for every one. And yet in both there are endless diversities and varieties, and neither the heaven nor the hell of one person is ever exactly like that of another;

just as no man, spirit, or angel is ever exactly like another. When I merely thought of there being two exactly alike or equal, horror was excited in the inhabitants of the world of spirits and of the angelic heaven, and they said that every unit is formed by the harmony of many components, and that such as is the harmony, such is the one, and that it is impossible for anything to subsist that is absolutely a one, but only a one that results from a harmony of component parts. Thus every society in the heavens forms a one, and so do all the societies together, that is, the universal heaven, and this from the Lord alone, through love. A certain angel enumerated the most universal only of the genera of the joys of spirits, that is, of the first heaven, to about four hundred and seventy-eight, from which we may infer how innumerable must be the less universal genera and the species in each genus. And as there are so many in that heaven, how illimitable must be the kinds of happiness in the heaven of angelic spirits, and still more so in the heaven of angels !

458. Evil spirits have sometimes supposed that there is another heaven besides that of the Lord, and they have been permitted to seek for it wherever they could, but to their confusion they could never find any other heaven. For evil spirits rush into insanities both from the hatred they bear to the Lord, and from their infernal suffering, and catch at such phantasies.

459. There are three heavens : the first is the abode of good spirits ; the second, of angelic spirits ; and the third, of angels. Spirits, angelic spirits, and angels are all distinguished into the celestial and the spiritual. The celestial are those

who through love have received faith from the Lord, like the men of the Most Ancient Church treated of above. The spiritual are those who through cognitions of faith have received charity from the Lord, and who act from what they have received.

A continuation of this subject will follow at the end of this chapter.

CHAPTER V.

1. This is the book of the generations of Man. In the day that God created Man, in the likeness of God made He him.

2. Male and female created He them, and blessed them, and called their name Man, in the day when they were created.

3. And Man lived a hundred and thirty years, and begat into his likeness, after his image, and called his name Seth.

4. And the days of Man after he begat Seth were eight hundred years ; and he begat sons and daughters.

5. And all the days that Man lived were nine hundred and thirty years ; and he died.

6. And Seth lived a hundred and five years, and begat Enosh.

7. And Seth lived after he begat Enosh eight hundred and seven years, and begat sons and daughters.

8. And all the days of Seth were nine hundred and twelve years ; and he died.

9. And Enosh lived ninety years, and begat Kenan.

10. And Enosh lived after he begat Kenan eight hundred and fifteen years ; and begat sons and daughters.

287

11. And all the days of Enosh were nine hundred and five years ; and he died.

12. And Kenan lived seventy years, and begat Mahalalel.

13. And Kenan lived after he begat Mahalalel eight hundred and forty years, and begat sons and daughters.

14. And all the days of Kenan were nine hundred and ten years ; and he died.

15. And Mahalalel lived sixty and five years, and begat Jared.

16. And Mahalalel lived after he begat Jared eight hundred and thirty years, and begat sons and daughters.

17. And all the days of Mahalalel were eight hundred ninety and five years ; and he died.

18. And Jared lived a hundred sixty and two years, and begat Enoch.

19. And Jared lived after he begat Enoch eight hundred years, and begat sons and daughters.

20. And all the days of Jared were nine hundred sixty and two years ; and he died.

21. And Enoch lived sixty and five years, and begat Methuselah.

22. And Enoch walked with God after he begat Methuselah three hundred years, and begat sons and daughters.

23. And all the days of Enoch were three hundred sixty and five years.

24. And Enoch walked with God, and he was no more, for God took him.

25. And Methuselah lived a hundred eighty and seven years, and begat Lamech.

26. And Methuselah lived after he begat Lamech seven hundred eighty and two years, and begat sons and daughters.

27. And all the days of Methuselah were nine hundred sixty and nine years ; and he died.

28. And Lamech lived a hundred eighty and two years, and begat a son ;

29. And he called his name Noah, saying, He shall comfort us from our work, and the toil of our hands, out of the ground which JEHOVAH hath cursed.

30. And Lamech lived after he begat Noah five hundred ninety and five years, and begat sons and daughters.

31. And all the days of Lamech were seven hundred seventy and seven years ; and he died.

32. And Noah was a son of five hundred years ; and Noah begat Shem, Ham, and Japheth.

THE CONTENTS.

460. This chapter treats specifically of the propagation of the Most Ancient Church through successive generations, almost to the flood.

461. The Most Ancient Church itself, which was celestial, is what is called " Man " (*homo*), and a " likeness of God " (verse 1).

462. A second church which was not so celestial as the Most Ancient Church, is called " Seth " (verses 2, 3).

463. A third church was called " Enosh " (verse 6) ; a fourth " Kenan " (verse 9) ; a fifth " Mahalalel " (verse 12) ; a sixth " Jared " (verse 15) ; a seventh " Enoch " (verse 18) ; and an eighth church " Methuselah " (verse 21).

464. The church called " Enoch " is described as framing doctrine from what was revealed to,

and perceived by, the Most Ancient Church, which doctrine, although of no use at that time, was preserved for the use of posterity. This is signified by its being said that " Enoch was no more, because God took him " (verses 22, 23, 24).

465. A ninth church was called " Lamech " (verse 25).

466. A tenth, the parent of three churches after the flood, was named " Noah." This church is to be called the Ancient Church (verses 28, 29).

467. " Lamech " is described as retaining nothing of the perception which the Most Ancient Church enjoyed ; and " Noah " is described as a new church (verse 29).

THE INTERNAL SENSE.

468. From what has been said and shown in the foregoing chapter, it is evident that by names are signified heresies and doctrines. Hence it may be seen that by the names in this chapter are not meant persons, but things, and in the present instance doctrines, or churches, which were preserved, notwithstanding the changes they underwent, from the time of the Most Ancient Church even to " Noah." But the case with every church is that in course of time it decreases, and at last remains among a few ; and the few with whom it remained at the time of the flood were called 2 " Noah." That the true church decreases and remains with but few, is evident from other churches which have thus decreased. Those who are left are in the Word called " remains," and a " remnant," and are said to be " in the midst," or " middle," " of the land." And as this is the case

in the universal, so also it is in the particular ; or
as it is with the church, so it is with every individual man ; for unless remains were preserved
by the Lord in every one, he must needs perish
eternally, since spiritual and celestial life are in the
remains. So also in the general or universal—if
there were not always some with whom the church,
or true faith, remained, the human race would
perish ; for, as is generally known, a city, nay,
sometimes a whole kingdom, is saved for the sake of
a few. It is in this respect with the church as it is
with the human body ; so long as the heart is
sound, life is possible for the neighbouring viscera,
but when the heart is enfeebled, the other parts of
the body cease to be nourished, and the man dies.
The last remains are those which are signified by
" Noah " ; for (as appears from verse 12 of the
following chapter, as well as from other places) the
whole earth had become corrupt. Of remains as 3
existing in each individual as well as in the church in
general, much is said in the Prophets ; as in *Isaiah* :

He that is left in Zion, and he that remaineth
in Jerusalem, shall be called holy to Him, even
every one that is written unto lives in Jerusalem,
when the Lord shall have washed the filth of
the daughters of Zion, and shall have washed
away the bloods of Jerusalem from the midst
thereof (iv. 3, 4).

In this passage holiness is predicated of the remains,
by which are signified the remains of the church,
and also of a man of the church ; for " those left "
in Zion and Jerusalem could not be holy merely
because they were " left." Again :

It shall come to pass in that day, that the
remains of Israel, and such as are escaped of the

291

house of Jacob, shall no more again stay upon
him that smote them, but shall stay upon
Jehovah the Holy One of Israel in truth. The
remains shall return, the remains of Jacob, unto
the mighty God (x. 20, 21).

In *Jeremiah* :

In those days, and in that time, the iniquity
of Israel shall be sought for, and there shall be
none ; and the sins of Judah, and they shall not
be found ; for I will pardon him whom I shall
make a remnant (l. 20).

In *Micah* :

The remains of Jacob shall be in the midst of
many peoples, as the dew from Jehovah, as the
showers upon the grass (v. 7).

4 The residue or remains of a man, or of the church,
were also represented by the tenths, which were
holy ; hence also a number with ten in it was holy,
and " ten " is therefore predicated of remains ;
as in *Isaiah* :

Jehovah shall remove man, and many things
[shall be] left in the midst of the land ; and yet
in it [shall be] a tenth part, and it shall return,
and shall be for exterminating ; as an oak, and
an ilex, when a stem is cast forth from them, the
seed of holiness is the stem thereof (vi. 12, 13).

Here the residue is called a " seed of holiness."

And in *Amos* :

Thus saith the Lord Jehovih, The city that
goeth forth a thousand shall have a hundred left,
and that which goeth forth a hundred shall have
ten left to the house of Israel (v. 3).

In these and many other passages, in the internal
sense, are signified the " remains " of which we

have been speaking. That a city is preserved for the sake of the remains or the church, is evident from what was said to Abraham concerning Sodom :

Abraham said, Peradventure ten may be found there ; and He said, I will not destroy it for ten's sake (*Gen.* xviii. 32).

469. Verse 1. **This is the book of the generations of Man. In the day that God created Man, in the likeness of God made He him.** The " book of the generations," is an enumeration of those who were of the Most Ancient Church ; " in the day that God created Man," denotes his being made spiritual ; and " in the likeness of God made He him," signifies that he was made celestial : thus it is a description of the Most Ancient Church.

470. That the " book of the generations " is an enumeration of those who were of the Most Ancient Church, is very evident from what follows, for from this to the eleventh chapter, that is, to the time of Eber, names never signify persons, but actual things. In the most ancient time mankind were distinguished into houses, families, and nations ; a house consisting of the husband and wife with their children, together with some of their family who served ; a family of a greater or smaller number of houses, that lived not far apart and yet not together ; and a nation, of a larger or smaller number of families.

471. The reason why they dwelt thus alone by themselves, distinguished only into houses, families, and nations, was that by this means the church might be preserved entire, that all the houses and families might be dependent on their parent, and thereby remain in love and in true worship. It

293

is to be remarked also that each house was of a peculiar genius, distinct from every other ; for it is well known that children, and even remote descendants, derive from their parents a particular genius, and such marked characteristics that they can be distinguished by the face, and by many other peculiarities. Therefore, in order that there might not be a confounding, but an exact distinction, it pleased the Lord that they should dwell in this manner. Thus the church was a living representative of the kingdom of the Lord ; for in the Lord's kingdom there are innumerable societies, each one distinct from every other, according to the differences of love and faith. This, as observed above, is what is meant by " living alone," and by " dwelling in tents." For the same reason also it pleased the Lord that the Jewish Church should be distinguished into houses, families, and nations, and that every one should contract marriage within his own family ; but concerning this, of the Lord's Divine mercy, we will treat hereafter.

472. That by the " day in which God created Man," is signified his being made spiritual, and that by " God making him in His likeness," is signified his being made celestial, appears from what was said and shown above. The expression to " create " properly relates to man when he is being created anew, or regenerated ; and the word " make," when he is being perfected ; wherefore in the Word there is an accurate distinction observed between " creating," " forming," and " making," as was shown above in the second chapter, where it is said of the spiritual man made celestial that " God rested from all His work, which God created in making " ; and in other passages also, to " create " relates to the spiritual man, and to " make," that is, to perfect, to the celestial man. (See n. **16**, and 88.)

473. That a " likeness of God " is a celestial man, and an " image of God," a spiritual man, has also been previously shown. An " image " is preparatory to a " likeness," and a " likeness " is a real resemblance, for a celestial man is entirely governed by the Lord, as His " likeness."

474. Since, therefore, the subject here treated of is the birth or propagation of the Most Ancient Church, this is first described as coming from a spiritual to a celestial state, for the propagations follow from this.

475. Verse 2. **Male and female created He them, and blessed them, and called their name Man, in the day when they were created.** By " male and female," is signified the marriage between faith and love ; by " calling their name Man," is signified that they were the church, which, in an especial sense, is called " Man " (*homo*).

476. That by " male and female " is signified the marriage between faith and love was declared and proved above, where it was shown that the male or man (*vir*) signifies the understanding and whatever belongs to it, consequently everything of faith ; and that the female or woman signifies the will, or the things pertaining to the will, consequently whatever has relation to love ; wherefore, she was called Eve, a name signifying life, which is of love alone. By the female therefore is also signified the church, as has been previously shown ; and by the male, a man (*vir*) of the church. The subject here is the state of the church when it was

spiritual, and which was afterwards made celestial, wherefore " male " is mentioned before " female," as also in Chapter I, 26, 27. The expression to " create " also has reference to the spiritual man ; but afterwards when the marriage has been effected, that is, when the church has been made celestial, it is not said " male and female," but " man " (*homo*), who, by reason of their marriage, signifies both ; wherefore it presently follows, " and He called their name Man," by which is signified the church.

477. That " Man " is the Most Ancient Church has been often said and shown above ; for in the highest sense the Lord Himself alone is Man. From this the celestial church is called Man, as being a likeness, and from this the spiritual church is afterwards so called because it was an image. But in a general sense every one is called a man who has human understanding ; for man is man by virtue of understanding, and according thereto one person is more a man than another, although the distinction of one man from another ought to be made according to his faith as grounded in love to the Lord. That the Most Ancient Church, and every true church, and hence those who belong to the church, or who live from love to the Lord and from faith in Him, are especially called " man," is evident from the Word, as in *Ezekiel* :

I will cause man to multiply upon you, all the house of Israel, all of it ; I will cause to multiply upon you man and beast, that they may be multiplied and bear fruit ; and I will cause you to dwell according to your antiquities ; and I will do better unto you than at your beginnings ; and I will cause man to walk upon you, My people Israel (xxxvi. 10, 11, 12).

Here by " antiquities " is signified the Most Ancient Church ; by " beginnings," the Ancient Churches ; by the " house of Israel " and " people Israel," the primitive church, or Church of the Gentiles ; all which churches are called " Man." So in *Moses* :   3

Remember the days of eternity, understand ye the years of generation and generation ; when the Most High would give the nations an inheritance, when He would set apart the sons of man, He set the bounds of the peoples according to the number of the sons of Israel (*Deut.* xxxii. 7, 8).

Here by the " days of eternity " is meant the Most Ancient Church ; by " generation and generation," the Ancient Churches ; the " sons of man " are those who were in faith towards the Lord, which faith is the " number of the sons of Israel." That a regenerate person is called " man," appears from *Jeremiah* :

I beheld the earth, and lo it was empty and void ; and the heavens, and they had no light ; I beheld, and lo, no man, and all the birds of the heavens were fled (iv. 23, 25).

Here " earth " signifies the external man ; " heaven " the internal ; " man " the love of good ; the " birds of the heavens " the understanding of truth. Again :   4

Behold the days come that I will sow the house of Israel, and the house of Judah, with the seed of man, and with the seed of beast (xxxi. 27).

Here " man " signifies the internal man, " beast " the external. In *Isaiah* :

Cease ye from man in whose nostrils is breath, for wherein is he to be accounted of (ii. 22).

Here by " man " is signified a man of the church.
Again :

> Jehovah shall remove man far away, and
> many things shall be left in the midst of the
> land (vi. 12).

This treats of the vastation of man, so that there
should no longer exist either good or truth. Again :

> The inhabitants of the earth shall be burned,
> and man shall be left very little (xxiv. 6).

Here " man " signifies those who have faith.
Again :

> The paths have been desolated, the farer on
> the path hath ceased, he hath made vain the
> covenant, he hath despised the cities, he hath
> not regarded man, the earth mourneth and lan-
> guisheth (xxxiii. 8, 9).

This denotes the man who in the Hebrew tongue
is " Enosh." Again :

> I will make a man more precious than· fine
> gold, and a man than the gold of Ophir ; there-
> fore I will shake the heavens, and the earth shall
> be moved out of her place (xiii. 12, 13).

Here the word for man in the first place is " Enosh,"
and in the second is " Adam."

478. The reason why he is called " Adam " is
that the Hebrew word " Adam " signifies " man " ;
but that he is never properly called " Adam " by
name, but " Man," is very evident from this passage
and also from former ones, so that [in some cases]
he is not spoken of in the singular number, but
in the plural, and also from the fact that the term
is predicated of both the man and the woman, both
together being called " Man." That it is predicated
of both, every one may see from the words, for it

is said, " He called their name Man, in the day
that they were created " ; and in like manner in
the first chapter : " Let us make man in our
image, and let them have dominion over the fish
of the sea " (27, 28).   Hence also it is evident that
the subject treated of is not the creation of some
one man who was the first of mankind, but the
Most Ancient Church.

479. By "calling a name," or "calling by
name." is signified in the Word to know the quality
of things, as was shown above, and in the present
case it has relation to the quality of the Most
Ancient Church, denoting that man was taken
from the ground, or regenerated by the Lord, for
the word " Adam " means " ground " ; and that
afterwards, when he was made celestial, he became
most eminently " Man," by virtue of faith originating in love to the Lord.

480. That they were called " Man " in the day
that they were created, appears also from the first
chapter (verses 26, 27), that is, at the end of the
sixth day, which answers to the evening of the
sabbath, or when the sabbath or seventh day
began ; for the seventh day, or sabbath, is the
celestial man, as was shown above.

481. Verse 3. **And Man lived a hundred and
thirty years, and begat into his likeness, after his
image, and called his name Seth.** By a " hundred
and thirty years " there is signified the time before
the rise of a new church, which, being not very
unlike the Most Ancient, is said to be born " into
its likeness, and after its image " ; but the term
" likeness " has relation to faith, and " image " to
love. This church was called " Seth."

482. What the "years," and the "numbers of years," which occur in this chapter, signify in the internal sense, has hitherto been unknown. Those who abide in the literal sense suppose them to be secular years, whereas from this to the twelfth chapter there is nothing historical according to its appearance in the literal sense, but all things in general and every single thing in particular contain other matters. And this is the case not only with the names, but also with the numbers. In the Word frequent mention is made of the number three, and also of the number seven, and wheresoever they occur they signify something holy or most sacred in regard to the states which the times or other things involve or represent ; and they have the same signification in the least intervals of time as in the greatest, for as the parts belong to the whole, so the least things belong to the greatest, for there must be a likeness in order that the whole may properly come forth from the parts, or the greatest from the least parts. Thus in *Isaiah* :

Now hath Jehovah spoken, saying, Within three years, as the years of a hireling, and the glory of Moab shall be rendered worthless (xvi. 14).

Again :

Thus hath the Lord said unto me, Within a year, according to the years of a hireling, and all the glory of Kedar shall be consumed (xxi. 16).

Here both the least and the greatest intervals are signified. In *Habakkuk* :

Jehovah, I have heard Thy renown, and was afraid ; O Jehovah, revive Thy work in the midst of the years, in the midst of the years make known (iii. 2).

Here the " midst of the years " signifies the Lord's
advent. In lesser intervals it signifies every coming
of the Lord, as when man is being regenerated ;
in greater, when the church of the Lord is arising
anew. (It is likewise called the " year of the
redeemed," in *Isaiah* :

> The day of vengeance is in My heart, and the
> year of My redeemed is come (lxiii. 4).

So also the thousand years in which Satan was to
be bound (*Rev.* xx. 2, 7), and the thousand years of
the first resurrection (*Rev.* xx. 4, 5, 6), by no means
signify a thousand years, but their states ; for as
" days " are used to express states, as shown above,
so also are " years," and the states are described
by the number of the years. Hence it is evident
that the times in this chapter also involve states ;
for every church was in a different state of perception from the rest, according to the differences
of disposition, hereditary and acquired.

483. By the names which follow : " Seth,"
" Enosh,"   " Kenan,"   " Mahalalel," " Jared,"
" Enoch," " Methuselah," " Lamech," " Noah,"
are signified so many churches, of which the first
and principal was called " Man." The chief
characteristic of these churches was perception,
wherefore the differences of the churches of that
time were chiefly differences of perception. I may
here mention concerning perception, that in the
universal heaven there reigns nothing but a perception of good and truth, which is such as cannot
be described, with innumerable differences, so
that no two societies enjoy similar perception ;
the perceptions there existing are distinguished into
genera and species, and the genera are innumerable, and the species of each genus are likewise

301

innumerable : but concerning these, of the Lord's
Divine mercy, we will treat hereafter. Since then
there are innumerable genera, and innumerable
species in each genus, and still more innumerable
varieties in the species, it is evident how little—so
little that it is almost nothing—the world at this
day knows concerning things celestial and spiritual,
since they do not know even what perception is,
and if they are told, they do not believe that any
such thing exists ; and so with other things also.
The Most Ancient Church represented the celestial
kingdom of the Lord, even as to the generic and
specific differences of perception ; but whereas
the nature of perception, even in its most general
aspect, is at this day utterly unknown, any account
of the genera and species of the perceptions of
these churches would necessarily appear dark and
strange.   At that time they were distinguished
into houses, families, and nations, and contracted
marriage within their houses and families, in
order that genera and species of perceptions might
exist, and be derived from the parents precisely
as are the propagations of native character ; wherefore those who were of the Most Ancient Church
dwell together in heaven.

484. That the church called " Seth " was very
nearly like the Most Ancient Church, is evident
from its being said that the man begat in his
likeness, according to his image, and called his
name Seth ; the term " likeness " having relation
to faith, and " image " to love ; for that this
church was not like the Most Ancient Church with
regard to love and its derivative faith, is plain
from its being said just before, " Male and female
created He them, and blessed them, and called

their name Man," by which is signified the spiritual
man of the sixth day, as was said above, so that
the likeness of this man was to the spiritual man
of the sixth day, that is, love was not so much the
principal, but still faith was conjoined with love.

485. That a different church is here meant by
" Seth " from that which was described above
(iv. 25), may be seen at n. 435. That churches of
different doctrine were called by the same name,
is evident from those which in the foregoing chapter
(verses 17 and 18) were called " Enoch " and
" Lamech," while here other churches are in like
manner called " Enoch " and " Lamech " (verses
21, 30).

486. Verse 4. **And the days of Man after he
begat Seth were eight hundred years, and he begat
sons and daughters.** By " days " are signified
times and states in general; by " years," times and
states in particular ; by " sons and daughters " are
signified the truths and goods which they perceived.

487. That by " days " are signified times and
states in general, was shown in the first chapter,
where the " days " of creation have no other
signification. In the Word it is very usual to call
all time " days," as is manifestly the case in the
present verse, and in those which follow (5, 8, 11,
14, 17, 20, 23, 27, 31) ; and therefore the states of
the times in general are likewise signified by
" days " ; and when " years " are added, then
by the seasons of the years are signified the qualities of the states, thus states in particular. The
most ancient people had their numbers, by which
they signified various things relating to the church,
as the numbers " three," " seven," " ten,"
" twelve," and many that were compounded of

303

these and others, whereby they described the
states of the church ; wherefore these numbers
contain arcana which would require much time to
explain.　It was an account or reckoning of the
states of the church.　The same thing occurs in
many parts of the Word, especially the prophetical.　In the rites of the Jewish Church also
there were numbers, both of times and measures,
as for instance in regard to the sacrifices, meat-
offerings, oblations, and other things, which
everywhere signify holy things, according to their
application.　The things here involved, therefore,
in the number " eight hundred," and in the next
verse, in the number " nine hundred and thirty,"
and in the numbers of years in the verses following
—namely, the changes of state of their church as
applied to their own general state—are too many
to be recounted.　In a future part of this work, of
the Lord's Divine mercy, we shall take occasion
to show what the simple numbers up to " twelve "
signify, for until the signification of these is known,
it would be impossible to apprehend the signification of the compound numbers.

488. That " days " signify states in general,
and " years " states in particular, appears from
the Word, as in *Ezekiel* :

Thou hast caused thy days to draw near, and
art come even unto thy years (xxii. 4).

This treats of those who commit abominations,
and fill up the measure of their sins, of whose state
in general are predicated " days," and in particular
" years."　So in *David* :

Thou shalt add days to the days of the king,
and his years as of generation and generation
(*Ps.* lxi. 6).

This treats of the Lord and of His kingdom, where also " days " and " years " signify the state of His kingdom. Again :

I have considered the days of old, the years of the ages (*Ps.* lxxvii. 5).

Here " days of old " signify states of the Most Ancient Church, and " years of the ages," states of the Ancient Church. In *Isaiah* :

The day of vengeance is in My heart, and the year of My redeemed is come (lxiii. 4).

This treats of the last times, where the " day of vengeance " signifies a state of damnation, and the " year of the redeemed " a state of blessedness. Again :

To proclaim the acceptable year of the Lord, and the day of vengeance of our God ; to comfort all that mourn (lxi. 2).

Here both " days " and " years " signify states. In *Jeremiah* :

Renew our days as of old (*Lam.* v. 21).

Here state is plainly meant. In *Joel* :   2

The day of Jehovah cometh, for it is nigh at hand, a day of darkness and of thick darkness, a day of cloud and of obscurity ; there hath not been ever the like, neither shall be after it, even to the years of generation and generation (ii. 1, 2).

Here " day " signifies a state of darkness and of thick darkness, of cloud and of obscurity, with each one in particular, and with all in general. In *Zechariah* :

I will remove the iniquity of that land in one day ; in that day shall ye cry a man to his companion under the vine, and under the fig-tree (iii. 9, 10).

And in another place :

> It shall be one day which is known to Jehovah,
> not day nor night, and it shall come to pass that
> at evening time it shall be light (xiv. 7).

Here it is plain that state is meant, for it is said
that there shall be a day that is "neither day nor
night, at evening time it shall be light." The same
appears from expressions in the Decalogue :

> Honour thy father and thy mother, that thy
> days may be prolonged, and that it may be
> well with thee upon the ground (*Deut.* v.
> 16 ; xxv. 15).

3 Here to have the "days prolonged" does not
signify length of life, but a happy state. In the
literal sense it must needs appear as if "day"
signifies time, but in the internal sense it signifies
state. The angels, who are in the internal sense,
do not know what time is, for to them the sun and
moon are not for the distinguishing of time ;
consequently they do not know what days and
years are, but only what states are and the changes
thereof ; and therefore before the angels, who are
in the internal sense, everything relating to matter,
space, and time disappears, as in the literal sense
of this passage in *Ezekiel* :

> The day is near, even the day of Jehovah is
> near, a day of cloud ; it shall be the time of the
> nations (xxx. 3).

And of this in *Joel* :

> Alas for the day ! for the day of Jehovah is
> at hand, and as vastation shall it come (i. 15).

Here a "day of cloud" signifies a cloud, or falsity ;
the "day of the nations" signifies the nations, or
wickedness ; the "day of Jehovah" signifies
vastation. When the notion of time is removed,

there remains the notion of the state of the things
which existed at that time. The case is the same
with regard to the " days " and " years " that
are so often mentioned in this chapter.

489. That by " sons and daughters " are signified
the truths and goods of which they had a perception, and indeed by " sons " truths, and by
" daughters " goods, is evident from many
passages in the Prophets ; for in the Word, as
also in olden time, the conceptions and births of
the church are called " sons and daughters," as
in *Isaiah* :

The Gentiles shall come to thy light, and kings
to the brightness of thy rising ; lift up thine eyes
round about and see ; all they gather themselves
together and come to thee ; thy sons shall come
from far, and thy daughters shall be nursed at
thy side ; then thou shalt see and flow together,
and thy heart shall be amazed, and shall be
enlarged (lx. 3, 4, 5).

In this passage " sons " signify truths, and
" daughters " goods. In *David* : 2

Deliver me and rescue me from the hand of
the sons of the stranger, whose mouth speaketh
vanity ; that our sons may be as plants grown
up in their youth, that our daughters may be
as corner-stones hewn in the form of a temple
(*Ps.* xliv. 11, 12).

Here the " sons of the stranger " signify spurious
truths, or falsities ; " our sons " signify doctrinals
of truth ; " our daughters," doctrinals of good.
In *Isaiah* : 3

I will say to the north, Give up, and to the
south, Keep not back ; bring My sons from far,

and My daughters from the ends of the earth ;
bring forth the blind people, and they shall
have eyes ; the deaf, and they shall have ears
(xliii. 6, 8).

In this passage " sons " signify truths ; " daughters," goods ; the " blind," those who would see
truths ; and the " deaf," those who would obey
4 them. In *Jeremiah* :

Shame hath devoured the labour of our fathers
from our youth ; their flocks, their herds, their
sons, and their daughters (iii. 24).

Here " sons " and " daughters " signify truths
and goods. That " children " and " sons " signify
truths, is plain from *Isaiah* :

Jacob shall not now be ashamed, neither shall
his face now wax pale ; for when he shall see
his children the work of. My hands in the midst
of him, they shall sanctify My name, and shall
sanctify the Holy One of Jacob, and shall fear
the God of Israel ; they also that erred in spirit
shall know understanding (xxix. 22, 23, 24).

Here the " Holy One of Jacob, the God of Israel,"
signifies the Lord ; " children " signify the
regenerate, who have the understanding of good
5 and truth, as is indeed explained. Again :

Sing, O barren, thou that didst not bear, for
more are the sons of the desolate than the sons
of the married wife (liv. 1).

Here the " sons of the desolate " signify the truths
of the primitive Church, or that of the Gentiles ;
the " sons of the married wife," the truths of the
6 Jewish Church. In *Jeremiah* :

My tent is laid waste and all My cords are
plucked out ; My sons are gone forth of Me, and
are not (x. 20).

Here " sons " signify truths. Again :

His sons shall be as aforetime, and their congregation shall be established before Me (xxx. 20).

Here " sons " signify the truths of the Ancient
Church. In *Zechariah* :

I will stir up thy sons, O Zion, with thy sons,
O Javan, and make thee as the sword of a
mighty man (ix. 13).

This signifies the truths of the faith of love.

490. In the Word " daughters " frequently
denote goods ; as in *David* :

Kings' daughters were among thy precious
ones ; at thy right hand doth stand the queen
in the best gold of Ophir ; the daughter of Tyre
with a gift ; the king's daughter is all glorious
within ; of eyelet work of gold is her raiment ;
instead of thy fathers shall be thy sons (*Ps.*
xiv. 10–17).

Here the good and beauty of love and faith are
described by the " daughter."   Hence churches
are called " daughters " by virtue of goods, as the
" daughter of Zion " and the " daughter of Jerusalem " (*Isa.* xxxvii. 22, and in many other places) ;
they are also called " daughters of My people "
(*Isa.* xxii. 4), the " daughter of Tarshish " (*Isa.*
xxiii. 10), the " daughter of Sidon " (verse 12),
and " daughters in the field " (*Ezek.* xxvi. 6, 8).

491. The same things are signified by " sons "
and " daughters " in this chapter (verses 4, 7, 10,
13, 16, 19, 26, 30), but such as is the church, such
are the " sons and daughters," that is, such are
the goods and truths ; the truths and goods here
spoken of are such as were distinctly perceived,
because they are predicated of the Most Ancient

Church, the principal and parent of all the other and succeeding churches.

492. Verse 5. **And all the days that Man lived were nine hundred and thirty years, and he died.** By " days " and " years " are here signified times and states, as above ; by " Man's dying " is signified that such perception no longer existed.

493. That by " days " and " years " are signified times and states needs no further explanation, except to say that in the world there must needs be times and measures, to which numbers may be applied because they are in the ultimates of nature ; but whenever they are applied in the Word, the numbers of the days and years, and also of the measures, have a signification abstractedly from the times and measures, in accordance with the signification of the number ; as where it is said that there are six days of labour, and that the seventh is holy, of which above ; that the jubilee should be proclaimed every forty-ninth year, and should be celebrated in the fiftieth ; that the tribes of Israel were twelve, and the apostles of the Lord the same ; that there were seventy elders, and as many disciples of the Lord ; and so in many other instances where the numbers have a special signification abstractedly from the things to which they are applied ; and when thus abstracted, then it is states that are signified by the numbers.

494. That he " died," signifies that there was no longer such perception, is evident from the signification of the word " die," which is, that a thing ceases to be such as it has been. Thus in *John* :

Unto the angel of the church in Sardis write, These things saith He that hath the seven

310

spirits, and the seven stars; I know thy works, that thou art said to live, but art dead; be watchful, and strengthen the things which remain, that are ready to die; for I have not found thy works perfect before God (*Rev.* iii. 1, 2).

In *Jeremiah* :

I will cast out thy mother that bare thee, into another country where ye were not begotten, and there shall ye die (xxii. 26).

Here " mother " signifies the church. For as we have said, the case with the church is that it decreases and degenerates, and loses its pristine integrity, chiefly by reason of the increase of hereditary evil, for every succeeding parent adds new evil to that which he has inherited. All the actual evil in the parents puts on a kind of nature, and when it often recurs, becomes natural to them, and is added to their hereditary evil, and is transmitted into their children, and so to posterity. In this way the hereditary evil is immensely increased in the descendants. That this is so is evident from the fact that the evil dispositions of children are exactly like those of their progenitors. Quite false is the opinion of those who think that there is no hereditary evil except that which they allege to have been implanted in us from Adam (see n. 313). The truth is that every one makes hereditary evil by his own actual sins, and adds it to the evils that he has inherited, and in this way it accumulates, and remains in all the descendants, nor is it abated except in those who are being regenerated by the Lord. In every church this is the principal cause of degeneration, and it was so in the Most Ancient Church.

495. How the Most Ancient Church decreased cannot appear unless it be known what perception is, for it was a perceptive church, such as at this day does not exist. The perception of a church consists in this, that its members perceive from the Lord what is good and true, like the angels; not so much what the good and truth of civic society is, but the good and truth of love to the Lord and of faith in Him. From a confession of faith that is confirmed by the life it can be seen what perception is, and whether it has any existence.

496. Verse 6. **And Seth lived a hundred and five years, and begat Enosh.** "Seth," as was observed, is a second church, less celestial than the Most Ancient Church, its parent, yet one of the most ancient churches; that he "lived a hundred and five years," signifies, as before, times and states; that he "begat Enosh," signifies that from them there descended another church that was called "Enosh."

497. That "Seth" is a second church less celestial than the Most Ancient Church, its parent, yet one of the most ancient churches, may appear from what was said above concerning Seth (verse 3). The case with churches, as we have said, is that by degrees, and in process of time, they decrease as to essentials, owing to the cause above mentioned.

498. That be "begat Enosh" signifies that from them there descended another church called "Enosh," is evident from the fact that in this chapter the names signify nothing else than churches.

499. Verses 7, 8. **And Seth lived after he begat Enosh eight hundred and seven years, and begat**

sons and daughters. And all the days of Seth were nine hundred and twelve years, and he died. The " days " and number of " years " signify here as before the times and states. " Sons and daughters " too have the same signification as before ; and so likewise has the statement that he " died."

500. Verse 9. **And Enosh lived ninety years, and begat Kenan.** By " Enosh," as before said, is signified a third church, still less celestial than the church " Seth," yet one of the most ancient churches ; by " Kenan " is signified a fourth church, which succeeded the former ones.

501. As regards the churches that in course of time succeeded one another, and of which it is said that one was born from another, the case with them was the same as it is with fruits, or with their seeds. In the midst of these, that is, in their inmost parts, there are as it were fruits of the fruits, or seeds of the seeds, from which live as it were in regular order the successive parts. For the more remote these are from the inmost towards the circumference, the less of the essence of the fruit or of the seed is there in them, until finally they are but the cuticles or coverings in which the fruits or seeds terminate. Or as in the case of the brain, in the inmost parts of which are subtle organic forms called the cortical substances, from which and by which the operations of the soul proceed ; and from which in regular order the purer coverings follow in succession, then the denser ones, and finally the general coverings called meninges, which are terminated in coverings still more general, and at last in the most general of all, which is the skull.

313

502. These three churches, " Man," " Seth," and " Enosh," constitute the Most Ancient Church, but still with a difference of perfection as to perceptions ; the perceptive faculty of the first church gradually diminished in the succeeding churches, and became more general, as observed concerning fruit or its seed, and concerning the brain. Perfection consists in the faculty of perceiving distinctly, which faculty is diminished when the perception is less distinct and more general ; an obscurer perception then succeeds in the place of that which was clearer, and thus it begins to vanish away.

503. The perceptive faculty of the Most Ancient Church consisted not only in the perception of what is good and true, but also in the happiness and delight arising from well-doing ; without such happiness and delight in doing what is good the perceptive faculty has no life, but by virtue of such happiness and delight it receives life. The life of love, and of the derivative faith, such as the Most Ancient Church enjoyed, is life while in the performance of use, that is, in the good and truth of use : from use, by use, and according to use, is life given by the Lord ; there can be no life in what is useless, for whatever is useless is cast away. In this respect the most ancient people were likenesses of the Lord, and therefore in perceptive powers they became images of Him. The perceptive power consists in knowing what is good and true, consequently what is of faith : he who is in love is not delighted in knowing, but in doing what is good and true, that is, in being useful.

504. Verses 10, 11. **And Enosh lived after he begat Kenan eight hundred and fifteen years, and**

314

begat sons and daughters. And all the days of Enosh were nine hundred and five years, and he died. Here in like manner the " days " and numbers of " years," and also " sons and daughters," and his " dying," signify like things.

505. " Enosh," as before observed, is a third church, yet one of the most ancient churches, but less celestial, and, consequently, less perceptive, than the church " Seth " ; and this latter was not so celestial and perceptive as the parent church, called " Man." These three are what constitute the Most Ancient Church, which, relatively to the succeeding ones, was as the kernel of fruits, or seeds, whereas the succeeding churches are relatively as the membranous parts of these.

506. Verse 12. **And Kenan lived seventy years, and begat Mahalalel.** By " Kenan " is signified a fourth church, and by " Mahalalel " a fifth.

507. The church called " Kenan " is not to be so much reckoned among those three more perfect ones, inasmuch as perception, which in the former churches had been distinct, began now to become general, comparatively as are the first and softer membranes relatively to the kernel of fruits or seeds ; which state is not indeed described, but still is apparent from what follows, as from the description of the churches called " Enoch " and " Noah."

508. Verses 13, 14. **And Kenan lived after he begat Mahalalel eight hundred and forty years, and begat sons and daughters. And all the days of Kenan were nine hundred and ten years, and he died.** The " days " and numbers of " years " have the same signification here as before. " Sons and

315

daughters" here also signify truths and goods, whereof the members of the church had a perception, but in a more general manner. That he "died" signifes in like manner the cessation of such a state of perception.

509. It is here only to be remarked, that all things are determined by their relation to the state of the church.

510. Verse 15. **And Mahalalel lived sixty and five years, and begat Jared.** By "Mahalalel" is signified, as before said, a fifth church; by "Jared" a sixth.

511. As the perceptive faculty decreased, and from being more particular or distinct, became more general or obscure, so also did the life of love or of uses; for as is the life of love or of uses, so is the perceptive faculty. From good to know truth is celestial; the life of those who constituted the church called "Mahalalel" was such that they preferred the delight from truths to the delight from uses, as has been granted me to know by experience among their like in the other life.

512. Verses 16, 17. **And Mahalalel lived after he begat Jared eight hundred and thirty years, and begat sons and daughters. And all the days of Mahalalel were eight hundred ninety and five years, and he died.** It is the same with these words as with the like words before.

513. Verse 18. **And Jared lived a hundred sixty and two years, and begat Enoch.** By "Jared," as before said, is signified a sixth church; by "Enoch" a seventh.

514. Concerning the church called "Jared" nothing is related; but its character may be known from the church "Mahalalel" which preceded it,

and the church " Enoch " which followed it, between which two it was intermediate.

515. Verses 19, 20. **And Jared lived after he begat Enoch eight hundred years, and begat sons and daughters. And all the days of Jared were nine hundred sixty and two years, and he died.** The signification of these words also is similar to that of the like words above. That the ages of the antediluvians were not so great, as that of Jared nine hundred and sixty-two years, and that of Methuselah nine hundred and sixty-nine years, must appear to every one, especially from what of the Lord's Divine mercy will be said at verse 3 of the next chapter, where we read, " Their days shall be a hundred and twenty years " ; so that the number of the years does not signify the age of any particular man, but the times and states of the church.

516. Verse 21. **And Enoch lived sixty and five years, and begat Methuselah.** By " Enoch," as before said, is signified a seventh church ; and by " Methuselah " an eighth.

517. The quality of the church " Enoch " is described in the following verses.

518. Verse 22. **And Enoch walked with God after he begat Methuselah three hundred years, and begat sons and daughters.** To " walk with God " signifies doctrine concerning faith. That he " begat sons and daughters " signifies doctrinal matters concerning truths and goods.

519. There were some at that time who framed doctrines from the things that had been matters of perception in the most ancient and succeeding churches. in order that such doctrine might serve

317

as a rule whereby to know what was good and
true : such persons were called " Enoch." This
is what is signified by the words, " and Enoch
walked with God " ;   and so did they call that
doctrine ; which is likewise signified by the name
" Enoch," which means to " instruct." The same
is evident also from the signification of the expression to " walk," and from the fact that he is said
to have " walked with God," not " with Jehovah " :
to " walk with God " is to teach and live according
to the doctrine of faith, but to " walk with Jehovah " is to live the life of love. To " walk " is a
customary form of speaking that signifies to live,
as to " walk in the law," to " walk in the statutes,"
to " walk in the truth." To " walk " has reference
properly to a way, which has relation to truth,
consequently to faith, or the doctrine of faith.
What is signified in the Word by " walking," may
in some measure appear from the following passages.
2 In *Micah* :

> He hath showed thee, O man, what is good, and
> what doth Jehovah require of thee, but to do
> judgment and the love of mercy, and to humble
> thyself by walking with thy God ? (vi. 8).

Here to " walk with God " signifies to live according
to the things here indicated ; here however it is
said " with God," while of Enoch another word is
used which signifies also " from with God," so
that the expression is ambiguous. In *David* :

> Thou hast delivered my feet from falling,
> that I may walk before God in the light of the
> living (*Ps.* lvi. 13).

Here to " walk before God " is to walk in the truth
of faith, which is the " light of the living." In
like manner in *Isaiah* :

318

The people that walk in darkness see a great light (ix. 1).

So the Lord says by *Moses*:

I will walk in the midst, and will be your God, and ye shall be My people (*Lev.* xxvi. 12).

This signifies that they should live according to the doctrine of the law. In *Jeremiah*:   3

They shall spread them before the sun, and the moon, and to the hosts of the heavens, whom they have loved, and whom they have served, and after whom they have walked, and whom they have sought (viii. 2).

Here a clear distinction is made between the things of love, and those of faith ; the things of love being expressed by " loving " and " serving " ; and those of faith by " walking " and " seeking." In all the prophetical writings every expression is used with accuracy, nor is one term ever used in the place of another. But to " walk with Jehovah," or " before Jehovah," signifies, in the Word, to live the life of love.

520. Verses 23, 24. **And all the days of Enoch were three hundred sixty and five years. And Enoch walked with God, and he was no more, for God took him.** By " all the days of Enoch being three hundred sixty and five years," is signified that they were few. By his " walking with God," is signified, as above, doctrine concerning faith. By " he was no more, for God took him," is signified the preservation of that doctrine for the use of posterity.

521. As to the words " he was no more, for God took him " signifying the preservation of that doctrine for the use of posterity, the case with Enoch, as already said, is that he reduced to

319

doctrine what in the Most Ancient Church had been a matter of perception, which in the time of that church was not allowable ; for to know by perception is a very different thing from learning by doctrine. Those who are in perception have no need to learn by formulated doctrine that which they know already. For example : he who knows how to think well, has no occasion to be taught to think by any rules of art, for in this way his faculty of thinking well would be impaired, as is the case with those who stick fast in scholastic dust. To those who learn by perception, the Lord grants to know what is good and true by an inward way ; but to those who learn from doctrine, know-ledge is given by an external way, or that of the bodily senses ; and the difference is like that between light and darkness. Consider also that the perceptions of the celestial man are such as to admit of no description, for they enter into the most minute and particular things, with all variety according to states and circumstances. But as it was foreseen that the perceptive faculty of the Most Ancient Church would perish, and that after-wards mankind would learn by doctrines what is true and good, or by darkness would come to light, it is here said that " God took him," that is, preserved the doctrine for the use of posterity.

522. The state and quality of the perception with those who were called " Enoch " have also been made known to me. It was a kind of general obscure perception without any distinctness ; for in such a case the mind determines its view outside of itself into the doctrinal things.

523. Verse 25. **And Methuselah lived a hundred eighty and seven years, and begat Lamech.** By

320

" Methuselah " is signified an eighth church, and by " Lamech " a ninth.

524. Nothing is mentioned concerning the quality of this church ; but that its perceptive faculty was general and obscure, is evident from the description of the church called " Noah " ; so that perfection decreased, and with perfection wisdom and intelligence.

525. Verses 26, 27. **And Methuselah lived after he begat Lamech seven hundred eighty and two years, and begat sons and daughters. And all the days of Methuselah were nine hundred sixty and nine years, and he died.** These words have a like signification.

526. Verse 28. **And Lamech lived a hundred eighty and two years, and begat a son.** By " Lamech " is here signified a ninth church, wherein the perception of truth and good was so general and obscure that it was next to none, so that the church was vastated. By the " son " is signified the rise of a new church.

527. That by " Lamech " is signified a church wherein the perception of truth and good was so general and obscure as to be next to none, consequently, a church vastated, appears from what was said in the preceding chapter, and from what follows in the next verse. " Lamech " in the preceding chapter has nearly the same signification as in this, namely, vastation (concerning which see verses 18, 19, 23, 24 of that chapter) ; and he who begat him is also called by nearly the same name, " Methusael," so that the things signified by the names are nearly the same. By " Methusael " and " Methuselah " is signified something that is about to die ; and by " Lamech " what is destroyed.

L   321

528. Verse 29. And he called his name Noah, saying, He shall comfort us from our work, and the toil of our hands, out of the ground which Jehovah hath cursed. By " Noah " is signified the Ancient Church. By " comforting us from our work and the toil of our hands, out of the ground which Jehovah hath cursed," is signified doctrine, whereby what had been perverted would be restored.

529. That by " Noah " is signified the Ancient Church, or the parent of the three churches after the flood, will appear from the following pages, where many things concerning Noah are treated of.

530. By the names in this chapter, as we have said, are signified churches, or what is the same, doctrines ; for the church exists and has its name from doctrine ; thus by " Noah " is signified the Ancient Church, or the doctrine that remained from the Most Ancient Church. How the case is with churches or doctrines has already been stated, namely, that they decline, until there no longer remains anything of the goods and truths of faith, and then the church is said in the Word to be vastated. But still remains are always preserved, or some with whom the good and truth of faith remain, although they are few ; for unless the good and truth of faith were preserved in these few, there would be no conjunction of heaven with mankind. As regards the remains that are in a man individually, the fewer they are the less can the things of reason and knowledge that he possesses be enlightened, for the light of good and truth flows in from the remains, or through the remains, from the Lord. If there were no remains

in a man he would not be a man, but much viler than a brute ; and the fewer remains there are, the less is he a man, and the more remains there are, the more is he a man. Remains are like some heavenly star, which, the smaller it is the less light it gives, and the larger, the more light. The few things that remained from the Most Ancient Church were among those who constituted the church called Noah ; but these were not remains of perception, but of integrity, and also of doctrine derived from the things of perception in the most ancient churches. Therefore a new church was now raised up by the Lord, which being of an entirely different genius from the most ancient churches, is to be called the Ancient Church—Ancient from the fact that it existed at the close of the ages before the flood, and during the first period after it. Of this church, by the Divine mercy of the Lord, more will be said hereafter.

531. That by " comforting us from our work and the toil of our hands, out of the ground which Jehovah hath cursed," is signified doctrine, whereby what had been perverted would be restored, will also appear, of the Lord's Divine mercy, in the following pages. By " work " is signified that they could not perceive what is true except with labour and distress. By the " toil of the hands out of the ground which Jehovah hath cursed," is signified that they could do nothing good. Thus is described " Lamech," that is, the vastated church. There is " work and labour of the hands " when, from themselves or from their proprium, men must seek out what is true and do what is good. That which comes of this is the " ground which Jehovah hath cursed," that is, nothing comes of

323

it but what is false and evil. (But what is signified
by " Jehovah cursing," may be seen above, n. 245.)
To " comfort " has reference to the " son," or
Noah, whereby is signified a new regeneration,
thus a new church, which is the Ancient Church.
By this church, or " Noah," is therefore likewise
signified rest, and comfort that comes from rest,
just as it was said of the Most Ancient Church that
it was the seventh day, in which the Lord rested.
(See n. 84 to n. 88.)

532. Verses 30, 31. **And Lamech lived after he
begat that Noah** (*illum Noachum*) **five hundred
ninety and five years, and begat sons and daughters.
And all the days of Lamech were seven hundred
seventy and seven years, and he died.** By
" Lamech," as before said, is signified the church
vastated. By " sons and daughters," are signified
the conceptions and births of such a church.

533. As nothing more is related concerning
Lamech than that he begat sons and daughters,
which are the conceptions and births of such a
church, we shall dwell no longer on the subject.
What the births were, or the " sons and daughters,"
appears from the church ; for such as is the church,
such are the births from it. Both the churches
called " Methuselah " and " Lamech " expired just
before the flood.

534. Verse 32. **And Noah was a son of five
hundred years; and Noah begat Shem, Ham, and
Japheth.** By " Noah," as has been said, is signified
the Ancient Church. By " Shem, Ham, and
Japheth " are signified three Ancient Churches,
the parent of which was the Ancient Church called
" Noah."

535. That the church called " Noah " is not to be numbered among the churches that were before the flood, appears from verse 29, where it is said that it should " comfort them from their work and the toil of their hands, out of the ground which Jehovah hath cursed." The " comfort " was that it should survive and endure. But concerning Noah and his sons, of the Lord's Divine mercy, we will treat hereafter.

536. As in the foregoing pages much has been said about the perception possessed by the churches that existed before the flood, and as at this day perception is a thing utterly unknown, so much so that some may imagine it to be a kind of continuous revelation, or to be something implanted in men ; others that it is merely imaginary, and others other things ; and as perception is the very Celestial itself given by the Lord to those who are in the faith of love, and as in the universal heaven there is perception of endless variety : therefore in order that there may be among men some conception of what perception is, of the Lord's Divine mercy, I may in the following pages describe the principal kinds of perception that exist in the heavens.

————

CONTINUATION CONCERNING HEAVEN AND
HEAVENLY JOY.

537. A certain spirit attached himself to my left side, and asked me whether I knew how he could get into heaven. I was permitted to tell him that admission into heaven belongs solely to the Lord, who alone knows what a man's quality is. Very many arrive from the world who make it their sole pursuit to get into heaven, being quite ignorant of what heaven is, and of what heavenly joy is,

that heaven is mutual love, and that heavenly joy is the derivative joy. Therefore, those who do not know this are first instructed about it by actual experience. For example, there was a certain spirit, newly arrived from the world, who in like manner longed for heaven, and, in order that he might perceive what the nature of heaven is, his interiors were opened so that he should feel something of heavenly joy. But as soon as he felt it he began to lament and to writhe, and begged to be delivered, saying that he could not live on account of the anguish ; and therefore his interiors were closed towards heaven, and in this way he was restored. From this instance we may see with what pangs of conscience and with what anguish those are tortured who are admitted even but a little way, if they are not prepared for it.

538. There were some who sought admission into heaven without knowing what heaven is. They were told that unless they were in the faith of love, to enter heaven would be as dangerous as going into a flame ; but still they sought for it. When they arrived at the first entrance court, that is to say, the lower sphere of angelic spirits, they were smitten so hard that they threw themselves headlong back, and in this way were taught how dangerous it is merely to approach heaven until prepared by the Lord to receive the affections of faith.

539. A certain spirit who during his life in the body had made light of adulteries, was in accordance with his desire admitted to the first threshold of heaven. As soon as he came there he began to suffer and to be sensible of his own cadaverous stench, until he could endure it no longer. It seemed to him that if he went any further he

326

should perish, and he was therefore cast down
to the lower earth, enraged that he should feel
such torment at the first threshold of heaven,
merely because he had arrived in a sphere that was
contrary to adulteries.   He is among the unhappy.

540. Almost all who come into the other life are
ignorant of the nature of heavenly happiness and
bliss, because they know not the nature and quality
of inward joy.   They form a conception of it
merely from the delights and joys of the body and
the world.   What they are ignorant of they suppose
to be nothing, the truth being that bodily and
worldly joys are relatively non-existent and foul.
In order, therefore, that those who are well disposed may learn and may know what heavenly
joy is, they are taken in the first place to paradises
that surpass every conception of the imagination
(concerning which, of the Lord's Divine mercy,
we will treat hereafter), and they suppose that
they have arrived in the paradise of heaven ; but
they are taught that this is not true heavenly
happiness, and are therefore permitted to experience interior states of joy which are perceived by
their inmost being.   They are then transported into
a state of peace, even to their inmost being, and
they confess that nothing of it is at all expressible
or conceivable.   And finally they are introduced
into a state of innocence, also to their inmost
feeling.   In this way are they permitted to learn
the nature of true spiritual and celestial good.

541. Certain spirits who were ignorant of the
nature of heavenly joy were unexpectedly taken
up into heaven after they had been brought into
such a state as to render this possible, that is to
say, a state in which their bodily things and fanciful

notions were lulled into quiescence. From there I heard one saying to me that now for the first time he felt how great is the joy in heaven, and that he had been very greatly deceived in having a different idea of it, but that now he perceived in his inmost being a joy immeasurably greater than he had ever felt in any bodily pleasure such as men are delighted with in the life of the body, and which he called foul.

542. Those who are taken up into heaven in order that they may know its quality either have their bodily things and fanciful notions lulled to quiescence—for no one can enter heaven with the bodily things and fanciful notions that they take with them from this world—or else they are surrounded by a sphere of spirits who miraculously temper such things as are impure, and that cause disagreement. With some the interiors are opened. In these and other ways they are prepared, according to their lives and the nature thereby acquired.

543. Certain spirits longed to know the nature of heavenly joy, and were, therefore, allowed to perceive their own inmost joy, to such a degree that they could bear no more ; and yet it was not angelic joy, being scarcely equal to the least angelic joy, as was given me to perceive by a communication of their joy. It was so slight as to be as it were chilly, and yet being their inmost joy they called it most heavenly. From this it was evident not only that there are degrees of joys, but also that the inmost of one scarcely approaches the outmost or middle of another, and that when any one receives his own inmost joy, he is in his heavenly joy, and cannot endure that which is still more interior, for it becomes painful.

544. Certain spirits who were admitted into the heaven of innocence of the first heaven spoke to me thence, and confessed that the state of joy and gladness was such as they never could have conceived any idea of. Yet this was only in the first heaven, and there are three heavens, and states of innocence in each, with their innumerable varieties.

545. But in order that I might know the nature and quality of heaven and of heavenly joy, frequently and for long periods I have been permitted by the Lord to perceive the delights of heavenly joys, so that as I know them from actual experience I can indeed know them, but can by no means describe them. However, in order to give some idea of it I may say that heavenly joy is an affection of innumerable delights and joys that form one general simultaneous joy, in which general joy, that is, in which general affection, there are harmonies of innumerable affections that do not come distinctly to perception, but obscurely, because the perception is very general. Yet I was permitted to perceive that there are things innumerable within it, in such order as can never be described, these innumerable things being such as flow from the order of heaven. Such order exists in the most minute things of the affection, all of which together are presented and perceived as a very general affection according to the capacity of him who is the subject of it. In a word, in every general joy or affection there are illimitable things ordinated in a most perfect form, and there is nothing that is not alive or that does not affect even the inmost things of our being, for heavenly joys proceed from inmost things. I perceived also that the joy and deliciousness came as if from

L*   329

the heart, and very softly diffused themselves through all the inmost fibres, and so into the congregated fibres, with such an inmost sense of delight that the fibre is as it were nothing but joy and deliciousness, and the whole derivative perceptive and sensitive sphere the same, being alive with happiness. In comparison with these joys the joy of bodily pleasures is like gross and pungent dust as compared with a pure and gentle breeze.

546. In order that I might know how the case is with those who desire to be in heaven and are not such that they can be there, once when I was in a heavenly society, an angel appeared to me as an infant with a chaplet of bright blue flowers about its head, and girded about the breast with wreaths of other colours. By this I was given to know that I was in a society where there was charity. Some well-disposed spirits were then admitted into the same society, who, the moment they entered, became much more intelligent, and spoke like angelic spirits. Afterwards, some were admitted who desired to be innocent from themselves, whose state was represented to me by an infant that vomited milk out of its mouth. Such is their state. Then some were admitted who supposed that they were intelligent from themselves, and their state was represented by their faces, which appeared sharp, but fair enough; and they seemed to wear a peaked hat from which a sharp point projected, but their faces did not appear to be of human flesh, but as if carved out and devoid of life. Such is the state of those who believe that they are spiritual from themselves, that is, able from themselves to have faith. Other spirits were admitted who could not remain there, but were dismayed, became distressed, and fled away.

CHAPTER THE SIXTH.

CONCERNING HEAVEN AND HEAVENLY JOY.

547. The souls who come into the other life are all ignorant of the nature of heaven and of heavenly joy. Very many suppose it to be a kind of joy into which any can be admitted no matter how they have lived, even those who have borne hatred against their neighbour and have passed their lives in adulteries, being quite unaware of the fact that heaven is mutual and chaste love, and that heavenly joy is the derivative happiness.

548. I have sometimes spoken with spirits fresh from the world concerning the state of eternal life, telling them how important it was for them to know who is the Lord of that kingdom, and what is the nature and form of its government, just as those in this world who go into another kingdom are especially interested to know who and of what sort is the king, what is the nature of the government, and many other things that belong to the kingdom ; and how much more should they be interested in this kingdom, where they are to live forever. I told them that the Lord alone rules both heaven and the universe, for He who rules the one must rule the other ; and that the kingdom in which they were now is the Lord's kingdom, the laws of which are eternal truths, all of which are based on the one great law that men shall love the Lord above all things and their neighbour as themselves, and now even more than themselves, for

331

if they would be as the angels this is what they must do. To all this they could make no reply because in their bodily life they had heard something of the kind, but had not believed it. They marvelled that there is such love in heaven, and that it is possible for any one to love his neighbour more than himself, seeing that they had heard that they were to love their neighbour as themselves. But they were instructed that in the other life all goods are immeasurably increased, and that the life in the body is such that men can go no further than loving the neighbour as themselves, because they are in the things of the body, but that when these are removed, the love becomes purer, and at last angelic, which consists in loving the neighbour more than themselves. The possibility of such love is evident from the conjugial love that exists with some persons, who would suffer death rather than let their married partner be injured ; and also from the love of parents for their children, in that a mother will endure starvation rather than see her infant hunger, and this even among birds and animals ; and likewise from sincere friendship, in that perils will be undergone for our friends ; and even from polite and feigned friendship, that would emulate real friendship in offering the better things to those to whom we wish well, making great professions even when they do not come from the heart. And finally its possibility is evident from the very nature of love, which finds its joy in being of service to others, not for the sake of self but for the love's own sake. But all this could not be comprehended by those who loved themselves more than others, and who in the bodily life had been greedy for gain, and least of all by the avaricious.

549. The angelic state is such that every one communicates his own bliss and happiness to others. For in the other life there is a most exquisite communication and perception of all the affections and thoughts, so that each person communicates his joy to all, and all to each, so that each one is, as it were, the centre of all. This is the heavenly form. And, therefore, the more there are who constitute the Lord's kingdom, the greater is the happiness, for it increases in proportion to the numbers, and this is why heavenly happiness is unutterable. There is this communication of all with each and of each with all when every one loves others more than himself. But if any one wishes better for himself than for others the love of self reigns, which communicates nothing to others from itself except the idea of self, which is very foul, and when this is perceived the person is at once banished and rejected.

550. Just as in the human body all things both in general and particular contribute to the general and individual uses of all the rest, so is it in the Lord's kingdom, which is constituted like a man, and in fact is called the Grand Man. In this way every one there contributes either more nearly or more remotely, and in many ways, to the happiness of all, and this in accordance with the order instituted and, consequently, maintained by the Lord alone.

551. From the universal heaven bearing relation to the Lord, and all there in both general and particular bearing relation to the Very and Only Being both in the universal as a whole and in its most individual constituents, there comes order, there comes union, there comes mutual love, and there

comes happiness ; for thus each person regards the welfare and happiness of all, and all that of each one.

552. That all the joy and happiness in heaven are from the Lord alone, has been shown me by many experiences, of which the following may be related. I saw that with the utmost diligence some angelic spirits were fashioning a lampstand with its lamps and flowers of the richest ornamentation in honour of the Lord. For an hour or two I was permitted to witness with what great pains they laboured to make everything about it beautiful and representative, they supposing that they were doing it of themselves. But to me it was given to perceive that of themselves they could devise nothing at all. At last after some hours they said that they had formed a very beautiful representative candelabrum in honour of the Lord, whereat they rejoiced from their very hearts. But I told them that of themselves they had devised and formed nothing at all, but the Lord alone for them. At first they would scarcely believe this, but being angelic spirits they were enlightened, and confessed that it was so. So it is with all other representative things, and with everything of affection and thought in both general and particular, and also with heavenly joys and felicities—even the very smallest of them is from the Lord alone.

553. Those who are in mutual love in heaven are continually advancing to the springtime of their youth, and to a more and more gladsome and happy spring the more thousands of years they live, and this with continual increase to eternity, according to the advance and degree of mutual love, charity, and faith. Those of the female sex who have died in old age and enfeebled with

years, and who have lived in faith in the Lord, in charity towards the neighbour, and in happy conjugial love with their husbands, after a succession of years come more and more into the bloom of youth and early womanhood, and into a beauty that surpasses all idea of beauty such as is ever perceptible to the natural sight ; for it is goodness and charity forming and presenting their own likeness, and causing the delight and beauty of charity to shine forth from every least feature of the countenance, so that they are the very forms of charity ; some have seen them and been amazed. The form of charity, as is seen to the life in the other world, is such that it is charity itself that portrays and is portrayed, and this in such a manner that the whole angel, and especially the face, is as it were charity, the charity both plainly appearing to the view and being perceived by the mind. When this form is beheld, it is unutterable beauty that affects with charity the very inmost life of the beholder's mind. Through the beauty of this form the truths of faith are presented to view in an image, and are even perceived from it. Such forms, or such beauties, do those become in the other life who have lived in faith in the Lord, that is, in the faith of charity. All the angels are such forms, with countless variety, and of such is heaven.

CHAPTER VI.

1. And it came to pass that man began to multiply himself upon the faces of the ground, and daughters were born unto them.

2. And the sons of God saw the daughters of

335

man that they were good; and they took to
themselves wives of all that they chose.

3. And Jehovah said, My spirit shall not reprove
man forever, for that he is flesh; and his days
shall be a hundred and twenty years.

4. There were Nephilim in the earth in those
days; and most especially after the sons of God
went in unto the daughters of man, and they bare
to them; the same became mighty men, who were
of old, men of renown.

5. And Jehovah saw that the evil of man was
multiplied on the earth, and that all the imagination of the thoughts of his heart was only evil
every day.

6. And it repented Jehovah that He had made
man on the earth, and it grieved Him at His heart.

7. And Jehovah said, I will destroy man whom I
have created, from upon the faces of the ground, both
man and beast, and creeping thing, and fowl of the
heavens; for it repenteth Me that I have made them.

8. And Noah found grace in the eyes of Jehovah.

THE CONTENTS.

554. The subject here treated of is the state of
the people before the flood.

555. That with man, where the church was,
lusts—which are the "daughters"—began to
reign.   Also that they conjoined the doctrinal
things of faith with their lusts, and thus confirmed
themselves in evils and falsities, which is signified
by "the sons of God taking to themselves wives of
the daughters of man" (verses 1, 2).

556. And whereas there were thus no remains of
good and truth left, it is foretold that man should

be differently formed, in order that he might have remains, which are " a hundred and twenty years " (verse 3).

557. Those who immersed the doctrinal things of faith in their lusts, and in consequence of this as well as of the love of self conceived dreadful persuasions of their own greatness in comparison with others, are signified by the " Nephilim " (verse 4).

558. In consequence of this there no longer remained any will or perception of good and truth (verse 5).

559. The mercy of the Lord is described by " repenting and grieving at heart " (verse 6). That they became such that their lusts and persuasions must needs prove fatal to them (verse 7). Therefore, in order that the human race might be saved, a new church should arise, which is " Noah " (verse 8).

THE INTERNAL SENSE.

560. Before proceeding further we may mention how the case was with the church before the flood. Speaking generally, it was as with succeeding churches, as with the Jewish Church before the Lord's advent, and the Christian Church after His advent, in that it had corrupted and adultered the knowledges of true faith; but specifically, as regards the man of the church before the flood, he in course of time conceived direful persuasions, and immersed the goods and truths of faith in foul lusts, insomuch that there were scarcely any remains in them. When they came into this state they were suffocated as if of themselves, for man cannot live without remains; for, as we have said, it is in the remains that the life of man is superior to that

337

of brutes. From remains, that is, through remains from the Lord, man is able to be as man, to know what is good and true, to reflect upon matters of every kind, and consequently to think and to reason; for in remains alone is there spiritual and celestial life.

561. But what are remains? They are not only the goods and truths that a man has learned from the Lord's Word from infancy, and has thus impressed on his memory, but they are also all the states thence derived, such as states of innocence from infancy; states of love towards parents, brothers, teachers, friends; states of charity towards the neighbour, and also of pity for the poor and needy; in a word, all states of good and truth. These states together with the goods and truths impressed on the memory, are called remains, which are preserved in man by the Lord and are stored up, entirely without his knowledge, in his internal man, and are completely separated from the things of man's proprium, that is, from evils and falsities. All these states are so preserved in man by the Lord that not the least of them is lost, as I have been granted to know from the fact that every state of a man, from his infancy to extreme old age, not only remains in the other life, but also returns, in fact his states return exactly as they were while he lived in this world. Not only do the goods and truths of memory thus remain and return, but also all states of innocence and charity. And when states of evil and falsity recur—for each and all of these, even the smallest, also remain and return—then these states are tempered by the Lord by means of the good states. From all this it is evident that if a man had no remains he

must necessarily be in eternal damnation. (See what was said before at n. 468.)

562. The people before the flood were such that at last they had almost no remains, because they were of such a genius that they were filled with direful and abominable persuasions concerning all things that occurred to them or came into their thought, so that they would not go back from them one whit ; for they were possessed with the most excessive love of self, and supposed themselves to be as gods, and that whatever they thought was Divine. No such persuasion has ever existed in any people before or since, for it is deadly or suffocating, and, therefore, in the other life the antediluvians cannot be with any other spirits, for when they are present they take away from them all power of thought by injecting their fearfully determined persuasions, not to mention other matters which, of the Lord's Divine mercy, shall be spoken of in what follows.

563. When such a persuasion takes possession of a man, it is like a glue which catches in its sticky embrace the goods and truths that otherwise would be remains, the result of which is that remains can no longer be stored up, and those which have been stored up can be of no use ; and, therefore, when these people arrived at the summit of such persuasion they became extinct of their own accord, and were suffocated by an inundation not unlike a flood ; and, therefore, their extinction is compared to a " flood," and also, according to the custom of the most ancient people, is described as one.

564. Verse 1. **And it came to pass that man began to multiply himself upon the faces of the ground, and daughters were born unto them.** By " man "

339

(*homo*) is here signified the race of mankind existing at that time. By the " faces of the ground " is signified all that tract where the church was. By " daughters " are here signified the things appertaining to the will of that man, consequently, lusts.

565. That by " man " is here signified the race of mankind existing at that time, and indeed a race which was evil or corrupt, appears from the following passages : " My spirit shall not reprove man forever, for that he is flesh " (verse 3). " The evil of man was multiplied on the earth, and the imagination of the thoughts of his heart was only evil " (verse 5). " I will destroy man whom I have created " (verse 7) ; and in the following chapter (verses 21, 22), " All flesh died that crept upon the earth, and every man, in whose nostrils was the breath of the spirit of lives." Of man it has already been said that the Lord alone is Man, and that from Him every celestial man, or celestial church, is called " man." So with all other churches ; and so is every one, whatever his faith, to distinguish him from the brutes. But still a man is not a man, and distinct from the brutes, except by virtue of remains, which are of the Lord. From these also a man is called man, and inasmuch as he is so called by reason of remains, which belong to the Lord, it is from Him that he has the name of man be he ever so wicked, for a man is by no means man, but the vilest of brutes, unless he has remains.

566. That by the " faces of the ground " is signified all that region where the church was, is evident from the signification of " ground " ; for in the Word there is an accurate distinction made between " ground " and " earth " ; by " ground "

is everywhere signified the church, or something belonging to the church ; and from this comes the name of " man," or " Adam," which is " ground " ; by " earth " in various places is meant where there is no church, or anything belonging to the church, as in the first chapter, where " earth " only is named, because as yet there was no church, or regenerate man. The " ground " is first spoken of in the second chapter, because then there was a church. In like manner it is said here, and in the following chapter (verses 4, 23), that " every substance should be destroyed from off the faces of the ground," signifying in the region where the church was ; but in verse 3, speaking of a church about to be created, it is said, " to keep seed alive on the faces of the ground." " Ground " has the same signification everywhere in the Word ; as in *Isaiah* :

Jehovah will have mercy on Jacob, and will yet choose Israel, and will set them upon their own ground, and the peoples shall take them, and shall bring them to their place, and the house of Israel shall inherit them on the ground of Jehovah (xiv. 1, 2).

This treats of the church that has been established ; whereas where there is no church it is in the same chapter called " earth " (verses 9, 12, 16, 20, 21, 25, 26). Again :   2

And the ground of Judah shall be a terror unto Egypt ; in that day there shall be five cities in the land of Egypt speaking with the lip of Canaan (xix. 17, 18).

Here " ground " signifies the church, and " land " where there is no church. In the same :

The earth shall reel to and fro like a drunkard ; Jehovah shall visit upon the army of the height

in the height, and upon the kings of the ground
on the ground (xxiv. 20, 21).

In *Jeremiah* :

> Because of the ground that is worn, because
> there was no rain on the earth, the husbandmen
> were ashamed, they covered their heads, yea,
> the hind also calved in the field (xiv. 4, 5).

Here " earth " is that which contains the " ground,"
and " ground " that which contains the " field."
3 In the same :

> He brought the seed of the house of Israel
> from the northern land, from all the lands whither
> I have driven them, and they shall dwell on
> their own ground (xxiii. 8).

Here " land " and " lands " are where there are no
churches ; " ground " where there is a church or
true worship. Again :

> I will give the remains of Jerusalem, them
> that are left in this land, and them that dwell
> in the land of Egypt, and I will deliver them to
> commotion, for evil to all the kings of the earth,
> and I will send the sword, the famine, and pesti-
> lence among them, till they be consumed from
> off the ground which I gave to them and to their
> fathers (xxiv. 8, 9, 10).

Here " ground " signifies doctrine and the worship
thence derived ; and in like manner in the same
4 Prophet, chapter xxv. 5.   In *Ezekiel* :

> I will gather you out of the lands wherein ye
> have been scattered, and ye shall know that I
> am Jehovah when I shall bring you again into
> the ground of Israel, into the land for which I
> lifted up My hand to give it to your fathers
> (xx. 41, 42).

Here " ground " signifies internal worship ; it is called " land " when there is no internal worship. In *Malachi* :

> I will rebuke him that consumeth for your sakes, and he shall not corrupt for you the fruit of the ground, nor shall the vine be bereaved for you in the field ; and all nations shall call you blessed, because ye shall be a delightsome land (iii. 11, 12).

Here " land " denotes the containant, and therefore it plainly denotes man, who is called " land " when " ground " denotes the church, or doctrine. In *Moses* : 5

> Sing, O ye nations, His people, He will make expiation for His ground, His people (*Deut.* xxxii. 43).

Evidently this signifies the Church of the Gentiles, which is called " ground." In *Isaiah* :

> Before the child shall know to refuse the evil and choose the good, the ground shall be forsaken, which thou abhorrest in presence of both her kings (vii. 16).

This treats of the advent of the Lord ; that the " ground will be forsaken " denotes the church, or the true doctrine of faith. That " ground " and " field " are so called from being sown with seed, is evident ; as in *Isaiah* :

> Then shall He give rain of thy seed wherewith thou shalt sow the ground ; the oxen also and the young asses that labour on the ground (xxx. 23, 24).

And in *Joel* :

> The field is laid waste, and the ground hath mourned, because the corn is laid waste (i. 10).

Hence then it is evident that " man," who in the Hebrew tongue is called " Adam," from " ground," signifies the church.

567. All that region is called the region of the church where those live who are instructed in the doctrine of true faith ; as the land of Canaan, when the Jewish Church was there, and Europe, where the Christian Church now is ; the lands and countries outside of this are not the region of the church, or the " faces of the ground." Where the church was before the flood, may also appear from the lands which the rivers encompassed that went forth from the garden of Eden, by which in various parts of the Word are also described the boundaries of the land of Canaan ; and also from what follows concerning the Nephilim that were " in the land " ; and that these Nephilim dwelt in the land of Canaan is evident from what is said of the sons of Anak : that they were " of the Nephilim " (*Num.* xiii. **33**).

568. That " daughters " signify such things as are of the will of that man, consequently lusts, is evident from what was said and shown concerning " sons and daughters " in the preceding chapter (verse **4**), where " sons " signify truths, and " daughters," goods. " Daughters," or goods, are of the will, but such as a man is, such is his understanding and such his will, thus such are the " sons and daughters." The present passage treats of man in a corrupt state, who has no will, but mere lust instead of will, which is supposed by him to be will, and is also so called. What is predicated is in accordance with the quality of the thing whereof it is predicated, and that the man of whom the daughters are here predicated was a corrupt man, has been shown before. The reason why

344

" daughters " signify the things of the will, and,
where there is no will of good, lusts ; and why
" sons " signify the things of the understanding,
and, where there is no understanding of truth,
phantasies, is that the female sex is such, and so
formed, that the will or lust reigns in them more
than the understanding.   Such is the entire disposition of their fibres, and such their nature,
whereas the male sex is so formed that the intellect
or reason rules, such also being the disposition of
their fibres, and such their nature.   Hence the
marriage of the two is like that of the will and
the understanding in every man ; and since at this
day there is no will of good, but only lust, and
still something intellectual, or rational, can be
given, this is why so many laws were enacted in
the Jewish Church concerning the prerogative of
the husband (*vir*), and the obedience of the wife.

569. Verse 2. **And the sons of God saw the
daughters of man that they were good, and they took
to themselves wives of all that they chose.** By the
" sons of God " are signified the doctrinal things
of faith, by " daughters," here as before, lusts.
By the " sons of God seeing the daughters of man
that they were good, and taking to themselves
wives of all that they chose," is signified that the
doctrinal things of faith conjoined themselves
with cupidities, in fact with any lusts whatsoever.

570. That by the " sons of God " are signified
doctrinal things of faith, is evident from the signification of " sons " (concerning which see just above,
and also in the preceding chapter, verse 4, where
" sons " signify the truths of the church).   The
truths of the church are doctrinal things, which
regarded in themselves were truths, because those

here treated of had them by tradition from the most ancient people, and, therefore, they are called the " sons of God " ; they are so called also relatively, because lusts are called the " daughters of man." The quality of the members of this church is here described, namely, that they immersed the truths of the church, which were holy, in their lusts, and thereby defiled them ; and in this way they confirmed the principles of which they were so strongly persuaded. How this occurred may be easily conceived by any one, from observing what passes in himself and others : those who persuade themselves in regard to any subject, confirm themselves in such persuasion by everything which they imagine to be true, even by what they find contained in the Word of the Lord ; for while they cling to principles which they have received, and have become persuaded of, they make everything favour and assent to them. And the more any one is under the influence of self-love, the more firmly he holds them. Such was this race, concerning whom, of the Lord's Divine mercy, we will treat hereafter, when we come to treat of their direful persuasions, which, strange to say, are such that they are never allowed to flow in by reasonings, but only from lusts, for otherwise they would kill everything rational in the spirits present. Hence it appears what is signified by the " sons of God seeing the daughters of man that they were good, and taking to themselves wives of all that they chose," namely, that they conjoined the doctrinal things of faith with their lusts, in fact with any lusts.

571. When a man is such that he immerses the truths of faith in his insane lusts, he then profanes

the truths, and deprives himself of remains, which although they remain yet cannot be brought forth, for as soon as they are brought forth they are again profaned by things that are profane; for profanations of the Word produce, as it were, a callosity, which causes an obstruction, and which absorbs the goods and truths of remains. Therefore, let man beware of the profanation of the Word of the Lord, which contains the eternal truths wherein is life, although one who is in false principles does not believe that they are truths.

572. Verse 3. **And Jehovah said, My spirit shall not reprove man forever, for that he is flesh; and his days shall be a hundred and twenty years.** By " Jehovah's saying My spirit shall not always reprove man," is signified that man would not be so led any longer; " for that he is flesh," signifies because he had become corporeal; " and his days shall be a hundred and twenty years," signifies that he ought to have remains of faith. It is also a prediction concerning a future church.

573. That by **Jehovah's saying, My spirit shall not forever reprove man** is signified that man would not be so led any longer, is evident from what has gone before and from what follows; from what has gone before in that men had become such, through the immersion in lusts of the doctrinal things or truths of faith, that they could no longer be reproved, that is, know what evil is. All capacity to perceive truth and good had been extinguished through their persuasions, so that they believed that only to be true that was in conformity with their persuasions; and in regard to what follows, that after the flood the man of the church became different, in that with him conscience

347

succeeded in place of perception, through which
he could be reproved. " Reproof by the spirit
of Jehovah " therefore signifies an inward dictate,
a perception, or a conscience ; and the " spirit of
Jehovah " signifies the influx of what is true and
good ; as also in *Isaiah* :

> I will not contend to eternity, neither will
> I be forever wroth, for the spirit would over-
> whelm before me, and the souls I have made
> (lvii. 16).

574. That " flesh " signifies that man had
become corporeal, appears from the signification
of " flesh " in the Word, where it is used to signify
both every man in general, and also, specifically,
the corporeal man.   It is used to signify every man,
in *Joel* :

> I will pour out My spirit upon all flesh, and
> your sons and your daughters shall prophesy
> (ii. 28).

Here " flesh " signifies man, and " spirit " the
influx of truth and good from the Lord.   In *David* :

> Thou that hearest prayers, unto Thee shall
> all flesh come (*Ps.* lxv. 2).

Here " flesh " denotes every man.   In *Jeremiah* :

> Cursed is the man that trusteth in man, and
> maketh flesh his arm (xvii. 5).

Here " flesh " signifies man, and " arm " power.
In *Ezekiel* :

> That all flesh may know (xxi. 4, 5).

In *Zechariah* :

> Be silent, all flesh, before Jehovah (ii. 13).

2 Here " flesh " denotes every man.   That it signifies
348

specifically the corporeal man, is evident from *Isaiah*:

The Egyptian is man and not God, and his horses are flesh and not spirit (xxxi. 3).

This signifies that their knowledge (*scientificum*) is corporeal ; " horses " here and elsewhere in the Word denoting the Rational. Again :

He shall withdraw to the right hand, and shall be hungry ; and he shall devour on the left hand, and they shall not be satisfied ; they shall eat every one of the flesh of his own arm (ix. 20).

This signifies such things as are man's own, which are all corporeal. In the same :

He shall consume from the soul, and even the flesh (x. 18).

Here " flesh " signifies corporeal things. Again :

The glory of Jehovah shall be revealed, and all flesh shall see it together ; the voice said, Cry ; and he said, What shall I cry ? All flesh is grass (xl. 5, 6).

" Flesh " here signifies every man who is corporeal. In the same : 3

In fire will Jehovah dispute, and with His sword with all flesh, and the slain of Jehovah shall be multiplied (lxvi. 16).

Here " fires " signifies the punishment of lusts ; the " sword," the punishment of falsities ; and " flesh " the corporeal things of man. In *David* :

God remembered that they were flesh, a breath that passeth away, and cometh not again (*Ps.* lxxviii. 39).

This treats of the people in the wilderness desiring flesh, because they were corporeal ; their desiring flesh represented that they desired only things corporeal (*Num.* xi. 32, 33, 34).

575. That by the **days of man being a hundred and twenty years** is signified that he ought to have remains of faith, appears from what has been said in the foregoing chapter (verses 3 and 4), concerning " days " and " years " signifying times and states ; and also from the circumstance of the most ancient people denoting states and changes of states in the church from numbers variously compounded ; but the nature of their ecclesiastical computation is now totally lost. Here in like manner numbers of years are mentioned, whose signification it is impossible for any one to understand, unless he be first acquainted with the hidden meaning of each particular number from " one " to " twelve," and so on. It plainly appears that they contain within them something else that is secret, for that men were to live a " hundred and twenty years " has no connection with the preceding part of the verse, nor did they live one hundred and twenty years, as is evident from the people after the flood (chapter xi.), where it is said of Shem that " he lived after he begat Arphaxad five hundred years " ; and that Arphaxad lived after he begat Selah " four hundred and three years " ; and that Selah lived after he begat Eber " four hundred and three years " ; and that Eber lived after he begat Peleg " four hundred and thirty years " ; and that Noah lived after the flood " three hundred and fifty years " (chapter ix. 28), and so on. But what is involved in the number " one hundred and twenty," appears only from the meaning of " ten " and " twelve," which being multiplied together make one hundred and twenty, and from the signification of these component numbers it may be seen that " one hundred and twenty " signifies the remains of faith. The number " ten " in the Word, as also

350

" tenths," signify and represent remains, which are preserved by the Lord in the internal man, and which are holy, because they are of the Lord alone ; and the number " twelve " signifies faith, or all things relating to faith in one complex ; the number therefore that is compounded of these, signifies the remains of faith.

576. That the number " ten," and also " tenths," signify remains, is evident from the following passages of the Word :

> Many houses shall be a desolation, great and fair, without an inhabitant ; for ten acres of vineyard shall yield one bath, and the seed of a homer shall yield an ephah (*Isa.* v. 9, 10).

This treats of the vastation of things spiritual and celestial : " ten acres of vineyard making a bath," signifies that the remains of things spiritual were so few ; and " the seed of a homer yielding an ephah," signifies that there were so few remains of celestial things.   In the same :

> And many things are forsaken in the midst of the land, yet in it shall be a tenth part, and it shall return, and nevertheless it shall be consumed (vi. 12, 13).

Here the " midst of the land " signifies the internal man ; a " tenth part " signifies the smallness of the remains.   In *Ezekiel* :

> Ye shall have balances of justice, and an ephah of justice, and a bath of justice ; the ephah and the bath shall be of one measure, the bath to contain the tenth of a homer, and an ephah the tenth of a homer ; the measure thereof shall be after the homer ; and the ordinance of oil, a bath of oil, the tenth of a

bath out of a kor, ten baths to the homer, for ten baths are a homer (xlv. 10, 11, 14).

In this passage the holy things of Jehovah are treated of by measures, whereby are signified the kinds of the holy things ; by " ten " are here signified the remains of celestial and of the derivative spiritual things ; for unless such holy arcana were contained herein, what could be the use or intent of describing so many measures determined by numbers, as is done in this and the former chapters in the same Prophet, where the subject is the heavenly Jerusalem and the New Temple ?

2 In *Amos* :

The virgin Israel is fallen, she shall no more rise. Thus saith the Lord Jehovih, The city that went out a thousand shall have a hundred remaining, and that which went out a hundred, shall have ten remaining to the house of Israel (v. 2, 3).

Here, speaking of remains it is said that very little would be left, being only a " tenth part," or remains of remains. Again :

I abhor the pride of Jacob and his palaces, and will shut up the city, and its fullness, and it shall come to pass if there shall be left ten men in one house they shall even die (vi. 8, 9).

This treats of remains which should scarcely continue. In *Moses* :

An Ammonite or Moabite shall not come into the congregation of Jehovah, even the tenth generation of them shall not come into the congregation of Jehovah to eternity (*Deut.* xxiii. 3).

" An Ammonite and a Moabite," signify the profanation of the celestial and spiritual things of

352

faith, the " remains " of which are spoken of in
what precedes.   Hence it appears also that 3
" tenths " represent remains.   And so in *Malachi* :

> Bring ye all the tithes [tenths] into the treasure-
> house, that there may be booty in My house, and
> let them prove Me, bestir ye in this, if I will not
> open for you the cataracts of heaven, and pour
> you out a blessing (iii. 10).

" That there may be booty in My house," signifies
remains in the internal man, which are compared to
" booty," because they are insinuated as by stealth
among so many evils and falsities ; and it is by
these remains that all blessing comes.   That all
man's charity comes by the remains which are in
the internal man, was also represented in the
Jewish Church by this statute : that when they
had made an end of tithing all the tithes, they
should give to the Levite, to the stranger, to the
fatherless, and to the widow (*Deut*. xxvi. 12 *seq*.). 4
Inasmuch as remains are of the Lord alone, therefore the tenths are called " holiness to Jehovah " ;
as in *Moses* :

> All the tenths of the land, of the seed of the
> land, of the fruit of the tree, they are Jehovah's,
> holiness to Jehovah : all the tenths of the herd
> and of the flock, whatsoever passeth under the
> (pastoral) rod, the tenth shall be holiness to
> Jehovah (*Lev*. xxvii. 30, 31).

That the Decalogue consisted of " ten " precepts,
or " ten " words, and that Jehovah wrote them
on tables (*Deut*. x. 4), signifies remains, and their
being written by the hand of Jehovah signifies
that remains are of the Lord alone ; their being
in the internal man was represented by the
tables.

M   353

577. That the number " twelve " signifies faith, or the things of love and the derivative faith in one complex, might also be confirmed by many passages from the Word, as from the " twelve " sons of Jacob and their names, the " twelve " tribes of Israel, and the Lord's " twelve " apostles ; but concerning these of the Lord's Divine mercy we will treat hereafter, especially in *Genesis* xxix. and xxx.

578. From these numbers alone it is evident what the Word of the Lord contains in its bosom and interior recesses, and how many arcana are concealed therein which do not at all appear to the naked eye. And so it is everywhere : there are similar things in every word.

579. That with the antediluvians here treated of there were few and almost no remains, will be manifest from what, of the Lord's Divine mercy, will be said of them hereafter ; and as no remains could be preserved among them, it is here foretold of the new church called " Noah " that it should have remains ; concerning which also, of the Lord's Divine mercy, we will treat hereafter.

580. Verse 4. **There were Nephilim in the earth in those days; and especially after the sons of God went in unto the daughters of man, and they bare to them, the same became mighty men, who were of old, men of renown.** By " Nephilim " are signified those who through a persuasion of their own loftiness and pre-eminence made light of all things holy and true ; " and especially after the sons of God went in unto the daughters of man, and they bare to them," signifies that this occurred when they immersed the doctrinals of faith in their lusts, and formed persuasions of what is false ;

354

they are called " mighty men " from their love of self ; " of old, men of renown," signifies that there had been such before.

581. That by the " Nephilim " are signified those who through a persuasion of their own lofti- ness and pre-eminence made light of all things holy and true, appears from what precedes and what follows, namely, that they immersed the doctrinals of faith in their lusts, signified by the " sons of God going in unto the daughters of man, and their bearing unto them." Persuasion concerning self and its phantasies increases also according to the multitude of things that enter into it, till at length it becomes indelible ; and when the doc- trinals of faith are added thereto, then from prin- ciples of the strongest persuasion they make light of all things holy and true, and become " Nephilim." That race, which lived before the flood, is such that they so kill and suffocate all spirits by their most direful phantasies (which are poured forth by them as a poisonous and suffo- cating sphere) that the spirits are entirely deprived of the power of thinking, and feel half dead ; and unless the Lord by His coming into the world had freed the world of spirits from that poisonous race, no one could have existed there, and consequently the human race, who are ruled by the Lord through spirits, would have perished. They are, therefore, now kept in a hell under, as it were, a misty and dense rock, under the heel of the left foot, nor do they make the slightest attempt to rise out of it. Thus is the world of spirits free from this most dangerous crew, concerning which and its most poisonous sphere of persuasions, of the Lord's Divine mercy, we will treat hereafter. These are

those who are called " Nephilim," and who make
light of all things holy and true. Further mention
is made of them in the Word, but their descendants
were called " Anakim " and " Rephaim." That they
were called " Anakim " is evident from *Moses* :

> There we saw the Nephilim, the sons of Anak,
> of the Nephilim, and we were in our own eyes as
> grasshoppers, and so we were in their eyes
> (*Num.* xiii. 33).

That they were called " Rephaim " appears also
from *Moses* :

> The Emim dwelt before in the land of Moab,
> a people great, and many, and tall, as the
> Anakim, who also were accounted Rephaim,
> as the Anakim, and the Moabites called them
> Emim (*Deut.* ii. 10, 11).

The Nephilim are not mentioned any more, but
the Rephaim are, and are described by the prophets
to be such as are above stated ; as in *Isaiah* :

> Hell low down has been in commotion for
> thee, to meet thee in coming, it hath stirred up
> the Rephaim for thee (xiv. 9).

This treats of the hell which is the abode of such
spirits. In the same :

> Thy dead shall not live, the Rephaim shall not
> arise, because thou hast visited and destroyed
> them, and made all their memory to perish
> (xxvi. 14).

Here also their hell is referred to, from which they
shall no more rise again. In the same :

> Thy dead shall live, my corpse, they shall rise
> again ; awake and sing, ye that dwell in the dust,
> for the dew of herbs is thy dew ; but thou shalt
> cast out the land of the Rephaim (xxvi. 19).

356

" The land of the Rephaim " is the hell above
spoken of. In *David* :

> Wilt Thou show a wonder to the dead ? Shall
> the Rephaim arise, shall they confess to Thee ?
> (*Ps.* lxxxviii. 10).

This treats in like manner concerning the hell of
the Rephaim, and that they cannot rise up and
infest the sphere of the world of spirits with the
very direful poison of their persuasions. But it
has been provided by the Lord that mankind should
no longer be filled with such dreadful phantasies
and persuasions. Those who lived before the flood
were of such a nature and genius that they could
be infilled, for a reason as yet unknown, concerning
which, of the Lord's Divine mercy, we will treat
hereafter.

582. **After that the sons of God came in unto the
daughters of men, and they bare to them.** That this
signifies that they became Nephilim when they
had immersed the doctrinals of faith in their lusts,
is evident from what was said and shown above in
verse 2, namely, that the " sons of God " signify
the doctrinal things of faith, and that " daughters "
signify lusts. The birth thereby produced must
needs make light of and profane the holy things of
faith, for the lusts of man, being those of the love
of self and of the world, are altogether contrary to
what is holy and true. For when in man lusts
prevail, so that what is holy and true, and is
acknowledged to be such, is immersed in lusts,
it is all over with the man, for the lusts cannot be
rooted out and separated ; they cling to every
idea, and in the other life it is ideas that are communicated from one to another, so that as soon as
any idea of what is holy and true is brought forth,

what is profane and false is joined to it, which is
instantly perceived. Therefore such persons have
to be separated and thrust down into hell.

583. That the Nephilim are called " mighty men "
f.om the love of self, is evident from various
passages of the Word, where such are called
" mighty " ; as in *Jeremiah* :

> The mighty ones of Babel have ceased to
> fight, they sit in their holds, their might faileth,
> they are become as women (li. 30).

Here the " mighty ones of Babel " denote those
who are eaten up with the love of self. In the
same :

> A sword is against the liars, and they shall be
> insane, a sword is against her mighty ones, and
> they shall be dismayed (l. 36).

Again :

> I saw them dismayed, and turning away back,
> their mighty ones were broken in pieces, and
> have been put to flight, and looked not back,
> fear was round about, the swift shall not flee
> away, nor the mighty one escape ; come up, ye
> horses, and rage, ye chariots, and let the mighty
> ones go forth, Cush, Put, the Lydians (xlvi.
> 5, 6, 9).

This treats of persuasion from reasonings. Again :

> How say ye, We are mighty, and men of
> strength for war ? Moab is laid waste (xlvii.
> 14, 15).

Again :

> The city is taken, and the strongholds, it has
> been seized, and the heart of the mighty men of
> Moab in that day is become as the heart of a
> woman in her pangs (xlviii. 41).

358

In like manner it is said :

The heart of the mighty ones of Edom (xlix. 22).

Again :

Jehovah hath redeemed Jacob, and hath avenged him from the hand of him that was mightier than he (xxxi. 11).

Here " mighty " is expressed by another term. That the Anakim, who were of the Nephilim, were called " mighty ones," is evident from *Moses* :

Thou passest over Jordan to-day, to go in to possess nations greater and more numerous than thyself, cities great and fortified to heaven, a people great and tall, the sons of the Anakim, whom thou knewest, and of whom thou hast heard ; who shall stand before the sons of Anak ? (*Deut.* ix. 1, 2).

584. Verse 5. **And Jehovah saw that the evil of man was multiplied in the earth, and that all the imagination of the thoughts of his heart was only evil every day.** " Jehovah saw that the evil of man was multiplied on the earth," signifies that there began to be no will of good ; " all the imagination of the thoughts of his heart was only evil every day," signifies that there was no perception of truth and good.

585. That by **the evil of man being multiplied in the earth** is signified that there began to be no will of good, is evident from what was said above, namely, that there was no longer any will, but only lust ; and from the signification of " man in the earth." In the literal sense, the " earth " is where man is. In the internal sense, it is where the love is, and as love is of the will, or of the lust, the earth

is taken to mean the will itself of man. For man is
man from willing, and not so much from knowing
and understanding, because these flow out from
his will ; whatever does not flow out from his will
he is willing neither to know nor understand ; nay,
even when he is speaking or doing something that
he does not will, still there is something of the will
remote from the speech or action that governs him.
That the " land of Canaan," or the " holy land,"
denotes love, and consequently the will of the
celestial man, might be confirmed by many
passages from the Word ; in like manner, that the
lands of various nations denote their loves, which
in general are the love of self and the love of the
world ; but as this subject so often recurs, it need
not be dwelt upon here. Hence it appears that by
" the evil of man on the earth " is signified his
natural evil, which is of the will, and which is said
to be " multiplied " because it was not so depraved
in all but that they wished good for others, yet
for the sake of themselves ; but that the perversion
becomes complete, is signified by the " imagination
of the thoughts of the heart."

586. **The imagination of the thoughts of the
heart was only evil every day,** signifies that there
was no perception of truth and good, for the reason,
as before said and shown, that they immersed the
doctrinal things of faith in their filthy lusts, and
when this occurred all perception was lost, and in
place thereof a dreadful persuasion succeeded, that
is, a most deep-rooted and deadly phantasy, which
was the cause of their extinction and suffocation.
This deadly persuasion is here signified by " the
imagination of the thoughts of the heart " ; but
by " the imagination of the heart," without the

360

word " thoughts," is signified the evil of the love of self, or of lusts, as in the following chapter, where Jehovah said, after Noah had offered a burnt-offering : " I will not again curse the ground for man's sake, because the imagination of the heart of man is evil from his childhood " (viii. 21). An " imagination " is that which man invents for himself, and of which he persuades himself ; as in *Habakkuk* :

What profiteth a graven image, that the fashioner thereof hath graven it ? the molten image and teacher of lies, that the fashioner trusteth to his imagination, to make dumb idols (ii. 18).

A " graven image " signifies false persuasions originating in principles conceived and hatched out by one's self ; the " fashioner " is one who is thus self-persuaded, of whom this " imagination " is predicated. In *Isaiah* :

Your subversion : shall the potter be reputed as the clay, that the work should say to him that made it, He made me not ; and the thing fashioned say to him that fashioned it, He had no understanding ? (xxix. 16).

The " thing fashioned " here signifies thought originating in man's proprium, and the persuasion of what is false thence derived. A " thing fashioned " or " imagined," in general, is what a man invents from the heart or will, and also what he invents from the thought or persuasion, as in *David* :

Jehovah knoweth our fashioning (*figmentum*), He remembereth that we are dust (*Ps.* ciii. 14).

In *Moses* :

I know his imagination that he doeth this day, before I bring him into the land (*Deut.* xxxi. 21).

M*   361

586A. Verse 6. **And it repented Jehovah that He made man on the earth, and it grieved Him at His heart.** That He " repented," signifies mercy ; that He " grieved at the heart," has a like signification ; to " repent " has reference to wisdom ; to " grieve at the heart " to love.

587. That **it repented Jehovah that He made man on the earth** signifies mercy, and that " He grieved at the heart " has a like signification, is evident from this, that Jehovah never repents, because He foresees all things from eternity both in general and in particular ; and when He made man, that is, created him anew, and perfected him till he became celestial, He also foresaw that in process of time he would become such as is here described, and because He foresaw this He could not repent. This appears plainly from what Samuel said :

> The invincible One of Israel doth not lie, nor repent, for He is not a man that He should repent (1 *Sam.* xv. 29).

And in *Moses* :

> God is not a man that He should lie, or the son of man that He should repent ; hath He said, and shall He not do ? or hath He spoken, and shall He not make it good ? (*Num.* xxiii. 19).

But to " repent " signifies to be merciful. The mercy of Jehovah, or of the Lord, includes everything that is done by the Lord towards mankind, who are in such a state that the Lord pities them, each one according to his state ; thus He pities the state of him whom He permits to be punished, and pities him also to whom He grants the enjoyment of good ; it is of mercy to be punished, because mercy turns all the evil of punishment into good ; and

it is of mercy to grant the enjoyment of good,
because no one merits anything that is good ; for
all mankind are evil, and of himself every one would
rush into hell ; wherefore it is of mercy that he is
delivered thence ; nor is it anything but mercy,
inasmuch as He has need of no man. Mercy has its
name from the fact that it delivers man from
miseries and from hell ; thus it is called mercy in
respect to mankind, because they are in such a
state of misery, and it is the effect of love towards
them all, because all are so.

588. But it is predicated of the Lord that He
" repents," and " is grieved at heart," because
there appears to be such a feeling in all human
mercy, so that what is said here of the Lord's
" repenting " and " grieving " is spoken according
to the appearance, as in many other passages in the
Word. What the mercy of the Lord is none can
know, because it infinitely transcends the understanding of man ; but what the mercy of man is
we all know to be to repent and grieve ; and unless
a man were to form his idea of mercy according to
his own apprehension, he could not have any conception of it, and thus he could not be instructed ;
and this is the reason why human qualities are
often predicated of the attributes of Jehovah or the
Lord, as that Jehovah or the Lord punishes, leads
into temptation, destroys, and is angry ; when yet
He never punishes any one, never leads any into
temptation, never destroys any, and is never angry.
But as even such things as these are predicated of
the Lord, it follows that repentance also and
grief may be predicated of Him ; for the predication
of the one follows from that of the other, as plainly
appears from the following passages in the Word.

2 In *Ezekiel* :

> Mine anger shall be consummated, I will make
> my wrath to rest, and it shall repent Me (v. 13).

Here, because " anger " and " wrath " are predicated, " repentance " is predicated also.   In
Zechariah :

> As I thought to do evil when your fathers
> provoked Me to anger, saith Jehovah Zebaoth,
> and it repented Me not, so again I will think
> in those days to do good unto Jerusalem and to
> the house of Judah (viii. 14, 15).

Here it is said that Jehovah " thought to do evil,"
and yet He never thinks to do evil to any, but good
to all and every one.   In *Moses*, when he prayed
forbearance of the face of Jehovah :

> Turn from the wrath of Thine anger and repent
> Thee of this evil against Thy people ; and
> Jehovah repented of the evil which He said He
> would do unto His people (*Exod.* xxxii. 12, 14).

Here also the " wrath of anger " is attributed
to Jehovah, and consequently " repentance."   In
Jonah, the king of Nineveh said :

> Who knoweth whether God will not turn and
> repent, and turn from the heat of His anger, that
> we perish not ? (iii. 9).

In like manner here " repentance " is predicated
3 because " anger " is.   In *Hosea* :

> My heart is turned within me ; My repentings
> are kindled together ; I will not execute the
> wrath of Mine anger (xi. 8, 9).

Here also it is said of the heart that " repentings
were kindled," just as in the passage we are considering it is said that He " grieved at heart."

" Repentings " plainly denote great mercy.   So
in *Joel* :

> Turn unto Jehovah your God ; for He is
> gracious and compassionate, slow to anger and
> plenteous in mercy, and repenteth of the evil
> (ii. 13).

Here also to " repent " manifestly denotes mercy.
In *Jeremiah* :

> If so be they will hearken, and turn every man
> from his evil way, and it repent Me of the evil
> (xxvi. 3).

This signifies to have mercy.   Again :

> If that nation turn from their evil, it shall
> repent Me of the evil (xviii. 8).

Here also to " repent " denotes to have mercy
provided they would turn.   For it is man who turns
the Lord's mercy away from himself : the Lord
never turns it away from man.

589. From these and many other passages it is
evident that the Word was spoken according to
the appearances with man.   Whoever, therefore,
desires to confirm false principles by the appearances
according to which the Word was spoken, can do so
by passages without number.   But it is one thing to
confirm false principles by the Word, and another
to believe in simplicity what is in the Word.   He
who confirms false principles, first assumes a principle which he will not at all recede from, nor yield
in the least, but scrapes together and accumulates
confirmations wherever he can, also from the
Word, until he so strongly persuades himself that
he can no longer see the truth.   But he who simply
or with simple heart believes, does not first assume
principles, but thinks that because the Lord has

thus said it is true ; and if instructed from other passages of the Word how it is to be understood, he acquiesces and rejoices in his heart. Even the man who in simplicity believes that the Lord is angry, punishes, repents, and grieves, and so believing is afraid of evil and does good, takes no harm ; for this belief causes him to believe also that the Lord sees everything ; and being in such a belief he is afterwards enlightened in other matters of faith in the other life, if not before. Very different is the case with those who, in agreement with a foul love of self or of the world, persuade themselves to believe certain things that are deduced from the principles they have already adopted.

590. That " repenting " has reference to wisdom, and " grieving at heart," to love, cannot be explained to human apprehension, save in accordance with the things that are with man, that is, by means of appearances. In every idea of thought in man there is something from the understanding and from the will, or from his thought and his love. Whatever idea does not derive anything from his will or love is not an idea, for he cannot think at all otherwise than from his will. There is a kind of perpetual and indissoluble marriage, between the thought and the will, so that in the ideas of man's thought there inhere and adhere the things that are of his will or his love. From this state of things in man it may, as it were, be known, or rather it seems possible to form some idea of what is contained in the Lord's mercy, namely, wisdom and love. Thus in the Prophets, especially in *Isaiah*, there are, almost everywhere, double expressions concerning everything, one involving what **is**

spiritual, the other what is celestial. The spiritual of the Lord's mercy is wisdom; the celestial is love.

591. Verse 7. **And Jehovah said, I will destroy man whom I have created, from upon the faces of the ground; both man and beast, and creeping thing, and fowl of the heavens; for it repenteth Me that I have made them.** " Jehovah said, I will destroy man," signifies that man would extinguish himself; " whom I have created, from upon the faces of the ground," signifies the man of the posterity of the Most Ancient Church; " both man and beast, and creeping thing," signifies that whatsoever is of the will would extinguish him; " and fowl of the heavens," is whatever belongs to the understanding or thought; " for it repenteth Me that I have made them," signifies compassion, as before.

592. **Jehovah said, I will destroy man.** That this signifies that man would extinguish himself, is evident from what has been explained before, namely, that it is predicated of Jehovah or the Lord that He punishes, that He tempts, that He does evil, that He destroys or kills, and that He curses. As for example, that He slew Er, Judah's firstborn; and Onan, another son of Judah (*Gen.* xxxviii. 7, 10); that Jehovah smote all the first-born of Egypt (xii. 12, 29). And so in *Jeremiah* :

Whom I have slain in Mine anger and in My wrath (xxxiii. 5).

In *David* :

He cast upon them the wrath of His anger; vehement anger, and fury and straitness, a sending of evil angels (*Ps.* lxxviii. 49).

367

In *Amos* :

> Shall evil befall a city, and Jehovah hath not done it ? (iii. 6).

In *John* :

> Seven golden vials full of the wrath of God who liveth forever and ever (*Rev.* xv. 1, 7 ; xvi. 1).

All these things are predicated of Jehovah, although entirely contrary to His nature. They are predicated of Him for the reason explained before ; and also in order that men may first form the very general idea that the Lord governs and disposes all things both in general and in particular ; and may afterwards learn that nothing of evil is from the Lord, much less does He kill ; but that it is man who brings evil upon himself, and ruins and destroys himself—although it is not man, but evil spirits who excite and lead him ; and yet it is man, because he believes that he is himself the doer. So now here it is said of Jehovah that He would " destroy man," when in fact it was man who 2 would destroy and extinguish himself. The state of the case may be very evident from those in the other life who are in torment and in hell, and who are continually lamenting and attributing all the evil of punishment to the Lord. So in the world of evil spirits there are those who make it their delight, even their greatest delight, to hurt and punish others ; and those who are hurt and punished think it is from the Lord. But they are told, and it is shown them, that not the least of evil is from the Lord, but they bring it upon themselves ; for such is the state and such the equilibrium of all things in the other life that evil returns upon him who does evil, and becomes the evil of punishment ; and for the same reason it is inevitable. This is said to be permitted for the sake of the amendment of the evil. But still the Lord turns all the evil of punishment into good ; so that there is never anything but good from the Lord. But hitherto no one has known what permission is ; what is permitted is believed to be done by Him who permits, because He permits. But the fact is quite otherwise, concerning which, of the Lord's Divine mercy, we will treat hereafter.

593. **Whom I have created, from upon the faces of the ground.** That this signifies the man from the posterity of the Most Ancient Church, is evident not only from its being said, the man whom He had " created," that is, whom He had regenerated ; and afterwards whom He had " made," that is, had perfected, or regenerated until he became celestial ; but also from its being said " from upon the faces of the ground." The " ground " is where the church is, as has been shown before. The same is evident from the fact that those are treated of who immersed the doctrinal things of faith in their lusts ; and those who had not doctrinal things of faith could not do so. Those who are outside the church are in ignorance of truth and good, and those who are in ignorance may be in a kind of innocence while speaking and acting somewhat contrary to the truths and goods of faith ; for they may act from a certain zeal for the worship which they have been taught from infancy, and which they therefore believe to be true and good. But the case is entirely different with those who have the doctrine of faith among them. These can mingle truths with falsities, and holy things with profane. Hence their lot in the other life is much worse than the lot of those who are called Gentiles,

369

concerning whom, of the Lord's Divine mercy, we
will treat hereafter.

594. **Both man and beast, and creeping thing.**
That this signifies that whatsoever is of the will
would extinguish him, is evident from the signification of "man," of "beast," and of "creeping
thing." Man is man solely from the will and
understanding, by which he is distinguished from
brutes ; in all other respects he is very similar to
them. In the case of these men all will of good
and understanding of truth had perished. In place
of a will of good there followed insane lusts, in
place of an understanding of truth insane phantasies ;
and these were commingled with their lusts, so
that after they had thus as it were destroyed
remains, they could not but be extinguished. That
all things of the will are called "beasts" and
"creeping things," is evident from what has been
said before concerning beasts and creeping things.
But here, because of the character of the man
treated of, good affections are not signified by
"beasts," but evil, consequently lusts ; and by
"creeping things," pleasures, both bodily and
sensuous. That such things are signified by
"beasts" and "creeping things" needs no
further confirmation from the Word, because they
have been treated of before (see n. 45, 46, 142, 143).

595. That **the fowl of the heavens** signifies
whatever belongs to the understanding, that is, to
thought, may also be seen above (n. 40).

596. Verse 8. **And Noah found grace in the eyes
of Jehovah.** By "Noah" is signified a new church.
That he "found grace in the eyes of Jehovah,"
signifies that the Lord foresaw that the human
race might thus be saved.

597. By " Noah " is signified a new church, which is to be called the Ancient Church, for the sake of distinction between the Most Ancient Church, which was before the flood, and that which was after the flood. The states of these two churches were entirely different. The state of the Most Ancient Church was such that they had from the Lord a perception of good and the derivative truth. The state of the Ancient Church, or " Noah," became such that they had a conscience of good and truth. Such as is the difference between having perception and having conscience, such was the difference of state of the Most Ancient and the Ancient Church. Perception is not conscience : the celestial have perception ; the spiritual have conscience. The Most Ancient Church was celestial, the Ancient was spiritual. The Most Ancient Church had immediate revela- 2 tion from the Lord by consort with spirits and angels, as also by visions and dreams ; whereby it was given them to have a general knowledge of what was good and true ; and after they had acquired a general knowledge, these general leading principles, as we may call them, were confirmed by things innumerable, by means of perceptions ; and these innumerable things were the particulars or individual things of the general principles to which they related. Thus were the general leading principles corroborated day by day ; whatever was not in agreement with the general principles they perceived not to be so ; and whatever was in agreement with them they perceived to be so. Such also is the state of the celestial angels. The 3 general principles of the Most Ancient Church were heavenly and eternal truths,—as that the Lord governs the universe, that all good and truth is from

the Lord, that all life is from the Lord, that man's proprium is nothing but evil, and in itself is dead ; with many others of similar character. And they received from the Lord a perception of countless things that confirmed and supported these truths. With them love was the chief thing of faith. By love it was given them by the Lord to perceive whatever was of faith, and hence with them faith was love, as was said before. But the Ancient Church became entirely different, concerning which of the Lord's Divine mercy we will treat hereafter.

598. **He found grace in the eyes of Jehovah,** signifies that the Lord foresaw that the human race might thus be saved. The Lord's mercy involves and looks to the salvation of the whole human race ; and it is the same with His " grace," and therefore the salvation of the human race is signified. By " Noah " is signified not only a new church, but also the faith of that church, which was the faith of charity. Thus the Lord foresaw that through the faith of charity the human race might be saved (concerning which faith we will 2 treat hereafter). But there is a distinction in the Word between " mercy " and " grace," and this in accordance with the difference that exists in those who receive them ; " mercy " being applied to those who are celestial, and " grace " to those who are spiritual ; for the celestial acknowledge nothing but mercy, and the spiritual scarcely anything but grace. The celestial do not know what grace is ; the spiritual scarcely know what mercy is, which they make one and the same with grace. This comes from the ground of the humiliation of the two being so different ; those who are in humiliation of heart implore the Lord's mercy ;

but those who are in humiliation of thought beseech His grace ; and if these implore mercy, it is either in a state of temptation, or is done with the mouth only and not from the heart. Because the new church called " Noah " was not celestial but spiritual, it is not said to have found " mercy," but " grace," in the eyes of Jehovah. That there is a distinction in the Word between " mercy " and " grace," is evident from many passages where Jehovah is called " merciful and gracious " (as in *Ps.* ciii. 8 ; cxi. 4 ; cxlv. 8 ; *Joel* ii. 13). The distinction is likewise made in other places, as in *Jeremiah* :

Thus saith Jehovah, The people which were left of the sword found grace in the wilderness, when I went to give rest to him, to Israel. Jehovah appeared unto me from afar ; and I have loved thee with an everlasting love ; therefore in mercy have I drawn thee (xxxi. 2, 3).

Here " grace " is predicated of the spiritual, and " mercy " of the celestial. In *Isaiah* :

Therefore will Jehovah wait that He may give grace unto you, and therefore will He exalt Himself that He may have mercy upon you (xxx. 18).

Here likewise " grace " regards the spiritual, and " mercy " the celestial. So in the chapter presently following, where Lot says to the angel :

Behold, I pray, thy servant hath found grace in thine eyes, and thou hast made great thy mercy which thou hast wrought with me, to make alive my soul (*Gen.* xix. 19).

That " grace " relates to spiritual things, which are of faith, or of the understanding, is evident here also in that it is said, he " hath found grace in

thine eyes "; and that " mercy " relates to
celestial things which are of love, or of the will, is
evident from the fact that the angel is said to have
" wrought mercy," and to have " made alive the
soul."

———

9. These are the generations of Noah ; Noah
was a man righteous and perfect in his generations :
Noah walked with God.

10. And Noah begat three sons : Shem, Ham,
and Japheth.

11. And the earth was corrupt before God ; and
the earth was filled with violence.

12. And God saw the earth, and behold it was
corrupt, for all flesh had corrupted its way upon
the earth.

13. And God said unto Noah, The end of all flesh
is come before Me, for the earth is filled with violence from their faces, and behold I will destroy
them with the earth.

14. Make thee an ark of gopher woods ; mansions shalt thou make the ark, and shalt pitch it
within and without with pitch.

15. And thus shalt thou make it : three hundred
cubits the length of the ark, fifty cubits its breadth,
and thirty cubits its height.

16. A window shalt thou make to the ark, and
to a cubit shalt thou finish it from above ; and the
door of the ark shalt thou set in the side thereof ;
with lowest, second, and third stories shalt thou
make it.

17. And I, behold I do bring the flood of waters
upon the earth, to destroy all flesh wherein is
the breath of lives from under the heavens ; everything that is in the earth shall expire.

18. And I will set up My covenant with thee ; and thou shalt enter into the ark, thou and thy sons, and thy wife, and thy sons' wives with thee.

19. And of every living thing of all flesh, pairs of all shalt thou make to enter into the ark, to keep them alive with thee ; they shall be male and female.

20. Of the fowl after its kind, and of the beast after its kind, of every creeping thing of the ground after its kind, pairs of all shall enter unto thee, to keep them alive.

21. And take thou unto thee of all food that is eaten, and gather it to thee, and it shall be for food for thee and for them.

22. And Noah did according to all that God commanded him ; so did he.

THE CONTENTS.

599. The subject here treated of is the state of the church called " Noah," before its regeneration.

600. The man of that church is described as being such that he could be regenerated (verse 9) ; but that there arose thence three kinds of doctrine, which are " Shem, Ham, and Japheth " (verse 10).

601. That the man who was left from the Most Ancient Church could not be regenerated, on account of his direful persuasions and foul lusts (verses 11, 12) ; whereby he would utterly destroy himself (verse 13).

602. But the man of the church called " Noah," who is described by the " ark," was not so (verse 14) ; and the remains with him are described

375

by the measures (verse 15) ; the things of his understanding, by the " window," " door," and " mansions " (verse 16).

603. That he would be preserved when the rest
would perish by an inundation of evil and falsity
(verse 17).

604. And that the truths and goods which were
with him would be saved (verse 18) ; and thus
whatever was of the understanding and whatever
was of the will, by regeneration (verses 19, 20) ;
for receiving which he was to be prepared
(verse 21) ; and that it was so done (verse 22).

THE INTERNAL SENSE.

605. The subject now treated of is the formation
of a new church, which is called " Noah " ; and
its formation is described by the ark into which
living things of every kind were received. But
as is wont to be the case, before that new church
could arise it was necessary that the man of the
church should suffer many temptations, which are
described by the lifting up of the ark, its fluctuation, and its delay upon the waters of the flood.
And finally, that he became a true spiritual man
and was set free, is described by the cessation of
the waters, and the many things that follow. No
one can see this who adheres to the sense of the
letter only, in consequence (and especially is this
the case here) of all things being historically connected, and presenting the idea of a history of
events. But such was the style of the men of that
time, and most pleasing to them was it that all
things should be wrapped up in representative

376

figures, and that these should be arranged in the form of history ; and the more coherent the historical series, the better suited it was to their genius. For in those ancient times men were not so much inclined to knowledges as at this day, but to profound thoughts, of which the offspring was such as has been described.. This was the wisdom of the ancients.

606. That the " flood," the " ark," and therefore the things described in connection with them, signify regeneration, and also the temptations that precede regeneration, is in some degree known among the learned at this day, who also compare regeneration and temptations to the waters of a flood.

607. But the character of this church will be described hereafter. That an idea of it may be presented here, it shall be briefly said that the Most Ancient Church was celestial, as already shown, but this church became spiritual. The Most Ancient Church had a perception of good and truth ; this, or the Ancient Church, had not perception, but in its place another kind of dictate, which may be called conscience. But what is as yet unknown 2 in the world, and is perhaps difficult to believe, is that the men of the Most Ancient Church had internal respiration, and only tacit external respiration. Thus they spoke not so much by words, as afterwards and as at this day, but by ideas, as angels do ; and these they could express by innumerable changes of the looks and face, especially of the lips. In the lips there are countless series of muscular fibres which at this day are not set free, but being free with the men of that time, they could so present, signify, and represent ideas by them as to

express in a minute's time what at this day it
would require an hour to say by articulate sounds
and words, and they could do this more fully and
clearly to the apprehension and understanding of
those present than is possible by words, or series of
words in combination. This may perhaps seem
incredible, but yet it is true. And there are many
others, not of this earth, who have spoken and at
this day speak in a similar manner ; concerning
whom, of the Lord's Divine mercy, we will treat
3 hereafter. It has been granted me to know the
nature of that internal respiration, and how in
process of time it was changed. As these most
ancient people had a respiration such as the angels
have, who breathe in a similar manner, they were
in profound ideas of thought, and were able to
have such perception as cannot be described ; and
even if it could be described such as it really was,
it would not be believed, because it would not be
comprehended. But in their posterity this internal
respiration little by little came to an end ; and
with those who were possessed with dreadful
persuasions and phantasies, it became such that
they could no longer present any idea of thought
except the most debased, the effect of which was
that they could not survive, and therefore all
became extinct.

608. When internal respiration ceased, external
respiration gradually succeeded, almost like that
of the present day ; and with external respiration
a language of words, or of articulate sound, into
which the ideas of thought were determined. Thus
the state of man was entirely changed, and became
such that he could no longer have similar perception, but instead of perception another kind of

378

dictate which may be called conscience ; for it
was like conscience, though a kind of intermediate
between perception and the conscience known to
some at this day. And when such determination
of the ideas of thought took place, that is to say,
into spoken words, they could no longer be instructed, like the most ancient man, through the
internal man, but through the external. And,
therefore, in place of the revelations of the Most
Ancient Church, doctrinal things succeeded, which
could first be received by the external senses, and
from them material ideas of the memory could be
formed, and from these, ideas of thought, by which
and according to which they were instructed. Hence
it was that this church which followed had an
entirely different genius from that of the Most
Ancient Church, and if the Lord had not brought
the human race into this genius, or into this state,
no man could have been saved.

609. As the state of the man of this church which
is called " Noah " was altogether changed from
that of the man of the Most Ancient Church, he
could no longer—as before said—be informed and
enlightened in the same way as the most ancient
man ; for his internals were closed, so that he no
longer had communication with heaven, except
such as was unconscious. Nor, for the same reason,
could he be instructed except as before said by
the external way of sense or of the senses. On this
account, of the Lord's providence, doctrinal matters
of faith, with some of the revelations to the Most
Ancient Church, were preserved for the use of this
posterity. These doctrinal things were first
collected by " Cain," and were stored up that they
might not be lost ; and therefore it is said of Cain

that a " mark was set upon him, lest any one should slay him " (concerning which see what was said at that place, chapter iv. 15). These doctrinal matters were afterwards reduced. into doctrine by " Enoch " ; but because this doctrine was of use to no one at that time, but was for posterity, it is said that " God took him." (See also chapter v. 24.) These doctrinal matters of faith are what were preserved by the Lord for the use of this posterity or church ; for it was foreseen by the Lord that perception would be lost, and therefore it was provided that these doctrinal things should remain.

610. Verse 9. **These are the nativities of Noah; Noah was a man righteous and perfect in his generations; Noah walked with God.** By " the nativities of Noah," is signified a description of the reformation or regeneration of the new church. That " Noah was a man just and perfect in his generations," signifies that he was such that he could be endowed with charity ; " just " (or " righteous ") has relation to the good of charity, and " perfect " to the truth of charity. The " generations " are those of faith. To " walk with God " signifies here as before, when said of Enoch, the doctrine of faith.

611. That by " the nativities of Noah " is signified a description of the reformation or regeneration of the new church, is evident from what has been said before (at chapter ii. 4, and v. 1).

612. **Noah was a man righteous and perfect (integer) in his generations.** That this signifies that he was such that he could be endowed with charity, is evident from the signification of " just and perfect," " just " having regard to the good of charity, and " perfect " to the truth of charity ;

and also from the essential of that church being
charity, concerning which, of the Lord's Divine
mercy, we will treat hereafter. That " just " has
regard to the good of charity, and " perfect " to
the truth of charity, is evident from the Word, as
in *Isaiah* :

> They will seek Me daily and desire knowledge
> of My ways, as a nation that doeth righteous-
> ness, and forsaketh not the judgment of their
> God ; they will ask of Me the judgments of
> righteousness, and will long for the approach of
> God (lviii. 2).

Here " judgment " denotes the things which are
of truth, and "righteousness" those which are
of good. " Doing judgment and righteousness "
became as it were an established formula for doing
what is true and good (as in *Isa.* lvi. 1 ; *Jer.* xxii. 3,
13, 15 ; xxiii. 5 ; xxxiii. 14, 16, 19). The Lord
said :

> The righteous shall shine forth as the sun, in
> the kingdom of My Father (*Matt.* xiii. 43).

" The righteous " means those who are endowed
with charity ; and concerning the consummation
of the age He said :

> The angels shall go forth and shall sever the
> wicked from among the righteous (v. 49).

Here also the " righteous " denote those who are
in the good of charity. But " perfect " signifies 2
the truth which is from charity, for there is truth
from many another origin ; but that which is
from the good of charity from the Lord is called
" perfect " and a " perfect man," as in *David* :

> Who shall sojourn in Thy tent, who shall
> dwell in the mountain of Thy holiness ? He

that walketh perfect, and worketh righteousness, and speaketh the truth in his heart (*Ps.* xv. 1, 2).

The " perfect " man is here described. Again :

With the holy Thou wilt show Thyself holy ; with the perfect man Thou wilt show Thyself perfect (xviii. 25).

Here the " perfect man " is one who is so from holiness, or the good of charity. And again :

Jehovah will withhold no good from them that walk in perfectness (*integritate*) (lxxxiv. 11).

3 That a " perfect man " is one who is true from good, or who speaks and does truth from charity, is evident from the words " walk " and " way " being often applied to what is perfect, that is, to wholeness or entirety, and also the words " upright " or " uprightness," which words pertain to truth. As in *David* :

I will teach the perfect in the way how far he shall come unto me. I will walk within my house in the perfectness of my heart (*Ps.* ci. 2).

And in the sixth verse :

He that walketh in the way of the perfect, he shall minister unto me.

Again :

Blessed are the perfect in the way, who walk in the law of Jehovah (*Ps.* cxix. 1).

And again :

Perfectness and uprightness shall guard me (xxv. 21).

And in another place :

Mark the perfect man, and behold the upright, for the end of that man is peace (xxxvii. 37).

382

It is evident from these passages that he is called " righteous " who does what is good, and that he is called " perfect " who does what is true therefrom, which also is to " do righteousness and judgment." " Holiness " and " righteousness " are the celestial of faith ; " perfectness " and " judgment " are the spiritual things thence derived.

613. That the " generations " are those of faith, does not appear from the sense of the letter, which is historical ; but as internal things only are here treated of, generations of faith are signified. It is also evident from the connection that the generations here are no others. It is the same in other passages of the Word, as in *Isaiah* :

They that shall be of thee shall build the waste places of old ; thou shalt raise up the foundations of generation and generation ; and thou shalt be called, Tne repairer of the breach, The restorer of paths to dwell in (lviii. 12).

All these things signify what is of faith ; the " waste places of old " signify celestial things of faith ; the " foundations of generation and generation," spiritual things of faith. Those which had lapsed from the ancient times have a similar signification. Again :

They shall build the old wastes, they shall raise up the former desolations, they shall renew the waste cities, the desolations of generation and generation (lxi. 4).

This has a similar signification. And again :

They shall not labour in vain, nor bring forth for trouble ; for they are the seed of the blessed of Jehovah, and their offspring with them (lxv. 23).

Here also "bringing forth (*generare*)" is predicated of the things of faith; "labouring," of those of love. Of the latter it is said that they are "the seed of the blessed of Jehovah"; of the former, that they are "offspring."

614. That "to walk with God" signifies the doctrine of faith, may be seen from what was said before respecting Enoch (chapter v. 22, 24), of whom also it is said that he "walked with God"; and there it signifies the doctrine of faith preserved for the use of posterity. And as this is the posterity for whose use it was preserved, the subject is now here taken up again.

615. The quality of the man of this church is here described in general; not that he was such as yet—for his formation is treated of in what follows—but that he might become such: that is to say, that by cognitions of faith he could be endowed with charity, and so act from charity, and from the good of charity know what is true. For this reason the good of charity or "righteous" precedes, and the truth of charity or "perfect" follows. Charity, as before said, is love towards the neighbour and mercy; and it is a lower degree of the love of the Most Ancient Church, which was love to the Lord. Thus love now descended and became more external, and is to be called charity.

616. Verse 10. **And Noah begat three sons: Shem, Ham, and Japheth.** "Noah begat three sons," signifies that three kinds of doctrine thence arose, which are meant by "Shem, Ham, and Japheth."

384

617. **Noah begat three sons.** That this signifies that three kinds of doctrine thence arose, is evident from all that has been shown before about names signifying nothing else than churches, or, what is the same, doctrines. So it is here ; but here they are merely mentioned for the sake of the series or connection with the things that precede, which are, that it was foreseen by the Lord that the man of this genius could be endowed with charity ; but yet that three kinds of doctrines would thence have birth, which doctrines, of the Lord's Divine mercy, shall be described hereafter, where Shem, Ham, and Japheth are treated of.

618. That " Noah was righteous and perfect," that he " walked with God," and in this verse that he " begat three sons," is all said in the past tense, and yet these expressions look to the future. It should be known that the internal sense is such that it has no relation to times ; and this the original language favours, where sometimes one and the same word is applicable to any time whatever, without using different words, for by this means interior things appear more evidently. The language derives this from the internal sense, which is more manifold than any one could believe ; and therefore it does not suffer itself to be limited by times and distinctions.

619. Verse 11. **And the earth was corrupt before God ; and the earth was filled with violence.** By the " earth " is signified the race mentioned before. It is said to be " corrupt " on account of their dreadful persuasions ; and to be " filled with violence," on account of their foul lusts. Here and in the following verses of this chapter it is said " God." because there was now no church.

620. That by the " earth " is signified the race which has been treated of before, is evident from what has already been told respecting the signification of "earth" and of "ground." The "earth" is a term very often used in the Word ; and by it is signified the " land " where the true church of the Lord is, as the " land " of Canaan ; also a " land " where there is not a church, as the " land " of Egypt, and of the Gentiles. Thus it denotes the race that dwells there ; and as it denotes the race, it denotes likewise every one of the race who is there. The church is called the " land " from celestial love, as the " land of Canaan " ; and the " land of the Gentiles " from impure loves. But it is called " ground " from faith which is implanted ; for, as has been said, the land or country is the containant of the ground, and the ground is the containant of the field, just as love is the containant of faith, and faith is the containant of the cognitions of faith which are implanted. Here the " earth " is taken for a race in which everything of celestial love and of the church had perished. What is predicated is known from the subject.

621. That the earth is said to be " corrupt " on account of their dreadful persuasions, and " filled with violence " because of their foul lusts, is evident from the signification of the verb to " corrupt " and of the word " violence." In the Word one term is never taken for another, but uniformly that word is employed which fitly expresses the thing of which it is predicated ; and this so exactly that from the words alone which are used, what is in the internal sense at once appears, as here from the words " corrupt " and " violence." " Corrupt " is predicated of the things of the

386

understanding when it is desolated ; " violence,"
of the things of the will, when vastated. Thus " to
corrupt " is predicated of persuasions ; and
" violence," of lusts.

622. That " to corrupt " is predicated of persuasions, is evident in *Isaiah* :

They shall not hurt, nor corrupt, in all the
mountain of My holiness ; for the earth shall
be full of the knowledge of Jehovah (xi. 9).

And so in lxv. 25, where " to hurt " has relation
to the will, or to lusts, and " to corrupt " to the
understanding, or to persuasions of falsity. Again :

Woe to the sinful nation, a people laden with
iniquity, a seed of evildoers, sons that are
corrupters (i. 4).

Here, as in other places, " nation " and the " seed
of evildoers " denote evils which are of the will,
or of lusts ; " people," and " sons that are corrupters," falsities which are of the understanding, or
of persuasions. In *Ezekiel* :

Thou wast more corrupt than they in all thy
ways (xvi. 47).

Here " corrupt " is predicated of things of the
understanding, of the reason, or of the thought ;
for " way " is a word that signifies truth. In
David :

They have done what is corrupt, and have done
abominable work (*Ps.* xiv. 1).

Here " what is corrupt " denotes dreadful persuasions, and " abominable " the foul lusts which are
in the work, or from which the work is done. In
Daniel :

After sixty and two weeks shall the Messiah
be cut off, and there shall be none belonging to

Him ; and the people of the leader that shall
come shall corrupt the city and the sanctuary,
and the end thereof shall be with a flood (ix. 26).

Here likewise " to corrupt " denotes persuasions
of what is false, of which a " flood " is predicated.

623. **The earth was filled with violence.** That
this is said on account of their foul lusts, and most
of all on account of those which come of the
love of self, or of inordinate arrogance, is evident
from the Word. It is called " violence " when men
do violence to holy things by profaning them, as
did these antediluvians who immersed the doctrinal
things of faith in all kinds of lusts. As in *Ezekiel* :

My faces will I turn from them, and they shall
profane My secret [place], and robbers shall
enter into it and profane it. Make the chain ;
for the land is full of the judgment of bloods, and
the city is full of violence (vii. 22, 23).

The " violent " are here described as to who they
are, and that they are such as we have stated.
Again :

They shall eat their bread in solicitude, and
drink their waters in desolation, that her land
may be devastated from its fullness, because of the
violence of all them that dwell therein (xii. 19).

The " bread which they shall eat in solicitude," is
the celestial things, and the " waters which they
shall drink in desolation " are the spiritual things,
to which they have done violence, or which they
2 have profaned. In *Isaiah* :

Their webs shall not be for garments ; neither
shall they be covered in their works ; their
works are works of iniquity, and the deed of
violence is in their hands (lix. 6).

388

Here " webs " and " garments " are predicated of things of the understanding, that is, of the thought ; " iniquity " and " violence," of things of the will, that is, of works. In *Jonah* :

Let them turn every one from his evil way, and from the violence that is in their hands (iii. 8).

Here the " evil way " is predicated of falsities, which are of the understanding ; and " violence," of evils, which are of the will. In *Jeremiah* :

A rumour shall come in one year, and violence in the land (li. 46).

" A rumour " denotes things of the understanding, " violence," those of the will. In *Isaiah* : 2

He hath done no violence, neither was there any deceit in His mouth (liii. 9).

Here also " violence " denotes the things of the will ; " deceit in His mouth," those of the understanding.

624. That a state not of the church is here treated of, is evident from the fact that here and in the following verses of this chapter the name " God " is used, but in preceding verses " Jehovah." When there is not a church " God " is the term used, and when there is a church " Jehovah " ; as in the first chapter of *Genesis*, when there was no church, it is said " God " ; but in the second chapter, when there was a church, it is said " Jehovah God." The name " Jehovah " is most holy, and belongs only to the church ; but the name " God " is not so holy, for there was no nation that had not gods, and therefore the name God was not so holy. No one was permitted to speak the name " Jehovah " unless he had a cognition of the true faith ; but any one might speak the name " God."

625. Verse 12. **And God saw the earth, and behold it was corrupt, for all flesh had corrupted its way upon the earth.** "God saw the earth," signifies that God knew man; "it was corrupt," signifies that there was nothing but falsity; "for all flesh had corrupted its way upon the earth," signifies that the corporeal nature of man had destroyed all the understanding of truth.

626. **God saw the earth.** That this signifies that God knew man, is evident to every one; for God who knows all things and everything from eternity, has no need to see whether man is such. To "see" is human, and therefore—as has been said at the sixth verse and elsewhere—the Word is spoken in accordance with the appearance of things to man; and this to such a degree that God is even said to "see with eyes."

627. **For all flesh had corrupted its way upon the earth.** That this signifies that man's corporeal nature had destroyed all the understanding of truth, is evident from the signification of "flesh" (concerning which see verse 3), which in general means every man, and in particular the corporeal man, or all that is of the body; and from the signification of a "way" as being the understanding of truth, that is, truth itself. That a "way" is predicated of the understanding of truth, that is, of truth, is evident from passages which have been adduced in different places before, and also from the following. In *Moses*:

Jehovah said, Arise, get thee down quickly from hence; for thy people have corrupted themselves; they have suddenly turned back out of the way which I commanded them; they have made them a molten image (*Deut.* ix. 12, 16).

This means that they had turned away from the commandments, which are truths. In *Jeremiah* : 2

Whose eyes are open upon all the ways of the sons of man, to give every man according to his ways, and according to the fruit of his works (xxxii. 19).

The " ways " here are a life according to the commandments ; " the fruit of his works," is a life from charity. Thus a " way " is predicated of truths, which are those of the precepts and commandments. And the meaning of " son of man " (*homo*) and of " man " (*vir*) is as has been shown above. So in *Jeremiah* vii. 3, and xvii. 10. In *Hosea* :

I will visit upon him his ways, and render to him his works (iv. 9).

In *Zechariah* :

Return ye from your evil ways, and from your evil works. Like as Jehovah Zebaoth thought to do unto us according to our ways, and according to our works (i. 4, 6).

Here the sense is similar, but the opposite of the former, because they are evil " ways " and evil " works." In *Jeremiah* :

I will give them one heart, and one way (xxxii. 39).

" Heart " denotes goods, and " way " truths. In *David* :

Make me to understand the way of Thy commandments ; remove from me the way of falsehood ; and grant me Thy law graciously. I have chosen the way of truth. I will run the way of Thy commandments (cxix. 27, 29, 30, 32).

391

Here the "way of the commandments and precepts" is called the "way of truth," opposed to
3 which is the "way of falsehood." Again :

> Make known to me Thy ways, O Jehovah,
> teach me Thy paths. Lead my way in Thy
> truth, and teach me (*Ps.* xxv. 4, 5).

Here likewise a "way" manifestly denotes truth.
In *Isaiah* :

> With whom did Jehovah take counsel, and
> who instructed Him, and taught Him the path
> of judgment, and taught Him knowledge and
> made Him to know the way of understanding ?
> (xl. 14).

This manifestly means the understanding of truth.
In *Jeremiah* :

> Thus hath said Jehovah, Stand ye upon the
> ways and see, and ask for the old paths, where
> is the good way, and go therein (vi. 16).

Here likewise "way" is put for the understanding
of truth. In *Isaiah* :

> I will lead the blind in a way that they knew
> not, in paths that they have not known I will
> lead them (xlii. 16).

The terms "way," "path (*semita*)," "path
(*trames*)," "street (*platea*)," and "street (*vicus*),"
are predicated of truth, because they lead to truth :
as also in *Jeremiah* :

> They have caused them to stumble in their
> ways, in the ancient paths, to walk in by-paths,
> in a way not cast up (xviii. 15).

So in the book of *Judges* :

> In the days of Jael the paths ceased, and they
> that walked in paths went through crooked
> paths. The streets ceased in Israel (v. 6).

392

628. The internal sense here is that every man whatsoever, in the land where the church was, " had corrupted his way," so that he did not understand truth. For every man had become corporeal, not only those referred to in the preceding verse, but also those called " Noah," who are specifically treated of here and in the following verse, for such they were before they were regenerated. These things are said first, because in the following verses their regeneration is treated of. And because but little of the church remained, " God " is now named, not " Jehovah." In this verse is signified that there was nothing true, and in the following verse, that there was nothing good, except in the remains which they had who are called " Noah " (for without remains there is no regeneration), and also in the doctrinal matters that they knew. But there was no understanding of truth, as there never can be except where there is a will of good. Where the will is not, there is not understanding ; and as the will is, such is the understanding. The most ancient people had a will of good, because they had love to the Lord ; and from this they had an understanding of truth, but this understanding wholly perished with the will. A kind of rational truth however, as well as natural good, remained with those who are called " Noah," and therefore they could be regenerated.

629. Verse 13. **And God said unto Noah, The end of all flesh is come before Me, for the earth is filled with violence from their faces, and behold I destroy them with the earth.** " God said," signifies that it was so ; " the end of all flesh is come before Me," signifies that the human race must surely perish ; " for the earth is filled with

violence," signifies that they no longer had a will of good ; " behold I destroy them with the earth," signifies that the human race would perish with the church.

630. That " God said " signifies that it was so, is evident from the fact that in Jehovah there is nothing but Being (*Esse*).

631. That **the end of all flesh is come before Me** signifies that the human race must surely perish, is evident from the words themselves, and from the signification of " flesh," which means every man is general, and specifically the corporeal man, as already shown.

632. That **the earth is filled with violence** signifies that they no longer had a will of good, is evident from what has been said and shown before concerning the signification of " violence " (at verse 11). In the preceding verse the understanding of truth was spoken of, and here the will of good, because both had perished with the man of the church.

633. The case is this : With no man is there any understanding of truth and will of good, not even with those who were of the Most Ancient Church. But when men become celestial it appears as if they have a will of good and understanding of truth, and yet this is of the Lord alone, as they also know, acknowledge, and perceive. So is it with the angels also. So true is this that whoever does not know, acknowledge, and perceive that it is so, has no understanding of truth or will of good whatever. With every man, and with every angel, even the most celestial, his proprium is nothing but falsity and evil ; for it is known that the heavens are not clean before the Lord [*Job* xv. 15], and

that all good and all truth are of the Lord alone.
But so far as a man or an angel is capable of being
perfected, so far of the Lord's Divine mercy he is
perfected, and receives, as it were, an understanding
of truth and a will of good ; but his having these
is only an appearance. Every man can be perfected—and consequently receive this gift of the
Lord's mercy—in accordance with the actual
deeds of his life, and in a manner suited to the
hereditary evil implanted by his parents.

634. But it is extremely difficult to say, in a
manner to be apprehended, what is the understanding of truth and the will of good in the proper
sense, for the reason that a man supposes everything he thinks to be of the understanding, since
he calls it so ; and everything that he desires he
supposes to be of the will, since he calls it so. And
it is the more difficult to explain this so as to be
apprehended, because most men at this day are
also ignorant of the fact that what belongs to the
understanding is distinct from what belongs to
the will, for when they think anything they say
they will it, and when they will a thing they say
they think it. This is one cause of the difficulty,
and another reason why this subject can with
difficulty be comprehended is that men are solely
in what is of the body, that is, their life is in the
most external things. And for these reasons they 2
do not know that there is in every man something
that is interior, and something still interior to
that, and indeed an inmost ; and that his corporeal
and sensuous part is only the outermost. Desires
and things of the memory are interior ; affections
and rational things are interior still to these ; and
the will of good and understanding of truth are

inmost. And these are so distinct from one another that nothing can ever be more distinct. The corporeal man makes all these into a one, and confounds them. This is why he believes that when his body dies all things will die ; though in fact he then first begins to live, and this by his interiors following one another closely in their order. If his interiors were not thus distinct, and did not thus succeed each other, men could never be in the other life spirits, angelic spirits, and angels, these being thus distinguished according to their interiors. For this reason there are three heavens, quite distinct from one another. From these considerations it may now in some measure be evident what, in the proper sense, are the understanding of truth and the will of good ; and that they can be predicated only of the celestial man, or of the angels of the third heaven.

635. What is said in the preceding verse and in this one signifies that in the end of the days of the antediluvian church all understanding of truth and will of good had perished, so that among the antediluvians who were imbued with dreadful persuasions and filthy lusts not even a vestige appeared. But with those who are called " Noah " there continued to be remains, which, however, could not bring forth anything of understanding and will, but only rational truth and natural good. For the operation of remains is according to the nature of the man. Through remains these people could be regenerated ; and persuasions did not obstruct and absorb the Lord's operation through remains. Persuasions, or principles of falsity, when inrooted, impede all operation ; and unless these are first eradicated the man can never be

396

regenerated ; concerning which subject, of the Lord's Divine mercy, we will treat hereafter.

636. I will destroy them with the earth. That this signifies that together with the church the human race would perish, is evident from its being said " with the earth " ; for the " earth " in a wide sense signifies love, as before said, and thus the celestial of the church. Here, since no love and nothing whatever that is celestial remained, the " earth " signifies the love of self, and whatever is contrary to the celestial of the church. And yet there was a man of the church, for they had doctrinal things of faith. For, as before stated, the earth is the containant of the ground, and the ground is the containant of the field ; as love is the containant of faith, and faith is the containant of the knowledges of faith.

637. That " I will destroy them with the earth " signifies that together with the church the human race would perish, is on this account : If the Lord's church should be entirely extinguished on the earth, the human race could by no means exist, but one and all would perish. The church, as before said, is as the heart : so long as the heart lives, the neighbouring viscera and members can live ; but as soon as the heart dies, they one and all die also. The Lord's church on earth is as the heart, whence the human race, even that part of it which is outside the church, has life. The reason is quite unknown to any one, but in order that something of it may be known, it may be stated that the whole human race on earth is as a body with its parts, wherein the church is as the heart ; and that unless there were a church with which as with a heart the Lord might be united through

heaven and the world of spirits, there would be
disjunction ; and if there were disjunction of the
human race from the Lord, it would instantly
perish. This is the reason why from the first
creation of man there has always been some church,
and whenever the church has begun to perish it
2 has yet remained with some. This was also the
reason of the Lord's coming into the world. If
in His Divine mercy He had not come, the whole
human race on this earth would have perished, for
the church was then at its last extremity, and there
was scarcely any good and truth surviving. The
reason why the human race cannot live unless it
is conjoined with the Lord through heaven and
the world of spirits, is that regarded in himself
man is much viler than the brutes. If left to himself
he would rush into the ruin of himself and of all
things ; for he desires nothing but what would
make for the destruction of himself and of all. His
order should be, that one should love another as
himself ; but now every one loves himself more
than others, and thus hates all others. But with
brute animals the case is quite different : their order
is that according to which they live. Thus they live
quite according to the order in which they are, and
man entirely contrary to his order. Therefore, unless
the Lord should have compassion on him, and conjoin him with Himself through angels, he could not
live a single moment ; but this he does not know.

638. Verse 14. **Make thee an ark of gopher
woods, mansions shalt thou make the ark, and shalt
pitch it within and without with pitch.** By the
" ark " is signified the man of that church ; by
" gopher wood " his lusts ; by the " mansions "
are signified the two parts of the man, which are

the will and the understanding; by " pitching it within and without " is signified his preservation from an inundation of lusts.

639. That by the " ark " is signified the man of that church, or the church called " Noah," is sufficiently evident from the description of it in the following verses ; and from the fact that the Lord's Word everywhere involves spiritual and celestial things ; that is, that the Word is spiritual and celestial. If the ark with its coating of pitch, its measurement, and it construction, and the flood also, signified nothing more than the letter expresses, there would be nothing at all spiritual and celestial in the account of it, but only something historical, which would be of no more use to the human race than any similar thing described by secular writers. But because the Word of the Lord everywhere in its bosom or interiors involves and contains spiritual and celestial things, it is very evident that by the ark and all the things said about the ark, are signified hidden things not yet revealed. It is the same in other places, as in the 2 case of the little ark in which Moses was concealed, which was placed among the sedge by the river side (*Exod.* ii. 3) ; and to take a more lofty instance, it was the same with the holy ark in the wilderness, that was made after the pattern shown to Moses on Mount Sinai. If each and all things in this ark had not been representative of the Lord and His kingdom, it would have been nothing but a sort of idol, and the worship idolatrous. Similarly the temple of Solomon was not holy at all of itself, or on account of the gold, silver, cedar, and stone in it, but on account of all the things which these represented. And so here—if the ark and its

construction, with its several particulars, did not signify some hidden thing of the church, the Word would not be the Word of the Lord, but a kind of dead letter, as in the case of any profane writer. Therefore it is evident that the ark signifies the man of the church, or the church called " Noah."

640. That by " gopher woods " are signified lusts, and by the " mansions " the two parts of this man, which are the will and the understanding, no one has hitherto known. Nor can any one know how these things are signified, unless he is first told how the case was with that church. The Most Ancient Church, as has often been said, knew from love whatever was of faith ; or what is the same, from a will of good had understanding of truth. But their posterity received also by inheritance that lusts, which are of the will, ruled over them, in which they immersed the doctrinal things of faith, and thus became " Nephilim." When, therefore, the Lord foresaw that if man continued to be of such a nature he would perish eternally, He provided that the will should be separated from the understanding, and that man should be formed, not as before by a will of good, but through an understanding of truth should be endowed with charity, which appears as a will of good. Such became this new church which is called " Noah," and thus it was of an entirely different nature from the Most Ancient Church. Besides this church, there were other churches also at that time, as that which is called " Enosh " (see chapter iv. 26), and others also of which no such mention and description is extant. Only this church " Noah " is here described, because it was of another and entirely different nature from the Most Ancient Church.

641. As this man of the church must be reformed as to that part of man which is called the understanding, before he could be reformed as to the other part which is called the will, it is here described how the things of the will were separated from those of the understanding, and were, as it were, covered over and reserved, lest anything should touch the will. For if things of the will, that is of lust, had been excited, the man would have perished, as will appear, of the Lord's Divine mercy, hereafter. These two parts—the will and the understanding—are so distinct in man that nothing could be more distinct, as has been granted me also to know with certainty from the fact that things of the understanding of spirits and angels flow into the left part of the head or brain, and things of the will into the right ; and it is the same with respect to the face. When angelic spirits flow in, they do so gently like the softest breaths of air ; but when evil spirits flow in, it is like an inundation into the left part of the brain with dreadful phantasies and persuasions, and into the right with lusts, their influx being, as it were, an inundation of phantasies and lusts.

642. From all this it is evident what this first description of the ark involves, with its construction of gopher wood, its mansions, and its coating within and without with pitch, namely, that one part, that of the will, was preserved from inundation ; and only that part opened which is of the understanding, and it is described, in verse 16, by the window, the door, and the lowest, second, and third stories. These things are not easily believed, because hitherto no one has had any idea of them. And yet they are most true. But these

are the least and most general of the hidden meanings which man is ignorant of. If the individual particulars were told him, he could not apprehend even one of them.

643. But as regards the signification itself of the words : that " gopher wood " signifies lusts, and the " mansions " the two parts of man, is evident from the Word. Gopher wood is a wood abounding in sulphur,* like the fir, and others of its kind. On account of its sulphur it is said that it signifies lusts, because it easily takes fire. The most ancient people compared things in man (and regarded them as having a likeness) to gold, silver, brass, iron, stone, and wood—his inmost celestial to gold, his lower celestial to brass, and what was lowest, or the corporeal therefrom, to wood. But his inmost spiritual they compared, and regarded as having a likeness, to silver, his lower spiritual to iron, and his lowest to stone. And such in the internal sense is the signification of these things when they are mentioned in the Word, as in *Isaiah* :

> For brass I will bring gold, and for iron I will bring silver, and for wood brass, and for stones iron ; I will also make thine officers peace, and thine exactors righteousness (lx. 17).

Here the Lord's kingdom is treated of, in which there are not such metals, but spiritual and celestial things ; and that these are signified is very evident from the mention of " peace " and " righteousness." " Gold," " brass," and " wood " here correspond to one another, and signify things celestial or of the will, as before said ; and " silver," " iron," and

---

* The word "sulphur" was formerly used not exclusively as the name of the element, but also as a general term for any inflammable substance.

" stone " correspond to one another, and signify
things spiritual or of the understanding. In *Ezekiel* : 2

> They shall make a spoil of thy riches and make
> a prey of thy merchandise ; thy stones, and thy
> wood (xxvi. 12).

It is very manifest that by " riches " and " mer-
chandise " are not meant worldly riches and mer-
chandise, but celestial and spiritual ; and the same
by the " stones " and " wood "—the " stones "
being those things which are of the understanding,
and the " wood " those which are of the will.
In *Habakkuk* :

> The stone crieth out of the wall, and the beam
> out of the wood answereth (ii. 11).

The " stone " denotes the lowest degree of the
understanding ; and the " wood " the lowest of the
will, which " answers " when anything is drawn from
sensuous knowledge (*scientifico sensuali*).   Again :

> Woe unto him that saith to the wood, Awake ;
> and to the dumb stone, Arise, this shall teach.
> Behold, it is fastened with gold and silver, and
> there is no breath in the midst of it. But Jehovah
> is in the temple of His holiness (ii. 19, 20).

Here also " wood " denotes lust ; "stone " denotes
the lowest of the understanding, and therefore
to be " dumb " and to " teach " are predicated of
it ; " there is no breath in the midst of it," signifies
that it represents nothing celestial and spiritual,
just as a temple wherein are stone and wood, and
these bound together with gold and silver, is to
those who think nothing of what they represent.
In *Jeremiah* :						3

> We drink our waters for silver ; our wood
> cometh for price (*Lam.* v. 4).

Here " waters " and " silver " signify the things of the understanding ; and " wood " those of the will. Again :

Saying to wood, Thou art my father ; and to the stone, Thou hast brought us forth (*Jer.* ii. 27).

Here " wood " denotes lust, which is of the will, whence is the conception ; and " stone " the sensuous knowledge (*scientifico sensuali*), from which is the " bringing forth." Hence, in different places in the Prophets, " serving wood and stone " is put for worshipping graven images of wood and stone, by which is signified that they served lusts and phantasies ; and also " committing adultery with wood and stone," as in *Jeremiah* (iii. 9). In *Hosea* :

My people inquire of their wood, and the staff thereof declareth unto them ; because the spirit of whoredoms hath led them away (iv. 12).

This means that they make inquiry of graven 4 images of wood, or of cupidities. In *Isaiah* :

Tophet is prepared from yesterday, the pile thereof is fire and much wood, the breath of Jehovah is like a stream of burning sulphur (xxx. 33).

Here " fire," " sulphur," and " wood " stand for foul lusts. In general, " wood " signifies the things of the will which are lowest ; the precious woods, such as cedar and the like, those which are good, as for example the cedar wood in the temple, and the cedar wood employed in the cleansing of leprosy (*Lev.* xiv. 4, 6, 7), also the wood cast into the bitter waters at Marah, whereby the waters became sweet (*Exod.* xv. 25), concerning which, of the Lord's Divine mercy, we will treat in those places. But woods that were not precious, and those that were made into graven images, as well as those used for funeral piles and the like, signify lusts ; as in this place does the gopher wood, on account of its sulphur.   So in *Isaiah* :

The day of vengeance of Jehovah ; the streams thereof shall be turned into pitch, and the dust thereof into sulphur, and the land thereof shall become burning pitch (xxxiv. 9).

" Pitch " stands for dreadful phantasies ; " sulphur " for abominable lusts.

644. That by the " mansions " are signified the two parts of man, which are the will and the understanding, is evident from what has been stated before : that these two parts, the will and the understanding, are quite distinct from each other, and that for this reason, as before said, the human brain is divided into two parts, called hemispheres. To its left hemisphere belong the intellectual faculties, and to the right those of the will.   This is the most general distinction.   Besides this, both the will and the understanding are distinguished into innumerable parts, for so many are the divisions of the intellectual things of man, and so many those of the will, that they can never be described or enumerated even as to the universal genera, still less as to their species.   A man is a kind of least heaven, corresponding to the world of spirits and to heaven, wherein all the genera and all the species of the things of the understanding and of the will are distinguished by the Lord in the most perfect order, so that even the least of them is distinguished, concerning which, of the Lord's Divine mercy, we will treat hereafter.   In heaven these divisions are called Societies, in the Word " habitations," and by the Lord " mansions "

(*John* xiv. 2).   Here also they are called " mansions," because they are predicated of the ark, which signifies the man of the church.

645. That to " pitch it within and without with pitch," signifies preservation from an inundation of lusts, is evident from what has been said before. For the man of this church was first to be reformed as to the things of his understanding, and therefore he was preserved from an inundation of lusts, which would destroy all the work of reformation. In the original text it is not indeed said that it was to be " pitched with pitch," but a word is used which denotes " protection," derived from " expiate " or " propitiate," and therefore it involves the same. The expiation or propitiation of the Lord is protection from the inundation of evil.

646. Verse 15. **And thus shalt thou make it : three hundred cubits the length of the ark, fifty cubits its breadth, and thirty cubits its height.** By the numbers here as before are signified remains, that they were few ; the " length " is their holiness, the " breadth " their truth, and the " height " their good.

647. That these particulars have such a signification, as that the numbers " three hundred," " fifty," and " thirty " signify remains, and that they are few ; and that " length," " breadth," and " height " signify holiness, truth, and good, cannot but appear strange to every one, and very remote from the letter. But in addition to what was said and shown above concerning numbers (at verse 3 of this chapter, that a " hundred and twenty " there signify remains of faith), it may be evident to every

406

one also from the fact that those who are in the internal sense, as are good spirits and angels, are beyond all such things as are earthly, corporeal, and merely of the world, and thus are beyond all matters of number and measure, and yet it is given them by the Lord to perceive the Word fully, and this entirely apart from such things. And this being true, it may, therefore, be very evident that these particulars involve things celestial and spiritual which are so remote from the sense of the letter that it cannot even appear that there are such things. Such are celestial and spiritual things both in general and in particular. And from this a man may know how insane it is to desire to search into those things which are matters of faith, by means of the things of sense and knowledge (*sensualia et scientifica*) ; and to be unwilling to believe unless he apprehends them in this way.

648. That in the Word numbers and measures signify things celestial and spiritual, is very evident from the measurement of the New Jerusalem and of the Temple, in *John*, and in *Ezekiel*. Any one may see that by the "New Jerusalem" and the "new Temple" is signified the kingdom of the Lord in the heavens and on earth, and that the kingdom of the Lord in the heavens and on earth is not subject to earthly measurement ; and yet its dimensions as to length, breadth, and height are designated by numbers. From this any one may conclude that by the numbers and measures are signified holy things, as in *John* :

> There was given me a reed like unto a rod ; and the angel stood, and said unto me, Rise, and measure the temple of God, and the altar, and them that worship therein (*Rev.* xi. 1).

And concerning the New Jerusalem :

> The wall of the New Jerusalem was great and high, having twelve gates, and over the gates twelve angels, and names written, which are the names of the twelve tribes of the sons of Israel ; on the east three gates, on the north three gates, on the south three gates, on the west three gates. The wall of the city had twelve foundations, and in them the names of the twelve apostles of the Lamb. He that talked with me had a golden reed, to measure the city, and the gates thereof, and the wall thereof. The city lieth four square, and the length thereof is as great as the breadth. And he measured the city with the reed, twelve thousand furlongs ; the length and the breadth and the height thereof are equal. He measured the wall thereof, a hundred and forty and four cubits, which is the measure of a man, that is, of an angel (*Rev.* xxi. 12–17).

2 The number " twelve " occurs here throughout, which is a very holy number because it signifies the holy things of faith (as said above, at verse 3 of this chapter, and as will be shown, of the Lord's Divine mercy, at the twenty-ninth and thirtieth chapters of *Genesis*). And, therefore, it is added that this measure is the " measure of a man, that is, of an angel." It is the same with the new Temple and new Jerusalem in *Ezekiel*, which are also described as to their measures (xl. 3, 5, 7, 9, 11, 13, 14, 22, 25, 30, 36, 42, 47 ; xli. 1 to the end ; xlii. 5–15 ; *Zech.* ii. 1, 2). Here, too, regarded in themselves the numbers signify nothing but the holy celestial and spiritual, abstractedly from the numbers. So with all the numbers of the dimensions of the ark (*Exod.* xxv. 10) ; of the mercy seat ;

of the golden table ; of the tabernacle ; and of the
altar (*Exod.* xxv. 10, 17, 23 ; xxvi., and xxvii. 1) ;
and all the numbers and dimensions of the temple
(1 *Kings* vi. 2, 3), and many others.

649. But here the numbers or measures of the
ark signify nothing but the remains that were with
the man of this church when he was being reformed,
and that they were but few. This is evident from
the fact that in these numbers *five* predominates,
which in the Word signifies some or a little, as in
Isaiah :

> There shall be left therein gleanings, as the
> shaking of an olive-tree, two or three berries in
> the top of the uppermost bough, four or five in
> the branches of a fruitful one (xvii. 6).

Here " two or three " and " five " denote a few.
Again :

> One thousand at the rebuke of one ; at the
> rebuke of five shall ye flee ; until ye be left as a
> pole upon the top of a mountain (xxx. 17).

Here also " five " denotes a few. So too the least
fine, after restitution, was a " fifth part " (*Lev.* v.
16 ; vi. 5 ; xxii. 14 ; *Num.* v. 7). And the least
addition when they redeemed a beast, a house, a
field, or the tithes, was a " fifth part " (*Lev.* xxvii.
13, 15, 19, 31).

650. That " length " signifies the holiness,
" breadth " the truth, and " height " the good of
whatever things are described by the numbers,
cannot so well be confirmed from the Word, because
they are each and all predicated according to the
subject or thing treated of. Thus " length " as
applied to time signifies perpetuity and eternity,
as " length of days " in *Ps.* xxiii. 6, and xxi. 4 ;

but as applied to space it denotes holiness, as follows therefrom. And the same is the case with "breadth" and "height." There is a trinal dimension of all earthly things, but such dimensions cannot be predicated of celestial and spiritual things. When they are predicated, greater or less perfection is meant, apart from the dimensions, and also the quality and quantity; thus here the quality, that they were remains; and the quantity, that they were few.

651. Verse 16. **A window shalt thou make to the ark, and to a cubit shalt thou finish it from above; and the door of the ark shalt thou set in the side thereof; with lowest, second, and third stories shalt thou make it.** By the " window " which was to be finished " to a cubit from above," is signified the intellectual part; by the " door at the side," is signified hearing; by the " lowest, second, and third stories," are signified the things of knowledge, of reason, and of understanding (*scientifica, rationalia, et intellectualia*).

652. That the " window " signifies the intellectual part, and the " door " hearing, and thus that in this verse the intellectual part of man is treated of, is evident from what has been stated before; that the man of that church was reformed in this way. There are two lives in man; one is of the will, the other of the understanding. They become two lives when there is no will, but lust in place of a will. Then it is the other or intellectual part that can be reformed; and afterwards through this a new will can be given, so that the two may still constitute one life, namely, charity and faith. Because man was now such that he had no will, but mere lust in place of it, the part

410

which belongs to the will was closed—as stated at verse 14—and the other or intellectual part was opened ; which is the subject treated of in this verse.

653. The case is this : When a man is being reformed, which is effected by combats and temptations, such evil spirits are associated with him as excite nothing but his things of knowledge and reason ; and spirits that excite lusts are kept entirely away from him. For there are two kinds of evil spirits, those who act upon man's reasonings, and those who act upon his lusts. The evil spirits who excite a man's reasonings bring forth all his falsities, and endeavour to persuade him that they are true, and even turn truths into falsities. A man must fight against these when he is in temptation ; but it is really the Lord who fights, through the angels who are adjoined to the man. As soon as the falsities are separated, and as it were dispersed, by these combats, the man is prepared to receive the truths of faith. For so long as falsities prevail, a man never can receive the truths of faith, because the principles of falsity stand in the way. When he has thus been prepared to receive the truths of faith, then for the first time can celestial seeds be implanted in him, which are the seeds of charity. The seeds of charity can never be implanted in ground where falsities reign, but only where truths reign. Thus is it with the reformation or regeneration of the spiritual man, and so it was with the man of this church which is called " Noah." Hence it is that here the " window " and " door " of the ark are spoken of, and its " lowest, second, and third stories," which all pertain to the spiritual or intellectual man.

411

654. This agrees with what is at this day known in the churches; that faith comes by hearing. But faith is by no means the cognitions of the things that are of faith, or that are to be believed. This is only knowledge; whereas faith is acknowledgment. There can, however, be no acknowledgment with any one unless the chief thing of faith is in him, which is charity, that is, love towards the neighbour and mercy. When there is charity, then there is acknowledgment, or faith. He who apprehends otherwise is as far away from a knowledge of faith as earth is from heaven. When charity is present, which is the goodness of faith, then acknowledgment is present, which is the truth of faith. When therefore a man is being regenerated according to the things of knowledge, of reason, and of understanding, it is to the end that the ground may be prepared—that is, his mind— for receiving charity; from which, or from the life of which, he thereafter thinks and acts. Then he is reformed or regenerated, and not before.

655. That the " window " which was to be " finished to a cubit from above " signifies the intellectual part, any one may see from what has now been said; and also from the fact that when the construction of the ark is being treated of, and by the " ark " is signified the man of the church, the intellectual part cannot be otherwise compared than to a " window from above." And so in other parts of the Word: the intellectual part of man, that is, his internal sight, whether it be reason, or mere reasoning, is called a " window." Thus in *Isaiah*:

O thou afflicted, tossed with tempest and not comforted, I will make thy suns (windows) of

rubies, and thy gates of carbuncles, and all thy
border of pleasant stones (liv. 11, 12).

Here " suns " are put for " windows," from the
light that is admitted, or transmitted. The
" suns " or " windows " in this passage are intellectual things that come from charity, and therefore they are likened to a " ruby " ; the " gates "
are rational things thence derived ; and the
" border " is that which is of knowledge and the
senses. The Lord's church is here treated of. All 2
the windows of the temple at Jerusalem represented the same : the highest of them the intellectual things ; the middle, rational things ; and
the lowest, the things of knowledge and the senses ;
for there were three stories (1 *Kings* vi. 8). Likewise the windows of the new Jerusalem in *Ezekiel*
(xl. 16, 22, 25, 33, 36). In *Jeremiah* :

Death is come up into our windows, it is
entered into our palaces ; to cut off the little
child from the street, the young men from the
streets (*vicis*) (ix. 21).

Windows of the middle story are here meant, which
are rational things, it being meant that they are
extinguished ; the " little child in the street," is
truth beginning. Because " windows " signify 3
things intellectual and rational that are of truth,
they signify also reasonings that are of falsity.
Thus in the same Prophet :

Woe unto him that buildeth his house in what
is not righteousness, and his chambers in what
is not judgment ; who saith, I will build me a
house of measures, and spacious chambers, and
he cutteth him out windows, and it is floored
with cedar, and painted with vermilion (xxii.
13, 14).

413

Here "windows" denote principles of falsity. In *Zephaniah* :

> Droves of beasts shall lie down in the midst of her, every wild animal of his kind, both the cormorant and the bittern shall lodge in the pomegranates thereof ; a voice shall sing in the window ; wasting shall be upon the threshold (ii. 14).

This is said of Asshur and Nineveh ; "Asshur" denotes the understanding, here vastated ; a "voice singing in the windows," reasonings from phantasies.

656. That by the "door at the side" is signified hearing is now, therefore, evident, and there is no need that it should be confirmed by similar examples from the Word. For the ear is to the internal organs of sense as a door at the side is to a window above ; or what is the same, the hearing which is of the ear, is so to the intellectual part which is of the internal sensory.

657. That by the "lowest, second, and third stories," are signified things of knowledge, of reason, and of understanding, follows also from what has been shown. There are three degrees of intellectual things in man ; the lowest is that of knowledge ; the middle is the Rational ; the highest, the Intellectual. These are so distinct from one another that they should never be confounded. But man is not aware of this, for the reason that he makes life consist in what is of sense and knowledge only ; and while he cleaves to this, he cannot even know that his rational part is distinct from that which is concerned with knowing ; and still less that his intellectual part is so.

414

And yet the truth is that the Lord flows through man's Intellectual into his Rational, and through his Rational into the knowledge of the memory, whence comes the life of the senses of sight and of hearing. This is the true influx, and this is the true intercourse of the soul with the body. Without influx of the Lord's life into the things of the understanding in man—or rather into things of the will and through these into those of understanding —and through things of understanding into things rational, and through things rational into his knowledges which are of the memory, life would be impossible to man. And even though a man is in falsities and evils, yet there is an influx of the Lord's life through the things of the will and of the understanding ; but the things that flow in are received in the rational part according to its form ; and this influx gives man the ability to reason, to reflect, and to understand what truth and good are. But concerning these things, of the Lord's Divine mercy, we will treat hereafter ; and also how the case is with the life that pertains to brutes.

658. These three degrees, which in general are called those of man's intellectual things, namely, understanding, reason, and knowledge, are likewise signified, as before said, by the windows of the three stories of the temple at Jerusalem (1 *Kings* vi. 4, 6, 8), and also as above by the rivers which went forth out of the Garden of Eden in the east. The " east " there signifies the Lord ; " Eden " love, which is of the will ; the " garden " intelligence thence derived ; the " rivers " wisdom, reason, and knowledge (concerning which see what was said before, at chapter ii. verses 10 to 14).

415

659. Verse 17. **And I, behold I do bring the flood of waters upon the earth, to destroy all flesh wherein is the breath of lives from under the heavens ; everything that is on the earth shall expire.** By the " flood " is signified an inundation of evil and falsity ; " to destroy all flesh wherein is the breath of lives from under the heavens," signifies that the whole posterity of the Most Ancient Church would destroy themselves ; " everything that is in the earth shall expire," signifies those who were of that church and had become such.

660. That by the " flood " is signified an inundation of evil and falsity, is evident from what has been stated before concerning the posterity of the Most Ancient Church ; that they were possessed with foul lusts, and that they immersed the doctrinal things of faith in them, and in consequence had persuasions of falsity which extinguished all truth and good, and at the same time closed up the way for remains, so that they could not operate ; and therefore it could not be otherwise than that they would destroy themselves. When the way for remains is closed, man is no longer man, because he can no longer be protected by angels, but is totally possessed by evil spirits, whose sole study and desire it is to extinguish man. Hence came the death of the antediluvians, which is described by a flood, or total inundation. The influx of phantasies and lusts from evil spirits is not unlike a kind of flood ; and therefore it is called a " flood " or inundation in various places in the Word, as, of the Lord's Divine mercy, will be seen in what is premised to the following chapter.

661. **To destroy all flesh wherein is the breath of lives from under the heavens.** That this signifies
416

that the whole posterity of the Most Ancient Church
would destroy themselves, is evident from what is
said above, and from the description of them
given before : that they derived by inheritance
from their parents in succession such a genius that
they more than others were imbued with direful
persuasions ; and especially for the reason that
they immersed the doctrinal things of faith that
they possessed in their lusts. It is otherwise
with those who have no doctrinal things of faith,
but live entirely in ignorance ; these cannot so
act, and therefore cannot profane holy things,
and thereby close up the way for remains ; and
consequently they cannot drive away from themselves the angels of the Lord. Remains, as has 2
been said, are all things of innocence, all things of
charity, all things of mercy, and all things of the
truth of faith, which from his infancy a man has
had from the Lord, and has learned. Each and
all of these things are treasured up ; and if a man
had them not, there could be nothing of innocence,
of charity, and of mercy, and therefore nothing of
good and truth in his thought and actions, so that
he would be worse than the savage wild beasts.
And it would be the same if he had had the remains
of such things and had closed up the way by foul
lusts and direful persuasions of falsity, so that they
could not operate. Such were the antediluvians
who destroyed themselves, and who are meant
by " all flesh wherein is the breath of lives, under
the heavens." " Flesh," as before shown, signifies 3
every man in general, and the corporeal man in
particular. The " breath of lives " signifies all
life in general, but properly the life of those who
have been regenerated, consequently, in the present
case, the last posterity of the Most Ancient Church.

Although there was no life of faith remaining among them, yet as they derived from their parents something of seed therefrom which they stifled, it is here called the " breath of lives," or (as in chapter vii. 22), " in whose nostrils was the breathing of the breath of lives." " Flesh under the heavens," signifies what is merely corporeal ; the " heavens " are the things of the understanding that are of truth and the things of the will that are of good, on the separation of which from the Corporeal a man can no longer live. What sustains man is his conjunction with heaven, that is, through heaven with the Lord.

662. **Everything that is in the earth shall expire.** This signifies those who were of that church and had become of this character. It has been shown before that the " earth " does not mean the whole world, but only those who were of the church. Thus no deluge was meant here, still less a universal deluge, but the expiring or suffocation of those who existed there, when they were separated from remains, and thereby from the things of the understanding that are of truth and the things of the will that are of good, and therefore from the heavens. That the " earth " signifies the region where the church is, and therefore those who live there, may be confirmed by the following passages from the Word, in addition to those already cited. In *Jeremiah* :

Thus hath said Jehovah, The whole earth shall be desolate ; yet will I not make a consummation. For this shall the earth mourn, and the heavens above shall be black (iv. 27, 28).

Here the " earth " denotes those who dwell where the church is that is vastated. In *Isaiah* :

418

I will move the heavens, and the earth shall be shaken out of her place (xiii. 13).

The " earth " denotes the man who is to be vastated, where the church is. In *Jeremiah* :

The slain of Jehovah shall be at that day from the end of the earth even unto the end of the earth (xxv. 33).

Here the " end of the earth " does not signify the whole world, but only the region where the church was, and consequently the men who were of the church. Again :

I will call for a sword upon all the inhabitants of the earth ; a tumult shall come even to the end of the earth ; for Jehovah hath a controversy with the nations (xxv. 29, 31).

In this passage, in like manner, the whole world is not meant, but only the region where the church is, and therefore the inhabitant or man of the church ; the " nations " here denote falsities. In *Isaiah* :

Behold, Jehovah cometh forth out of His place to visit the iniquity of the inhabitant of the earth (xxvi. 21).

Here the meaning is the same. Again :

Have ye not heard ? hath it not been told you from the beginning ? have ye not understood the foundations of the earth ? (xl. 21).

Again :

Jehovah, that createth the heavens, God Himself that formeth the earth and maketh it, He establisheth it (xlv. 18).

419

The " earth " denotes the man of the church. In *Zechariah* :

> The saying of Jehovah, who stretcheth out the heavens, and layeth the foundation of the earth, and formeth the spirit of man in the midst of him (xii. 1).

Here the " earth " manifestly denotes the man of the church. The " earth " is distinguished from the " ground " as are the man of the church and the church itself, or as are love and faith.

663. Verse 18. **And I will set up My covenant with thee ; and thou shalt enter into the ark, thou, and thy sons, and thy wife, and thy sons' wives with thee.** To " set up a covenant," signifies that he would be regenerated ; that " he, and his sons, and his sons' wives," should " come into the ark," signifies that he would be saved. " Sons " are truths ; " wives " are goods.

664. In the preceding verse those who destroyed themselves were treated of, but here those who were to be regenerated and thus saved, who are called " Noah."

665. That to " set up a covenant " signifies that he would be regenerated, is very evident from the fact that there can be no covenant between the Lord and man other than conjunction by love and faith, and therefore a " covenant " signifies conjunction. For it is the heavenly marriage that is the veriest covenant ; and the heavenly marriage, or conjunction, does not exist except with those who are being regenerated ; so that in the widest sense regeneration itself is signified by a " covenant." The Lord enters into

a covenant with man when He regenerates him ; and therefore among the ancients a covenant represented nothing else. Nothing can be gathered from the sense of the letter but that the covenant with Abraham, Isaac, and Jacob, and so many times with their descendants, was concerned with them personally, whereas they were such that they could not be regenerated ; for they made worship consist in external things, and supposed the externals of worship to be holy, without internal things being adjoined to them. And, therefore, the covenants made with them were only representatives of regeneration. It was the same with their rites, and with Abraham himself, and with Isaac, and Jacob, who represented the things of love and faith. Likewise the high priests and priests, whatever their character, even those that were wicked, could represent the heavenly and most holy priesthood. In representatives the person is not regarded, but the thing that is represented. Thus all the kings of Israel and of Judah, even the worst, represented the royalty of the Lord ; and even Pharaoh too, who set Joseph over the land of Egypt. From these and many other considerations, concerning which, of the Lord's Divine mercy, we will treat hereafter, it is evident that the covenants so often entered into with the sons of Jacob were only religious rites that were representative.

666. That a " covenant " signifies nothing but regeneration and the things pertaining to regeneration, is evident from various passages in the Word where the Lord Himself is called the " Covenant," because it is He alone who regenerates, and who is looked to by the regenerate man, and is the all

421

in all of love and faith. That the Lord is the Covenant itself is evident in *Isaiah* ·

I, Jehovah, have called thee in righteousness, and will hold thy hand, and will keep thee, and will give thee for a covenant to the people, for a light of the nations (xlii. 6).

Here a " covenant " denotes the Lord ; " a light of the nations " is faith. So in chapter xlix. 6, 8. In *Malachi* :

Behold I send Mine angel, and the Lord whom ye seek shall suddenly come to His temple, even the Angel of the covenant whom ye desire ; behold He cometh ; who may abide the day of His coming ? (iii. 1, 2).

Here the Lord is called the " Angel of the Covenant." The sabbath is called a " perpetual covenant " (*Exod.* xxxi. 16), because it signifies the Lord Himself, and the celestial man regenerated

2 by Him. Since the Lord is the very covenant itself, it is evident that all that which conjoins man with the Lord is of the covenant—as love and faith, and whatever is of love and faith—for these are of the Lord, and the Lord is in them ; and so the covenant itself is in them, where they are received. These have no existence except with a regenerated man, with whom whatever is of the Regenerator or of the Lord is of the covenant, or is the covenant. As in *Isaiah* :

My mercy shall not depart from thee, neither shall the covenant of My peace be removed away (liv. 10).

Here " mercy " and the " covenant of peace " denote the Lord and what belongs to Him. Again :

Incline your ear and come unto Me, hear, and your soul shall live, and I will make a covenant of eternity with you, the sure mercies of David ; behold, I have given Him for a witness to the peoples, a leader and a law-giver to the nations (lv. 3, 4).

" David " here denotes the Lord ; the " covenant of eternity " is in those things and by those things which are of the Lord, and these are meant by going to Him and hearing, that the soul may live. In *Jeremiah* : 3

I will give them one heart, and one way, that they may fear Me all the days, for good to them, and to their sons after them. And I will make an everlasting covenant with them, that I will not turn away from them, to do them good ; and I will put My fear in their heart (xxxii. 39, 40).

This is said of those who are to be regenerated, and of things that belong to them, namely, " one heart and one way," that is, charity and faith, which are of the Lord and so of the covenant. Again :

Behold the days come, saith Jehovah, that I will make a new covenant with the house of Israel and with the house of Judah ; not according to the covenant that I made with their fathers, for they rendered My covenant vain : but this is the covenant that I will make with the house of Israel after these days ; I will put My law in the midst of them, and write it on their heart ; and I will be their God, and they shall be My people (xxxi. 31–33).

Here the meaning of a " covenant " is clearly explained, that it is the love and faith in the Lord which is with those who are to be regenerated.

423

4 And again in *Jeremiah*, love is called the " covenant of the day," and faith the " covenant of the night " (xxxiii. 20). In *Ezekiel* :

> I, Jehovah, will be their God, and My servant David a prince in the midst of them, and I will make with them a covenant of peace, and I will make the evil beast to cease out of the land ; and they shall dwell secure in the wilderness, and sleep in the forests (xxxiv. 24, 25).

Here regeneration is evidently treated of. " David " denotes the Lord. Again :

> David shall be a prince to them to eternity ; I will make a covenant of peace with them. It shall be a covenant of eternity with them ; I will set My sanctuary in the midst of them to eternity (xxxvii. 25, 26).

Here likewise regeneration is treated of. " David " and the " sanctuary " denote the Lord. And again :

> I entered into a covenant with thee, and thou wast Mine ; and I washed thee with waters, and washed away thy bloods from upon thee, and I anointed thee with oil (xvi. 8, 9).

Here regeneration is plainly meant. In *Hosea* :

> In that day will I make a covenant for them with the wild beast of the field, and with the fowl of the heavens, and with the creeping thing of the earth (ii. 18).

This means regeneration ; the " wild beast of the field," denotes the things that are of the will ; " the fowl of the heavens," those that are of the understanding. In *David* :

> He hath sent redemption unto His people ; He hath commanded His covenant to eternity (*Ps.* cxi. 9).

424

This also means regeneration. It is called a
" covenant " because it is given and received.
But of those who are not regenerated, or what is 5
the same, who make worship consist in external
things, and esteem and worship themselves and
what they desire, and think as if they were gods,
it is said that they render the covenant vain,
because they separate themselves from the Lord.
And in *Jeremiah* :

> They have forsaken the covenant of Jehovah
> their God, and have bowed themselves down to
> other gods, and served them (xxii. 9).

In *Moses* :

> He who should transgress the covenant by
> serving other gods—the sun, the moon, the
> host of the heavens—should be stoned (*Deut.*
> xvii. 2, *seq.*).

The " sun " denotes the love of self ; the " moon "
principles of falsity ; the " host of the heavens "
falsities themselves. From all this it is now evident
what the " ark of the covenant " signified wherein
was the " covenant," or " testimony," namely,
that it signified the Lord Himself ; and that the
" book of the covenant " also signified the Lord
Himself (*Exod.* xxiv. 4–7 ; xxxiv. 27 ; *Deut.*
iv. 13, 23) ; and likewise that by the " blood of
the covenant " (*Exod.* xxiv. 6, 8) was signified the
Lord Himself, who alone is the Regenerator.
Hence the " covenant " denotes regeneration
itself.

667. **Thou shalt enter into the ark, thou and thy
sons, and thy wife, and thy sons' wives with thee.**
That this signifies that he would be saved, is
evident from what has been said before and from

o* 425

what follows : that he was saved because regenerated.

668. That " sons " signify truths, and " daughters " goods, has also been shown before—at chapter v. verse 4—where " sons " and " daughters " were spoken of. But here it is " sons " and " wives," because " wives " are the goods that are adjoined to truths ; for no truth can be produced unless there is a good or delight from which it is. In good and in delight there is life ; but not in truth, except that which it has from good and delight. From this, truth is formed and begotten, and so is faith, which is of truth, formed and begotten by love, which is of good. It is with truth exactly as it is with light : there is no light except from the sun or a flame ; it is from this that light is formed. Truth is only the form of good ; and faith is only the form of love. Truth is formed from good according to the quality of the good, and faith is formed from love according to the quality of the love or charity. This then is the reason why a " wife " and " wives " are mentioned, which signify goods adjoined to truths. And hence it is said in the following verse that pairs of all were to enter into the ark, a male and a female ; for without goods adjoined to truths there is no regeneration.

669. Verse 19. **And of every living thing of all flesh, pairs of all shalt thou make to enter into the ark, to keep them alive with thee ; they shall be male and female.** By the " living soul " are signified the things of the understanding ; by " all flesh," those of the will ; " pairs of all shalt thou make to enter into the ark," signifies their regeneration ; the " male " is truth ; the " female," good.

426

670. That by the "living soul" are signified the things of the understanding, and by "all flesh" those of the will, is evident from what has been said before, and from what follows. By "living soul" in the Word is signified every living creature in general, of every kind (as in chapter i. verses 20–24, and ii. 19) ; but here, being immediately connected with "all flesh," it signifies the things which are of the understanding ; for the reason mentioned above that the man of this church was to be regenerated first as to intellectual things. And, therefore, in the following verse the "fowl," which signifies intellectual or rational things, is mentioned first, and afterwards the "beasts," which are things of the will. "Flesh" specifically signifies that which is corporeal, which is of the will.

671. **Pairs of all shalt thou make to enter into the ark, to keep them alive.** That this signifies their regeneration, is evident from what has been said in connection with the preceding verse : that truths cannot be regenerated except through goods and delights ; nor, therefore, the things of faith, except through those which are of charity. And for this reason it is said here that "pairs" of all should enter in, that is, both of truths which are of the understanding, and of goods which are of the will. A man who is not regenerated has no understanding of truth or will of good, but only what appear to be such, and in common speech are so called. He can, however, receive rational truths and scientifics, but they are not living. He may also have a kind of goods of the will, such as exist in the Gentiles, and even in brutes, but neither are these living ; they are merely analogous.

Such goods in man are not living until he is regenerated, and they are thus made alive by the Lord. In the other life it is very manifestly perceived what is not alive and what is alive. Truth that is not alive is instantly perceived as something material, fibrous, closed up ; and good not alive, as something woody, bony, stony. But truth and good made living by the Lord are open, vital, full of the spiritual and celestial, open and manifest even from the Lord ; and this in every idea and in every act, yea, in the least of either of them. This then is why it is said that pairs should enter into the ark, to keep them alive.

672. That the male means truth and the female good, has been said and shown before. In every least thing of man there is the likeness of a kind of marriage. Whatever is of the understanding is thus coupled with something of the will, and without such a coupling or marriage nothing at all is brought forth.

673. Verse 20. **Of the fowl after its kind, and of the beast after its kind, of every creeping thing of the ground after its kind, pairs of all shall enter unto thee, to keep them alive.** The " fowl," signifies things intellectual ; the " beast," things of the will ; the " creeping thing of the ground," signifies both, but what is lowest of them ; " pairs of all shall come unto thee, to keep them alive," signifies, as before, their regeneration.

674. That the " fowl " signifies things intellectual or rational has been shown before (n. 40), and that the " beast " signifies things of the will, or affections (n. 45, 46, 143, 144, 246). That the " creeping thing of the ground " signifies both,

428

but what is lowest of them, may be plain to any one from the fact that creeping on the ground is what is lowest. That " pairs of all shall enter unto thee, to keep them alive " signifies their regeneration, has been shown in the preceding verse.

675. As to its being said " the fowl after its kind," " the beast after its kind," and " the creeping thing after its kind," be it known that in every man there are innumerable genera, and still more innumerable species, of the things of understanding and of will, and that all these are quite distinct from one another, although man does not know it. But during the regeneration of man the Lord draws them out, each and all in their order, and separates and disposes them so that they may be bent towards truths and goods and may be conjoined with them, and this with diversity according to the states, which also are innumerable. All these things can never become perfect even to eternity, as each genus, each species, and each state, comprehends things illimitable even when uncompounded, and still more in combination. A man does not so much as know this fact ; still less can he know in what manner he is regenerated. This is what the Lord says to Nicodemus concerning man's regeneration :

The wind bloweth where it listeth, and thou hearest the sound thereof, but knowest not whence it cometh, or whither it goeth. So is every one that is born of the spirit (*John* iii. 8).

676. Verse 21. **And take thou unto thee of all food that is eaten, and gather it to thee ; and it shall be for food, for thee and for them.** That he

should " take to himself of all food that is eaten,"
signifies goods and delights; that he should
" gather to himself," signifies truths; that it
should be " for food for him and for them," signifies
both.

677. As regards the food of the man who is to
be regenerated, the case is this : before a man can
be regenerated he needs to be furnished with all
things that may serve as means—with the goods
and delights of the affections as means for the will ;
and with truths from the Word of the Lord, and
also with confirmatory things from other sources,
as means for the understanding. Until a man is
furnished with such things he cannot be regenerated, these being for food. This is the reason why
a man is not regenerated until he comes to adult
age. But each man has his peculiar and, as it
were, his own food, which is provided for him by
the Lord before he is regenerated.

678. That his " taking to himself of all food that
is eaten " signifies goods and delights, is evident
from what has been said above : that goods and
delights constitute man's life ; and not so much
truths, for truths receive their life from goods
and delights. From infancy to old age nothing of
knowledge or of reason is ever instilled except by
means of what is good and delightful, and such
things are called " food," because the soul lives
and derives its sustenance from them ; and they
are food, for without them a man's soul cannot
possibly live, as any one may know if he will but
pay attention to the matter.

679. That " gathering to himself " means truths,
is therefore evident ; for " gathering " is predicated

of the things that are in man's memory, where they are gathered together. And the expression further implies that both goods and truths should be gathered in man before he is regenerated ; for without goods and truths gathered together, through which as means the Lord may operate, a man can never be regenerated, as has been said. From this then it follows that " it shall be for food for thee and for them," signifies both goods and truths.

680. That goods and truths are the genuine foods of man must be evident to every one, for he who is destitute of them has no life, but is dead. When a man is spiritually dead the foods with which his soul is fed are delights from evils and pleasures from falsities—which are foods of death— and are also those which come from bodily, worldly, and natural things, which also have nothing of life in them. Moreover, such a man does not know what spiritual and celestial food is, because whenever " food " or " bread " is mentioned in the Word he supposes the food of the body to be meant ; as in the Lord's prayer, the words, " Give us our daily bread," he supposes to mean only sustenance for the body ; and those who extend their ideas further say it includes also other necessaries of the body, such as clothing, property, and the like. They even sharply deny that any other food is meant ; although they see plainly that the words preceding and following involve only celestial and spiritual things, and that the Lord's kingdom is spoken of ; and besides, they might know that the Word of the Lord is celestial and spiritual. From this and other similar examples 2 it must be sufficiently evident how corporeal is

431

man at the present day ; and that, like the Jews, he is disposed to take everything that is said in the Word in the most gross and material sense. The Lord Himself clearly teaches what is meant in His Word by " food " and " bread." Concerning " food " He thus speaks in *John* :

> Jesus said, Labour not for the meat which perisheth, but for that meat which endureth unto eternal life, which the Son of man shall give unto you (vi. 27).

And concerning " bread " He says, in the same chapter :

> Your fathers did eat manna in the wilderness, and are dead. This is the Bread which cometh down from heaven, that a man may eat thereof and not die. I am the living Bread which came down from heaven ; if any man eat of this Bread he shall live for ever (vi. 49–51, 58).

But at the present day there are men like those who heard these words and said : " This is a hard saying ; who can hear it ? " and who " went back and walked no more with Him " (*ib.* verses 60, 66), 3 to whom the Lord said : " The words that I speak unto you they are spirit and they are life " (verse 63). And so with respect to " water," which signifies the spiritual things of faith, and concerning which the Lord thus speaks in *John* :

> Jesus said, Every one that drinketh of this water shall thirst again ; but whosoever drinketh of the water that I shall give him shall never thirst ; but the water that I shall give him shall become in him a fountain of water springing up unto eternal life (iv. 13, 14).

But at the present day there are those who are
like the woman with whom the Lord spoke at the
well, and who answered, " Lord, give me this water,
that I thirst not, neither come hither to draw "
(verse 15). That in the Word " food " means 4
no other than spiritual and celestial food, which is
faith in the Lord, and love, is evident from many
passages in the Word, as in *Jeremiah* :

> The enemy hath spread out his hand upon all
> the desirable things of Jerusalem ; for she hath
> seen that the nations are entered into her
> sanctuary, concerning whom Thou didst com-
> mand that they should not enter into Thy
> congregation. All the people groan, they seek
> bread ; they have given their desirable things
> for food to refresh the soul (*Lam.* i. 10, 11).

No other than spiritual bread and food are here
meant, for the subject is the sanctuary. Again :

> I have cried out for my lovers, they have
> deceived me ; my priests and mine elders in the
> city expired, for they sought food for themselves,
> to refresh their soul (i. 19).

This has the same meaning. In *David* :

> These wait all upon Thee, that Thou mayest
> give them their food in its season ; Thou givest
> them, they gather ; Thou openest thine hand,
> they are satisfied with good (*Ps.* civ. 27, 28).

Here likewise spiritual and celestial food is meant. 5
In *Isaiah* :

> Ho, every one that thirsteth, come ye to the
> waters ; and he that hath no silver ; come ye,
> buy and eat ; yea, come, buy wine and milk
> without silver, and without price (lv. 1).

433

Here " wine " and " milk " denote spiritual and celestial drink. Again :

> A virgin shall conceive and bear a Son, and thou shalt call His name Immanuel ; butter and honey shall He eat, that He may know to refuse the evil and choose the good ; and it shall come to pass that for the abundance of milk that they shall give they shall eat butter ; for butter and honey shall every one eat that is left in the midst of the land (vii. 14, 15, 22).

Here to " eat honey and butter " is to appropriate what is celestial spiritual ; " they that are left " denote remains, concerning whom also in *Malachi* :

> Bring ye all the tithes into the treasure-house, that there may be food in My house (iii. 10).

" Tithes " denote remains. (Concerning the signification of " food," see above, n. 56–58, 276).

681. The nature of celestial and spiritual food can best be known in the other life. The life of angels and spirits is not sustained by any such food as there is in this world, but by " every word that proceedeth out of the mouth of the Lord," as the Lord teaches in *Matthew* iv. 4. The truth is that the Lord alone is the life of all, and that from Him come all things both in general and in particular that angels and spirits think, say, and do, and also what evil spirits think, say, and do. The reason why these latter say and do evil things is that they so receive and pervert all the goods and truths that are of the Lord. Reception and affection are according to the form of the recipient. This may be compared to the various objects that receive the light of the sun, some of which turn

the light received into unpleasing and disagreeable
colours, while others turn it into pleasing and
beautiful colours, according to the form, determination, and disposition of their parts.   The
whole heaven and the entire world of spirits thus
live by everything that proceeds out of the mouth
of the Lord, and from this each individual has
his life ; and not only the whole heaven and the
world of spirits, but also the whole human race.
I know that these things will not be believed,
nevertheless from the continuous experience of
years I can assert that they are most true.   Evil
spirits in the world of spirits are not willing to
believe that this is so ; and therefore it has often
been demonstrated to them—to the life—even
until they have acknowledged with indignation
that it is true.   If angels, spirits, and men were
deprived of this food they would expire in a moment.

682. Verse 22.   **And Noah did according to all
that God commanded him ; so did he.** " Noah
did according to all that God commanded him,"
signifies that thus it came to pass.   That it is
twice said he " did " involves both [good and
truth].

683. As regards the repetition of " did," that
it involves both [good and truth], it should be
known that in the Word, especially in the Prophets,
one thing is described in a twofold manner.   Thus
in *Isaiah* :

He passed through in peace, a way that He
had not gone with His feet ; who hath wrought
and done it (xli. 3, 4) ?

Here one expression relates to good, and the other
to truth ; or, one relates to what is of the will, and

435

the other to what is of the understanding ; that
is to say, " he passed over in peace," involves
what is of the will, and " a way he had not gone
with his feet," involves what is of the understanding ; and it is the same with the words " wrought "
and " done."   Thus the things that pertain to the
will and to the understanding, or to love and faith,
or what is the same, celestial and spiritual things,
are so conjoined together in the Word that in each
and everything there is a likeness of a marriage,
and a relation to the heavenly marriage.   It is
so here, in that the one word is repeated.

CONCERNING THE SOCIETIES WHICH CONSTITUTE
HEAVEN.

684. There are three heavens : the First is the
abode of good spirits, the Second of angelic spirits,
and the Third of angels.   And one heaven is more
interior and pure than another, so that they are
quite distinct.   Each heaven, the first, the second,
and the third, is distinguished into innumerable
societies ;   and each society consists of many
individuals, who by their harmony and unanimity
constitute, as it were, one person ;   and all the
societies together are as one man.   The societies
are distinct from one another according to the
differences of mutual love, and of faith in the
Lord.   These differences are so innumerable that
not even the most general kinds of them can be
computed ;   and there is not the least difference
that is not disposed in most perfect order, so as to
conspire most harmoniously to a common unity,
and the common unity to unanimity of individuals,
and thereby to the happiness of all from each, and
of each from all.   Each angel and each society is

therefore an image of the universal heaven, and is, as it were, a little heaven.

685. There are wonderful consociations in the other life which may be compared to relationships on earth : that is to say, they recognize one another as parents, children, brothers, and relations by blood and by marriage, the love being according to such varieties of relationship. These varieties are endless, and the communicable perceptions are so exquisite that they cannot be described. The relationships have no reference at all to the circumstance that those who are there had been parents, children, or kindred by blood and marriage on earth ; and they have no respect to person, no matter what any one may have been. Thus they have no regard to dignities, nor to wealth, nor to any such matters, but solely to varieties of mutual love and of faith, the faculty for the reception of which they had received from the Lord while they had lived in the world.

686. It is the Lord's mercy, that is, His love towards the whole heaven and the whole human race, thus it is the Lord alone who determines all things both in general and in particular into societies. This mercy it is which produces conjugial love, and from this the love of parents for children, which are the fundamental and chief loves. From these come all other loves, with endless variety, which are arranged most distinctly into societies.

687. Such being the nature of heaven, no angel or spirit can have any life unless he is in some society, and thereby in a harmony of many. A society is nothing but a harmony of many, for no one has any life separate from the life of others.

Indeed no angel or spirit, or society can have any life (that is, be affected by good, exercise will, be affected by truth, or think), unless there is a conjunction thereof through many of his society with heaven and with the world of spirits. And it is the same with the human race : no man, no matter who and what he may be, can live (that is, be affected by good, exercise will, be affected by truth, or think), unless in like manner he is conjoined with heaven through the angels who are with him, and with the world of spirits, nay, with hell, through the spirits that are with him. For every man while living in the body is in some society of spirits and of angels, though entirely unaware of it. And if he were not conjoined with heaven and with the world of spirits through the society in which he is, he could not live a moment. The case in this respect is the same as it is with the human body, any portion of which that is not conjoined with the rest by means of fibres and vessels, and thus by means of functions, is not a part of the body, but is instantly separated and rejected, as having no vitality. The very societies in and with which men have been during the life of the body, are shown them when they come into the other life. And when, after the life of the body, they come into their society, they come into the actual life which they had in the body, and from this life begin a new life ; and so according to their life which they have lived in the body they either go down into hell, or are raised up into heaven.

688. As there is such conjunction of all with each and of each with all, there is also a similar conjunction of the least things of affection and the least things of thought.

689. There is, therefore, an equilibrium of all and of each with respect to celestial, spiritual, and natural things ; so that no one can think, feel, and act except by conjunction with many others, and yet every one supposes that he does so of himself, most freely. Similarly there is nothing which is not balanced by its opposite, and opposites by intermediates, so that each by himself, and many together, live in most perfect equilibrium. And therefore no evil can befall any one without being instantly counterbalanced ; and when there is a preponderance of evil, the evil or evildoer is chastised by the law of equilibrium, as of himself, but solely for the end that good may come. Heavenly order consists in such a form and the consequent equilibrium ; and that order is formed, disposed, and preserved by the Lord alone, to eternity.

690. It should be known, moreover, that there is never one society entirely and absolutely like another, nor is there one person like another in any society, but there is an accordant and harmonious variety of all ; and the varieties are so ordered by the Lord that they conspire to one end, which is effected through love and faith in Him. Hence their unity. For the same reason the heaven and heavenly joy of one is never exactly and absolutely like that of another ; but according to the varieties of love and faith, such are the heaven and the heavenly joy in those varieties.

691. These things in general respecting the heavenly societies are from manifold and daily experience, concerning which specifically, of the Lord's Divine mercy, we will treat hereafter.

CHAPTER THE SEVENTH.

CONCERNING HELL.

692. As in regard to heaven, so in regard to hell, man has only a very general idea, which is so obscure that it is almost nothing. It is such as those who have not been beyond their huts in the woods may have of the earth. They know nothing of its empires and kingdoms, still less of its forms of government, of its societies, or of the life in the societies. Until they know these things they can have but the most general idea of the earth, so general as to be almost nothing. The case is the same in regard to people's ideas about heaven and hell, when yet in each of them there are things innumerable and indefinitely more numerous than in any earthly world. How numberless they are may be evident from this alone ; that just as no one ever has the same heaven, so no one has the same hell as another, and that all souls who have lived in the world since the first creation come there and are gathered together.

693. As love to the Lord and towards the neighbour, together with the joy and happiness thence derived constitute heaven, so hatred against the Lord and the neighbour, together with the consequent punishment and torment, constitute hell. There are innumerable genera of hatreds, and still more innumerable species ; and the hells are just as innumerable.

694. As heaven from the Lord, through mutual love, constitutes, as it were, one man, and one

440

soul, and thus has regard to one end, which is the
conservation and salvation of all to eternity, so,
on the other hand, hell, from man's proprium,
through the love of self and of the world, that is,
through hatred, constitutes one devil and one
mind, and thus also has regard to one end, which
is the destruction and damnation of all to eternity.
That such is their endeavour has been perceived
thousands and thousands of times, so that unless
the Lord preserved all every instant, they would
perish.

695. But the form and the order imposed by the
Lord on the hells is such that all are held bound
and tied up by their lusts and phantasies, in which
their very life consists ; and this life, being a life
of death, is turned into dreadful torments, so
severe that they cannot be described. For the
greatest delight of their life consists in being able
to punish, torture, and torment one another, and
this by arts unknown in the world, whereby they
know how to induce exquisite suffering, just as if
they were in the body, and at the same time dreadful and horrid phantasies, with terrors and horrors
and many such torments. The diabolical crew
take so great a pleasure in this that if they could
increase and extend the pains and torments to
infinity, they would not even then be satisfied,
but would burn yet again to infinity ; but the
Lord frustrates their endeavours, and alleviates
the torments.

696. Such is the equilibrium of all things in the
other life in both general and particular that evil
punishes itself, so that in evil there is the punishment of evil. It is the same with falsity, which
returns upon him who is in falsity. Hence every

441

one brings punishment and torment upon himself, and rushes at the same time among the diabolical crew who inflict such torment. The Lord never sends any one to hell, but would lead all away from hell ; and still less does He lead into torment. But as the evil spirit rushes into it himself, the Lord turns all the punishment and torment to good, and to some use. No penalty is ever possible unless the Lord has in view some use as an end ; for the Lord's kingdom is a kingdom of ends and uses. But the uses which the infernals can perform are the lowest uses ; and when they are engaged in them they are not in so much torment, but on the cessation of the use they are sent back into hell.

697. There are with every man at least two evil spirits and two angels. Through the evil spirits man has communication with hell ; and through the angels, with heaven. Without communication with both no man can live a moment. Thus every man is in some society of infernals, although he is unaware of it. But their torments are not communicated to him, because he is in a state of preparation for eternal life. The society in which a man has been is sometimes shown him in the other life ; for he returns to it, and thereby into the life that he had in the world ; and from thence he either tends towards hell, or is raised up towards heaven. Thus a man who does not live in the good of charity, and does not suffer himself to be led by the Lord, is one of the infernals, and after death also becomes a devil.

698. Besides the hells there are also vastations, concerning which there is much in the Word. For, as a result of actual sins, a man takes with him into the other life innumerable evils and falsities,

442

which he accumulates and joins to himself. It is so even with those who have lived uprightly. Before these can be taken up into heaven, their evils and falsities must be dissipated, and this dissipation is called vastation. There are many kinds of vastations, and longer and shorter periods of vastation. Some are taken up into heaven in a comparatively short time, and some immediately after death.

699. That I might witness the torment of those who are in hell, and the vastation of those who are in the lower earth, I have at different times been let down thither. To be let down into hell is not to be carried from one place to another, but to be let into some infernal society, the man remaining in the same place. But I may here relate only this experience : I plainly perceived that a kind of column surrounded me, and this column was sensibly increased, and it was intimated to me that this was the " wall of brass " spoken of in the Word.* The column was formed of angelic spirits in order that I might safely descend to the unhappy. When I was there I heard piteous lamentations, such as, O God ! O God ! take pity on us ! take pity on us ! and this for a long time. I was permitted to speak to those wretched ones, and this for a considerable time. They complained especially of evil spirits, because they desired and burned for nothing else than to torment them. They were in despair, saying that they believed their torment would be eternal ; but I was permitted to comfort them.

700. The hells being as we have stated so numerous, in order to give some regular account

* Jer. i. 18 ; xv. 20.

of them, they shall be treated of as follows:
I. Concerning the hells of those who have lived a
life of hatred, revenge, and cruelty. II. Concerning
the hells of those who have lived in adulteries
and lasciviousness; and concerning the hells of
the deceitful, and of sorceresses. III. Concerning
the hells of the avaricious; and the filthy Jerusalem there, and the robbers in the wilderness;
also concerning the excrementitious hells of those
who have lived in mere pleasures. IV. Afterwards
concerning other hells which are distinct from the
above.   V. Finally concerning those who are in
vastation.   The description of these will be found
prefixed and appended to the following chapters.

CHAPTER VII.

1. And Jehovah said unto Noah, Enter thou
and all thy house into the ark; for thee have I
seen righteous before Me in this generation.

2. Of every clean beast thou shalt take to thee by
sevens, the man (*vir*) and his wife; and of the beast
that is not clean by twos, the man and his wife.

3. Of the fowl of the heavens also by sevens,
male and female, to keep seed alive upon the faces
of the whole earth.

4. For in yet seven days I will cause it to rain
upon the earth forty days and forty nights; and
every substance that I have made will I destroy
from off the faces of the ground.

5. And Noah did according to all that Jehovah
commanded him.

*   *   *   *   *

6. And Noah was a son of six hundred years, and
the flood of waters was upon the earth.

7. And Noah went in, and his sons, and his wife, and his sons' wives with him, into the ark, from before the waters of the flood.

8. Of the clean beast, and of the beast that is not clean, and of the fowl, and of everything that creepeth upon the ground,

9. There went in two and two unto Noah into the ark, male and female, as God had commanded Noah.

10. And it came to pass after the seven days that the waters of the flood were upon the earth.

*　　*　　*　　*　　*

11. In the six hundredth year of Noah's life, in the second month, in the seventeenth day of the month, in that day were all the fountains of the great deep broken up, and the cataracts of heaven were opened.

12. And the rain was upon the earth forty days and forty nights.

*　　*　　*　　*　　*

13. In the self-same day entered Noah, and Shem, and Ham, and Japheth, the sons of Noah, and Noah's wife, and the three wives of his sons with them, into the ark.

14. They, and every wild animal after its kind, and every beast after its kind, and every creeping thing that creepeth upon the earth after its kind ; and every fowl after its kind, every flying thing, every winged thing.

15. And they went in unto Noah into the ark, two and two of all flesh wherein is the breath of lives.

*　　*　　*　　*　　*

16. And they that went in, went in male and female of all flesh, as God had commanded him. And Jehovah shut after him.

445

17. And the flood was forty days upon the earth, and the waters increased, and bare up the ark, and it was lifted up from off the earth.

18. And the waters were strengthened, and were increased exceedingly upon the earth ; and the ark went upon the face of the waters.

*   *   *   *   *

19. And the waters were strengthened very exceedingly upon the earth, and all the high mountains that were under the whole heaven were covered.

20. Fifteen cubits upward did the waters prevail, and covered the mountains.

21. And all flesh died that creepeth upon the earth, as to fowl, and as to beast, and as to wild animal, and as to every creeping thing that creepeth upon the earth ; and every man.

22. All in whose nostrils was the breathing of the breath of lives, of all that was in the dry [land], died.

23. And He destroyed every substance that was upon the faces of the ground, from man even to beast, even to creeping thing, and even to the fowl of the heavens ; and they were destroyed from the earth ; and Noah only was left, and that which was with him in the ark.

24. And the waters were strengthened upon the earth a hundred and fifty days.

THE CONTENTS.

701. The subject here treated of in general is the preparation of a new church. As the subject before was the intellectual things of that church, so here it is the things of the will (verses 1 to 5).

702. Next its temptations are treated of, which are described as to its intellectual things from verses 6 to 10, and as to the things of the will in verses 11, 12.

703. Afterwards the protection of this church is treated of, and its preservation (verses 13 to 15). But what its state was, that it was fluctuating, is described in verses 16 to 18.

704. Finally the last posterity of the Most Ancient Church is treated of in regard to its character : that it was possessed by persuasions of falsity and by lusts of the love of self to such a degree that it perished (verses 19 to 24).

THE INTERNAL SENSE.

705. The subject here specifically treated of is the " flood," by which is signified not only the temptations which the man of the church called " Noah " had to undergo before he could be regenerated, but also the desolation of those who could not be regenerated. Both temptations and desolations are compared in the Word to " floods " or " inundations " of waters, and are so called. Temptations are denoted in *Isaiah* :

> For a small moment have I forsaken thee, but in great compassions will I gather thee again. In an inundation of anger I hid my faces from thee for a moment ; but in the mercy of eternity will I have compassion upon thee, saith Jehovah thy Redeemer. For this is the waters of Noah unto Me, to whom I have sworn that the waters of Noah should no more go over the earth, so have I sworn that I would not be wroth with thee

and rebuke thee, O thou afflicted and tossed with
tempests and not comforted (liv. 7–9, **11**).

This is said of the church that is to be regenerated,
and concerning its temptations, which are called
the " waters of Noah." The Lord Himself also
2 calls temptations " flood," in *Luke* :

Jesus said, Every one that cometh unto Me,
and heareth My sayings and doeth them is like
unto a man building a house, who digged, and
went deep, and laid a foundation upon the rock ;
and when a flood came, the stream beat upon
that house, but could not shake it, because it
had been founded upon the rock (vi. 47, 48).

That temptations are here meant by " flood " must
be evident to every one. Desolations are also
denoted in *Isaiah* :

The Lord bringeth up upon them the waters
of the river, strong and many, the king of
Asshur and all his glory ; and he riseth up above
all his channels, and shall go over all his banks :
and he shall go through Judah ; he shall inundate and go through ; he shall reach even to
the neck (viii. 7, 8).

" The king of Asshur " here stands for phantasies,
principles of falsity, and the derivative reasonings,
which desolate man, and which desolated the
3 antediluvians. In *Jeremiah* :

Thus hath said Jehovah, Behold waters rise
up out of the north, and shall become an inundating stream, and shall inundate the land and
the fullness thereof, the city and them that dwell
therein (xlvii. 2, 3).

This is said of the Philistines, who represent those
who take up false principles, and reason from them

concerning spiritual things, which reasonings inundate man, as they did the antediluvians. The reason why both temptations and desolations are compared in the Word to " floods " or " inundations " of waters, and are so called, is that they are similarly circumstanced ; it being evil spirits who flow in with their persuasions and the false principles in which they are, and excite such things in man. With the man who is being regenerated, these are temptations ; but with the man who is not being regenerated they are desolations.

706. Verse 1. **And Jehovah said unto Noah, Enter thou and all thy house into the ark ; for thee have I seen righteous before Me in this generation.** " Jehovah said unto Noah," signifies that so it came to pass ; " Jehovah " is named because charity is now treated of ; " enter thou and all thy house into the ark," signifies the things that belong to the will, which is the " house " ; to " enter into the ark," here signifies to be prepared ; " for thee have I seen righteous in this generation," signifies that he had good, whereby he might be regenerated.

707. Here, as far as the fifth verse, are found almost the same things that were said in the previous chapter, merely changed in some little measure, and it is the same in the verses that follow. One who is not acquainted with the internal sense of the Word cannot but think that this is merely a repetition of the same thing. Similar instances occur in other parts of the Word, especially in the Prophets, where the same thing is expressed in different words ; and sometimes is also taken up again and described a second time. But, as before said, the reason is that there are two faculties in man which are quite distinct from each other—the

P   449

will, and the understanding—and the two are treated of in the Word distinctively. This is the reason of the repetition. That this is the case here will be evident from what follows.

708. Jehovah said unto Noah. That this signifies that so it came to pass, is evident from the consideration that with Jehovah there is nothing else but Being (*Esse*) : that which He says comes to pass and is done ; just as in the preceding chapter at verse 13, and elsewhere, where the expression " Jehovah said " means that it came to pass and was done.

709. The name " Jehovah " is here used because the subject now treated of is charity. In the preceding chapter, from the ninth verse to the end it is not said " Jehovah," but " God," for the reason that the subject there treated of is the preparation of " Noah," that is, of the man of the church called " Noah," as to the things of his understanding, which relate to faith ; whereas the subject here treated of is his preparation as to the things of the will, which pertain to love. When the things of the understanding, or the truths of faith, are the subject treated of, the name " God " is used, but when the things of the will, or the goods of love are treated of, the name " Jehovah " is used. For the things of the understanding, or of faith, do not constitute the church, but the things of the will, which pertain to love. Jehovah is in love and charity, and not in faith unless it is a faith of love or of charity. And, therefore, in the Word faith is compared to " night," and love to " day " ; as in the first chapter of *Genesis*, where the " great lights " are spoken of, it is said that the " greater light," or the sun, which signifies

love, should rule the day, and the " lesser light,"
or the moon, which signifies faith, should rule the
night (*Gen.* i. 14, 16) ; and it is the same in the
Prophets (*Jer.* xxxi. 35 ; xxxiii. 20 ; *Ps.* cxxxvi.
8, 9 ; *Rev.* viii. 12).

710. Enter thou and all thy house into the ark.
That this signifies the things of the will, is therefore
evident.　In the preceding chapter, where the
things of the understanding are meant, it is
expressed differently, namely : " Thou shalt come
into the ark, thou and thy sons, and thy wife, and
thy sons' wives with thee " (verse 18).　That a
" house " signifies the will and what is of the will,
is evident in various places in the Word ; as in
Jeremiah :

> Their houses shall be turned over unto others,
> their fields and their wives together (vi. 12).

Here " houses " and also " fields " and " wives "
relate to things which are of the will.　Again :

> Build ye houses and dwell in them ; and
> plant gardens and eat the fruit of them (xxix.
> 5, 28).

Here " building houses and dwelling in them "
relates to the will ; " planting gardens," to the
understanding : and it is the same in other passages.
And the " house of Jehovah " is frequently mentioned as signifying the church wherein love is the
chief thing ; the " house of Judah," as signifying
the celestial church ; and the " house of Israel,"
as signifying the spiritual church.　As " house "
signifies the church, the mind of the man of the
church (wherein are the things of the will and of the
understanding, or of charity and faith), is also
signified by " house."

711. That to "enter into the ark," is to be prepared, has been stated before, at verse 18 of the preceding chapter. But there it signified that he was prepared for salvation as to things of the understanding, which are truths of faith ; but here as to things of the will, which are goods of charity. Unless a man is prepared, that is, furnished with truths and goods, he can by no means be regenerated, still less undergo temptations. For the evil spirits who are with him at such a time excite his falsities and evils ; and if truths and goods are not present, to which they may be bent by the Lord, and by which they may be dispersed, he succumbs. These truths and goods are the remains that are reserved by the Lord for such uses.

712. **For thee have I seen righteous in this generation.** That this signifies that he had good whereby he might be regenerated, was stated and shown at the ninth verse of the preceding chapter. In that place "righteous" or "just" signifies the good of charity ; and "perfect" the truth of charity. It is there said "generations," in the plural, because things of the understanding are treated of ; and here, "generation," in the singular, because things of the will are treated of. For the will comprehends in itself the things of the understanding, but the understanding does not comprehend in itself those of the will.

713. Verse 2. **Of every clean beast thou shalt take to thee by sevens, the man** (*vir*) **and his wife ; and of the beast that is not clean by twos, the man and his wife.** By "every clean beast," are signified affections of good ; by "sevens," is signified that they are holy ; by "man and his wife," that the

truths were conjoined with goods. By the " beast
not clean," are signified evil affections ; by " two,"
that they are relatively profane ; by " man and
wife," falsities conjoined with evils.

714. That affections of good are signified by
" every clean beast " is evident from what has
been said and shown before respecting beasts
(n. 45, 46, 142, 143, 246). The reason why affections
are thus signified is that man in himself, and regarded in his proprium, is nothing but a beast. He
has very similar senses, appetites, desires ; and
all his affections are very similar. His good,
and even his best loves, are very similar ; as the
love for companions of his own kind, the love of
his children, and of his wife ; so that they do not
at all differ. But his being man, and more than
beast, consists in his having an interior life, which
beasts never have nor can have. This life is the
life of faith and love from the Lord. And if this
life were not within everything that he has in
common with beasts, he would not be anything
else. Take only one example—love towards companions : if he should love them only for the sake
of himself, and there were nothing more heavenly
or Divine in his love, he could not from this be
called a man, because it is the same with beasts.
And so with all the rest. If, therefore, there were
not the life of love from the Lord in his will, and
the life of faith from the Lord in his understanding,
he would not be a man. By virtue of the life which
he has from the Lord he lives after death ; because
the Lord adjoins him to Himself. And thus he
can be in His heaven with the angels, and live to
eternity. And even if a man lives as a wild beast,
and loves nothing whatever but himself and what

regards himself, yet so great is the Lord's mercy— for it is Divine and Infinite—that He does not leave him, but continually breathes into him His own life, through the angels ; and even supposing that he receives it no otherwise, it still causes him to be able to think, to reflect, to understand whether a thing is good or evil—in relation to what is moral, civil, worldly, or corporeal—and, therefore, whether it is true or false.

715. As the most ancient people knew, and when they were in self-humiliation acknowledged, that they were nothing but beasts and wild beasts, and were men solely by virtue of what they had from the Lord, therefore, whatever pertained to them-selves they not only likened to but called beasts and birds ; things of the will they compared to beasts, and called beasts ; and things of the understanding they compared to and called birds. But they distinguished between good affections and evil affections. Good affections they compared to lambs, sheep, kids, she-goats, he-goats, rams, heifers, oxen—for the reason that they were good and gentle, and serviceable to life, since they could be eaten, and their skins and wool could furnish clothing. These are the principal clean beasts. But those that are evil and fierce, and not service-able to life, are unclean beasts.

716. That holy things are signified by " seven " is evident from what has been said before respecting the seventh day, or the sabbath (n. 84–87), namely, that the Lord is the seventh day ; and that from Him every celestial church, or celestial man, is a seventh day, and indeed the celestial itself, which is most holy because it is from the Lord alone. For this reason, in the Word, " seven " signifies what

is holy ; and in fact, as here, in the internal sense, partakes not at all of the idea of number. For those who are in the internal sense, as angels and angelic spirits are, do not even know what number is, and therefore not what seven is. Therefore it is not meant here that seven pairs were to be taken of all the clean beasts ; or that there was so much of good in proportion to evil as seven to two ; but that the things of the will with which this man of the church was furnished were goods, which are holy, whereby he could be regenerated, as was said above. That " seven " signifies what 2 is holy, or holy things, is evident from the rituals in the representative church, wherein the number seven so frequently occurs. For example, they were to sprinkle of the blood and the oil seven times, as related in *Leviticus* :

Moses took the anointing oil, and anointed the tabernacle and all that was therein, and sanctified them ; and he sprinkled thereof upon the altar seven times, and anointed the altar and all its vessels, to sanctify them (viii. 10, 11).

Here " seven times " would be entirely without significance if what is holy were not thus represented. And in another place : When Aaron came into the holy place it is said :

He shall take of the blood of the bullock and sprinkle with his finger upon the faces of the mercy-seat toward the east ; and before the mercy-seat shall he sprinkle of the blood with his finger seven times.

And so at the altar :

He shall sprinkle of the blood upon it with his finger seven times, and cleanse it and sanctify it (*Lev.* xvi. 14, 19).

The particulars here, each and all, signify the Lord Himself, and, therefore, the holiness of love ; that is to say, the " blood," the " mercy-seat," and also the " altar," and the " east," towards which the blood was to be sprinkled, and therefore also 3 " seven times." And likewise in the sacrifices, of which we read in *Leviticus* :

If a soul shall sin through error, and if the anointed priest shall sin so as to bring guilt on the people, he shall slay the bullock before Jehovah, and the priest shall dip his finger in the blood, and sprinkle of the blood seven times before Jehovah, toward the veil of the sanctuary (iv. 2, 3, 6).

Here also " seven " signifies what is holy ; because the subject treated of is expiation, which is of the Lord alone, and, therefore, the subject treated of is the Lord. Similar rites were also instituted in respect to the cleansing of leprosy, concerning which we read in *Leviticus* :

Of the blood of the bird, with cedar wood, and scarlet, and hyssop, the priest shall sprinkle upon him that is to be cleansed from the leprosy seven times, and shall make him clean. In like manner he was to sprinkle of the oil that was upon the palm of his left hand seven times before Jehovah. And so in a house where there was leprosy, he was to take cedar wood and hyssop and scarlet, and with the blood of the bird sprinkle seven times (xiv. 6, 7, 27, 51).

Here any one may see that there is nothing at all in the " cedar wood," the " scarlet," the " oil," the " blood of a bird," nor yet in " seven," except from the fact that they are representative of holy things. Take away from them what is holy, and

all that remains is dead, or profanely idolatrous.
But when they signify holy things there is Divine
worship therein, which is internal, and is only
represented by the externals. The Jews indeed
could not know what these things signified ; nor
does any one at the present day know what was
signified by the " cedar wood," the " hyssop," the
" scarlet," and the " bird." But if they had only
been willing to think that holy things were involved
which they did not know, and so had worshipped
the Lord, or the Messiah who was to come, who
would heal them of their leprosy—that is, of their
profanation of holy things—they might have been
saved. For those who so think and believe are
at once instructed in the other life, if they desire,
as to what each and all things represented. And 4
in like manner it was commanded respecting the
red heifer :

> The priest shall take of her blood with his
> finger and sprinkle of her blood toward the
> face of the tent of meeting seven times (*Num.*
> xix. 4).

As the " seventh day " or " sabbath " signified the
Lord, and from Him the celestial man, and the
Celestial itself, the seventh day in the Jewish
Church was of all religious observances the most
holy ; and hence came the " sabbath of sabbath,"
in the seventh year (*Lev.* xxv. 4), and the " jubilee "
that was proclaimed after the seven sabbaths of
years, or after seven times seven years (xxv. 8, 9).
That, in the highest sense, " seven " signifies
the Lord, and hence the holy of love, is evident
also from the golden candlestick and its seven
lamps (concerning which in *Exod.* xxv. 31–33,
37 ; xxxvii. 17–19, 23 ; *Num.* viii. 2, 3 ;

P*   457

Zech. iv. 2) and of which it is thus written by *John* :

> Seven golden lampstands ; and in the midst of the seven lampstands One like unto the Son of man (*Rev.* i. 12, 13).

It very clearly appears in this passage that the " lampstand with the seven lamps " signifies the Lord, and that the " lamps " are the holy things of love, or celestial things ; and therefore they
5 were " seven." And again :

> Out of the throne went forth seven torches of fire, burning before the throne, which are the seven spirits of God (*Rev.* iv. 5).

Here the " seven torches " that went forth out of the throne of the Lord are the seven lights, or lamps. The same is signified wherever the number " seven " occurs in the Prophets, as in *Isaiah* :

> The light of the moon shall be as the light of the sun, and the light of the sun shall be seven-fold, as the light of seven days, in the day that Jehovah bindeth up the breach of His people (xxx. 26).

Here the " sevenfold light, as the light of seven days," does not signify sevenfold, but the holy thing of the love signified by the " sun." See also what was said and shown above respecting the number " seven " (chapter iv. verse 15). From all this again it is clearly evident that whatever numbers are used in the Word never mean numbers (as was also shown before, chapter vi. verse 3).

717. It is also evident from all this that the subject here treated of is the things of man's will, or the good and holy things in him which are predicated of the will. For it is said that he

should " take of the clean beast by sevens " ; and the same is said in the following verse concerning the " fowl." But in the preceding chapter (verses 19, 20), it is not said that he should " take by sevens," but by " twos," or pairs ; because there things of the understanding are treated of, which are not holy in themselves, but are holy from love, which is of the will.

718. That by " man (*vir*) and wife " is signified that the truths were conjoined with goods, is evident from the signification of " man " as being truth, which is of the understanding, and from the signification of " wife " as being good, which pertains to the will (concerning which see before), and also from the fact that man has not the least of thought, nor the least of affection and action, in which there is not a kind of marriage of the understanding and the will. Without a kind of marriage, nothing ever exists or is produced. In the very organic forms of man, both composite and simple, and even in the most simple, there is a passive and an active, which, if they were not coupled as in a marriage, like that of man and wife, could not even be there, still less produce anything, and the case is the same throughout the whole of nature. These perpetual marriages derive their source and origin from the heavenly marriage ; and thereby there is impressed upon everything in the whole of nature, both animate and inanimate, an idea of the Lord's kingdom.

719. That evil affections are signified by the " beasts not clean," is evident from what has been said and shown before respecting the clean beasts. They are called " clean " because they are gentle, good, and useful. The unclean—of which

there are genera and species—are the contrary, being fierce, evil, and not useful. In the Word also they are described as wolves, bears, foxes, swine, and many others ; and various lusts and evil dispositions are signified by them. As to its being here said that unclean beasts also, that is, evil affections, should be brought into the ark, the truth is that the man of that church is here described such as he was in character, and this by the ark, and, therefore, by the things that were in the ark, or that were brought into the ark ; that is to say, the things are described that were in the man before he was regenerated. There were in him the truths and goods with which he had been furnished and gifted by the Lord before regeneration ; for without truths and goods no one can ever be regenerated. But here the evils that were in him are spoken of, and are signified by the unclean beasts. There are evils in man that must be dispersed while he is being regenerated, that is, which must be loosened and attempered by goods ; for no actual and hereditary evil in man can be so dispersed as to be abolished. It still remains implanted ; and can only be so far loosened and attempered by goods from the Lord as not to do injury, and not to appear : this is an arcanum hitherto unknown. Actual evils are those which are loosened and attempered, and not hereditary evils ; which also is a thing unknown.

720. That " pairs " signify things relatively profane, is evident from the signification of the number " two." A " pair," or " two," not only signifies marriage (and is, when predicated of the heavenly marriage, a holy number), but it also signifies the same as " six." That is to say, as

the six days of labour are related to the seventh
day of rest, or the holy day, so is the number
" two " related to " three " ; and therefore the
third day in the Word is taken for the seventh,
and involves almost the same, on account of the
Lord's resurrection on the third day. And hence
the Lord's coming into the world, and in glory,
and every coming of the Lord, is described equally
by the " seventh " and by the " third " day. For
this reason the two days that precede are not
holy, but relatively are profane. Thus in *Hosea* :

> Come and let us return unto Jehovah, for
> He hath wounded, and He will heal us ; He
> hath smitten and He will bind us up. After two
> days He will revive us ; on the third day He
> will raise us up, and we shall live before Him
> (vi. 1, 2).

And in *Zechariah* :

> It shall come to pass in all the land, saith
> Jehovah, that two parts therein shall be cut
> off and die, and the third shall be left therein ;
> and I will bring the third part through the fire,
> and will refine them as silver is refined (xiii. 8, 9).

And that silver was most pure when purified seven
times appears in *Psalm* xii. 6 ; from all of which
it is plain that as " seven " does not signify seven,
but things that are holy, so by " pairs " are
signified not pairs, but things relatively profane ;
and therefore the meaning is not that the unclean
beasts, or evil affections, in comparison with the
clean beasts, or good affections, were few in the
proportion of two to seven, for the evils in man
are far more numerous than the goods.

721. That by " man and wife " are signified
falsities conjoined with evils, is evident from what

was said just above. For here " man and wife "
is predicated of the unclean beasts ; but before of
the clean ; and, therefore, the expression there
signified truths conjoined with goods, but here
falsities conjoined with evils. Such as is the
subject, such is the predication.

722. Verse 3. **Of the fowl of the heavens also
by sevens, male and female, to keep seed alive upon
the faces of the whole earth.** By " the fowl of the
heavens," are signified things of the understanding ;
by " sevens," those which are holy ; by " male
and female," truths and goods ; " to keep seed
alive upon the faces of the whole earth," signifies
truths of faith.

723. That the " fowl of the heavens " signifies
things of the understanding, has been shown
before, and therefore need not be dwelt upon.

724. Likewise that " sevens " signifies things
that are holy, and here holy truths, which are
holy from the fact that they come from goods.
No truth is holy unless it comes from good. A
man may utter many truths from the Word, and
thus from memory, but if it is not love or charity
that brings them forth, nothing holy can be said
of them. But if he has love and charity, then he
acknowledges and believes, and this from the
heart. And it is the same with faith, of which so
many say that it alone saves : if there is no love
or charity from which the faith comes, there is
no faith. Love and charity are what make faith
holy. The Lord is in love and charity, but not in
faith that is separated from charity. In faith
separated is the man himself, in whom there is
nothing but uncleanness. For when faith is

separated from love, his own praise, or his own advantage, is the moving cause in his heart, and from which he speaks. This every one may know from his own experience. Whoever tells any one that he loves him, that he prefers him to others, that he acknowledges him as the best of men, and the like, and yet in heart thinks otherwise, does this only with his mouth, and in heart denies, and sometimes makes sport of him. And it is the same with faith. This has been made very well known to me by much experience. Those who in the life of the body have preached the Lord and faith with so much eloquence, together with feigned devoutness, as to astonish their hearers, and have not done it from the heart, in the other life are among those who bear the greatest hatred towards the Lord, and who persecute the faithful.

725. That by " male and female " are signified truths and goods, is evident from what has been said and shown before, namely, that " man " and " male " signify truth, and " wife " and " female " good. But " male and female " are predicated of things of the understanding, and " man and wife," of things of the will, for the reason that marriage is represented by man and wife, and not so much by male and female. For truth can never of itself enter into marriage with good, but good can with truth ; because there is no truth which is not produced from good and thus coupled with good. If you withdraw good from truth, nothing whatever remains but words.

726. **To keep seed alive upon the faces of the whole earth.** That this signifies truths of faith, is evident from the seed being kept alive by this

463

church. By "seed" is meant faith. The rest of the descendants of the Most Ancient Church destroyed the celestial and spiritual seed within them, by foul cupidities and direful persuasions. But that celestial seed might not perish, those who are called "Noah" were regenerated, and this by means of spiritual seed. These are the things that are signified. Those are said to be "kept alive" who receive the Lord's life, because life is in those things only which are of the Lord, as must be evident to every one from the fact that there is no life in those things which are not of eternal life, or which do not look to eternal life. Life that is not eternal is not life, but in a brief time perishes. Nor can being (*esse*) be predicated of things that cease to be, but only of those that never cease to be. Thus living and being are within those things only which are of the Lord, or Jehovah ; because all being and living, to eternity, are of Him. By eternal life is meant eternal happiness, respecting which see what was said and shown above (n. 290).

727. Verse 4. **For in yet seven days I will cause it to rain upon the earth forty days and forty nights ; and every substance that I have made will I destroy from off the faces of the ground.** " In yet seven days," signifies the beginning of temptation ; "to rain," signifies temptation ; "forty days and nights," signifies the duration of temptation ; "I will destroy every substance that I have made from off the faces of the ground," signifies the proprium of man, which is, as it were, destroyed when he is being regenerated. The same words signify also the extinction of those of the Most Ancient Church who destroyed themselves.

728. That " in yet seven days " here signifies the beginning of temptation, is evident from the internal sense of all things mentioned in this verse, in that the temptation of the man called " Noah " is treated of. It treats in general both of his temptation and of the total vastation of those who were of the Most Ancient Church, and had become such as has been described. Therefore, " in yet seven days," signifies not only the beginning of temptation, but also the end of vastation. The reason why these things are signified by " in yet seven days," is that " seven " is a holy number, as was said and shown before (at verse 2 of this chapter, and in chapter iv., verses 15, 24, and at n. 84–87). " In seven days," signifies the Lord's coming into the world, also His coming into glory, and every coming of the Lord in particular. It is an attendant feature of every coming of the Lord that it is a beginning for those who are being regenerated, and is an end for those who are being vastated. Thus to the man of this church the Lord's coming was the beginning of temptation ; for when man is tempted he begins to become a new man and to be regenerated. And at the same time it was the end of those of the Most Ancient Church who had become such that they could not but perish. Just so when the Lord came into the world—the church at that time was in its last state of vastation, and was then made new. That these things are signified by " in yet seven days," is evident in *Daniel* :   **2**

Seventy weeks are decreed upon thy people, and upon the city of thy holiness, to consummate the transgression, to seal up sins, and to purge away iniquity, and to bring in the righteousness

of the ages, and to seal up vision and prophet,
and to anoint the holy of holies. Know therefore and perceive, from the going forth of the
word to restore and to build Jerusalem, unto
Messiah the Prince, shall be seven weeks
(ix. 24, 25).

Here "seventy weeks" and "seven weeks"
signify the same as "seven days," namely, the
coming of the Lord. But as here there is a manifest
prophecy, the times are still more sacredly and
certainly designated by septenary numbers. It
is evident then not only that "seven" thus applied
to times signifies the coming of the Lord, but that
the beginning also of a new church at that time
is signified by the "anointing of the holy of
holies," and by Jerusalem being "restored and
built." And at the same time the last vastation
is signified by the words, "Seventy weeks are
decreed upon the city of holiness, to consummate
3 the transgression, and to seal up sins." So in
other places in the Word, as in *Ezekiel*, where he
says of himself :

I came to them of the captivity at Tel-abib,
that sat by the river Chebar, and I sat there
astonished among them seven days ; and it
came to pass at the end of seven days
that the word of Jehovah came unto me
(iii. 15, 16).

Here also "seven days" denote the beginning of
visitation ; for after seven days, while he sat
among those who were in captivity, the word of
Jehovah came unto him. Again :

They shall bury Gog, that they may cleanse
the land, seven months ; at the end of seven
months they shall search (xxxix. 12, 14).

466

Here likewise " seven " denotes the last limit of vastation, and the first of visitation. In *Daniel* :

> The heart of Nebuchadnezzar shall they change from man, and the heart of a beast shall be given unto him, and seven times shall pass over him (iv. 16, 25, 32).

In like manner, this denotes the end of vastation, and the beginning of a new man. The " seventy 4 years " of Babylonish captivity represented the same. Whether the number is " seventy " or " seven " it involves the same, be it seven days or seven years, or seven ages which make seventy years. Vastation was represented by the years of captivity ; the beginning of a new church by the liberation and the rebuilding of the temple. Similar things were also represented by the service of Jacob with Laban, where these words occur :

> I will serve thee seven years for Rachel ; and Jacob served seven years for Rachel ; and Laban said, Fulfil this week, and I will give thee her also, for the service which thou shalt serve with me yet seven other years ; and Jacob did so, and fulfilled this week (*Gen.* xxix. 18, 20, 27, 28).

Here the " seven years " of service involve the same, and also that after the days of seven years came the marriage and freedom. This period of seven years was called a " week," as also in *Daniel*. 5 The same was also represented in the command that they should compass the city of Jericho " seven times," and the wall would then fall down ; and it is said that :

> On the seventh day they rose with the dawn and compassed the city after the same manner seven times, and it came to pass at the seventh

467

time the seven priests blew the seven trumpets and the wall fell down (*Joshua* vi. 10–20).
If these things had not also such a signification, the command that they should compass the city seven times, and that there should be seven priests and seven trumpets would never have been given. From these and many other passages (as *Job* ii. 13 ; *Rev.* xv. 1, 6, 7 ; xxi. 9), it is evident that " in seven days " signifies the beginning of a new church, and the end of the old. In the passage before us, as it treats both of the man of the church called " Noah " and his temptation, and of the last posterity of the Most Ancient Church, which destroyed itself, " in yet seven days," can have no other signification than the beginning of Noah's temptation, and the end or final devastation and expiration of the Most Ancient Church.

729. That by " raining " is signified temptation, is evident from what was said and shown in the introduction to this chapter, namely, that a " flood " or " inundation " of waters, which is here described by " rain," signifies not only temptation, but also vastation. And the same will also appear from what is to be said concerning the flood in the following pages.

730. That by " forty days and nights " is signified the duration of temptation, is plainly evident from the Word of the Lord. That " forty " signifies the duration of temptation, comes from the fact that the Lord suffered Himself to be tempted for forty days (as is stated in *Matthew* iv. 1, 2 ; *Luke* iv. 2 ; *Mark* i. 13). And as the things instituted in the Jewish and the other representative churches before the coming of the Lord were each and all types of Him, so also were the forty

days and nights—in that they represented and signified in general all temptation—and specifically the duration of the temptation, whatever that might be. And because a man when in temptation is in vastation as to all things that are of his proprium, and of the body (for the things that are of his proprium and of the body must die, and this through combats and temptations, before he is born again a new man, or is made spiritual and heavenly), for this reason also " forty days and nights " signify the duration of vastation ; and it is the same here where the subject is both the temptation of the man of the new church, called " Noah," and the devastation of the antediluvians. That the number " forty " signifies the duration 2 of both temptation and vastation, whether greater or less, is evident in *Ezekiel* :

Thou shalt lie on thy right side, and shalt bear the iniquity of the house of Judah forty days, each day for a year have I appointed it unto thee (iv. 6).

" Forty " denotes here the duration of the vastation of the Jewish Church, and also a representation of the Lord's temptation ; for it is said that he should " bear the iniquity of the house of *Judah.*" Again :

I will make the land of Egypt wastes, a waste of desolation ; no foot of man shall pass through it, nor foot of beast shall pass through it, and it shall not be inhabited forty years ; and I will make the land of Egypt a desolation in the midst of the desolate lands, and her cities in the midst of the cities that are laid waste shall be a solitude forty years (xxix. 10–12).

Here also " forty " denotes the duration of vastation and desolation ; and in the internal sense

469

forty years are not meant, but only, in general, the
desolation of faith, whether within a shorter or
longer time. In *John* :

> The court that is without the temple cast out
> and measure it not ; for it hath been given
> unto the nations, who shall tread the holy city
> under foot forty and two months (*Rev.* xi. 2).

3 And again :

> There was given unto the beast a mouth
> speaking great things and blasphemies ; and
> there was given unto him power to make war
> forty and two months (xiii. 5).

This denotes the duration of vastation, for any
one may know that forty-two months of time is
not meant. But the origin of the use of the number
" forty-two " in this passage (which has the same
signification as the number " forty ") is that
" seven days " signify the end of vastation, and
a new beginning, and " six days " signify labour,
from the six days of labour or combat. Seven are,
therefore, multiplied by six, and thus give rise
to the number forty-two, which signifies the duration of the vastation and the duration of the
temptation, or the labour and combat, of the man
who is to be regenerated, in which there is holiness.
But, as is evident from these passages in the
Apocalypse, the round number " forty " was
taken for the not so round number " forty-two."

4 That the Israelitish people were led about for
forty years in the wilderness before they were
brought into the land of Canaan, in like manner
represented and signified the duration of temptation, and also the duration of vastation ; the
duration of temptation, by their being afterwards
brought into the holy land ; the duration of vasta-

tion, by the fact that all above the age of twenty years, who went out of Egypt, except Joshua and Caleb, died in the wilderness (*Num.* xiv. 33–35 ; xxxii. 8–14). The things against which they so often murmured signify temptations, and the plagues and destruction that so frequently came upon them signify vastations. That these signify temptations and vastations will, of the Lord's Divine mercy, be shown in that place. Of these things it is written in *Moses*:

> Thou shalt remember all the way which Jehovah thy God hath led thee these forty years in the wilderness, to afflict thee, to tempt thee, to know what was in thine heart, whether thou wouldest keep His commandments, or no (*Deut.* viii. 2, 3, 16).

That Moses was forty days and forty nights upon Mount Sinai, also signifies the duration of the temptation, that is, it signifies the Lord's temptation, as is evident from his abiding in the mount forty days and forty nights, neither eating bread nor drinking water, supplicating for the people that they might not be destroyed (*Deut.* ix. 9, 11, 18, 25 to the end ; x. 10).

The reason why "forty days" signify the 5 duration of temptation is, as just said, that the Lord suffered Himself to be tempted of the devil forty days. And therefore—as all things were representative of the Lord—when the idea of temptations was present with the angels, that idea was represented in the world of spirits by such things as are in this world, as is the case with all angelic ideas during their descent into the world of spirits : they being presented representatively. And in the same way the idea of

temptation was presented by the number " forty "
because the Lord was to be tempted forty days.
With the Lord, and, consequently, with the
angelic heaven, it is the same whether a thing is
present or is to come ; what is to come is present,
or what is to be done is done. From this came the
representation of temptations, as also of vastations,
in the representative church, by " forty." But
these things cannot as yet be very well comprehended, because the influx of the angelic heaven
into the world of spirits is not known, nor that
such is the nature of this influx.

731. **Every substance that I have made will I
destroy from off the faces of the ground.** That
this signifies man's proprium, which is as if destroyed when vivified, is evident from what has
been said before respecting this proprium. Man's
proprium is entirely evil and falsity. So long as
this continues, the man is dead ; but when he
comes into temptations it is dispersed, that is,
loosened and tempered by truths and goods from
the Lord, and thus is vivified and appears as if it
were not present. That it does not appear and
is no longer hurtful, is signified by " destroyed " ;
and yet it is not destroyed, but remains. It is
almost as with black and white, which when
variously modified by the rays of light are turned
into beautiful colours—such as blue, yellow, and
purple—whereby, according to their arrangements
are presented lovely and agreeable tints, as in
flowers, yet remaining radically and fundamentally
black and white. But as here at the same time the
final vastation of those who were of the Most
Ancient Church is treated of, by " I will destroy
every existing thing that I have made, from off

472

the face of the ground," are signified those who perished (as likewise in the following verse, 23). The " substance that I have made," is all that, or every man, in which there was heavenly seed, or who was of the church ; and therefore, both here and in the following verse, " ground " is mentioned, which signifies the man of the church in whom good and truth have been implanted. This seed, in those called " Noah "—evils and falsities being dispersed, as before said—gradually grew up ; but with the antediluvians who perished it was extinguished by tares.

732. Verse 5. **And Noah did according to all that Jehovah commanded him.** This signifies as before, that thus it came to pass. Compare the preceding chapter, verse 22, where it is said twice that Noah " did," here only once ; and there the name " God " is used, but here " Jehovah." The reason is that there things of the understanding are treated of, and here those of the will. Things of the understanding regard those of the will as being different and distinct from themselves ; but things of the will regard those of the understanding as being united, or as one, with them ; for the understanding is from the will. This is the reason why it is there twice said he " did," and here only once ; and also why the name " God " is used, and here " Jehovah."

733. Verse 6. **And Noah was a son of six hundred years, and the flood of waters was upon the earth.** " Noah was a son of six hundred years," signifies his first state of temptation ; " the flood of waters was upon the earth," signifies the beginning of temptation.

734. In the preceding chapter (verse 13 to the end) the truths of the understanding are treated of, in which the man of the church called " Noah " was instructed by the Lord before he was regenerated ; and next in this chapter (verses 1–5), the goods of the will are treated of, with which also he was endowed by the Lord. As both are treated of, it appears like a repetition. But now in verses 6 to 11 his temptation is treated of, and here the first state and thus the beginning of temptation ; and, as every one can see, a repetition occurs again. For it is said in this verse that " Noah was a son of six hundred years," when the flood came upon the earth ; and in the eleventh verse that it was " in the six hundredth year of his life, in the second month, in the seventeenth day of the month." And so in the seventh verse it is said that Noah went into the ark with his sons and their wives, and likewise in the thirteenth verse. Again it is said in the eighth and ninth verses that the beasts went in unto Noah into the ark ; and also in verses 14 to 16. From which it is evident that here also there is a repetition of what was said before. Those who abide in the sense of the letter alone cannot know but that it is a matter of history thus repeated. But here as elsewhere there is not the least word that is superfluous and vain ; for it is the Word of the Lord. There is, therefore, no repetition, except with another signification. And here, in fact, as before, the signification is that it is the first temptation, which is temptation as to things of his understanding ; but afterwards it is his temptation as to things of the will. These temptations follow one after the other with him who is to be regenerated. For to be tempted as to things of the understanding is quite another thing from being

474

tempted as to what is of the will. Temptation as to things of the understanding is light ; but temptation as to things of the will is severe.

735. The reason why temptation as to things of the understanding, or as to the falsities in a man, is light, is that man is in the fallacies of the senses, and the fallacies of the senses are such that they cannot but enter, and are therefore also easily dispelled. Thus it is with all who abide in the sense of the letter of the Word where it speaks according to the apprehension of man, and therefore according to the fallacies of his senses. If they simply have faith in these things because it is the Word of the Lord, then notwithstanding their being in fallacies they easily suffer themselves to be instructed. As for example : a man who believes that the Lord is angry and punishes and does evil to the wicked, as he has derived this belief from the sense of the letter, he can easily be informed what the real truth is. And so if one simply believes that he can do good of himself, and that if of himself he is good he will receive reward in the other life, he also can easily be instructed that the good which he does is from the Lord, and the Lord in His mercy gives the reward gratuitously. And, there-fore, when such come into temptation as to matters of the understanding, or as to such fallacies, they can be only lightly tempted. And this is the first temptation—and it hardly appears as temptation—which is now treated of. But it is otherwise with those who do not in simplicity of heart believe the Word, but confirm themselves in fallacies and falsities because they favour their lusts ; and who being impelled by this motive bring together many reasonings from themselves and their

scientifics, and afterwards confirm the same by the Word, and thus impress upon themselves, and persuade themselves, that what is false is true.

736. As regards "Noah," or the man of this new church, he was of such character that he believed in simplicity what he had from the Most Ancient Church, which were matters of doctrine, collected and reduced to some doctrinal form by those who were called "Enoch." And he was of an entirely different genius from the antediluvians who perished, called "Nephilim," who immersed the doctrinal things of faith in their foul lusts, and thereby conceived direful persuasions, from which they would not recede, however much instructed by others and shown the falsity of those persuasions. There are at this day also men of the one genius, or disposition, and men of the other. Those of the one may easily be regenerated, but those of the other with difficulty.

737. **Noah was a son of six hundred years.** That this signifies his first state of temptation, is evident, because here and as far as to Heber in the eleventh chapter, numbers and periods of years and names mean nothing but actual things; just as do also the ages and all the names in the fifth chapter. That "six hundred years" here signify the first state of temptation, is evident from the dominant numbers in six hundred, which are ten and six, twice multiplied into themselves. A greater or less number from the same factors changes nothing. As regards the number "ten," it has been shown already (at chapter vi. verse 3) that it signifies remains; and that "six" here signifies labour and combat is evident from many passages in the Word. For the case is this: In what has gone

before the subject is the preparation of the man called "Noah" for temptation—that he was furnished by the Lord with truths of the understanding and goods of the will. These truths and goods are remains, which are not brought out so as to be recognized until the man is being regenerated. In the case of those who are being regenerated through temptations, the remains in a man are for the angels that are with him, who draw out from them the things wherewith they defend the man against the evil spirits who excite the falsities in him, and thus assail him. As the remains are signified by "ten," and the combats by "six," for this reason the years are said to be "six hundred," in which the dominant numbers are ten and six, and signify a state of temptation. As regards the number "six" in particular, that 2 it signifies combat is evident from the first chapter of *Genesis*, where the six days are described in which man was regenerated, before he became celestial, and in which there was continual combat, but on the seventh day, rest. It is for this reason that there are six days of labour and the seventh is the sabbath, which signifies rest. And hence it is that a Hebrew servant served six years, and the seventh year was free (*Exod.* xxi. 2 ; *Deut.* xv. 12 ; *Jer.* xxxiv. 14) ; also that six years they sowed the land and gathered in the fruits thereof, but the seventh year omitted to sow it (*Exod.* xxiii. 10–12), and dealt in like manner with the vineyard ; and that in the seventh year was "a sabbath of sabbath unto the land, a sabbath of Jehovah" (*Lev.* xxv. 3, 4). As "six" signifies labour and combat, it also signifies the dispersion of falsities, as in *Ezekiel* :

Behold six men came from the way of the

477

upper gate which looketh toward the north, and every one had his weapon of dispersion in his hand (ix. 2).

And again, against Gog :

I will make thee to turn again, and will make thee a sixth, and will cause thee to come up from the sides of the north (xxxix. 2).

Here " six " and " to reduce to a sixth," denote dispersion ; the " north," falsities ; " Gog," those who derive matters of doctrine from things external, whereby they destroy internal worship. In *Job* :

In six troubles He shall deliver thee, yea, in the seventh there shall no evil touch thee (v. 19).

3 This means the combat of temptations. But " six " occurs in the Word where it does not signify labour, combat, or the dispersion of falsities, but the holiness of faith, because of its relation to " twelve," which signifies faith and all things of faith in one complex ; and to " three," which signifies the holy ; whence is derived the genuine signification of the number " six " ; as in *Ezekiel* (chapter xl. verse 5), where the reed of the man, with which he measured the holy city of Israel, was " six cubits " ; and in other places. The reason of this derivation is that the holiness of faith is in the combats of temptation, and that the six days of labour and combat look to the holy seventh day.

738. Noah is here called " a son of six hundred years," because a " son " signifies truth of the understanding, as shown before. But in the eleventh verse he is not called a " son," because there his temptation as to things of the will is treated of.

478

739. That by the " flood of waters " is signified the beginning of temptation, is evident from temptation as to things of the understanding being here treated of, which temptation precedes, and, as before said, is light ; and for this reason it is called a " flood of waters," and not simply " a flood " as in the seventeenth verse. For " waters " signify especially the spiritual things of man, the intellectual things of faith, and the opposites of these, which are falsities ; as may be confirmed by very many passages from the Word. That a 2 " flood " or " inundation " of waters signifies temptation, is evident from what was shown in the introduction to this chapter. So also in *Ezekiel* :

> Thus saith the Lord Jehovih, I will make a stormy wind to break through in My fury, and an inundating rain shall there be in Mine anger, and hailstones in wrath, unto the consummation, that I may destroy the wall that ye have daubed with what is unfit (xiii. **13, 14**).

Here a " stormy wind," and an " inundating rain," denote the desolation of falsities ; the " wall daubed with what is unfit," denotes fiction appearing as truth. In *Isaiah* :

> Jehovah God is a protection from inundation, a shadow from the heat, for the breath of the violent is as an inundation against the wall (xxv. **4**).

An " inundation " here denotes temptation as to things of the understanding, and is distinguished from temptation as to things of the will, which is called " heat." Again :   3

> Behold the Lord hath a mighty and strong one, as an inundation of hail, a destroying

storm, as an inundation of mighty waters, over-
flowing (xxviii. 2).

Here degrees of temptation are described. And
again :

> When thou passest through the waters I will
> be with thee ; and through the rivers, they shall
> not overflow thee ; when thou walkest through
> the fire thou shalt not be burned, and the flame
> shall not kindle upon thee (xliii. 2).

" Waters " and " rivers " here denote falsities
and phantasies, " fire " and " flame " evils and
lusts. In *David* :

> For this shall every one that is holy pray unto
> Thee at a time of finding, so that in the inun-
> dation of many waters they shall not reach unto
> him ; Thou art my hiding place ; Thou wilt
> preserve me from trouble (*Ps.* xxxii. 6, 7).

Here the " inundation of waters " denotes temptation which is also called a " flood." In the
same :

> Jehovah sitteth at the flood ; yea, Jehovah
> sitteth King forever (*Ps.* xxix. 10).

From these passages, and from what was premised
at the beginning of this chapter, it is evident that
a " flood " or " inundation " of waters signifies
nothing but temptations and vastations, although
described historically, after the manner of the
most ancient people.

740. Verse 7. **And Noah went in, and his sons,
and his wife, and his sons' wives with him, into
the ark, from before the waters of the flood.** " Noah
went into the ark, from before the waters of the
flood," signifies that he was protected in temptation ; by " sons " are signified truths, as before ;

by " wife," goods ; by " sons' wives," truths
conjoined with goods.

**741. Noah went into the ark from before the
waters of the flood.** That this signifies that he
was protected, must be evident to every one.
Temptations are nothing but combats of evil spirits
with the angels who are with a man. Evil spirits
call up all the wrong things that a man has either
done or even thought from his infancy, thus both
his evils and his falsities, and condemn him, and
there is nothing that gives them greater delight
than to do this, for the very delight of their life
consists therein. But through angels the Lord
guards the man, and restrains the evil spirits and
genii from going beyond bounds, and inundating
the man beyond what he is able to bear.

742. That by " sons " are signified truths, by
" wife " goods, and by " sons' wives " truths
conjoined with goods, has been explained before
at the eighteenth verse of the preceding chapter,
where the same words occur. By truths and goods
(though here called " sons " and " wives ") are
meant those things which were in the man called
" Noah," and by means of which he was protected.
Such is the most ancient style of the Word, connected in the manner of history, but involving
heavenly arcana.

743. Verses 8, 9. **Of the clean beast, and of the
beast that is not clean, and of the fowl, and of
everything that creepeth upon the ground, there
went in two and two, to Noah into the ark, male
and female, as God had commanded Noah.** By
" the clean beast," affections of good are signified
as before ; by " the beast that is not clean," lusts ;

Q   481

by " the fowl," in general, thoughts ; by " everything that creepeth upon the ground," the sensuous
part and its every pleasure ; "two and two,"
signify things corresponding ; that they " went
into the ark," signifies that they were protected ;
" male and female," signify as before truth and
good ; " as God commanded Noah," signifies that
so it came to pass.

744. That affections of good are signified by
" the clean beast," has been stated and explained
before, at the second verse of this chapter, and
therefore need not be dwelt upon ; as also that
lusts, that is, evil affections, are signified by " the
beast not clean."

745. That by the " fowl," or " bird," in general
are signified thoughts, may be seen from what has
been said before concerning birds—that they
signify things of the understanding, or things
rational. But there they were called " fowls of the
heavens," and here only " the fowl " ; and, therefore, they signify thoughts in general. For there
are many kinds of birds, both clean and unclean,
which are distinguished in the fourteenth verse
into the " fowl," the " flying thing," and the
" winged thing." The clean birds are thoughts of
truth ; the unclean are false thoughts ; concerning
which, of the Lord's Divine mercy, we will treat
hereafter.

746. **Everything that creepeth upon the ground.**
That this signifies the sensuous part and its every
pleasure, has also been said and shown before.
The most ancient people compared and likened
the sensuous things of man and his pleasures to
reptiles and creeping things, and even called them

so, because they are the outermost things, and, as
it were, creep on the surface of a man, and must not
be permitted to raise themselves higher.

747. That " two and two " signify things that
correspond, any one may see from their being pairs ;
they cannot be pairs unless they correspond to each
other, as do goods and truths, and evils and falsities.   For there is in all things a semblance of
a marriage, or a coupling, as of truths with goods,
and of evils with falsities, because there is a
marriage of the understanding with the will, or
of the things of the understanding with those of
the will.   And indeed everything has its marriage
or its coupling, without which it could not possibly
subsist.

748. That their " going into the ark " signifies
that they were protected, was stated before at
the seventh verse, where it is said concerning Noah
and his sons and their wives.

749. That " male and female " signify truth
and good, may be seen from what has been said
before, at verses 2 and 3 of this chapter, where
" male and female " are predicated of fowls, and
" man and wife " of beasts.   The reason was also
then stated, namely, that there is a marriage of
the things of the will with those of the understanding, and not so much of the things of the understanding, in themselves regarded, with those of
the will.   The former are related as man and wife,
the latter as male and female.   And because the
subject here, as before said, is the temptation of
that man as to the things of his understanding,
it is said " male and female," and there is meant a
combat or temptation as to the things of the
understanding.

750. **As God commanded Noah.** That this signifies that so it came to pass, has been shown at verse 22 of the preceding chapter, and in this chapter at verse 5.

751. As the subject here treated of is the temptation of the man of the new church called " Noah," and as few if any know the nature of temptations (because at this day there are few who undergo such temptations, and those who do undergo them know not but that it is something inherent in themselves which thus suffers), the subject shall be briefly explained. There are evil spirits who, as before said, in times of temptation call up a man's falsities and evils, and in fact call forth from his memory whatever he has thought and done from his infancy. Evil spirits do this with a skill and a malignity so great as to be indescribable. But the angels with the man draw out his goods and truths, and thus defend him. This combat is what is felt and perceived by the man, causing
2 the pain and remorse of conscience. There are two kinds of temptations, one as to things of the understanding, the other as to those of the will. When a man is tempted as to things of the understanding, the evil spirits call up only the evil things he has been guilty of (here signified by the " unclean beasts "), and accuse and condemn him ; they do indeed also call up his good deeds (here signified by the " clean beasts "), but pervert them in a thousand ways. At the same time they call up what he has thought (here signified by the " fowl "), and such things also as are signified by " everything that creepeth upon the ground."
3 But this temptation is light, and is perceived only by the recalling of such things to mind and a

484

certain anxiety therefrom. But when a man is tempted as to the things of the will, his thoughts and doings are not so much called up, but there are evil genii (as evil spirits of this kind may be called) who inflame him with their lusts and foul loves with which he also is imbued, and thus combat by means of the man's lusts themselves, which they do so maliciously and secretly that it could not be believed to be from them. For in a moment they infuse themselves into the life of his lusts, and almost instantly invert and change an affection of good and truth into an affection of evil and falsity, so that the man cannot possibly know but that it is done of his own self, and comes forth of his own will. This temptation is most severe, and is perceived as an inward pain and tormenting fire. Of this more will be said hereafter. That such is the case has been given me to perceive and know by manifold experience ; and also when and how the evil spirits or genii were flowing in and inundating, and who and whence they were ; concerning which experiences, of the Lord's Divine mercy, special and particular mention will be made hereafter.

752. Verse 10. **And it came to pass after the seven days that the waters of the flood were upon the earth.** This signifies, as before, the beginning of temptation.

753. That by " seven days " is signified the beginning of temptation was shown above at the fourth verse ; and it has reference to what has gone before, namely, that this temptation, which was of the things of his understanding, was the beginning of temptation, or the first temptation ; and the conclusion is thus expressed. And because this first temptation was as to things of the

understanding, it is described by the " waters of the flood," as above at the seventh verse, and by the " flood of waters " at the sixth verse, which properly signify such temptation, as was there shown.

754. Verse 11. **In the six hundredth year of Noah's life, in the second month, in the seventeenth day of the month, in that day were all the fountains of the great deep broken up, and the cataracts of heaven were opened.** By " the six hundredth year, the second month, and the seventeenth day," is signified the second state of temptation; " all the fountains of the great deep were broken up," signifies the extreme of temptation as to the things of the will; " the cataracts of heaven were opened," signifies the extreme of temptation as to the things of the understanding.

755. That by " the six-hundredth year, the second month, and seventeenth day," is signified the second state of temptation, follows from what has hitherto been said; for from the sixth verse to this eleventh verse the first state of temptation is treated of, which was temptation as to things of his understanding. And that now the second state is treated of, namely, as to things of the will, is the reason why his age is told again. It was said before that he was " a son of six hundred years," and here that the flood came " in the six hundredth year of his life, in the second month, and in the seventeenth day." No one could suppose that by the years of Noah's age, of which the years, months, and days are specified, a state of temptation as to things of the will is meant. But as has been said, such was the manner of speech and of writing among the most ancient people; and especially were they delighted in being able to

486

specify times and names, and thereby construct a narrative similar to actual history ; and in this consisted their wisdom. Now it has been shown 2 above, at verse 6, that the " six hundred years " signify nothing but the first state of temptation, and so do the " six hundred years " here ; but in order that the second state of temptation might be signified, " months " and " days " are added ; and indeed two months or " in the second month," which signifies combat itself, as is evident from the signification of the number " two " in the second verse of this chapter, where it is shown that it signifies the same as " six," that is, labour and combat, and also dispersion. But the number " seventeen " signifies both the beginning of temptation and the end of temptation, because it is composed of the numbers seven and ten. When this number signifies the beginning of temptation, it involves the days up to seven, or a week of seven days ; and that this signifies the beginning of temptation has been shown above, at the fourth verse of this chapter. But when it signifies the end of temptation (as at verse 4 of chapter viii.), then " seven " is a holy number ; to which " ten " (which signifies remains) is adjoined, for without remains man cannot be regenerated. That the 3 number " seventeen " signifies the beginning of temptation, is evident in *Jeremiah*, when that prophet was commanded to buy a field from Hanameel his uncle's son, which was in Anathoth ; and he weighed him the money, seventeen shekels of silver (xxxii. 9). That this number also signifies the Babylonish captivity, which represents the temptation of the faithful and the devastation of the unfaithful, and so the beginning of temptation and at the same time the end of temptation, or

487

liberation, is evident from what follows in the
same chapter—the captivity in the thirty-sixth
verse, and the liberation in the thirty-seventh
and following verses. No such number would
have appeared in the prophecy if it had not, like
all the other words, involved a hidden meaning.

4 That " seventeen " signifies the beginning of temptation, is also evident from the age of Joseph, who
was a " son of seventeen years " when he was sent
to his brothers and sold into Egypt (*Gen.* xxxvii. 2).
His being sold into Egypt has a similar signification,
as of the Lord's Divine mercy will be shown in the
explanation of that chapter. There the historical
events are representative, which actually took
place as described ; but here significative historical
incidents are composed, and did not take place as
described in the sense of the letter. And yet the
actual events involve arcana of heaven, in fact
every word of them does so, exactly as do these
made-up histories. It cannot but appear strange
that this is so, because where any historical fact
or statement is presented, the mind is held in the
letter and cannot release itself from it, and so
thinks that nothing else is signified and represented.

5 But that there is an internal sense in which the
life of the Word resides (and not in the letter,
which without the internal sense is dead), must
be evident to any intelligent man. Without the
internal sense how does any historical statement
in the Word differ from history as told by any
profane writer ? And then of what use would it
be to know the age of Noah, and the month and
day when the flood took place, if it did not involve
a heavenly arcanum ? And who cannot see that
this saying : " all the fountains of the great deep
were broken up, and the cataracts of heaven were

488

opened," is a prophetical one ?   Not to mention other similar considerations.

756. That " all the fountains of the great deep were broken up," signifies the extreme of temptation as to things of the will, is evident from what has been said just above respecting temptations, that they are of two kinds, one as to things of the understanding, the other as to things of the will, and that the latter relatively to the former are severe ; and it is evident also from the fact that up to this point temptation as to things of the understanding has been treated of. It is similarly evident from the signification of the " deep," namely, lusts and the falsities thence derived (as before at n. 18), and it is evident also from the following passages in the Word. In *Ezekiel* :

> Thus saith the Lord Jehovih, When I shall make thee a desolate city, like the cities that are not inhabited, when I shall bring up the deep upon thee, and many waters shall cover thee (xxvi. 19).

Here the " deep " and " many waters " denote the extreme of temptation. In *Jonah* :

> The waters compassed me about, even to the soul ; the deep was round about me (ii. 5).

Here likewise the " waters " and the " deep " denote the extreme of temptation. In *David* :

> Deep calleth unto deep at the noise of Thy water-spouts ; all Thy breakers and all Thy waves are over me (*Ps.* xlii. 7).

Here also the " deep " manifestly denotes the extreme of temptation. Again :

> He rebuked the Red Sea also, and it was dried up ; and He made them go through the deeps

as in the wilderness, and He saved them from the hand of him that hated them, and redeemed them from the hand of the enemy, and the waters covered their adversaries (*Ps*. cxi. 9–11).

2 Here the " deep " denotes the temptations in the wilderness. In ancient times, hell was meant by the " deep " ; and phantasies and persuasions of falsity were likened to waters and rivers, as also to a smoke out of the deep. And the hells of some appear so, that is, as deeps and as seas ; concerning which, of the Lord's Divine mercy, we will treat hereafter. From those hells come the evil spirits that devastate, and also those that tempt man ; and their phantasies that they pour in, and the lusts with which they inflame a man, are as inundations and exhalations therefrom. For as before said, through evil spirits man is conjoined with hell, and through angels with heaven. And, therefore, when it is said that " all the fountains of the deep were broken up," such things are signified. That hell is called the " deep " and that the foul emanations therefrom are called " rivers," is evident in *Ezekiel* :

Thus saith the Lord Jehovih, In the day when he went down into hell I caused a mourning, I covered the deep above him, and I restrained the rivers thereof, and the great waters were stayed (xxxi. 15).

Hell is also called the " deep," or " abyss," in *John* (*Rev*. ix. 1, 2, 11 ; xi. 7 ; xvii. 8 ; xx. 1, 3).

757. The cataracts of heaven were opened. That this signifies the extreme of temptation as to things of the understanding, is also evident from the above. Temptation as to things of the will, or as to lusts, can by no means be separated

490

from temptation as to things of the understanding ;
for if separated there would not be any temptation,
but an inundation, such as there is with those who
live in the fires of lusts, in which they, like infernal
spirits, feel the delights of their life.   They are
called the " cataracts of heaven " from the inundation   of   falsities   or   reasonings ;   concerning
which also in *Isaiah* :

> He who fleeth from the noise of the fear shall
> fall into the pit ; and he that cometh up out of
> the midst of the pit shall be taken in the snare ;
> for the cataracts from on high are opened, and
> the foundations of the earth do shake (xxiv. 18).

758. Verse 12. **And the rain was upon the earth
forty days and forty nights.**   This signifies that
the temptation continued.   " Rain " is temptation ;
" forty days and forty nights," denotes its duration.

759. That the " rain " here is temptation is
evident from what has been said and shown above,
concerning a " flood " and an " inundation " ;
and also from the signification of the " fountains
of the deep were broken up," and the " cataracts
of heaven were opened," as being temptations.

760. That the " forty days and forty nights,"
signify its duration, was shown above, at verse 4.
By " forty," as before said, is signified every
duration of temptation, whether greater or less,
and indeed severe temptation, which is of the
things of the will.   For by continual pleasures,
and by the loves of self and of the world, consequently by the lusts that are the connected activi-
ties of these loves, man has acquired a life for
himself of such a kind that it is nothing but a life of
such things.   This life cannot possibly accord with

heavenly life ; for no one can love worldly and heavenly things at the same time, seeing that to love worldly things is to look downwards, and to love heavenly things is to look upwards. Much less can any one love himself and at the same time the neighbour, and still less the Lord. He who loves himself, hates all who do not render him service ; so that the man who loves himself is very far from heavenly love and charity, which is to love the neighbour more than one's self, and the Lord above all things. From this it is evident how far removed the life of man is from heavenly life, and, therefore, he is regenerated by the Lord through temptations, and is bent so as to bring him into agreement. This is why such temptation is severe, for it touches a man's very life, assailing, destroying, and transforming it, and is, therefore, described by the words : " the fountains of the deep were broken up, and the cataracts of heaven were opened."

761. That spiritual temptation in man is a combat of the evil spirits with the angels who are with him, and that this combat is commonly felt in his conscience, has been stated before, and concerning this combat it should also be known that angels continually protect man and avert the evils which evil spirits endeavour to do to him. They even protect what is false and evil in a man, for they know very well whence his falsities and evils come, namely, from evil spirits and genii. Man does not produce anything false and evil from himself, but it is the evil spirits with him who produce it, and at the same time make the man believe that he does it of himself. Such is their malignity. And what is more, at the moment when

they are infusing and compelling this belief, they accuse and condemn him, as I can confirm from many experiences. The man who has not faith in the Lord cannot be enlightened so as not to believe that he does evil of himself, and he therefore appropriates the evil to himself, and becomes like the evil spirits that are with him. Such is the case with man. As the angels know this, in the temptations of regeneration they protect also the falsities and evils of a man, for otherwise he would succumb. For there is nothing in a man but evil and the falsity thence derived, so that he is a mere assemblage and compound of evils and their falsities.

762. But spiritual temptations are little known at this day. Nor are they permitted to such a degree as formerly, because man is not in the truth of faith, and would therefore succumb. In place of these temptations there are others, such as misfortunes, griefs, and anxieties, arising from natural and bodily causes, and also sicknesses and diseases of the body, which in a measure subdue and break up the life of a man's pleasures and lusts, and determine and uplift his thoughts to interior and religious subjects. But these are not spiritual temptations, these being experienced by those only who have received from the Lord a conscience of truth and good. Conscience is itself the plane of temptations, wherein they operate.

763. Thus far temptations have been treated of; and now follows the end or purpose of the temptation, which was that a new church might arise.

764. Verse 13. **In the self-same day entered Noah, and Shem, and Ham, and Japheth, the sons of Noah, and Noah's wife, and the three wives of**

his sons with them, into the ark. That they
" entered into the ark," signifies here as before that
they were saved ; " Noah " signifies what was
of the church ; " Shem, Ham, and Japheth,"
what was of the churches that were thence derived ;
" the sons of Noah," signify doctrinal things ;
" the three wives of his sons with them," signify
the churches themselves that were thence derived.

765. Thus far the temptation of the man of the
church called " Noah " has been treated of :
first, his temptation as to things of the understanding, which are truths of faith (verses 6–10) ;
and then his temptation as to things of the will,
which have regard to the goods of charity (verses
11, 12). The end or purpose of the temptations
was that a man of the church or a new church
might be born again by their means ; seeing that
the Most Ancient Church had perished. This
church called " Noah " was, as before said, of a
different disposition from that of the Most Ancient
Church ; that is to say, it was spiritual, the characteristic of which is that man is born again by
means of doctrinal matters of faith, after the
implantation of which a conscience is instilled
into him, lest he should act against the truth and
good of faith ; and in this way he is endowed with
charity, which governs the conscience from which
he is thus beginning to act. From this it is evident
what a spiritual man is : that he is not one who
believes faith without charity to be saving, but one
who makes charity the essential of faith, and acts
from it. That such a man or such a church might
arise, was the end in view, and therefore that church
itself is now treated of. That the church is now
treated of is evident also from the repetition as

it were of the same matter ; for it is said here :
" in the self-same day entered Noah, and Shem,
and Ham, and Japheth, the sons of Noah, and
Noah's wife, and the three wives of his sons with
them, into the ark " ; and also above in verse 7,
but in these words : " and Noah went in, and his
sons, and his wife, and his sons' wives with him,
into the ark." But now, because the church is
treated of, the sons are named, " Shem, Ham, and
Japheth," who when thus named signify the man
of the church, but when called " sons," without
names, signify truths of faith. Besides, that which
was said in verses 8 and 9 about the beasts and the
fowls that went into the ark is repeated again,
in verses 14–16, but here with a difference accordant with and applicable to the subject of the church.

767. **They entered into the ark.** That this signifies that they were saved (namely, the man of
the church, who was " Noah," and the other
churches descending and derived from him which
are here spoken of), is evident from what has been
said before about " entering into the ark."

768. That by " Noah " is signified what pertained to the church, and by " Shem, Ham, and
Japheth " what pertained to the churches that
were derived therefrom, is evident from the fact
that here they are not called merely his " sons,"
as before in the seventh verse, but are called by
their names. When thus named they signify the
man of the church. The man of the church is not
merely the church itself, but is everything that
belongs to the church. It is a general term
comprehending whatever belongs to the church,
as was said before of the Most Ancient Church,
which was called " Man," and likewise of the other

churches that were named. Thus by " Noah,"
and by " Shem, Ham, and Japheth," is signified
whatever belongs to the church and to the churches
2 that were derived from it, as a whole. Such is the
style and mode of speaking in the Word. Thus
where " Judah " is named, in the Prophets, the
celestial church is mostly signified, or whatever
belongs to that church ; where " Israel " is named,
the spiritual church is mostly signified, or whatever
belongs to that church ; where " Jacob " is
named, the external church is signified ; for with
every man of the church there is an internal and an
external of the church, the internal being where
the true church is, and the external being what is
derived therefrom, and this latter is " Jacob."
3 But the case is different when the men are not
named. The reason why this is so is that when
named they refer representatively to the kingdom
of the Lord. The Lord is the only Man, and is the
all of His kingdom ; and as the church is His
kingdom on earth, the Lord alone is the all of the
church. The all of the church is love or charity ;
and therefore a man (or what is the same, one
called by name), signifies love or charity, that is,
the all of the church ; and then his " wife " signifies
simply the church thence derived. So it is here.
But what kind of churches are signified by " Shem,
Ham, and Japheth " will, of the Lord's Divine
mercy, be stated hereafter.

769. That by the " sons of Noah " are signified
doctrinal things, is evident from the signification
of " sons," as shown before ; for there can be no
church without doctrinal things. And, therefore,
they are not only named, but it is also added that
they are his " sons."

496

770. That by Noah's "wife" is signified the church itself, and by the "three wives of his sons with them," the churches themselves that were derived from that church, is evident from what has been said before, namely, that when the man of the church is named, the all of the church is meant, or, as it is termed, the head of the church ; and then his "wife" is the church itself, as shown before (n. 252, 253). It is otherwise when "man and wife," or "male and female," are named in the Word, for then by "man" and "male" are signified the things of the understanding, or the truths of faith ; and by "wife" and "female," the things of the will, or the goods of faith.

771. As every expression in the Word is from the Lord, and, therefore, has what is Divine within it, it is evident that there is no word, nor even an iota, that does not signify and involve something. And so it is here, when it is said "three wives," and the wives "of his sons," and also "with them." But what the particulars involve it would take too long to explain. It is sufficient to give only a general idea of their most general import.

772. Verses 14, 15. **They, and every wild animal after its kind, and every beast after its kind, and every creeping thing that creepeth upon the earth after its kind ; and every fowl after its kind, every flying thing, every winged thing. And they went in unto Noah into the ark, two and two, of all flesh wherein is the breath of lives.** By "they" is signified the man of the church in general ; by "every wild animal after its kind," is signified every spiritual good ; by "every beast after its kind," every natural good ; by "every creeping

497

thing that creepeth upon the earth after its kind,"
every sensuous and corporeal good; by "fowl
after its kind," every spiritual truth; by "flying
thing," natural truth; by "winged thing," sensuous truth. That "they went in unto Noah into
the ark," signifies as before that they were saved;
"two and two," signifies as before, pairs; "of all
flesh wherein is the breath of lives," signifies a new
creature, or that they received new life from the
Lord.

773. That by "they" is signified the man of the
church in general, or all that belonged to that
church, is evident from its referring to those who
were named just before, that is, to Noah, Shem,
Ham, and Japheth, who, although they are four,
yet together constitute a one. In "Noah," by
whom the Ancient Church in general is meant, are
contained, as in a parent or seed, the churches that
were derived from that church; and for this
reason by "they" is signified the Ancient Church.
All those churches which were called "Shem, Ham,
and Japheth," together constitute the church
which is called the Ancient Church.

774. That by the "wild animal after its kind," is
signified every spiritual good, and by "beast after
its kind," every natural good, and by "creeping
thing that creepeth upon the earth," every sensuous
and corporeal good, has been stated and shown
before (n. 45, 46, 142, 143, 246). At first view it
may appear as if it could not be that the "wild
animal" signifies spiritual good; yet that this
is the true signification appears from the series of
expressions, in that mention is first made of
"they," meaning the man of the church; next
of "wild animal"; then of "beast"; and lastly

498

of "creeping thing." So that "wild animal" involves what is of higher worth and excellence than "beast," the reason of which is that in the Hebrew language the expression "wild animal" means also an animal in which there is a living soul. And so here it does not mean a wild animal, but an animal in which there is a living soul, for it is the same word. That by "animals," "beasts," and "creeping things that creep upon the earth," are signified things pertaining to the will, has been stated and shown before, and will be further shown in what presently follows, where birds will be treated of.

775. It is said of each "after its kind," because there are genera and species of all goods, both spiritual and natural, and also of the derivative sensuous and corporeal goods. So many genera are there of spiritual goods, and so many genera likewise of spiritual truths, that they cannot be numbered ; still less can the species of the genera. In heaven all goods and truths, celestial and spiritual, are so distinct in their genera, and these in their species, that there is not the least of them which is not quite distinct ; and so innumerable are they, that the specific differences may be said to be unlimited. From this it may be seen how poor and almost nothing is human wisdom, which scarcely knows that there is such a thing as spiritual good or spiritual truth, much less what it is. From celestial and spiritual goods and their derivative truths, issue and descend natural goods and truths. For there is never any natural good and truth that does not spring from spiritual good, and this from celestial, and also subsist from the same. If the spiritual should withdraw from the natural, the

natural would be nothing. The origin of all things is in this wise : all things, both in general and in particular, are from the Lord ; from Him is the Celestial ; from Him through the Celestial comes forth the Spiritual ; through the Spiritual the Natural ; through the Natural the Corporeal and the Sensual. And as they all come forth from the Lord in this way, so also do they subsist from Him, for, as is well known, subsistence is a perpetual coming into existence. Those who have a different conception of the coming into existence and origin of things, like those who worship nature and deduce from her the origins of things, are in principles so deadly that the phantasies of the wild beasts of the forest may be called far more sane. Such are very many who appear to themselves to excel others in wisdom.

776. That " every fowl after its kind " signifies every spiritual truth, " flying thing " natural truth, and " winged thing " sensuous truth, is evident from what has been stated and shown before concerning " birds " (as at n. 40). The most ancient people likened man's thoughts to birds, because relatively to the things of the will, thoughts are like birds. As mention is made here of " fowl," " flying thing," and " winged thing," and of these in succession, like things intellectual, rational, and sensuous in man, in order that no one may doubt that they signify these things, some passages from the Word may be adduced in confirmation, from which it will also be plain that " beasts " signify
2 such things as have been stated. Thus in *David* :

Thou madest him to have dominion over the works of Thy hands : Thou hast put all things under his feet ; all sheep and oxen, yea, and the
500

beasts of the fields, the fowl of the heaven, and
the fish of the sea (*Ps.* viii. 6–8).

This is said of the Lord, whose dominion over man,
and over the things pertaining to man, is thus
described. Otherwise what would be the dominion
over " beasts " and " fowls " ? Again :

Fruitful trees and all cedars, the wild animal
and every beast, creeping things and flying
fowl, let them praise the name of Jehovah
(cxlviii. 9, 10, 13).

The " fruitful tree " denotes the celestial man ;
the " cedar," the spiritual man. The " wild
animal," and " beast," and " creeping thing," are
their goods, as in the history before us ; the " flying
fowl " is their truths ; from all of which they can
" praise the name of Jehovah." By no means can
the wild animal, the beast, the creeping thing, and
the bird do this. In profane writings such things
may be said hyperbolically, but there is nothing
hyperbolical in the Word of the Lord, but things
significative and representative. In *Ezekiel* :   3

The fishes of the sea, and the fowls of the
heaven, and the wild animal of the field, and all
creeping things that creep upon the earth, and
all the men that are upon the face of the earth,
shall shake at My presence (xxxviii. 20).

That such things are here signified by " beasts "
and " fowls " is very manifest ; for how would it
be to the glory of Jehovah if fishes, birds, and
beasts should shake ? Can any one suppose that
such sayings would be holy if they did not involve
holy things ? In *Jeremiah* :

I beheld, and lo there was no man, and all the
birds of the heavens were fled (iv. 25).

This denotes all good and truth; "man" also
denotes here the good of love. Again:

> They are burned up, so that none passeth
> through, neither can men hear the voice of the
> cattle; both the fowl of the heavens and the
> beast are fled, they are gone (ix. 10).

This denotes in like manner that all truth and
4 good have departed. And again:

> How long shall the land mourn, and the herb
> of every field wither? for the wickedness of
> them that dwell therein the beasts are consumed
> and the birds, because they said, He shall not
> see our latter end (xii. 4).

Here the "beasts" denote goods, and the "birds"
truths, which perished. In *Zephaniah*:

> I will consume man and beast, I will consume
> the fowls of the heaven and the fishes of the sea,
> and the stumbling-blocks with the wicked; and I
> will cut off man from off the face of the ground
> (i. 3).

Here "man and beast" denote the things of love
and its good; the "fowls of the heaven and the
fishes of the sea," the things of the understanding, thus which are of truth. These are called
"stumbling-blocks" because goods and truths are
stumbling-blocks to the wicked, but not beasts and
birds; and they are also plainly spoken of "man."
In *David*:

> The trees of Jehovah are satisfied, the cedars
> of Lebanon which He hath planted, where the
> birds make their nests (civ. 16, 17).

The "trees of Jehovah" and the "cedars of
Lebanon" denote the spiritual man; the "birds"
his rational or natural truths, which are as

" nests." It was, moreover, a common form of 5
expression that " birds would make their nests in
the branches," signifying truths, as in *Ezekiel* :

> In the mountain of the height of Israel will
> I plant it, and it shall lift up its bough, and
> bear fruit, and be a goodly cedar ; and under it
> shall dwell every bird of every wing ; in the
> shadow of the branches thereof shall they dwell
> (xvii. 23).

This denotes the church of the Gentiles, which was
spiritual. This is " the goodly cedar " ; the " bird
of every wing " denotes truths of every kind.
Again :

> All the birds of the heavens made their nests
> in his boughs, and under his branches all the
> wild animals of the field brought forth, and
> under his shadow dwelt all great nations
> (xxxi. 6).

This is said of Asshur, which is the spiritual church
and is called a " cedar " ; the " birds of the
heavens " denote its truths ; the " beasts " its
goods. In *Daniel* :

> The leaves thereof were fair, and the fruit
> thereof much, and it was meat for all ; the
> beasts of the field had shadow under it, and the
> fowls of heaven dwelt in the branches thereof
> (iv. 12, 21).

Here the " beasts " denote goods, the " fowls of
the heavens " truths, as must be evident to every
one ; for otherwise of what concern is it that the
bird and the beasts dwelt there ? And it is the
same with what the Lord says :

> The kingdom of God is like unto a grain of
> mustard seed, which a man took and cast into

his garden, and it grew, and became a tree, and the birds of the heaven lodged in the branches thereof (*Luke* xiii. 19; *Matt.* xiii. 31, 32; *Mark* iv. 31, 32).

777. It is now evident that the " fowl " signifies spiritual truth, the " flying thing " natural truth, and the " winged thing " sensuous truth ; and that truths are distinguished in this way. Sensuous truths, which are those of the sight and hearing, are called " winged things," because they are outermost ; and such is the signification of " wing " as applied to other things also.

778. Now as the " fowls of the heavens " signify truths of the understanding, and thus thoughts, they also signify their opposites, such as phantasies or falsities, which being of man's thought are also called " fowls," as for example when it is said that the wicked " shall be given for meat to the fowls of heaven and to the wild beasts," meaning phantasies and lusts (*Isa.* xviii. 6; *Jer.* vii. 33; xvi. 4; xix. 7; xxxiv. 20; *Ezek.* xxix. 5; xxxix. 4). The Lord Himself also compares phantasies and false persuasions to " fowls," where He says :

The seed that fell by the wayside was trodden under foot, and the fowls of heaven came and devoured it (*Matt.* xiii. 4; *Luke* viii. 5; *Mark* iv. 4, 15).

Here the " fowls of heaven " are nothing but falsities.

779. **And they went in unto Noah into the ark.** That this signifies that they were saved, has been already shown. That " two and two " signify pairs, and what they are, may be seen at chapter vi. verse 19.

780. **Of all flesh wherein is the breath of lives.**
That this signifies a new creature, or that they
received new life from the Lord, is evident from
the signification of " flesh " as being in general
all mankind, and specifically the corporeal man,
as before said and shown. Hence " flesh wherein
is the breath of lives," signifies a regenerated
man, for in his proprium there is the Lord's life,
which is the life of charity and faith. Every man
is only " flesh " ; but when the life of charity
and faith is breathed into him by the Lord, the
flesh is made alive, and becomes spiritual and
celestial, and is called a " new creature " (*Mark*
xvi. 15), from having been created anew.

781. Verse 16. **And they that went in, went in
male and female of all flesh, as God had commanded
him ; and Jehovah shut after him.** " They that
went in," signifies the things that were with the
man of the church ; " went in male and female
of all flesh," signifies that there were with him
truths and goods of every kind ; " as God had
commanded," signifies for the reception of which
he had been prepared ; " and Jehovah shut after
him," signifies that man no longer had such communication with heaven as had the man of the
celestial church.

782. Thus far, down to verse 11, the church
has been described as having been preserved in
those who were called " Noah." The state of the
church then follows, which is described, and first
in this passage, as already explained. Then is
described the quality of this state of the church.
The single verses and even single words involve
peculiarities of its state. And because the state
of the church is now treated of, what was said

just before is repeated, being said twice ; here, in the words " and they that went in, went in male and female of all flesh " ; while in the verse just preceding it is said, " and they went in unto Noah into the ark, two and two, of all flesh." This repetition in the Word signifies that another state is treated of. Otherwise, as any one may comprehend, it would be an entirely useless repetition.

783. That " they that went in," signifies the things that were with the man of the church, is therefore evident ; and it also follows that " went in male and female, of all flesh," signifies that there were with him goods and truths of every kind, for it has been stated and shown several times before that the " male " and the " female " signify truths and goods. " As God commanded him." That this signifies that he had been prepared to receive them, has also been mentioned before. With the Lord, to " command " is to prepare and do.

784. **And Jehovah shut after him.** That this signifies that man no longer had such communication with heaven as had the man of the celestial church, appears from the following statement of the case. The state of the Most Ancient Church was such that they had internal communication with heaven, and so through heaven with the Lord. They were in love to the Lord. Those who are in love to the Lord are like angels, with the difference only that they are clothed with a body. Their interiors were uncovered, and were opened even from the Lord. But this new church was different. They were not in love to the Lord, but in faith, and through faith were in charity toward the neighbour. Such cannot have internal

communication, like the most ancient man, but external. But the nature of internal and of external communication it would take too long to explain. Every man, even the wicked, has communication with heaven, through the angels with him (but with a difference as to degree, that is, nearer or more remote), for otherwise man could not exist. The degrees of this communication are without limit. A spiritual man cannot possibly have such communication as can the celestial man, for the reason that the Lord is in love, and not so much in faith. And this is what is signified by "Jehovah shut after him." And since those times heaven 2 has never been open in the way it was to the man of the Most Ancient Church. It is true that many afterwards spoke with spirits and angels: as Moses, Aaron, and others, but in an entirely different way, concerning which, of the Lord's Divine mercy we will treat hereafter. The reason why heaven was closed is deeply hidden, and why it is so closed at this day that man does not even know that there are spirits, still less that there are angels, with him, and supposes himself to be entirely alone when without companions in the world, and when he is thinking by himself. And yet he is continually in the company of spirits, who observe and perceive what the man is thinking, and what he intends and devises, as fully and plainly as if it were manifest before all in the world. This the man is ignorant of, so closed to him is heaven, and yet it is most true. The reason is that if heaven were not so closed to him while he is in no faith, still less in the truth of faith, and still less in charity, it would be most perilous to him. This is also signified by the words:

Jehovah God drove out the man, and He

507

placed at the east of the Garden of Eden the cherubim, and the flame of a sword that turned itself to keep the way of the tree of lives (chapter iii. 24 ; see also what is said n. 301–303).

785. Verses 17, 18. **And the flood was forty days upon the earth, and the waters increased, and bare up the ark, and it was lifted up from off the earth ; and the waters were strengthened, and increased greatly upon the earth ; and the ark went upon the faces of the waters.** By " forty days," is signified the duration of the church called " Noah " ; by " the flood," falsities which still inundated it ; that " the waters increased and bare up the ark, and it was lifted up from off the earth," signifies that such was its fluctuation ; " the waters were strengthened and increased greatly upon the earth, and the ark went upon the face of the waters," signifies that its fluctuations thus increased in frequency and strength.

786. That by " forty days " is signified the duration of the church called " Noah," was shown above (at verse 4). Here it is " forty days," there " forty days and forty nights " ; because in that place the duration of temptation was signified, in which the " nights " are anxieties.

787. That by the " flood " are signified falsities which still inundated the church, also follows from what was shown above ; for a " flood " or " inundation " is nothing but an inundation of falsities. Before (at verse 6), the " flood of waters " signified temptation, as was there shown ; which also is an inundation of falsities that evil spirits then excite in man. The case is the same here, but without temptation, and therefore it is said here simply the " flood," not the " flood of waters."

788. **The waters increased and bare up the ark, and it was lifted up from off the earth.** That this signifies the nature of its fluctuation, and that " the waters were strengthened and increased greatly upon the earth, and the ark went upon the face of the waters," signifies that its fluctuations thus increased in frequency and strength, cannot be seen unless there be first explained what was the state of this church which is called " Noah." " Noah " was not the Ancient Church itself, but was as the parent or seed of that church, as before said. " Noah " together with " Shem, Ham, and Japheth," constituted the Ancient Church, which immediately succeeded the Most Ancient. Every man of the church called " Noah " was of the posterity of the Most Ancient Church, and with respect to hereditary evil was, therefore, in a state nearly like that of the rest of the posterity, which perished ; and those who were in such a state could not be regenerated and made spiritual as could those who did not derive such quality by inheritance. What their hereditary quality was, has been stated above (n. 310). For example 2 (that the matter may be more clearly understood) : those who, like the Jews, are of the seed of Jacob, cannot so well be regenerated as can the Gentiles, for they have an inherent opposition to faith, not only from principles imbibed from infancy and afterwards confirmed, but from hereditary disposition also. That this inheres also from hereditary disposition, may in some measure be evident from their being of a different genius, of different manners, and also of different features, from other men, whereby they are distinguishable from others ; and these characteristics they have from inheritance. And it is the same with the

509

interior qualities, for manners and features are types of the interiors. Therefore converted Jews fluctuate more than others between truth and falsity. It was the same with the first men of the Ancient Church, who were called " Noah " because they were of the race and seed of the most ancient men. These are the fluctuations described here, and also in what follows : that Noah was a husbandman and planted a vineyard ; and that he drank of the wine, and was drunken, and lay uncovered within his tent (ix. 20, 21). That they were few, was made evident from the fact that the man of that church was represented in the world of spirits as a tall and slender man, clothed in white, in a chamber of small dimensions. And yet it was these who preserved and had among them the doctrinal things of faith.

789. The fluctuations of the man of this church are described here ; first, by its being said that the " waters (that is, falsities) increased " ; then, that they " bare up the ark," and that it was " lifted up from off the earth " ; afterwards, that the " waters were strengthened, and increased greatly upon the earth " ; and finally, that the " ark went upon the faces of the waters." But to explain each degree of the fluctuation would be unnecessary and too prolix. It is sufficient to know that they are here described. We will merely mention what is signified by the statement that the ark was lifted up from off the earth, and went upon the faces of the waters. As no one can know this unless he is informed how man is withheld from evils and falsities, and as this is a hidden thing, it shall be briefly explained. Speaking

generally, every man, even the regenerate, is such that if the Lord did not withhold him from evils and falsities he could cast himself headlong into hell. The very moment he is not withheld, he rushes headlong into it. This has been made known to me by experience, and was also represented by a horse (as before described, n. 187, 188). This withholding from evils and falsities is in effect a lifting up, so that evils and falsities are perceived below, and the man above. Concerning this elevation, of the Lord's Divine mercy, we will treat hereafter. It is this elevation which is signified by the "ark being lifted up from off the earth, and going upon the faces of the waters."

790. That the "waters" here and in the following verses signify falsities, is evident from the passages of the Word adduced at the beginning of this chapter, and at verse 6, where a "flood" or inundation of waters is treated of. It is there shown that inundations of waters signify desolations and temptations, which involve the same as falsities ; for desolations and temptations are nothing but inundations of falsities that are excited by evil spirits. That such "waters" signify falsities, is because in the Word "waters" in general signify what is spiritual, that is, what is of understanding, of reason, and of knowledge ; and as they signify these they also signify their contraries, for every falsity is a something pertaining to knowledge, and appears as a thing of reason and understanding, because it is of the thought. That 2 "waters" signify spiritual things, is evident from many passages in the Word ; and that they also signify falsities, let the following passages, in

addition to those already cited, serve for confirmation. In *Isaiah* :

> This people hath refused the waters of Shiloah that go softly ; therefore, behold, the Lord bringeth up upon them the waters of the river, strong and many, and he shall go over all his banks (viii. 6, 7).

The " waters that go softly," here denote things spiritual, " waters strong and many," falsities. Again :·

> Woe to the land shadowing with wings, which is beyond the rivers of Ethiopia ; that sendeth ambassadors upon the sea, and in vessels of papyrus upon the waters. Go, ye swift messengers, to a nation meted out and trodden down, whose land the rivers have spoiled (xviii. 1, 2).

This denotes the falsities which are of the " land
3 shadowing with wings." Again :

> When thou passest through the waters I will be with thee, and through the rivers they shall not overflow thee (xliii. 2).

The " waters " and " rivers " denote difficulties, and also falsities. In *Jeremiah* :

> What hast thou to do with the way of Egypt, to drink the waters of Shihor ? And what hast thou to do with the way of Assyria, to drink the waters of the river ? (ii. 18).

Here " waters " denote falsities from reasonings. Again :

> Who is this that riseth up as a river ? as the rivers his waters are in commotion. Egypt riseth up as a river, and as the rivers his waters toss themselves ; and he said, I will rise up, I will cover the earth, I will destroy the city and the inhabitants thereof (xlvi. 7, 8).

Here again " waters " denote falsities from reasonings. In *Ezekiel* :   4

> Thus saith the Lord Jehovih, When I shall make thee a desolate city, like the cities that are not inhabited, when I shall bring up the deep upon thee, and the great waters shall cover thee, then will I bring thee down with them that descend into the pit (xxvi. 19, 20).

" Waters " here denote evils and the falsities therefrom. In *Habakkuk* :

> Thou didst tread the sea with thine horses, the mire of many waters (iii. 15).

Here " waters " denote falsities. In *John* :

> And the serpent cast forth after the woman, out of his mouth, water as a river, that he might cause her to be carried away by the stream (*Rev.* xii. 15, 16).

Here " waters " denote falsities and lies. In *David* :

> Send Thine hand from above, rescue me and deliver me out of great waters, out of the hand of the sons of the stranger, whose mouth speaketh a lie, and their right hand is a right hand of falsehood (*Ps.* cxliv. 7, 8).

" Great waters " here manifestly denote falsities ; the " sons of the stranger " also signify falsities.

791. Thus far " Noah " has been treated of, or the regenerate men called " Noah," who were in the " ark," and were " lifted up above the waters." The subject will now be those descendants of the Most Ancient Church who were under the waters, or were submerged by the waters.

R   513

792. Verses 19, 20. **And the waters were strengthened very greatly upon the earth, and all the high mountains that were under the whole heaven were covered. Fifteen cubits upward did the waters prevail, and covered the mountains.** " And the waters were strengthened very greatly upon the earth," signifies that persuasions of falsity thus increased ; " and all the high mountains that were under the whole heaven were covered," signifies that all goods of charity were extinguished ; " fifteen cubits upward did the waters prevail, and covered the mountains," signifies that nothing of charity remained ; " fifteen " signifies so few as to be scarcely any.

793. The subject now treated of, up to the end of this chapter, is the antediluvians who perished, as is evident from the particulars of the description. Those who are in the internal sense can know instantly, and indeed from a single word, what subject is treated of ; and especially can they know this from the connection of several words. When a different subject is taken up, at once the words are different, or the same words stand in a different connection. The reason is that there are words peculiar to spiritual things, and words peculiar to celestial things ; or, what is the same, there are words peculiar to matters of understanding, and others to matters of will. For example : the word " desolation " is predicated of spiritual things, and " vastation " of celestial .things ; " city " is predicated of spiritual things, " mountain " of celestial things ; and so on. The case is the same with the connective expressions. And (what cannot fail to be a matter of surprise) in the Hebrew language the words are very often

distinguishable by their sound ; for in those which
belong to the spiritual class the first three vowels
are usually dominant, and in words that are of the
celestial class, the last two vowels.   That in these
verses a different subject is now treated of, appears
also from the repetition already spoken of (in that
it is here again said, as in the preceding verse,
" and the waters were strengthened very greatly
upon the earth "), and the same is evident also
from what follows.

794. **And the waters were strengthened very
greatly upon the earth.**   That this signifies that
persuasions of falsity thus increased, is evident
from what has been said and shown just above
about " waters," namely, that the waters of a
flood, or inundations, signify falsities.   Here,
because falsities or persuasions of what was false
were still more increased, it is said that the " waters
were strengthened very greatly," which in the
original language is the superlative.   Falsities are
principles and persuasions of what is false, and
that these had increased immensely among the
antediluvians, is evident from all that has been
said before concerning them.   Persuasions
immensely increase when men mingle truths
with lusts, or make them favour the loves of self
and of the world ; for then in a thousand ways
they pervert them and force them into agreement.
For who that has imbibed or framed for himself a
false principle does not confirm it by much that he
has learned ; and even from the Word ?   Is there
any heresy that does not thus lay hold of things to
confirm it ?   and even force, and in divers ways
explain and distort, things that are not in agreement, so that they may not disagree ?   For 2

example : he who adopts the principle that faith
alone is saving, without the goods of charity ;
can he not weave a whole system of doctrine out
of the Word ? and this without in the least caring
for, or considering, or even seeing, what the Lord
says, that " the tree is known by its fruit," and
that " every tree that bringeth not forth good
fruit is hewn down and cast into the fire " (*Matt.*
iii. 10 ; vii. 16–20 ; xii. 33). What is more pleasing
than to live after the flesh, and yet be saved if
only one knows what is true, though he does nothing
good ?   Every lust that a man favours forms the
life of his will, and every principle or persuasion
of falsity forms the life of his understanding. These
lives make one when the truths or doctrinals of
faith are immersed in lusts. Every man thus forms
for himself as it were a soul, and such after death
does his life become. Nothing, therefore, is of more
importance to a man than to know what is true.
When he knows what is true, and knows it so well
that it cannot be perverted, then it cannot be so
much immersed in lusts and have such deadly effect.
What should a man have more at heart than his life
to eternity ?   If in the life of the body he destroys
his soul, does he not destroy it to eternity ?

**795. All the high mountains that were under the
whole heaven were covered.** That this signifies
that all the goods of charity were extinguished, is
evident from the signification of mountains among
the most ancient people. With them mountains
signified the Lord, for the reason that they held
their worship of Him on mountains, because these
were the highest places on earth. Hence " mountains " signified celestial things (which also were
called the " highest "), consequently, love and

charity, and thereby the goods of love and charity, which are celestial. And in the opposite sense those also are called "mountains" who are vainglorious; and therefore a "mountain" stands for the very love of self. The Most Ancient Church is also signified in the Word by "mountains," from these being elevated above the earth and nearer as it were to heaven, to the beginnings of things. That "mountains" signify the Lord, and 2 all things celestial from Him, or the goods of love and charity, is evident from the following passages in the Word, from which it is plain what they signify in particular cases, for all things in the Word, both in general and in particular, have a signification according to the subject to which they are applied. In *David* :

> The mountains shall bring peace, and the hills, in righteousness (*Ps.* lxxii. 3).

"Mountains" denote here love to the Lord; "hills," love towards the neighbour, such as was with the Most Ancient Church, which, because of this character, is also signified in the Word by 'mountains" and "hills." In *Ezekiel* :

> In the mountain of My holiness, in the mountain of the height of Israel, saith the Lord Jehovih, there shall all the house of Israel serve Me, that whole land (xx. 40).

The "mountain of holiness" here denotes love to the Lord; the "mountain of the height of Israel," charity towards the neighbour. In *Isaiah* :

> It shall come to pass in the latter days that the mountain of the house of Jehovah shall be established in the top of the mountains, and shall be exalted above the hills (ii. 2).

517

Here " mountains " denote the Lord, and thence all that is celestial. Again :

> In this mountain shall Jehovah Zebaoth make unto all peoples a feast of fat things, and He will take away in this mountain the face of the covering (xxv. 6, 7).

" Mountain " here denotes the Lord, and hence
3 all that is celestial. Again :

> And there shall be upon every lofty mountain, and upon every high hill, rivers, streams of waters (xxx. 25).

Here " mountains " denote goods of love ; " hills," goods of charity, from which are truths of faith, which are the " rivers and streams of waters." Again :

> Ye shall have a song, as in the night when a holy feast is kept ; and gladness of heart, as when one goeth with a pipe to come into the mountain of Jehovah, to the Rock of Israel (xxx. 29).

The " mountain of Jehovah " here denotes the Lord with reference to the goods of love ; the " Rock of Israel," the Lord with reference to the goods of charity. Again :

> Jehovah Zebaoth shall come down to fight upon Mount Zion and upon the hill thereof (xxxi. 4).

" Mount Zion," here and elsewhere in many places, denotes the Lord, and hence all that is celestial, and which is love ; and " hills " denote what is
4 celestial of lower degree, which is charity. Again :

> O Zion that bringest good tidings, get thee up into the high mountain ; O Jerusalem that bringest good tidings, lift up thy voice with strength (xl. 9).

518

To " go up into the high mountain and bring good tidings," is to worship the Lord from love and charity, which are inmost, and are therefore also called " highest," because what is inmost is called highest. Again :

> Let the inhabitants of the rock sing, let them shout from the top of the mountains (xlii. 11).

The " inhabitants of the rock " denote those who are in charity ; to " shout from the top of the mountains " is to worship the Lord from love. Again :

> How beautiful upon the mountains are the feet of him that bringeth good tidings, that publisheth peace, that bringeth good tidings of good, that publisheth salvation ! (lii. 7).

To " bring good tidings upon the mountains," is likewise to preach the Lord from the doctrine of love and charity, and from these to worship Him. Again :

> The mountains and the hills shall break forth before you into singing, and all the trees of the field shall clap their hands (lv. 12).

This denotes worship of the Lord from love and charity, which are " the mountains and the hills " ; and from the faith thence derived, which are the " trees of the field." Again : 5

> I will make all My mountains a way, and My highways shall be exalted (xlix. 11).

Here " mountains " denote love and charity ; and " way " and " highways," the truths of faith thence derived, which are said to be " exalted " when they are from love and charity as their inmost. Again :

> He that putteth his trust in Me shall possess

the land as a heritage, and shall inherit the mountain of My holiness (lvii. 13).

This denotes the Lord's kingdom, wherein is nothing but love and charity. Again :

I will bring forth a seed out of Jacob, and out of Judah an inheritor of My mountains, and Mine elect shall possess it (lxv. 9).

" Mountains " here denote the Lord's kingdom and celestial goods ; " Judah," the celestial church. And again :

Thus saith the high and lofty One that inhabiteth eternity, whose name is holy, I dwell in the high and holy place (lvii. 15).

" High " here denotes what is holy ; and hence it is that on account of their height above the earth, mountains signify the Lord and His holy celestial things. And it was for this reason that the Lord promulgated the Law from Mount Sinai. Love and charity are also meant by the Lord, by " mountains," where, speaking of the consummation of the age, He says :

Then let them that are in Judea flee into the mountains (*Matt*. xxiv. 16 ; *Luke* xxi. 21 ; *Mark* xiii. 14).

Here " Judea " denotes the vastated church.

796. As the Most Ancient Church held holy worship upon mountains, the Ancient Church did the same. And hence in all the representative churches of that time, and in all the nations too, the custom prevailed of sacrificing upon mountains and of building high places, as is evident from what is related of Abram (*Gen*. xii. 1 ; xxii. 2) ; and of the Jews before the building of the temple (*Deut*.

xxvii. 4–7 ; *Joshua* viii. 30 ; 1 *Sam.* ix. 12–14,
19 ; x. 5 ; 1 *Kings* iii. 2–4) ; of the nations (*Deut.*
xii. 2 ; 2 *Kings* xvii. 9–11) ; and of the idolatrous
Jews (*Isa.* lvii. 7 ; 1 *Kings* xi. 7 ; xiv. 23 ; xxii. 43 ;
2 *Kings* xii. 3 ; xiv. 4 ; xv. 3, 4, 34, 35 ; xvi. 4 ;
xvii. 9–11 ; xxi. 5 ; xxiii. 5, 8, 9, 13, 15).

797. From all this it is now evident what is
signified by the " waters with which the mountains
were covered," namely, persuasions of falsity,
which extinguished all the good of charity.

798. **Fifteen cubits upward did the waters
prevail, and covered the mountains.** That this
signifies that nothing of charity remained ; and
that " fifteen " signifies so few as to be scarcely
any, is evident from the signification of the number
" five " (of which above, chapter vi. verse 15),
where it was shown that in the style of the Word,
or in the internal sense, " five " signifies a few ;
and since the number " fifteen " is composed of five,
signifying a few, and of ten, which signifies remains
(as was shown above, chapter vi. verse 3), therefore
" fifteen " signifies remains, which with this people
were scarcely any. For so many were the persuasions of falsity that they extinguished every
good. As for the remains with man, the fact was,
as already said, that principles of falsity, and still
more, persuasions of falsity, such as were with these
antediluvians, had so entirely shut in and hidden
away the remains that these could not be brought
out, and if brought out they would forthwith
have been falsified. For such is the life of persuasions that it not only rejects every truth and absorbs
every falsity, but also perverts every truth that
comes near.

R*

521

799. Verses 21, 22. **And all flesh died that creepeth upon the earth, as to fowl, and as to beast, and as to wild animal, and as to every creeping thing that creepeth upon the earth; and every man; all in whose nostrils was the breathing of the breath of lives, of all that was in the dry land, died.** " All flesh died that creepeth upon the earth," signifies that those who were of the last posterity of the Most Ancient Church became extinct ; " as to fowl, and as to beast, and as to wild animal, and as to every creeping thing that creepeth upon the earth," signifies their persuasions, wherein the " fowl " signifies affections of what is false, " beast " lusts, " wild animal " pleasures, and " creeping thing " corporeal and earthly things. These considered as one are called " every man." " All in whose nostrils was the breathing of the breath of lives," signifies the men who were of the Most Ancient Church, in whose nostrils was the " breathing of the breath of lives," that is, in whom was the life of love and of the derivative faith ; " of all that was in the dry land," signifies those men in whom there was no longer such life ; that they " died," signifies that they expired.

800. **And all flesh died that creepeth upon the earth.** That this signifies that those who were of the last posterity of the Most Ancient Church became extinct, is evident from what follows, where they are described as to their persuasions and their lusts. They are here first called " flesh that creepeth upon the earth," for the reason that they had become altogether sensuous and corporeal. Sensuous and corporeal things, as has been said, were likened by the most ancient men to creeping

things ; and, therefore, when " flesh moving upon the earth " is spoken of, such a man is signified as has become merely sensuous and corporeal. That " flesh " signifies all mankind in general, and specifically the corporeal man, has been said and shown before.

801. From the description of these antediluvians as here given, it may be seen what was the style of writing among the most ancient people, and hence what the prophetic style was. They are described here and up to the end of this chapter ; in these verses they are described in respect to their persuasions, and in verse 23 in respect to their lusts ; that is, they are first described in respect to the state of the things of their understanding, and then in respect to the state of the things of their will. And although with them there were in reality no things of understanding or of will, still the things contrary to them are so to be called ; that is to say, such things as persuasions of falsity, which are by no means things of understanding, and yet are things of thought and reason ; and also such things as lusts, which are by no means things of will. The antediluvians are described, I say, first as to their false persuasions, and then as to their lusts, which is the reason why the things contained in verse 21 are repeated in verse 23, but in a different order. Such also is the prophetic style. The reason is that with man there 2 are two lives ; one, of the things of the understanding ; the other, of the things of the will, and these lives are quite distinct from each other. Man consists of both, and although at this day they are separated in man, nevertheless they flow one into the other, and for the most part unite. That

they unite, and how they unite, can be established and made clear by many illustrations. Since man, therefore, consists of these two parts (the understanding and the will, of which the one flows into the other), when man is described in the Word, he is described with distinctiveness as to the one part and as to the other. This is the reason of the repetitions, and without them the description would be defective. And the case is the same with every other thing as it is here with the will and the understanding, for things are circumstanced exactly as are their subjects, seeing that they belong to their subjects because they come forth from them ; a thing separated from its subject, that is, from its substance, is nothing. And this is the reason why things are described in the Word in a similar way in respect to each constituent part, for in this way the description of each thing is full.

802. That persuasions are here treated of, and lusts in verse 23, may be known from the fact that in this verse " fowl " is first mentioned, and then " beast." For " fowl " signifies what is of the understanding, or of reason, and " beast " what is of the will. But when things belonging to lusts are described, as in verse 23, " beast " is first mentioned, and then " fowl " ; and this for the reason, as was said, that the one thus reciprocally flows into the other, and so the description of them is full.

803. **As to fowl, and as to beast, and as to wild animal, and as to every creeping thing that creepeth upon the earth.** That these signify the persuasions of those in whom " fowl " signifies affections of what is false, " beast " lusts, " wild animal "

pleasures, and " creeping thing " things corporeal
and earthly, is evident from what has been already
shown respecting the signification of " fowls " and
of " beasts " (concerning " fowls " in n. 40, and
above at verses 14 and 15 of this chapter ; concerning " beasts " also in the same place, and in
n. 45, 46, 142, 143, and 246). As " fowls " signify
things of understanding, of reason, and of knowledge, they signify also the contraries of these, as
what is of perverted reason, falsities, and affections
of what is false. The persuasions of the antediluvians are here fully described, namely, that there
were in them affections of what is false, lusts,
pleasures, corporeal and earthly things. That all
these are within persuasions, man is not aware,
believing a principle or a persuasion of what is
false to be but a simple thing, or one general thing ;
but he is much mistaken, for the case is very
different. Every single affection of a man derives
its existence and nature from things of his understanding and at the same time from those of his
will, so that the whole man, both as to all things of
his understanding and all things of his will, is in
his every affection, and even in the least particulars
or minutest things of his affection. This has been 2
made evident to me by many experiences, as for
example (to mention only one) that the quality of
a spirit can be known in the other life from one
single idea of his thought. Indeed angels have
from the Lord the power of knowing at once, when
they but look upon any one, what his character is,
nor is there any mistake. It is, therefore, evident
that every single idea and every single affection
of a man, even every least bit of his affection, is
an image of him and a likeness of him, that is,
there is present therein, nearly and remotely,

something from all his understanding and from all his will. In this way then are described the direful persuasions of the antediluvians : that there were in them affections of what is false, and affections of what is evil, or lusts, and also pleasures, and finally things corporeal and earthly. All these are within such persuasions ; and not only in the persuasions in general, but also in the least particulars or minutest things of the persuasions, in which things corporeal and earthly predominate. If man were to know how much there is within one principle and one persuasion of what is false, he would shudder. It is a kind of image of hell. But if it be from innocence or from ignorance, the falsities therein are easily shaken off.

804. It is added, " every man," by which is signified that these things were in that man. This is a general concluding clause which includes all that goes before. Such clauses are often added.

805. **All in whose nostrils was the breathing of the breath of lives.** That this signifies the men who belonged to the Most Ancient Church in whose nostrils was the breathing of the breath of lives, that is, the life of love and of the derivative faith, is evident from what has been said before (n. 96, 97). Among the most ancient people, life was signified by the " breath in the nostrils," or by " breathing," which is the life of the body corresponding to spiritual things, as the motion of the heart is the life of the body corresponding
2 to celestial things. It is here said, " in whose nostrils was the breathing of the breath of lives," because the antediluvians are treated of, in whom by inheritance from their progenitors there was seed from the celestial, but extinct or suffocated.

526

There is also a deeper meaning that lies hidden in
these words, of which we have already spoken
(n. 97), namely, that the man of the Most Ancient
Church had internal respiration, and thus respiration concordant with and similar to that of angels,
concerning which, of the Lord's Divine mercy, we
will treat hereafter. This respiration was varied
in accordance with all the states of the internal
man. But in process of time it was changed in
their posterity, until this last generation, wherein
all that was angelic perished. Then they could no
longer respire with the angelic heaven. This was
the real cause of their extinction ; and therefore
it is now said that they " expired," and that they
in whose nostrils was the breathing of the breath
of lives, " died." After these times internal respira- 3
tion ceased, and with it communication with
heaven and thereby celestial perception, and external respiration succeeded. And because communication with heaven thus ceased, the men of the
Ancient (or new) Church could no longer be celestial
men like the Most Ancient, but were spiritual.
But concerning these things, of the Lord's Divine
mercy, we will treat hereafter.

806. **Of all that was in the dry [land].** That this
signifies those in whom there was no longer such
life, and that their " dying " signifies that they
expired, now follows from what has been shown.
And because all the life of love and faith was
extinguished, it is here said the " dry [land]."
" Dry [land] " is where there is no water, that is,
where there is no longer anything spiritual, still
less celestial. A persuasion of falsity extinguishes
and as it were suffocates everything spiritual and
celestial ; as every one may know from much

527

experience, if he pays attention. Those who have
once conceived opinions, though quite false, cling
to them so obstinately that they are not even
willing to hear anything that is contrary to them ;
so that they never suffer themselves to be informed,
even if the truth be placed before their eyes. Still
more is this the case when they worship the false
opinion from a notion of its sanctity. Such are
those who spurn every truth, and that which they
admit they pervert, and thus immerse in phantasies. It is those who are signified here by the
" dry [land]," wherein there is no water and no
grass. So in *Ezekiel* :

> I will make the rivers dry, and will sell the
> land into the hand of evil men ; and I will make
> the land desolate, and the fullness thereof
> (xxx. 12).

To " make the rivers dry," signifies that there is
no longer anything spiritual. And in *Jeremiah* :

> Your land is become dry (xliv. 22).

" Dry " here denotes land that is desolated and
laid waste, so that there is no longer anything true
and good.

807. Verse 23. **And He destroyed every substance
that was upon the faces of the ground, from man
even to beast, even to creeping thing, and even to
the fowl of the heavens; and they were destroyed
from the earth; and Noah only was left, and that
which was with him in the ark.** " And He destroyed every substance," signifies lusts which are
of the love of self ; " that was upon the faces of
the ground," signifies the posterity of the Most
Ancient Church ; " from man even to beast, even
to creeping thing, and even to the fowl of the

heavens," signifies the nature of their evil ; " man
that nature itself, " beast " lusts, " creeping
thing " pleasures, " fowl of the heavens " falsities
therefrom ; " and they were destroyed from the
earth," is the conclusion—that the Most Ancient
Church expired. " Noah only was left, and that
which was with him in the ark," signifies that those
who constituted the new church were preserved ;
" that which was with him in the ark," signifies
all things that belonged to the new church.

808. **And he destroyed every substance.** That
this signifies lusts which are of the love of self, is
evident from what follows, where they are described
by representatives. " Substance " is predicated of
the things of the will, because from the will all
things with man arise, that is, come into existence
and subsist. The will is the very substance of man,
or the man himself. The lusts of the antediluvians
were of the love of self. There are two most
universal kinds of lusts : one kind belongs to the
love of self, the other to the love of the world.
A man desires nothing but what he loves, and
therefore lusts belong to his love. With these
men the love of self reigned, and consequently its
lusts. For they so loved themselves that they
believed themselves to be gods, not acknowledging
any God above themselves ; and of this they
persuaded themselves.

809. **That was upon the faces of the ground.**
That this signifies the posterity of the Most Ancient
Church, is evident from the signification of
" ground " (of which before) as being the church,
and therefore what belongs to the church. Here,
as " every substance that was upon the faces of
the ground " is said to be " destroyed," the

meaning is that those who were of the Most Ancient Church, and were of such a character, were destroyed. Here it is said " ground," though in the twenty-first verse it is said " earth," for the reason that the church is never predicated of things of the understanding, but of things of the will. Knowledge and rational conviction of faith by no means constitute the church or man of the church, but charity, which is of the will. All that is essential comes from the will ; and consequently neither does what is doctrinal make the church, unless both in general and in particular it looks to charity, for then charity becomes the end. From the end it is evident what kind of doctrine it is, and whether it is of the church or not. The church of the Lord, like the kingdom of the Lord in the heavens, consists of nothing but love and charity.

810. **Both man and beast, and creeping thing, and fowl of the heavens.** That these words signify the nature of their evil ; " man," that nature itself ; " beast," lusts ; " creeping thing," pleasures ; and " fowl of the heavens," falsities thence derived, is evident from the signification of all these things as given above, wherefore there is no need to dwell upon them.

811. **And they were destroyed from the earth.** That this is the conclusion, namely, that the Most Ancient Church expired ; and that by " Noah only was left, and that which was with him in the ark," is signified that those were preserved who constituted the new church ; and that by " that which was with him in the ark," are signified all things that were of the new church, needs no further explanation, being self-evident.

812. Verse 24. **And the waters were strengthened upon the earth a hundred and fifty days.** This signifies the last limit of the Most Ancient Church ; " a hundred and fifty " is the last limit, and the first.

813. That this signifies the last limit of the Most Ancient Church, and that " a hundred and fifty " is the last limit, and the first, cannot indeed be so well confirmed from the Word as can the more simple numbers, which frequently occur. And yet it is evident from the mention of the number " fifteen " (concerning which above at verse 20), which signifies so few as to be scarcely any ; and this is still more the case with the number a " hundred and fifty," composed of fifteen multiplied by ten, which last signifies remains. The multiplication of a few (like the multiplication of a half, a fourth, or a tenth), makes it still less, so that at length it becomes almost none, consequently the end or last limit. The same number occurs in the following chapter (viii. verse 3), where it is said : " the waters receded at the end of a hundred and fifty days," with the same signification. The numbers mentioned in the Word are to be understood in a sense entirely abstracted from that of the letter. They are introduced (as has been said and shown before) merely to connect together the historic series that is in the sense of the letter. Thus where " seven " occurs, it signifies what is holy, entirely apart from the times and measures with which the number is commonly joined. For the angels, who perceive the internal sense of the Word, know nothing of time and measure, still less of the number designated ; and yet they understand the Word fully, when it is being read

by man. When therefore a number anywhere occurs, they can have no idea of any number, but of the thing signified by the number. So here by this number they understand that it denotes the last limit of the Most Ancient Church ; and in the following chapter (verse 3), that it denotes the first limit of the Ancient or new Church.

CONTINUATION CONCERNING THE HELLS.

HERE, CONCERNING THE HELLS OF THOSE WHO HAVE PASSED THEIR LIFE IN HATRED, REVENGE, AND CRUELTIES.

814. Such spirits as cherish deadly hatred, and hence breathe out vengeance and nothing less than death to another, knowing no rest till then, are kept in the deepest cadaverous hell, where there is a noisome stench as of carcasses ; and, wonderful to say, such spirits are so delighted with the stench there that they prefer it to the most pleasing odours. Such is their dreadful nature, and their consequent phantasy. A like stench actually exhales from that hell. When the hell is opened (which occurs rarely, and then only for a short time), so great a stench pours forth from it that spirits cannot remain in the neighbourhood. Certain genii, or rather furies, who were sent forth thence in order that I might know their quality, infected the sphere with such poisonous and pestilent breath that the spirits about me could not stay ; and at the same time it so affected my stomach that I vomited. They manifested

themselves under the appearance of a little child, of not uncomely face, with a concealed dagger, whom they sent to me, bearing a cup in his hand. From this it was given me to know that they had a mind to murder, either with the dagger or with poison, under a show of innocence. Yet they themselves had naked bodies, and were very black. But presently they were sent back into their cadaverous hell, and it was then given me to observe how they sank down. They went on to the left, in the plane of the left temple, and to a great distance, without descending, and afterwards sank down ; first into what appeared as a fire, then into a fiery smoke as of a furnace, and then under that furnace, toward the front, where were many most gloomy caverns tending downward. On the way they were continually revolving and intending evils, and chiefly against the innocent, without cause. When they sank down through the fire they greatly lamented. That they may be well distinguished as to whence and what they are, when they are sent out they have a kind of ring to which are affixed points as of brass, which they press with the hands and twist about. This is a sign that they are of this nature, and are bound.

815. Those who so delight in hatred and the consequent revenge that they are not content to kill the body only, but desire to destroy the soul, which yet the Lord has redeemed, are sent down through a very dark opening towards the lowest parts of the earth, to a depth proportionate to the degree of their hatred and vindictiveness ; and there they are struck with grievous terror and horror, and at the same time are kept in the lust

for revenge ; and as this increases they are sent
down to lower depths. Afterwards, they are sent
into a place beneath Gehenna, where great and
dreadful thick-bellied serpents appear (so vividly
that it is just as if they were real), by whose bites
they are tormented, feeling them acutely. Such
things are keenly felt by spirits, answering to their
life just as things of the body do to the life of those
who are in the body. Meanwhile, they live in
direful phantasies for ages, until they no longer
know that they have been men. Their life, which
they have derived from such hatred and revenge,
cannot otherwise be extinguished.

816. As there are innumerable genera of hatreds
and revenge, and species still more innumerable,
and one genus has not the same hell as another, and
as it is therefore impossible to recount them singly
in their order, I may refer to what have been seen.
One came to me who appeared to be a noble.
(Those who appeared to me were seen as in clear
daylight, and even more clearly, but by my
internal sight ; for of the Lord's Divine mercy
it has been given me to be in company with spirits.)
At his first approach he pretended by signs that
he had much he wished to communicate to me,
asking whether I was a Christian ; to which I
replied that I was. He said that he was too, and
asked that he might be alone with me, to tell me
something that others might not hear. But I
answered that in the other life people cannot be
alone, as men think they are on earth, and that
many spirits were present. He now came nearer
and approached stealthily behind me to the back
of my head, and then I perceived that he was an
assassin. While he was there I felt as it were a

stab through the heart, and presently in the brain—
such a blow as might easily be the death of a man.
But as I was protected by the Lord, I feared
nothing. What device he used I do not know.
Thinking me dead, he told others that he had
just come from a man whom he had killed in that
way, and by a deadly stroke from behind, saying
that he was so skilful in the art that a man would
not know until he fell down dead, and it would
not be doubted that he himself was innocent. It
was given me to know from this that he had but
lately departed from life, where he had committed
such a deed. The punishment of such is dreadful.
After they have suffered infernal torments for
ages, they at length come to have a detestable and
most monstrous face—such as is not a face, but
a ghastly thing as of tow. Thus they put off
everything human, and then every one shudders
at the sight of them, and so they wander about
like wild beasts, in dark places.

817. There came one to me out of an infernal
apartment at the left side and spoke with me.
It was given me to perceive that he was of a
villainous crew. What he had done in the world
was disclosed in the following manner. He was
sent down somewhat deep into the lower earth,
in front, a little to the left, and there he began to
dig a grave, as is done for the dead who are to
be buried. From this arose a suspicion that in
the life of the body he had perpetrated some deadly
deed. Then there appeared a funeral bier covered
with a black cloth. Presently one rising from the
bier came to me, and in a devout manner related
that he had died, and that he believed he had
been killed by that man with poison, and that

535

he had thought so at the hour of his death, but did not know whether it was more than a suspicion. When the infamous spirit heard this, he confessed that he had committed such a deed. After the confession, punishment followed. He was twice rolled about in the dark hole he had dug, and became as black as an Egyptian mummy, both face and body, and in that state was taken up on high and carried about before spirits and angels, and the cry was heard : What a devil ! He also became cold, thus one of the cold infernals, and was sent down into hell.

818. There is a dreadful hell beneath the buttocks, where they seem to stab one another with knives, aiming the knives at one another's breasts like furies ; but in the act of striking the knife is continually taken away from them. They are those who have held others in such hatred that they burned to kill them cruelly ; and from this they had derived a nature so direful. This hell was opened to me (but only a little on account of their direful cruelties), so that I might see the nature of deadly hatred.

819. There is at the left, in a plane with the lower parts of the body, a kind of stagnant lake, large, and of greater length than breadth. About its bank in front there appear to those who are there monstrous serpents, such as inhabit stagnant waters, with pestilent breath. Farther away, on the left bank, appear those who eat human flesh, and devour one another, fastening with their teeth on one another's shoulders. Still farther away to the left appear great fishes, enormous whales, which swallow a man and vomit him out again. In the farthest distance, or on the opposite

shore, appear very ugly faces, too monstrous to be described, chiefly those of old women, who run about as if frenzied. On the right bank are those who are trying to butcher each other with cruel instruments, which vary in accordance with the direful feelings of their hearts. In the middle of the lake it is everywhere black, as if stagnant. Sometimes I have been surprised to see spirits brought to this lake, but was informed by some who came from it and told me, that they were those who had cherished intestine hatred against the neighbour ; and that their hatred burst forth as often as occasion offered, in which they perceived their greatest delight ; and that nothing had pleased them more than to bring a neighbour to judgment and cause punishment to be inflicted on him, and, if the penalties of the law had not deterred them, to put him to death. Into such things (as described above) are the hatreds and cruelties of men turned after the life of the body. The phantasies to which their hatreds and cruelties give rise have to them the reality of life.

820. In the other life those who have practised robbery and piracy love rank and fetid urine above all other liquids, and seem to themselves to dwell among such things, and among stagnant and stinking pools. A certain robber approached me, gnashing his teeth , the sound of which was as plainly heard as if it had proceeded from a man, which was strange, since they have no teeth.. He confessed that he would rather live in urinous filth than by the clearest waters, and that the smell of urine was what he delighted in. He said he would rather stay and have his home in urinous vats than anywhere else.

537

821. There are those who outwardly present an
honourable face and life, so that no one could
suspect them of being other than honourable,
studying in every way to appear so, for the sake
of being raised to honours, and of acquiring wealth
without the loss of reputation. They therefore
do not act openly ; but through others by deceitful
artifices they deprive men of their goods, caring
nothing if the families they despoil perish of
hunger ; and they would themselves be personal
agents in this villainy, without any conscience, if
they could escape public notice, so that they really
are of the same character as if they perpetrated it
by their own act. They are hidden robbers, and
the kind of hatred peculiar to them is joined with
scornful contempt for others, greed of gain, cruelty,
and deceit. In the other life such men desire to be
esteemed blameless, saying that they have done
nothing wrong, because it was not detected. And
to show themselves guiltless, they put off their
garments and present themselves naked—in this
way attesting their innocence. Yet while they
are being examined their quality is thoroughly
well perceived from every single word and every
single idea of their thought, without their being
aware of it. Such, in the other life, desire without
any conscience to murder whatever companions
.they fall in with. They have also an axe with
them, and a maul in their hand, and seem to
have another spirit with them whom they strike,
when on his back ; but not to the shedding of
blood, for they are afraid of death. And they
cannot cast these weapons out of their hands
although they strive to do so with all their might,
in order to prevent the actual ferocity of their
disposition from appearing before the eyes of

spirits and angels. They are at a middle distance under the feet, towards the front.

822. There is a kind of hatred against the neighbour, which finds its delight in injuring and harassing every one ; and the more mischief they can do the more delighted they are. There are very many such from the lowest of the common people. And there are those not of the common people who have a similar disposition, but outwardly are of better manners, from having been brought up in good society, and also from fear of legal penalties. After death, the upper part of the body of these spirits appears naked, and their hair dishevelled. They annoy one another by rushing forward and placing the palms of their hands on one another's shoulders, and they then leap over their heads, and soon come back and make a severe attack with their fists Those of whom it was said that they have better manners act in a similar way, but first exchange greetings, then go round behind their neighbour's back, and so attack with the fist ; but when they see each other face to face they make a salutation, and again go round behind the back and strike with the fist. In this way they keep up appearances. These appear at some distance towards the left side, at a middle height.

823. Whatever a man has done in the life of the body successively returns in the other life, and so does all that he has even thought. When his enmities, hatreds, and deceits return, the persons against whom he has indulged hatred and has clandestinely plotted are made present to him, and this in a moment. Such is the case in the other life ; but concerning this presence, of the Lord's Divine mercy, we will treat hereafter.

The thoughts a man has harboured against others make their appearance openly, for there is a perception of all thoughts. Hence come lamentable states, for there concealed hatreds break out openly. With the evil all their evil deeds and thoughts thus return, to the life ; but it is not so with the good. With these all their good states of friendship and love return, attended with the highest delight and happiness.

Titles Available
SWEDENBORG'S THEOLOGICAL WORKS

APOCALYPSE EXPLAINED, 3562 pages, 6 volumes.

This work sets forth the spiritual (symbolic) sense of the *Book of Revelation* up to chapter 19, verse 10, and in connection with that, the inner meaning of many other parts of the Scriptures, especially the Psalms, the Prophets and the Gospels. Towards its close, extensive and practical doctrinal discussions are introduced.

APOCALYPSE REVEALED, 1105 pages, 2 volumes.

Concentrates upon the spiritual (symbolic) exposition of the visions of John as set forth in the *Book of Revelation* in a way to make the teachings of this book of vital present interest and importance.

ARCANA CÆLESTIA (Heavenly Secrets), 7103 pages, 12 volumes.

An exposition of the spiritual sense of the *Genesis* and *Exodus,* showing that the stories of Creation, Eden, the Flood, the captivity of the chosen people in Egypt, their deliverance and the ritual of the Jewish religion, its sacrifices and observances are symbolic renderings of everlasting truth and religious experience.

CONJUGIAL LOVE, 612 pages.

This book treats of the relation of the sexes and of the sex extending to the spirit, of the nature and origin of love truly conjugial (marital) and of its indissoluble nature, of the marriage of the Lord and the Church and its spiritual significance, of sexual irregularities and the avoidance of them.

DIVINE LOVE AND WISDOM, 293 pages.

This book is an interpretation of the universe as a spiritual-natural or psycho-physical cosmos. It treats of the activity of God's love and wisdom in the creation of this cosmos and of the human being.

DIVINE PROVIDENCE, 376 pages.

Shows clearly the Lord's infinite care for man in all the affairs of his life; explains the existence of evil and why it is permitted. A rational answer to the question, Why do things happen?

FOUR DOCTRINES, 388 pages.

Swedenborg restates in this work four leading doctrines of the Christian religion: The Lord. The Sacred Scriptures. Life and Faith. These doctrines are drawn from, and substantiated by numerous passages from the divine Word, examined as a unified whole.

HEAVEN AND HELL, 455 pages.

Gives a clear and rational explanation of the nature of death, of man's entrance into the spiritual world, of the organization of that world and of the life there. The book excels all but the Scriptures for comfort to the bereaved.

MISCELLANEOUS THEOLOGICAL WORKS, 634 pages.

Bound together in this volume are treatises: *The New Jerusalem and its Heavenly Doctrine; Doctrine of the New Church; Intercourse between the Soul and the Body; White Horse Mentioned in the Apocalypse; Earths in the Universe; The Last Judgment.*

POSTHUMOUS THEOLOGICAL WORKS, 1196 pages, 2 volumes.
Contains a number of the small works which had not previously been in a form convenient for use, including a number of extracts from Swedenborg's correspondence.

THE SPIRITUAL LIFE, THE WORD OF GOD, 160 pages.
This volume consists of some extracts from Swedenborg's *The Apocalypse Explained* and makes devotional reading on the spiritual or regenerating life, the significance of the Ten Commandments, our possible profanation of good and truth, and the power of God's Word.

TRUE CHRISTIAN RELIGION, 1098 pages, 2 volumes.
This is Swedenborg's crowning work giving a complete and connected exposition of the doctrines of the New Christian Era. A powerful and massive presentation dealing with a broad spectrum of modern Christian concerns. It draws upon more than nine hundred passages from all parts of the Bible.

OTHER TITLES:

THE ESSENTIAL SWEDENBORG, by Sig Synnestvedt, 202 pages.
This work presents, in easy to read quotations, the basic elements of Swedenborg's thought within the confines of a brief compendium along with a biographical sketch of Swedenborg.

GIST OF SWEDENBORG, by Julian K. Smyth & William F. Wunsch, 110 pages.
A compilation of excellently chosen and well arranged quotations from Swedenborg's Works, dealing with a broad spectrum of modern Christian concerns such as God, Man, Regeneration, Marriage, Charity and Faith, Divine Providence, Death and the Resurrection, Heaven, Hell, The Church.

INTRODUCTION TO SWEDENBORG'S RELIGIOUS THOUGHT, by John Howard Spalding, 235 pages.
A clear, comprehensive and forcefully reasoned presentation of Swedenborg's teachings by a British layman and scientist.

MY RELIGION, by Helen Keller, 208 pages.
The beautifully written and inspiring account of the help which the teachings of Swedenborg have been to Miss Keller from her early years onward.

SWEDENBORG, LIFE AND TEACHINGS, by George Trobridge, 298 pages.
The most widely read biography of Emanuel Swedenborg, with summaries not only of his Theological Works but also of his Scientific and Philosophical Works.

Free Catalogue will be sent upon request from

SWEDENBORG FOUNDATION, INC.
139 E. 23rd Street
New York, New York 10010